Forces of Education

Walter Benjamin Studies

In this series devoted to the writings of Walter Benjamin each volume will focus on a theme central to contemporary work on Benjamin. The series aims to set new standards of work on Benjamin available in English for students and researchers in Philosophy, Cultural Studies and Literary Studies.

Series Editor: Andrew Benjamin, Anniversary Professor of Philosophy and the Humanities at Kingston University London and Distinguished Professor of Architectural Theory at the University of Technology, Sydney.

Editorial Board:

Howard Caygill, Kingston University, UK
Rebecca Comay, University of Toronto, Canada
Ilit Ferber, Tel Aviv University, Israel
Werner Hamacher, University of Frankfurt, Germany
Julia Ng, Goldsmiths College, University of London, UK
Gerhard Richter, Brown University, USA

Other titles in the series

Benjamin on Fashion, Philipp Ekardt
Modernism Between Benjamin and Goethe, Matthew Charles
Inheriting Walter Benjamin, Gerhard Richter

Forces of Education

Walter Benjamin and the Politics of Pedagogy

Edited by

Dennis Johannßen and Dominik Zechner

BLOOMSBURY ACADEMIC
Bloomsbury Publishing Plc
50 Bedford Square, London, WC1B 3DP, UK
1385 Broadway, New York, NY 10018, USA
29 Earlsfort Terrace, Dublin 2, Ireland

BLOOMSBURY, BLOOMSBURY ACADEMIC and the Diana logo are trademarks of
Bloomsbury Publishing Plc

First published in Great Britain 2023
This paperback edition published 2024

Copyright © Dennis Johannßen, Dominik Zechner, and Contributors 2023

Dennis Johannßen and Dominik Zechner have asserted their right under the Copyright, Designs and Patents Act, 1988, to be identified as Editors of this work.

Series design by Catherine Wood
Cover image: Old Fashioned Classroom © Johny Daniel / EyeEm / Getty Images)

All rights reserved. No part of this publication may be reproduced or transmitted in any form or by any means, electronic or mechanical, including photocopying, recording, or any information storage or retrieval system, without prior permission in writing from the publishers.

Bloomsbury Publishing Plc does not have any control over, or responsibility for, any third-party websites referred to or in this book. All internet addresses given in this book were correct at the time of going to press. The author and publisher regret any inconvenience caused if addresses have changed or sites have ceased to exist, but can accept no responsibility for any such changes.

A catalogue record for this book is available from the British Library.

A catalog record for this book is available from the Library of Congress.

ISBN: HB: 978-1-3502-7416-7
PB: 978-1-3502-7420-4
ePDF: 978-1-3502-7417-4
eBook: 978-1-3502-7418-1

Series: Walter Benjamin Studies

Typeset by RefineCatch Limited, Bungay, Suffolk

To find out more about our authors and books visit www.bloomsbury.com and sign up for our newsletters.

Contents

List of Abbreviations	vi
Preface: Pedagogy and Experience in Walter Benjamin *Michael W. Jennings*	vii
Editors' Introduction *Dennis Johannßen and Dominik Zechner*	1
Chronicle of Benjamin's School and Student Years *Dennis Johannßen and Dominik Zechner*	15

Part One Genealogies of Learning

1	Infans *Clemens-Carl Härle*	29
2	Learning from Experience: Elements of Self-Criticism in Benjamin's Works *Charles Gelman*	43
3	Leitmotif Siegfried *Laurence A. Rickels*	59
4	The Child in Benjamin: An Enduring Lesson *Henry Sussman*	73

Part Two Languages of Youth

5	Conversational Pedagogy in Benjamin and Nietzsche *Natasha Hay*	97
6	Speaking Silence: Historical Subjectivity in Nietzsche and Benjamin *Ian Fleishman*	111
7	Silence, Medium, Transmission: Benjamin's Metaphysics of Language and Youth *Adi Nester*	125
8	"In Voice Land": Benjamin on Air *Ilit Ferber*	143

Part Three Envisioning Pedagogical Futures

9	Unfulfilled Historical Time and the Self-Pedagogy of Critique *Gerhard Richter*	159
10	Against the Law: Youth and the Critical Pedagogy of Eternal Rebellion *Michael Powers*	177
11	Improvision *Thomas Schestag*	191
12	Walter Benjamin and the Anthropocene *Nitzan Lebovic*	211

List of Contributors	225
Index	229

Abbreviations

AP	*The Arcades Project*, trans. Howard Eiland and Kevin McLaughlin (Cambridge, MA: Belknap, 1999).
C	*The Correspondence of Walter Benjamin 1910–1940*, ed. Gershom Scholem and Theodor W. Adorno, trans. Manfred R. Jakobson and Evelyn M. Jakobson (Chicago, IL: University of Chicago Press, 1994).
EW	*Walter Benjamin: Early Writings 1910–1917*, trans. Howard Eiland et al. (Cambridge, MA: Belknap, 2011).
GB	*Gesammelte Briefe*, ed. Christoph Gödde and Henri Lonitz (Frankfurt a.M.: Suhrkamp, 1995–2000).
GS	*Walter Benjamin: Gesammelte Schriften*, ed. Rolf Tiedemann and Hermann Schweppenhäuser (Frankfurt a.M.: Suhrkamp, 1972–1989).
OT	*The Origin of the German Tragic Drama*, trans. John Osborne (London: Verso, 1998).
SW	*Walter Benjamin: Selected Writings*, ed. Michael W. Jennings (Cambridge, MA: Belknap, 1997–2003).

Preface: Pedagogy and Experience in Walter Benjamin

Michael W. Jennings

In an important sense, the entirety of Walter Benjamin's work can be understood as an investigation of the possibilities open to experience under conditions of modernity. Pedagogy, then, consists in the measures taken toward the realization of a genuine human experience—measures taken against powerful forces inimical to that very experience. Two important questions arise from this claim. First, to *what* is the human being educated, i.e., how does Benjamin conceive the subject that might emerge through the pedagogical process? And second, which human capacities and indeed even organs must be educated if this goal is to be achieved? Given the structure of Benjamin's thought—a structure that he once described as a "mobile and contradictory whole"—there is of course no single answer to these questions. I hope here to suggest instead two *trajectories* along which Benjamin considered these questions.

In answer to my first question, the editors of this volume put forward Youth as the "revolutionary subject" of Benjamin's earliest writings on pedagogy. Benjamin's conception of youth emerged as part of a broad historical interest in the young in the German-speaking nations; the most immediate context was provided by the Youth Movement in which Benjamin participated, but youth was more generally conceived in the arts and literature as the locus of utopian impulses. To name only one example, the journal *Jugend* (youth) began to appear in Munich in 1896 and lent its name to the movement in art and architecture known as *Jugendstil*. After Benjamin's break with his teacher Gustav Wyneken in 1914—and thus with the etymology of the term "pedagogy," which insists that the education of youth takes place through the actions of a strong leader—the general category of youth became increasingly concretized through the analysis of the *child* as the locus of utopian hope for the human subject. This early Rousseauian idealization of the child is most evident in *One-Way Street* (1923–26, published 1928) and in the remarkable series of meditations on children's toys and books in the second half of the 1920s; in the period of exile after 1933, the child is no longer conceived as proof against the depravations of the age. In Benjamin's masterpiece, *Berlin Childhood around 1900*, the child appears as always already entombed in a mausoleum and uniquely privy to a nihilistic insight: "Why is there anything at all in the world, why the world? With amazement, I realized that nothing in it could compel me to think the world. Its nonbeing would have struck me as not a whit more problematic than its being, which seemed to wink at nonbeing." A fundamental nihilism is never far from Benjamin's thought; it is the juxtaposition of utopianism and nihilism that lends that thought much of its complexity.

Leaving aside the analysis of childhood consciousness, Benjamin before 1923 adheres to a more or less traditional view of the humanist subject, although cracks begin increasingly to appear in the conception of a subject who is self-present and spatially and temporally coherent. Beginning in about 1923, though, Benjamin begins to complicate his understanding of the subject, moving slowly toward a conceptualization of the *collective* subject. If *Origin of German Trauerspiel* (written 1923–24, published 1928) presented the *via dolorosa* of the humanist subject and its final mortification, such texts as "Surrealism" of 1929 and "The Destructive Character" of 1931 prepared the way for the conception of the collective subject that dominated the writings in exile. In the texts that grew out of the unfinished project on the Parisian arcades—"The Work of Art in the Age of its Technological Reproducibility" and especially the great unfinished book *Charles Baudelaire: A Lyric Poet in the Era of High Capitalism*—Benjamin suggests that the "innervation of the collective" might offer the sole means of escape from the domination of the subject by the principle tools of capitalism: reification and phantasmagoria. The invocation of the term "innervation" brings us to the second of the two questions I posed at the outset, the question as to what capacities and indeed physiological bases would need "educating" if the new subject were to emerge.

Benjamin's early writings on pedagogy operate within a loosely Kantian framework, which is to say that the aim of pedagogy is a reform of the human rational capacities. From early essays such as "The Life of Students" (1912) through "On the Program of the Coming Philosophy" (1918) and his dissertation, *The Concept of Criticism in German Romanticism* (1920), Benjamin conceived education as a means to broaden the reach of human cognition, enabling it to encompass realms that traditional epistemology held to be the stuff of metaphysics. Benjamin's encounter with Georg Lukacs's *History and Class Consciousness* in 1923 marked a turning point; from this time on, Benjamin's writing evinces a profound skepticism regarding human reason—a tendency that aligned his thought first with that of Siegfried Kracauer and later with that of Theodor Adorno and Max Horkheimer. With the writing of *One-Way Street*, which occurred alongside the reading of Lukacs, the analysis of human reason gives way to a broad program focused on the pedagogical reform of the human *sensorium*. Much, though not all, of that program is linked to Benjamin's analysis of the potentials and the pitfalls of modern technological media, and of photography and film above all. If his early Kantianism saw him attempting to define new realms and objects for cognition, his work after 1923 saw him thinking toward vast new regions in which sense perception could operate in wholly new ways. In some essays—"To the Planetarium" of 1926 and "Doctrine of the Similar" of 1933—those regions were frankly cosmic and highly esoteric. In his writings on photography and film, though, Benjamin saw in these media the potential not just to educate human sensory capacities but to work physiological changes on the organs of perception. In these texts, the term "pedagogy" is relatively rare; its task is largely replaced by a notion of "training" (*Übung*). In "Little History of Photography" (1930), August Sanders's photobook *Face of our Time* is described as a "training manual" that could alert readers to the "provenance" of their political formation; in the story "Rastelli narrates," "Übung," as Hent de Vries has shown, is better translated as "exercise" with a broad connotative field that includes military exercises as well as spiritual ones (Loyola). These ideas on training receive their definitive formulation in "The Work of Art in the

Age of its Technological Reproducibility" (1935): "The function of film is to train human beings in the apperceptions and reactions needed to deal with a vast apparatus whose role in their lives is expanding almost daily." As the much-discussed footnote to this idea suggests, such training is the prerequisite for revolution: "Revolutions are innervations of the collective—or, more precisely, efforts at innervation on the part of the new, historically unique collective which has its organs in the new technology." Training—a materialist pedagogy—accelerates evolutionary changes in the human sensorium, potentiating innervation, which Miriam Hansen has defined as "a neurophysiological process that mediates between internal and external, psychic and motoric, human and machinic registers." At stake here is the very fate of the human sensorium in an environment "altered by technology and capitalist commodity production." And, for Walter Benjamin, the marshalling of innervation as a new and potentiated "contact zone" between the human and the increasingly inimical environment can only come about through pedagogy.

Editors' Introduction

Dennis Johannßen and Dominik Zechner

"It's for us that the university exists, for the dispossessed of the world."
John Williams, *Stoner*

"The pleasure of teaching is an act of resistance."
bell hooks, *Teaching to Transgress*

I

It is no coincidence that we consider the German Jewish critic and philosopher Walter Benjamin a seminal thinker of pedagogy at the precise moment when our pedagogical institutions are radically put to the test. If Benjamin's eighth thesis "On the Concept of History" holds "that the 'state of emergency' in which we live is not the exception but the rule," this historical diagnosis must be fathomed to include the educational circumstance.[1] Given the countless calamities pedagogical institutions are facing two decades into the twenty-first century, the statement that education is "in crisis" reads less like a proposition of true diagnostic value than the citation of an analytic cliché whose appearance within a critical discussion of the state of pedagogy is simply expected if not prescribed. Looking back at its recent history, we observe not only that the university has undergone grave transformations in terms of its self-understanding and institutional structure, but also that it appears as a site of active ruination and perpetuated calamity.[2] Reminding the reader of the birth of the modern university through Wilhelm von Humboldt's humanist visions seems like a tasteless joke if we consider the neoliberal agenda that the university, first and foremost in Anglo-American countries, has come to fulfill. As Werner Hamacher demonstrates, Humboldt saw universities as *Freistätten*, that is, places of freedom, whose task it was to host nothing but the spiritual life of humanity.[3] An affirmation of such freedom and its profession—in the declarative sense of *to profess*—can be discerned in Jacques Derrida's 1999 prospect of a *université sans condition*.[4]

The rather bleak reality of our current situation, however, makes these conceptions seem like increasingly distant fantasies. Even before the COVID-19 pandemic shook up the global educational landscape in unprecedented ways, the university had lost touch with its ideal. While the European Union instituted the so-called "Bologna Process," de facto assimilating the highly diverse European academic traditions to the Anglo-American paradigm, the latter went into neo-liberal overdrive, systematically diminishing the status of the public university and its mission.[5] Rather than establishing an entirely new principle, the pandemic and the university's way of "managing" it reveal themselves as mere accelerations of certain firmly pre-established tendencies. On the one hand, the pandemic has served as the solid justification for severe cuts and austerity measures imposed upon the university; on the other hand, it has delegitimized the pedagogical encounter between teachers and students by coercing it into the alienated spaces of a singularized online environment. In this environment, knowledge appears as a commodity suited for a transmission without reaction, rather than being acquired through an embodied experience. Embodied forms of conversational pedagogy, first and foremost the seminar, are receding.

The years leading up to these tectonic shifts in (higher) education were no less turbulent. Among the many quandaries that have marked the university over the past two decades, we would like to isolate three which we think are of particular significance: first, the financial crash of 2008 and its aftermath put great stress on the disproportionate cost of higher education, especially in the United States, and threw into sharp relief a still unresolved student loan crisis. The Great Recession further destabilized the academic job market in the humanities so drastically that even prior to the newest wave of hiring freezes it could hardly be said to have reconsolidated itself. Second, and more recently, the university has become the prime arena for the negotiation of questions concerning social justice and the transformation of free speech. These debates are closely connected to a rethinking of the Western tradition and its inherent potentials for violence and oppression, pressing us to critique and expose Eurocentric regimes of knowledge production and transmission. Lastly, the #MeToo movement, rapidly unfolding from the fall of 2017 onward, eventually also reached the university, disclosing the urgent need to redefine—or truly to define for the first time—an ethics of mentorship that would vehemently divulge and critique the structures of exploitation, material as well as emotional, that had been a central feature of campus life. We contend that the university campus is not simply one site of social interaction among others but that it manifests one of the most decisive contexts in which forms of sexism, misogyny, gender discrimination, homophobia, racism, and the general abuse of power become visible in unique ways, and where possible shifts toward ethical forms of coexistence can be anticipated, studied, and practiced.[6]

It is crucial to note that the impasses of the modern university system reach back far beyond the recent crises—yes, that the university's free and democratic ideal never had any true claim to reality. Emerging among pre-bourgeois societies, educational institutions from schools to universities fostered the idea of equal participation in knowledge, culture, and economic wealth, but this ideal was never actualized. From its inception to the present day, the university has remained the site and symptom of deep injustices and divisions along demarcations of class, race, gender, sexuality, and nationality. Karl Marx, who was keenly aware of the elevated and intricate importance of education for social transformation, indicated that society and the ideas we entertain about it should be considered as separate spheres—simply because "it is essential to educate the educators themselves."[7]

Although the recent debates regarding education are certainly driven by emancipatory motives, they also signal that the status of emancipation as such is in question as far as the university in its current condition is concerned. Emancipatory pedagogical practices like those of Paulo Freire or, in his wake, bell hooks, seem increasingly remote and unattainable.[8] Such a diagnosis is not meant to invite a nihilist defeatism. Rather, the current situation of variously entangled crises becomes readable as a watershed moment that urgently calls for the radical critique in tandem with a new vision of the university, an upending redefinition of what Barbara Johnson termed "the pedagogical imperative."[9] Hence, our volume on Walter Benjamin as pedagogue may be considered a contribution to the discourses that currently shape and reshape our understanding not only of the university but of the politics of education in general. The current moment urges us to reconsider the nexus between politics and pedagogy, and it is our sense that the work of Walter Benjamin constitutes an indispensable resource in this regard. In view of the catalogue of predicaments named above, we take our cue from Benjamin's unique stance that does not lament what is lost or vanishing amidst a permanent crisis, but instead highlights the missed opportunities and a dynamic of hidden forces that the decline engenders and sets free. Benjamin's pedagogy introduces practices of critique whose meaning for our current situation it is our task to recognize. Whether it is student life and its material conditions, the oppression inherent in tradition, or the possibility of an ethical community on campus, Benjamin has already confronted the precise ethical and political questions that haunt the concept of education to this day.

What are the concrete ways in which Benjamin's texts correspond to the ethical and political dimensions of our present educational and political condition? The conflict that Benjamin discerned between, on the one hand, the Enlightenment promise of free education, and, on the other, the rigid authoritarian structures of the Wilhelmine Empire in crucial ways reflects our own concerns regarding social inequality and the yet-to-be-realized demand for universal access to education. Benjamin's aspiration to endow the subjects of "youth" and "students" with the authority to reconfigure the institution from within, including the structure and content of an antiquated didactics and its curricula, can provide a model for our current struggles regarding the decentering, diversification, and decolonization of our inherited educational programs.

Benjamin's ideas on pedagogy strike us as particularly pertinent and urgent whenever the "use" of language is at stake. Since much of our current conversation regarding a peaceful coexistence on campus revolves around the critique of language, especially with regard to its injurious and scathing capacities, it may prove prudent to remember that language, for Benjamin, was not a means of communication, but a medium which first of all communicates *itself* and in which experience may take shape in a potentially nonviolent fashion. Benjamin's pedagogy furthermore puts great emphasis on the institution's de-hierarchization as he understands the encounter between teacher and student as reciprocal, encouraging us to explore the possibility of students teaching themselves.

Another dimension we would like to underscore is Benjamin's understanding of education's embeddedness within the larger surrounding world of media and technology. Inquiring about this connection is particularly important at a time when education is both forced into digital spaces to maintain itself and threatened by an unabashed far-right populism that abuses the possibilities of social media and platform capitalism to undermine any claim to scientifically secured or discursively stabilized knowledge.[10] This problem is particularly meaningful in the context of political education, and it affects students and instructors alike. Benjamin's analyses of media practices and technologies including photography, film, and radio appear as anything but obsolete messages from analogue antiquity as they help us to contextualize hyper-presentist media techniques with respect to the broader historical manifestations of social and political power, oppression, and resistance.

While we, as the editors of this volume, are situated within the compromised environment of the contemporary university and view our call to action as predominantly related to and aimed at the state of higher education, it is important to point out that Benjamin's pedagogy is not reducible to the project of reforming or restructuring a single institution. Although his early works on education do primarily target student life between German academic high school (*Gymnasium*) and the university, his later writings showed an increasing interest in early education and childhood. The contributions that are gathered in this volume certainly speak from an academic perspective, yet their concern reaches further and implies issues related to K-12 education and other settings of early schooling. For Benjamin, who started questioning the structure of education when he was only in middle school, the figure of the child had the capacity not only to upend outmoded and obsolete forms of education, but also to recast the shape of tradition and the ways in which generations relate to one another. In the anarchy of children's play, Benjamin saw pedagogical alternatives to the hierarchies and power-structures that scaffold the educational circumstance.

The proposal to consider Walter Benjamin a pedagogical thinker of critical import may certainly come as a surprise to some readers who will acknowledge Benjamin's voice as central to various aesthetic, historical, or media-theoretical debates but not necessarily to the field of education. While his impact on these matters remains undisputed, Benjamin's oeuvre, we propose, is permeated by a profound and long-standing critique of practices of education and their institutional enframing. This becomes especially clear when one considers his very early work, comprising a corpus of texts that were written during the years between 1910 and 1917. Himself a student activist at that time, Benjamin created a small yet considerably diverse and powerful dossier of writings during those years in which he dissects and attacks the bourgeois ideals and conventions of education.[11] Appended to this Introduction, we include a detailed biographical chronicle of Benjamin's school and student years that contextualizes his political and student-activist engagement during the years up until 1915.

Ambitious yet imbued with vicissitude, those early texts are *wild*—candid, idealistic, and metaphysically laden with messianic hope and boundless intellectual self-confidence. The concepts that Benjamin develops in these challenging writings include "religiosity," "value," "community," "language," "eros," and "life," as he attempts to capture the distinct school spirit of the German Youth Movement. Many of the themes that will accompany Benjamin through the unfolding of his mature oeuvre already come to the fore in these earliest philosophical and political writings—for instance, the problem of experience (*Erfahrung*) that captured Benjamin's teenage attention. Armed with this concept, he defended the spiritual ambition of the youngster against the sapped and impoverished quasi-wisdom of the philistine who tragically overcame the temptations of youth, leaving only resentment.[12] If one were to determine a "revolutionary subject" to carry out Benjamin's onslaught at education, it would thus have to be Youth. Correspondingly, these scattered and forceful early texts find one of their points of culmination in a piece titled "The Metaphysics of Youth" which several of our contributors identify as a touchstone for their analyses, not least due to the complex conversational pedagogy Benjamin develops in this text that insists on silence as youth's destined mode of self-articulation and critique.

It is pivotal to note, however, that the critical essays we gathered in this volume do not exhaust themselves through an exegesis of Benjamin's early work. Rather, we take this early corpus of politico-pedagogical writings as evidence of Benjamin as a prime thinker of the educational circumstance as we explore the unfolding of his pedagogy throughout his wider oeuvre. Just as the concept of "experience" will reappear in numerous later texts, most impactfully in Benjamin's writings on Baudelaire, the trope of youth and the focus on the student will give way to a sustained and far-reaching engagement with childhood and the figure of the child, including an exploration of practices of "play"; the early emphasis on the study of literature and philosophy will grow into the pedagogical experimentation with other media, particularly the acoustic spaces opened by the radio; and, as we show below, the intersection and interaction of education and violence that Benjamin first makes explicit in his juvenilia remains a central problem throughout his work.

II

If the title of our volume invokes Benjamin's "Forces of Education," the term "force," in this regard, ought to be understood as one of the semantic shades comprising the German word "Gewalt" with which Benjamin was occupied throughout many stages of his work, most importantly in his 1921 essay, "Critique of Violence" ("Zur Kritik der Gewalt"). While the German word "Gewalt" may certainly be translated as "violence," it opens a vast semantic field that includes the related yet distinct concepts of, among others, power, force, and cause.[13] It is therefore no surprise that the signifier starts drifting, especially when we consider Benjamin's work in other languages, for instance Edmund Jephcott's English translation, which oscillates eccentrically between the registers of "force," "power," and "violence."[14] As unsettling and destabilizing as this ambiguity may seem, we opted to make it productive for the purpose of our volume insofar as the "Forces of Education" that we invoke in the title do not remain stuck in an analysis of present systems of oppression and domination, instead pointing toward the revolutionary moments that allow for a reconfiguration of the educational enterprise as such. Liberating the "force" from the "violence" also opens the possibility of connecting this conceptual ambivalence to the "weak messianic power [*Kraft*]" Benjamin summons in his late work, insofar as the term "Kraft" partakes of the semantic movement of "Gewalt."[15]

Even though the phenomenon of a "force of education" remains as elusive as the shifts of its signifier, in what follows we would like to offer some reflections on a moment in Benjamin's "Critique of Violence" that establishes an explicit connection between his envisioned politics of pure means and the pedagogical circumstance. This moment is marked by the tentative introduction of an enigmatic term whose contours must remain vague as Benjamin does little to nothing toward offering a detailed definition. "Erzieherische Gewalt," the term in question, has been translated as "educative power" but may also be rendered as "educational violence" or "force of education."[16] Benjamin introduces this formulation at a very late point in the essay, and while he leaves its purpose and implications largely unexplained, it nonetheless can be said to take on a crucial role in terms of his broader argument.

Before elucidating this context any further, it is important to highlight the genealogy behind the nexus between education and violence within Benjamin's oeuvre. For it is indeed possible to argue that it does not simply appear ex nihilo at the end of "Critique of Violence," but that it was prepared already in his early writings. A text from 1912 titled "School Reform: A Cultural Movement," which may be considered a kind of manifesto Benjamin penned as a student under the influence of his ambiguous early mentor, the reform pedagogue Gustav Wyneken, has the young author explore the question regarding educational reform in terms of what he calls "the cultural problem." And he states: "It is a matter of finding a way out of the opposition between natural, truthful development, on the one hand, and the task of transforming the natural individual into the cultural individual, on the other hand, *a task that will never be completed without violence.*"[17] As far as we can see, this instance is the first in Benjamin's work where education and violence become essentially and explicitly intertwined; and it should not escape us that the term Benjamin uses in order to determine this connection marks a diversion from the traditional lexicon of humanist pedagogy: instead of *bilden* the passages speaks of *umbilden* (here translated as "transforming"). The neologism is necessary due to the structure of the problem which is presented as a Kantian antinomy: there is the "truthful" evolution of the natural individual on the one hand, and the "task" (this time not the "task of the translator" but the sheer task of *civilization*) to reshape the former according to the historical parameters of culture on the other. Education, thus, constitutes less a process of formation than one of violent *recasting*—the destruction of a pre-given form paired with the imposition of a new model, that of culture. Interestingly enough, the moment of violence does not coincide with the antinomy itself: according to Benjamin's passage, it is *not* the contrast between nature and culture that yields violence—but it is the pedagogical imperative *on the side of culture*, operating *on* the natural individual, that cannot do without the application of violence.

About a decade after this short essay on the school reform, Benjamin restates the problem of pedagogical violence in "Critique of Violence." There, he addresses the problem of education twice, and the two moments turn out to be hardly bridgeable. Yet both instances need to be read together in order for us to draw some preliminary conclusions about the nature of violence and its connection to the pedagogical imperative. The first distinction Benjamin puts to work resonates with his earlier text on the school reform and concerns the difference between natural and positive law. Seeking a way to develop the concept of legitimate violence ("rechtmäßige Gewalt") from the distinction of History versus Nature, he suggests calling only those acts of violence legitimate that are executed toward a legal end or "Rechtszweck." He goes on to discuss a potential conflict between the natural and legal functions of violence and offers a striking example: "[The legal] system strives to limit by legal ends even those areas in which natural ends are admitted in principle and within wide boundaries like that of education, as soon as these natural ends are pursued with an excessive measure of violence, as in the laws relating to the limits of educational authority to punish."[18] The problem is now inverted: education and educational violence reside on the site of nature and natural ends—and it is the prerogative of the institutions representing positive law to delimit, contain, and curb the application of violence for educational purposes. In other words, the realm of education is initially governed by natural ends whose realization requires a degree of violence—and only as a derivative or secondary measure will the state intervene and regulate the natural precinct of education so as to reduce excess amounts of violence set free in the pursuit of natural ends. Contextualizing this observation in terms of what has been said so far, we are confronted with the puzzling predicament that the location of educational violence vis-à-vis the institutions of culture, including those dedicated to pedagogy, cannot easily be determined. There is educational violence on the side of positive law to the extent that the cultivation of nature is at stake, as Benjamin argues in "School Reform"; yet, at the same time, there is the raw violence of rearing and upbringing that seeks to elude the posited institutions of culture in the violent pursuit of natural goals.

As though these inherent shifts in emphasis would not render the matter problematic enough, the concept of educational violence is readjusted a second time in the course of Benjamin's essay. As his argument unfolds, the author arrives at the famous distinction between two kinds of violence: the one that posits the law, and the one that preserves it ("rechtssetzende" and "rechtserhaltende Gewalt"). In addition, however, he introduces a third perspective on the problem, namely through the kind of violence that can *undo* the law, absolutely and without replacement. Benjamin calls it "divine" ("göttliche Gewalt"). As a pure means, divine violence is submitted neither to legal nor natural ends; its purpose aims neither at the conservation of any given nor at the founding of a new legal order. Undoing posited law and disintegrating the cultural institutions that order and govern our lives, this kind of violence is "rechtsvernichtend." It *annihilates*. Benjamin only offers very few clues toward making this kind of pure violence more fathomable. One of them is the proletarian general strike as a means of revolutionary politics that does not transform the given or negotiate the reform and improvement of a pre-established order, instead doing away with it in its entirety.[19] There is, however, another moment where Benjamin makes reference to an expressly *contemporary* example of pure (divine) violence, and its unexplained introduction is quite startling: "This divine violence is not only attested by religious tradition but is also found in present-day life in at least one sanctioned manifestation. The *educative violence*, which in its perfected form stands outside the law, is one of its manifestations."[20]

Paired with the proletarian general strike, Benjamin explicitly names *education* the only contemporary manifestation of divine violence. For our brief attempt to situate educational violence vis-à-vis the institutions of culture and of positive law, the implications of this passage could not be more momentous; and it is all the more vexing that instead of developing the argumentative import of his example, Benjamin merely posits it, letting it take effect without precisely measuring its reach. It remains up to the reader to appraise its ramifications.[21] If we take the passage at its word, there is the possibility of an educational violence completely stripped of any directedness toward a natural end while still remaining outside any posited law. This would be educational violence in its consummate expression—"was als erzieherische Gewalt *in ihrer vollendeten Form* außerhalb des Rechtes steht"—and it realizes itself as a manifestation of divine violence.

Benjamin's concept of educational violence thus goes through at least three stages of designation and redefinition: first, it is introduced as that which reshapes the natural individual into an agent of culture; second, it is remodeled according to pedagogical practices dedicated to the achievement of natural ends that need to be curbed through the intervention of culture, i.e., positive law. Instead of reaffirming the nature/culture divide, the problem of education, the way Benjamin conceptualizes it, scrambles this distinction, turning it irrecoverably blurry. In a third step of conceptual realignment, Benjamin introduces the ultimate possibility of educational violence as being *divine*, which implies that it neither functions as an agent of culture nor attempts to escape positive law in the pursuit of natural ends; instead, it announces the annihilation of all possible legitimacy. Education thus becomes legible as the possibility of abolishing all culture as we know it: it is the very prospect of undoing and dissolving the lawful institutions that order human existence. Education turns out to be the supreme site or scene, perhaps even one of the main inspirations, behind the triangular yet asymmetrical relationship between lawmaking, law-preserving, and divine violence. Divine violence appears on the site of education as *eluding* the clash between nature and culture, overcoming the dualism between legal and natural violence.[22] The "divine" instantiation of Benjamin's puzzling concept of "educational violence" gives us a sense of what it would mean to dream up a kind of education that would be truly revolutionary. Education as the force that reaches beyond the borders of what is given. Education as the radical impossibility of its institutions, no matter their form.

III

Forces of Education marks the culmination of a rich history of inspired collaboration on a global scale. Its primal scene dating back to a conversation on a bench in NYC's Washington Square Park in the fall of 2016, during which the editors first expressed the wish to pay closer attention to Walter Benjamin's early writings concerning school reform and the Youth Movement, our exploration of this early corpus of texts found its first expression in a seminar we proposed for the 2017 annual convention of the German Studies Association in Atlanta, titled "Benjamin's Pedagogy." This seminar brought together many of the volume's contributors and allowed us to launch a conversation that would accompany us for the years to come.

In 2018, our initiatives regarding the early Benjamin were recognized with the Young Scholars Prize, co-sponsored by the International Walter Benjamin Society, the Leibniz

Center for Literary and Cultural Research—ZfL Berlin, and the Walter Benjamin Archive Berlin. This generous grant allowed us to expand the purview of our network in order to unfold a conversation of global scope. Under the heading "Walter Benjamin and the Possibility of a Global Pedagogy," we organized an international conference co-hosted by the ZfL and the Walter Benjamin Archive in Berlin in early 2019. Led by our keynote speakers Ilit Ferber and Freddie Rokem, the conference brought together scholars from Austria, Brazil, Germany, Israel, Italy, the United Kingdom, and the United States. The collected volume we based on these events and conversations is to be understood not as their endpoint but as a first milestone as we continue our engagement with Benjamin and the heritage of his rich and provocative thought on the critique of education.

We would be remiss not to highlight those scholars whose decisive interventions paved the way for our explorations: in addition to the groundbreaking work of Michael Jennings—who so graciously agreed to preface our volume—we would like to make particular mention of Howard Eiland, who, together with Matthew Charles, recently edited an important issue of *boundary 2*, in which Benjamin's early works on education are contextualized for American audiences in a trailblazing effort. In their introduction, the editors criticize a tendency in Benjamin scholarship according to which readers often fail to ask whether Benjamin's early engagement with the Youth Movement and the writings he produced in this context "had any bearing on [his] subsequent philosophical and literary activity."[23] We share this observation and see our volume as both a historical and intellectual contextualization of Benjamin's early texts as well as an exploration of their "living on" (*Fortleben*) throughout his oeuvre. Eiland and Charles' special issue came in the wake of a dossier of texts published in *Pedagogy, Culture & Society*, edited by Carrie Paechter, Michael Rosen, and Tamara Bibby in 2016, that elucidates Benjamin's ideas about childhood and their importance for the broader discourse of pedagogy. In 2020, Tyson E. Lewis finally produced the first English-speaking monograph on the topic with *Walter Benjamin's Antifascist Education: From Riddles to Radio* (SUNY Press). Lewis's intervention is of particular importance, because it decidedly frames Benjamin's education as an inherently political project with a strong emphasis on its media-technological dimension. The book demonstrates that Benjamin's concept of education is not reducible to texts that explicitly critique the pedagogical circumstance and its institutional enframing, as he emphasizes that Benjamin's diverse cross-cultural curiosities about slapstick, riddles, urban architecture, theater, and radio are marked by a crucial pedagogical thrust. In the German academic context, Johannes Steizinger's monograph *Revolte, Eros und Sprache* (2016) contributed substantially to a comprehensive understanding of the young Benjamin and informed our volume especially in terms of the roles that the concept and metaphysics of youth play for a contemporary politics of education.[24]

The essays we gathered in *Forces of Education* significantly expand the ongoing conversation about Benjamin's pedagogy, and we are particularly proud to have been able to gather such contrasting voices in this book in order to unfold a complex conversation that brings together scholars from all stages in their careers, putting the ranks of established and high-profile Benjamin scholarship in touch with the perspective of a generation of newcomers. Rather than privileging one mode of reading or approaching Benjamin, the volume offers a multitude of methodologies, combining profound philological conscience and deconstructive sensitivity with a grounded sense for the historical and the inclusion of trans-medial perspectives.

As for the volume's structure, we decided to arrange the twelve chapters according to three sections, respectively titled "Genealogies of Learning," "Languages of Youth," and "Envisioning Pedagogical Futures." The first section starts with a contribution by Benjamin scholar and editor Clemens-Carl Härle, who interprets Benjamin's 1915 essay on "The Life of Students" as a turning point in his thinking that led him to a departure from his early work while nonetheless maintaining a sustained critique of the university and the form-giving power it exerts on its students' lives. Härle's intervention is framed by a thorough contextualization of Benjamin's essay in terms of Kant's transcendental dialectic. In the second chapter, Charles Gelman detects a similar "turn" in Benjamin's thought, which he interprets as a genuine development toward social critique. In his contribution, Gelman argues that in the years between "Moral Instruction" (1913) and "A Communist Pedagogy" (1927), Benjamin's engagement with the Marxist framework of thinking and writing took shape as a pedagogy of self-criticism, opposing the mental resistance characteristic of bourgeois ideology and the field of cultural production. Adding a crucial dimension to these philosophical-historical contexts, Laurence A. Rickels presents a psychoanalytic reading of the concept of youth as it emerges in Benjamin's early work. In particular, Rickels finds a compelling parallel between young Benjamin and the works of British psychoanalyst D.W. Winnicott, especially with regard to the latter's writings on adolescent development. Winnicott suggested that Nazism coincided with the superegoical evacuation of German adolescence, which Rickels sees anticipated and confirmed in Benjamin's encounter with clinical literature on psychosis, concretely with Alexander Mette's book *Language Peculiarities in Schizophrenia and Poetic Productions* which Benjamin reviewed in 1929. The volume's section on "Genealogies of Learning" concludes with an essay by Henry Sussman, whose contribution combines the philosophical-historical and psychoanalytic frames of reference shared by the preceding chapters while adding a deconstructive tone in a tour de force that follows the figure of the child in an attempt to present Benjamin as an inherently experimental, fragmentary, anti-systematic, and anti-institutional thinker.

In addition to his investment in Kant and Marx, the genealogical connection between Benjamin and Nietzsche marks one of the focal points of the volume's second section, "Languages of Youth." Both Natasha Hay and Ian Fleishman explore this important affinity, building on and adding to the vital insights that James McFarland's monograph presented on the matter.[25] Hay isolates the idea of a *Sprechsaal* ("conversation hall") that Benjamin realized with fellow students at the University of Berlin, interpreting it as a model for the autonomous discursive organization of an independent youth culture that allows for a renewed understanding of the aural and oral dimensions of education. As her argument unfolds, she draws a connection between Benjamin's aural activism and Nietzsche's famous critique in "On the Future of Our Educational Institutions" (1871). Invoking a second text of Nietzschean provenance, Ian Fleishman argues that the untimely and anti-institutional stance of "On the Advantage and Disadvantage of History for Life" (1874) served as a model for Benjamin's own attempt at "re-forming contemporary educational reform," as Fleishman puts it. He concludes with a thought that is taken up and explored in depth in Adi Nester's chapter, namely the sense that Benjamin's educational reform, whose subject is youth, does not articulate itself through slogans or concepts, but instead maintains a rigorous sigetics—a speaking in silence. Her comprehensive approach has Nester develop a detailed understanding of the "silence of youth" through Benjamin's concepts of history, language, and the possibility of experience and cognition, as she investigates a textual corpus that ranges from "The Metaphysics of Youth" to "On the Concept of History." That Benjamin's conversational pedagogy and his emphasis on the aural dimension of education are by no means reducible to his early writings is further emphasized by Ilit Ferber. Her chapter "In Voice Land" pays close attention to an often-neglected corpus of texts that Benjamin dedicated to the intersection of education and broadcasting. Ferber contextualizes Benjamin's radio plays as an experimental site that let him discover the potentialities of a "space that is solely acoustic," thus calling for an aural pedagogy that unfolds through sounds and voices. This adds an important media-technological dimension to the emphasis on the educative dimension of conversation and silence that Hay, Fleishman, and Nester elucidate in their contributions. It also displaces a reductive understanding of Benjamin's bearing on media studies that often privileges his reflections on visual media such as film, photography, and the stage at the expense of the aural dimension.

Opening the volume's final section, "Envisioning Pedagogical Futures," Gerhard Richter unfolds a concept of critique that finds its foundation in a practice of "self-pedagogy." Richter argues that Benjamin's early writings break open the concept of pedagogy from within. Concretely, Richter points out that pedagogy historically as well as etymologically implies a hierarchy according to which the pupil is led by another: the rearing subject, the subject of knowledge, the figure of authority. Richter's essay shows how Benjamin's pedagogical interventions reject this notion of "other-directedness," instead opting for a reconfigured understanding of the pedagogical relation as one that unfolds in a reflexive manner between self and self. The emerging process of self-pedagogy becomes aligned with the task of critique in that, to use Richter's formulation, it "places the critic in the simultaneous role of student and teacher." This argumentative thread is picked up in the subsequent chapter, in which Michael Powers pursues the subject of youth as one in "eternal rebellion" against society, the state, and the law. Pursuing the nonviolent and revolutionary "educative force" of Benjamin's pedagogy, Powers emphasizes the role-reversals between teacher and student that happen in scenes of improvisation and play. The idea that youth's rebellion is less subject to planned decree and prescription than *improvised* lawlessness is further explored in Thomas Schestag's reflection on the term "improvisation" as it appears in Benjamin's "On the Proletarian Children's Theater" (1929), a text written for the Latvian theater pedagogue Asja Lacis, whose work inspired Benjamin greatly. In his philological meditation, Schestag offers a detailed reading of Benjamin's text that pays close attention to the role the spectators play in Benjamin's envisioned theater, which the author proposes to read as a series of improvisations spawning "provisional visions," thus as *impro-vision*. At one moment, Benjamin calls the child's performance a "creative caesura" ("schöpferische Pause"), which Schestag suggests reading as a "*critical* pause" that allows for an understanding of the child's "improvisations" as so revolutionary that they revolt even against the very idea of revolution itself. Our volume concludes with a contribution by Nitzan Lebovic that emphasizes the *exigency* of Benjamin's pedagogical writings, not just in terms of a reform of our understanding of education and its institutions, but with respect to processes of a much wider scope that call for a redefinition of humanity's relationship with nature. Lebovic's argument relates Benjamin's writings on education to the discourse on the Anthropocene. Through a comprehensive reading that connects various tropes prevalent in Benjamin's early writings with later moments in his work, Lebovic suggests conceiving of Benjamin as a thinker characterized by a subtle premonition of the anthropocenic upheaval and a deep concern for ecocritical questions. Lebovic's contribution carries a sense of urgency stirred by a particular temporality that refuses to provide a neat kind of closure to our appraisal of Benjamin's politics of pedagogy. Instead, it serves as an invitation further to consider the corpus of his earliest texts and the ways in which they speak to our embattled present as well as our precarious futures.

*

Thinking of the many friends, colleagues, and mentors who accompanied the coming-together of this volume, we would like to emphasize our great gratitude for the reliable guidance we received from Peter Fenves and Mike Jennings, who supported us with solid advice and encouragement. We would also like to thank Elissa Marder, Kevin McLaughlin, and Freddie Rokem for enriching our conversations in sustained and always brilliant ways. We are immensely grateful to Daniel Weidner and the International Walter Benjamin Society; Ursula Marx, Nadine Werner, Erdmut Wizisla and the Walter Benjamin Archive; and Eva Geulen and the ZfL Berlin for generously funding and facilitating our research. We also thank our home institutions, the Department of Languages and Literary Studies at Lafayette College as well as the Department of German, Russian and East European Languages and Literatures at Rutgers University, for offering us the encouragement and support needed to put together this essay collection. Series editor Andrew Benjamin and our in-house editors Liza Thompson and Lucy Russell have been extraordinarily supportive in providing our work with the most exquisite home we could have hoped for, while Christopher Mayer offered crucial assistance with the initial copy-edits. We would like to thank Abby, Anselm, Tristan, and Elissa for being our motivating and, in many ways, educational forces throughout our work on this project. Lastly, our contributors are owed the greatest debt of gratitude: without your brilliant interventions this book would not exist. Thank you.

Notes

The epigraphs to this text are taken from: *Teaching to Transgress* by bell hooks, copyright © 1994 Routledge, reproduced by permission of Taylor & Francis Group; and *Stoner*, copyright © 1965 John Williams, reprinted by permission.

1. *SW* 4: 389–400.
2. Bill Readings, *University in Ruins* (Cambridge, MA and London: Harvard University Press, 1996).

3   See Werner Hamacher, "Freistätte," *Sprachgerechtigkeit* (Frankfurt am Main: Fischer, 2018), 283–322.
4   Jacques Derrida, "The University Without Condition," trans. Peggy Kamuf, *Without Alibi* (Stanford: Stanford University Press, 2002), 202–37.
5   See for instance Christopher Newfield, *The Great Mistake: How We Wrecked Public Universities and How We Can Fix Them* (Baltimore: Johns Hopkins University Press, 2016); and Wendy Brown, *Undoing the Demos: Neoliberalism's Stealth Revolution* (Brooklyn: Zone Books, 2015), esp. 175–222.
6   The literature on these matters is vast. For brevity's sake, we would like to mention, in particular, David Graeber's *Debt: The first 5,000 Years* (Brooklyn: Melvillehouse, 2011); Annie McClanahan, *Dead Pledges: Debt, Crisis, and Twenty-First Century Culture* (Stanford: Stanford University Press, 2016); Uncertain Commons, *Speculate This!* (Durham: Duke University Press, 2013); Stefano Harney and Fred Moten, *The Undercommons: Fugitive Planning and Black Study* (Wivenhoe/New York/Port Watson: Minor Compositions, 2013); and Jennifer Doyle, *Campus Sex/Campus Security* (South Pasadena: Semiotext(e), 2015).
7   Karl Marx, "Theses on Feuerbach," *The Marx-Engels Reader*, ed. Robert C. Tucker (New York: Norton, 1972), 144. Translation modified.
8   Paulo Freire, *Pedagogy of the Oppressed*, trans. Myra Bergman Ramos (New York and London: Bloomsbury, 2012); bell hooks, *Teaching to Transgress: Education as the Practice of Freedom* (New York: Routledge, 1994).
9   Barbara Johnson (ed.), *The Pedagogical Imperative: Teaching as a Literary Genre*, Yale French Studies 63 (1982).
10 Nick Srnicek, *Platform Capitalism* (Cambridge: Polity, 2017).
11 The first comprehensive English-language edition of these texts appeared in 2011 as *Early Writings: 1910–1917 (EW)*.
12 See "'Experience,'" *EW* 116–19.
13 Compare Grimm's definition: "vgl. angelsächsisch geweald, -wald m. n. (power, strength, might, efficacy ... empire, rule, dominion, mastery, sway, jurisdiction, government, protection, keeping, a bridle-bit, potestas, facultas, imperium, dictio, arbitrium, jus, cannus).... altnordisch vald n. (macht, gewalt, kraft, ursache)." Jacob and Wilhelm Grimm, *Deutsches Wörterbuch*, vol. 6 (Leibzig: Hirzel, 1911), ln. 5095.
14 See "Critique of Violence," *SW* 1: 236–52.
15 "Then, like every generation that preceded us, we have been endowed with a *weak* messianic power [eine *schwache* messianische Kraft], a power on which the past has a claim" ("On the Concept of History," *SW* 4: 390). The generational relation that Benjamin addresses here may become readable as inhabiting a pedagogical space since we cannot think education and pedagogy without at the same time considering the historical sequence of the generations and the transmission of knowledge and experience from the old to the young. Benjamin's perspective offers a renewed and critical understanding of this structure of historical succession. See also Jacques Derrida's insistence on the concept of "force" in the context of discussing Benjamin's argument about "Gewalt": "Force of Law," trans. Mary Quaintance, *Cardozo Law Review* 11 (1990), 920–1045.
16 *SW* 1: 250; *GS* 2: 200.
17 "School Reform," *EW* 59; *GS* 2: 14. Emphasis added ("Es gilt einen Ausweg zu finden aus dem Widerstreit zwischen natürlicher wahrhaftiger Entwicklung einerseits und der Aufgabe, das natürliche Individuum zum kulturellen umzubilden andererseits, jener Aufgabe, die ohne Gewalt niemals lösbar sein wird").

18 *SW* 1: 238; *GS* 2: 182 ("[Die] Rechtsordnung … drängt darauf, … Gebiete, für welche Naturzwecke prinzipiell in weiten Grenzen freigegeben werden, wie das der Erziehung, durch Rechtszwecke einzuschränken, sobald jene Naturzwecke mit einem übergroßen Maß von Gewalttätigkeit erstrebt werden, wie sie dies in den Gesetzen über die Grenzen der erzieherischen Strafbefugnis tut.").

19 See Werner Hamacher's analysis of Benjamin's politics of pure means and the way it forces us to rethink speech act theory and its understanding of performance in "Afformativ, Streik," trans. Dana Hollander, in *Cardozo Law Review* 13, no. 4 (1991), 1133–57.

20 *SW* 1: 250; *GS* 2: 200. Translation modified. Emphasis added ("Diese göttliche Gewalt bezeugt sich nicht durch die religiöse Überlieferung allein, vielmehr findet sie mindestens in einer geheiligten Manifestation sich auch im gegenwärtigen Leben vor. Was als erzieherische Gewalt in ihrer vollendeten Form außerhalb des Rechtes steht, ist eine ihrer Erscheinungsformen").

21 See Eva Geulen's insightful comments on the matter of education in the context of Benjamin's "Critique of Violence": "Legislating Education: Kant, Hegel, and Benjamin on 'Pedagogical Violence,'" in *Cardozo Law Review* 26, no. 3 (2005): 943–56. A more recent discussion of Benjamin's pedagogy with respect to the model and history of bourgeois education can be found in Sami Khatib's "Practice Makes Perfect: Undoing Bourgeois Pedagogy," in *boundary 2* 45, no. 2 (May 2018): 63–86. See also Mladen Gladić, "Erziehung, zweckfrei: Zur Medialität der Pädagogik bei Walter Benjamin," in *Walter Benjamins anthropologisches Denken*, ed. Carolin Duttlinger, Ben Morgan, and Anthony Phelan (Freiburg: Rombach, 2012), 215–41.

22 This thought-image anticipates a later formulation in *One-Way Street*: "But who would trust a cane wielder who proclaimed the mastery of children by adults to be the purpose of education? Is not education, above all, the indispensable ordering of the relationship between generations and therefore mastery (if we are to use this term) of that relationship and not of children?" (*SW* 1: 487). Matthew Charles attempts to disentangle precisely the contradiction between a rejection of the institutional forms of violence which mark the history of pedagogy and the conjuring of a violence that manifests itself as the revolutionary potential of true education. See Matthew Charles, "Towards a Critique of Educative Violence: Walter Benjamin and 'Second Education,'" *Pedagogy, Culture & Society* 24, no. 4 (2016): 525–36.

23 Matthew Charles and Howard Eiland, "Introduction," in *boundary 2* 45, no. 2 (May 2018): 1.

24 For an overview of the literature available on the topic, please consult our selected bibliography appended to the "Chronicle of Benjamin's School and Student Years" included in this volume.

25 James MacFarland, *Constellation: Friedrich Nietzsche and Walter Benjamin in the Now-Time of History* (New York: Fordham University Press, 2013).

Chronicle of Benjamin's School and Student Years

Dennis Johannßen and Dominik Zechner

Benjamin's early life and writings are surrounded by a nebulous aura. The years between 1912 and 1914, during which he became the leader of a radical intellectual subgroup of the German Youth Movement, are particularly opaque. Many commentators suspect that the various affiliations, disputes, and struggles of these years can no longer be fully reconstructed. Benjamin's own archive of these years, which could have shed further light on the period, was looted by the Nazis in 1933 when he was forced to leave Berlin. In addition, Benjamin's early years were shaped by his formative time at the Haubinda boarding school, of which not much is known, and by his perplexing decade-long commitment to the reform pedagogue Gustav Wyneken, who was dismissed from two teaching positions and convicted of sexual misconduct with minors in 1922.[1]

Earlier reconstructions of Benjamin's *Lehrjahre* emphasized the radicality of the cesura that occurred in the summer of 1914, which prompted him to break with the Youth Movement and Wyneken, cutting ties with almost all his friends. In particular, Benjamin's radical idealism, his defense of the indeterminacy and openness of spirit (*Geist*) against any kind of practical political activism, cannot easily be reconciled with his later engagement with Marxism. Even within the many changing and shifting orientations of the Youth Movement, Benjamin's uncompromising defense of spirit, which he developed in conversation with Wyneken's pedagogical doctrines, differed increasingly from the views of almost everyone around him. Interested in these inconsistencies, later commentators explored the continuities rather than the ruptures between Benjamin's thought before and after 1914, focusing on his unorthodox idealism, his stance towards Judaism and theology, and his unique philological attention to all things spiritual, cultural, and artistic.

Benjamin's thought during his early years resembles an "eddy" pulling in an astonishing number of ideas, perspectives, and impulses.[2] Some of his key concepts that link his earlier to his later writings, such as that of experience (*Erfahrung*), arose in the context of his engagement with questions of pedagogy and education. This engagement was informed by explorations of philosophy, literature, theater, media, and politics, and held together by his long-standing commitment to Wyneken and his vision of School Reform. Already before 1914, this vision became the backdrop upon which Benjamin formed his own perspective. During the 1920s and 1930s, Benjamin picked up many of the loose ends of his early years. Adorno wrote that the young Benjamin "reflected, absorbed, and educated himself on all the spiritual tendencies of his teenage years, while not belonging to any of them."[3] The following chronicle of Benjamin's teenage years, from his first private lessons to his break with Wyneken and his move to Munich in 1915, traces some of these "spiritual tendencies" as they relate to questions of pedagogy and education in Benjamin's works.

The First Years, 1892–1905. On July 15, 1892, Benjamin was born in Berlin, Charlottenburg into a wealthy assimilated family of Ashkenazi Jewish descent. His mother, Pauline Schoenflies, came from a family of cattle and wheat merchants in Mecklenburg. Benjamin described her as a mild and consoling person, and she entered *Berlin Childhood around 1900* as the archetype of the storyteller. His father, Emil, was a banker in Paris before he settled in Berlin as an art auctioneer and investor. Benjamin portrayed him as a primeval ruler using loud and violent language with clients on the phone, but he was also the impressive connoisseur who could tell the quality of a rug through the sole of his shoes. Benjamin's father passed away in 1926 and his mother in 1930.

Benjamin had two siblings, Georg and Dora. Georg, three years younger, was forced into suicide in the Mauthausen Concentration Camp in 1942. His sister Dora was nine years younger than Benjamin. She died in Switzerland in 1946. The three siblings grew up in considerable wealth. The family had maids from France, personal delivery personnel, and vacation homes in Potsdam and Neubabelsberg. In 1912, the year Benjamin graduated from high school, his father bought a fortress-like mansion in Berlin Grunewald, where the children, including Benjamin's later family, lived for extended periods of time. Benjamin's father, who owned several businesses, including an ice-skating rink with a bar, lost his entire fortune during the hyperinflation of 1923. The initial luxury and its subsequent loss deeply shaped Benjamin's life and work.

Benjamin received his primary school education from tutors in a small circle of children from privileged families, including children of noble descent. One of his first school essays was titled "On Nobility." To prepare him for public middle school, Benjamin received additional private lessons. In 1902, he joined the sixth grade at the Kaiser-Friedrich-Schule near Savignyplatz. Assigned seating, solitary confinement, and caning were prevalent. Benjamin disliked the school. With the outlook of a talented and privileged student, he described the nameless masses trudging up and down the stairs. His fellow students painted the Kaiser-Friedrich-Schule in different, much more agreeable colors.

In 1905, Benjamin's parents sent their thirteen-year-old son to the Landerziehungsheim Haubinda, a boarding school at the south-west border of Thuringia, founded by the reform pedagogue Hermann Lietz. Benjamin was struggling with poor health, which his parents hoped would improve in the country. For about a year, his teacher was the philosopher Gustav Wyneken, who had to leave Haubinda in 1906 because of conflicts with the administration. Wyneken went on to cofound the Free School Community Wickersdorf in a remote forest in Thuringia that existed through World War I, the Weimar Republic, the Third Reich, and the GDR until it was closed in 1991. At Haubinda, where he stayed until 1907, Benjamin began to engage with the German Youth Movement.

School Years at Haubinda and in Berlin, 1905–12. The German Youth Movement (*Deutsche Jugendbewegung*) originated around 1896 with the Wandervogel movement in Berlin, Stieglitz. The movement, which began with teachers who took their students on trips, so called "Fahrten," to the countryside, responded to the effects of industrialization, the rapid growth of urban centers, and the authoritarian social structures of the Wilhelmine Empire. The Wandervogel dominated the Youth Movement until about 1910, when a variety of smaller school, youth, and student groups came together to form the Free German Youth (*Freideutsche Jugend*), distinct from the eponymous movement founded in the GDR in 1946.

Part of the formation of the Free German Youth were rural boarding schools, or "Landerziehungsheime," like Haubinda, where students and teachers lived, learned, and worked together. In contrast to the strict hierarchical separation of rights and responsibilities in the Wilhelmine education system, the idea of a reciprocal and participatory relationship between students and teachers informed the underlying pedagogy. The professional and practical curriculum of the public schools was amended with music, dance, visual arts, and extensive physical exercise in the outdoors. Former attendees later likened the educational practices at the boarding schools to American colleges, just without the German nationalist pathos.[4] After 1923, the Bündische Jugend, a federation of youth groups based on the Wandervogel, became the main current of the Youth Movement. Large parts of the Bündische Jugend were absorbed by the Hitler Youth in 1933.

Benjamin used ambiguous language and images to describe his time at Haubinda.[5] It can hardly be overstated how important the encounter with Wyneken was for his intellectual formation. Benjamin credits him with inspiring his love for literature and philosophy, and he seems to have strengthened his sense for the power of the written word. After his return to the Kaiser-Friedrich-Schule in 1907, Benjamin founded a "Freundeskreis" (circle of friends)—a group of like-minded peers and students who met regularly for dramatic readings of canonical plays followed by open discussions. He read Wyneken's programmatic essay, "The Idea of the Free School Community" (1906–08), which messianically announces a new world order to be realized by the youth. Wyneken references Plato, Fichte, Schopenhauer, and Nietzsche, but at the center of his doctrine was Hegel's concept of objective spirit, which designates the manifestation of an epoch's ideas in its political, social, and cultural institutions.

Wyneken's vision was not the realization of small villages for alternative education, but the transformation of the entire public school system, and eventually of society as a whole, based on a heroic relation to Germany's cultural heritage and a new pedagogical eros. While he opposed the hierarchical and corporative education system of the Empire, Wyneken's pedagogy was founded on the principle of leadership ("Führerprinzip") that implied overcoming the authoritative border between student and teacher while paradoxically insisting on the students' subordination to their individually chosen mentors. Wyneken's doctrine became the foundation, if not the dogma, of Benjamin's early thought. He recommended Wyneken's essays to his friends and fellow students, and only began to question his teachings in the winter of 1913.

In 1910, Benjamin's first writings, among them the poem "The Poet" and the prose piece "At Night," were published in the first series of the journal *Der Anfang* ("The Beginning"). This journal existed in three different versions until the fall of 1914. It was one of the two outlets for Benjamin's work and engagement during his first student years, the other being his enthusiastic work for the School Reform branches in Freiburg and Berlin. In 1910, Wyneken was expelled from his position at the Free School Community Wickersdorf, after which he traveled and lectured across Germany. During this time, Benjamin intensified his exchange with Wyneken, describing him as the sole center of his thought and himself as "a strict and fanatic student."[6] He later mentioned Wyneken as one of the two most important people of his early years of philosophical apprenticeship, the other most likely being his friend, the poet C. F. Heinle.

Benjamin's earliest preserved letters, addressed to his friend Herbert Belmore, are from 1910 and 1911. They began as romanticized experiments in style, but soon became travel and reading diaries that show Benjamin's characteristic efforts to intensify the experience of his journeys in writing. The March 1911 issue of *Der Anfang* contained Benjamin's essay "Sleeping Beauty," which concerns, for the first time, questions of pedagogy and educational critique. In 1912, Benjamin completed his Abitur, the German high school diploma. Looking back at his school days, he lamented the absence of an "open, glad exchange between teachers and pupils," the kind of exchange he may have experienced at Haubinda.[7]

First Year of Studies in Freiburg and Berlin, 1912–13. During the next two years, Benjamin studied alternately at the University of Freiburg in the summer and at the Kaiser-Wilhelm-University, today's Humboldt University, in the winter. He first moved to Freiburg in the summer of 1912, where he declared a major in philology and attended courses in philosophy and history. Among his professors were the Neo-Kantian philosopher Heinrich Rickert and the nationalist historian Friedrich Meinecke.

Benjamin joined the local branch of the School Reform and continued to write essays on pedagogy and education, among them "School Reform: A Cultural Movement" (1912) and "Epilogue" (1912). From May to June, Benjamin traveled with two friends to Italy. This educational journey, common for students from well-situated families, gave Benjamin the opportunity to experiment further with the genre of the travel diary.

In August 1912, Benjamin went to Stolpmünde at the Northern Sea, today's Ustka, for a summer vacation. He met the poet and literary historian Ludwig Strauß, who tried to win him for the cause of Zionism. In his letters from the fall and winter, Benjamin shared that his first encounter with Judaism was through the experience of anti-Semitism and an abstract notion of piety, adding that he was unable to engage with Zionism because his life at that time could only have one spiritual center, Wyneken's School Reform.[8]

Disappointed with his professors and fellow students, Benjamin continued his studies in Berlin, where he attended lectures and courses by Georg Simmel, Ernst Cassirer, and the historian Kurt Breysig. Besides his studies, Benjamin dedicated these months primarily to his work for the third and last series of *Der Anfang*. The first issue of this series appeared in May 1913, containing Benjamin's essay "'Experience,'" one of the few early works that he later described as anticipatory.

Second Semester in Freiburg, Summer 1913. Upon his return to Freiburg in March or April 1913, Benjamin had Wyneken's support in taking over and reorganizing the Freiburg School Reform branch, which had been led by Benjamin's friend Philipp Kellner. Benjamin successively replaced Kellner, gave lectures on the novelist Carl Spitteler, and read from Wyneken's writings. During these months, he met the poet Christoph Friedrich Heinle, who followed him to Berlin in the fall, and with whom he developed an enigmatic and fateful friendship over the course of the next year. Benjamin attended lectures and seminars by Heinrich Rickert on logic and the metaphysics of Henri Bergson. Also present in these courses was Martin Heidegger, three years older than Benjamin, who defended his dissertation on Neo-Kantian logics of judgment a few months later.

In March 1913, the first *Sprechsaal* (conversation hall) discussion group was founded in Vienna by Siegfried Bernfeld, the leader of the Academic Committee for School Reform (ACS) and co-editor of the third series of *Der Anfang*. Bernfeld's later accounts are among the most illuminating materials on the Youth Movement milieu surrounding Benjamin.[9] The weekly meetings of the *Sprechsaal* formed the backdrop of Benjamin's pursuit of conversational modes of pedagogy; they were open to all students and provided a forum for different age groups and social backgrounds to discuss a broad variety of topics. Usually, the meetings began with a lecture on a general topic such as "Youth Culture," "The Esperanto Movement," or "On Reproductive Art," followed by an open discussion and administrative housekeeping.

On Pentecost, Benjamin visited Paris for the first time. The Louvre, the cafés, and the Grand Boulevard made the most profound impression on him. Later that spring, he visited Basel, where he saw Albrecht Dürer's *Melancholia I*. Various letters from this time show Benjamin grappling with questions of coeducation, gender, and sexuality. He advocated for a woman president of the School Reform branch, spoke up against erasing problems regarding misogyny and homosexuality from the curriculum, and he called Rickert's new philosophy of value a failure because it restricted the moral perfectibility of women. His own attempts to theorize prostitution are critical of objectification, but difficult to reconcile with an emancipatory perspective.[10]

In June, Benjamin responds to a request by Wyneken to review recent scholarship on coeducation in philosophical and pedagogical journals. With the precocious tone of a gifted undergraduate in the third semester, he attested a "colossal poverty of spirit" to the forty volumes of pedagogical literature that he scoured, bemoaning empty formulas regarding attitude (*Gesinnung*), society and individual, and the abstract goal of harmony. A year later, he described the orientation of the Freiburg School Reform chapter as being concerned not with pedagogical work, but with the "student question." He described "pedagogy" as a realm in which the movement found "at first almost symbolically and inwardly the subject matter to develop a youthful student attitude."[11]

On June 28, the *Sprechsaal Berliner Schüler* was founded. Together with the student Ernst Joël, who ran the social office of the student association, Benjamin rented an apartment, the "Heim," for their meetings. Along with his work for *Der Anfang*, from which he subsequently retreated due to internal conflicts, the Berlin *Sprechsaal* was the center of Benjamin's efforts and activities over the next months. A former member described the *Sprechsaal* as follows: "They had flowing hair, wore open shirts and velvet pants. They spoke, no, preached in celebratory, well-composed sentences of their renunciation of bourgeois life and of the youth's right to their own culture, corresponding to their value."[12]

Around July 1913, Benjamin began to articulate what he "was able to grasp of the essence of education." His letters to Carla Seligson, the sister of Heinle's girlfriend Rika (Frederika) Seligson, contain some of the most insightful formulations about his understanding of youth and youth culture. For Benjamin, youth culture is not a "movement," a word he used dismissively, but a transformed attitude toward spiritual life. "Being young means not so much to serve spirit, but to *await* it.... This permanently vibrating feeling for the abstractness of pure spirit is what I propose to call youth [*Dies ständige vibrierende Gefühl für die Abstraktheit des reinen Geistes möchte ich Jugend nennen*]."[13] In these sentences one can hear a distancing from Wyneken's reliance on Hegel's objective spirit. For Wyneken, serving spirit implied a practical, purpose-driven relation to the world, diminishing the radical indeterminacy of what Benjamin called spirit.

Berlin *Sprechsaal* and *Der Anfang*, 1913-14. Following his return to Berlin in September 1913, Benjamin's letters show further critical overtones and signs of distancing from Wyneken. In early October, Benjamin gave a lecture on the "Freiburg Orientation" at the First Pedagogical Student Conference in Breslau. On the way back, he attended the First Free German Youth Meeting, which took place on October 10-12 at Hanstein Castle and the Hoher Meißner near Kassel. In his article "Youth Was Silent" (1913), Benjamin denounces the failure to oppose the strong nationalism and anti-Semitism at the event. Bernfeld estimated that Wyneken's followers during these years comprised about 3,000 students, around one-third of which were Jewish.[14]

In November, Benjamin had a falling-out with Heinle. Most likely, they disagreed about the lecture "Youth" they wanted to give together. Heinle seems to have objected to Benjamin's draft, and they ended up giving two separate lectures on the same topic. They worked out their differences a few weeks later. Heinle approached him "in the name of love," while Benjamin "opposed him with the symbol," he wrote to Carla Seligson. "The goal remains to push [Heinle] out of the movement and leave the rest to spirit."[15]

In January 1914, the *Sprechsaal* for German-Aryan students was founded in Vienna. Benjamin opposed the decision and resigned from the ACS. In February, he was elected president of the Berlin Free Student Association. During the same month, Wyneken was publicly criticized, leading to a ban of *Der Anfang* from middle schools in Bavaria. On March 7-8, a Leadership Meeting (*Führertreffen*) took place in Marburg. This meeting, organized by the major figures of the various movements, brought together student and youth groups from across the country to give the Free German Youth a more rigorous organization. The majority of the participating groups voted to exclude Wyneken's groups, including the Freie Schulgemeinde Wickersdorf, the group around *Der Anfang*, and the Berlin *Sprechsaal*.

In March 1914, a revealing split occurred within *Der Anfang*. Formally, Benjamin was part of the same subgroup of Wyneken's School Reform as the journal's editors. Bernfeld was committed to working in solidarity with working class children and the economically disadvantaged. In the name of pure spirit, and seemingly contradicting his later engagement with Marxist thought, Benjamin opposed this practical social engagement. "I am thinking (not in the sense of socialism, but in some other sense) of the masses of those who are excluded [*Menge der Ausgeschlossenen*],"[16] he wrote to Carla Seligson. Later, in "The Life of Students" (1915–16), he added that he discerned "no internal or intrinsic connection between the spiritual existence of a student and, say, his concern for the welfare of workers' children or even for other students." Instead of engaging in social activism for the poor and the working class, Benjamin was committed to "making visible and ascendent in the present" the "most endangered, excoriated, and ridiculed creations and ideas."[17]

Between March and April, Heinle and another student, Simon Guttmann, attempted to take over the editorial board of *Der Anfang*. The impression arose that Wyneken would no longer serve as chief editor after he and his doctrines were publicly attacked. The coup failed. Benjamin, who had just been elected president, tried to mediate, but his sympathies were clearly with Heinle and Guttmann. After Georg Gretor, known as George Barbizon, a colleague in the Youth Reform movement and the editor of *Der Anfang*, confronted him, Benjamin wrote an open letter to Wyneken in which he declared that he was convinced of Heinle and Guttmann's innocence. He appealed to Wyneken as the only objective instance that could restore the integrity of the Youth Reform group, which he depicts as being compromised by Barbizon's unconfirmed accusations. The episode is an impressive example of Benjamin's diplomatic genius. It is unclear how involved he was in instigating the coup, but he emerged as the neutral and unscathed winner of the conflict.[18]

On May 4, Benjamin held the inaugural speech for his presidency, which he later included in the final version of "The Life of Students," published in Kurt Hiller's yearbook *Das Ziel* (The Goal). Benjamin gave the lecture again on June 14, presumably with revisions, at the Free Student Association meeting in Weimar. In the same month, he organized a discussion with Martin Buber and a lecture by Ludwig Klages on graphology. In May, Benjamin met his future wife, Dora Sophie Pollak (born Kellner). Their son Stefan Raphael, Benjamin's only child, was born in April 1918. The couple divorced in 1930.

C. F. Heinle's Suicide and Studies in Munich, 1914–15. On July 28, 1914, Austria-Hungry declared war on Serbia. On August 8, C. F. Heinle and Rika Seligson committed suicide in the "Heim" that Benjamin and Joël had rented for the *Sprechsaal*. In the morning, Benjamin received a note by Heinle, announcing their intention. Heinle's suicide had a traumatic effect on Benjamin. After months of epistolary silence, he broke ties with almost all of his friends and colleagues. Many commentators described Heinle's suicide as a deep rupture in Benjamin's life and work. In the years to come, he composed fifty-two posthumously published sonnets to commemorate Heinle's loss.

In the summer of 1914, Benjamin volunteered to join the army of the Second Reich, not out of enthusiasm, but in anticipation of his conscription and to remain with his friends. During the physical screening, he simulated palsy and his case was postponed. A second request came in January 1917. He again avoided induction by asking his future wife, Dora, to hypnotize him so he could pretend to have sciatica.

During the first months of 1915, Benjamin began his translation of Baudelaire's *Tableaux Parisiens* and wrote the essays "The Rainbow" and "Two Poems by Friedrich Hölderlin," the latter as a tribute to Heinle. In March, Benjamin finally openly broke with Wyneken because of his public support for the war. Six months earlier, Wyneken had given a lecture titled "War and Youth" (October 1914), in which he celebrated the war as an ethical experience of youth. Benjamin presented his separation from Wyneken as an act of faithfulness after the mentor had betrayed his own teachings by submitting the idea of youth to the state. At the end of June, Benjamin met his lifelong friend, Gershom Scholem, at a lecture by Kurt Hiller.

In the fall of 1915, Benjamin moved to Munich, where he studied with the art historian Heinrich Wölfflin, the phenomenologist Moritz Geiger, and, in a private seminar, with Walter Lehmann, an ethnologist, linguist, and specialist for Mesoamerican cultures. In Lehmann's seminar, which Benjamin described vividly, he sat a few seats away from Rainer Maria Rilke and met Werner Kraft and Felix Noeggerath. Benjamin attended a lecture by Heinrich Mann, who raised his voice moderately but distinctively at the point that concerned the war, a gesture that Benjamin called "politically grand and inciting [*im politischen Sinne groß und entflammend*]."[19]

"What became of us?" the physician and former member of the Berlin *Sprechsaal*, Martin Gumpert, asked in 1939. "One of us, the most talented, lives as an émigré philosopher in Paris and became a Marxist; another one runs an antique store in Rome; yet another one was a lawyer and now publishes newspapers in South Africa.... Many died in the murderous fire of Langemarck in 1914. No one, as far as I can see, became a Nazi. Yet this 'Free German Youth Movement,' as we later called it, bears a mythical complicity in the emergence of National Socialism."[20] Although Benjamin never fully subscribed to any branch of the Movement, he was an avid supporter of Youth Culture and Wyneken's School Reform. The critique of what Gumpert called "mythical complicity" accompanied and shaped Benjamin's entire critical project.

Notes

1 Besides Benjamin's writings, letters, and curricula vitae, this chronicle is based on the following biographical and historical sources: Howard Eiland and Michael W. Jennings, *Walter Benjamin: A Critical Life* (Cambridge, MA: The Belknap Press of Harvard University Press, 2014), 12–74; Howard Eiland, "Translator's Introduction," *EW* 1–13; Nadine Werner, "Zeit und Person," *Benjamin-Handbuch: Leben—Werk—Wirkung*, ed. Burkhardt Lindner (Stuttgart: Metzler, 2011), 3–5; Momme Brodersen, *Spinne im eigenen Netz: Walter Benjamin, Leben und Werk* (Bühl-Moos: Elster, 1990), 9–106; Bernd Witte, *Walter Benjamin* (Reinbek bei Hamburg: Rowohlt, 1985), 7–29; and "Anmerkungen der Herausgeber," *GS* 2: 825–88. For specific aspects such as Gustav Wyneken, Youth Movement, and Judaism in Benjamin's early years, see the selected bibliography.
2 Benjamin himself uses the image of the eddy (*Strudel*) to illustrate his understanding of "origin" (*Ursprung*) in *Origin of German Tragic Drama*. *OT* 45; *GS* 1: 226.

3   Theodor W. Adorno, "A l'écart de tous les courants," *Gesammelte Schriften*, ed. Rolf Tiedemann (Frankfurt am Main: Suhrkamp, 1970–86), vol. 20/1, 189. Our translation. "Alle geistigen Tendenzen seiner Jugendjahre hat er reflektierend in sich aufgenommen, an ihnen sich gebildet, keiner ist er zuzurechnen gewesen."
4   "Anmerkungen der Herausgeber," *GS* 2: 868.
5   "Landschaft von Haubinda," *GS* 6: 195; "Noch einmal," *GS* 4: 435.
6   *GB* 1: 64. Our translation.
7   "Epilog," *EW* 55.
8   *GB* 1: 69–70, 76.
9   "Anmerkungen der Herausgeber," *GS* 2: 845–52.
10 *GB* 1: 117, 125–33, 142; *GS* 2: 40.
11 "Ziele und Wege der studentisch-pädagogischen Gruppen an reichsdeutschen Universitäten," *GS* 2: 63. Our translation.
12 Martin Gumpert, quoted in "Anmerkungen der Herausgeber," *GS* 2: 867. Our translation.
13 "Letter to Carla Seligson, September 15, 1913," *GB* 1: 175. Our translation.
14 "Anmerkungen der Herausgeber," *GS* 2: 848. In Vienna, 450 out of the 500 members of the ACS were Jewish.
15 *GB* 1: 181. Our translation.
16 *GB* 1: 182. Our translation.
17 *EW* 200, 197.
18 *GB* 1: 198–213, 495–514.
19 *GB* 1: 302. Our translation.
20 "Anmerkungen der Herausgeber," *GS* 2: 868–9. Our translation.

Selected Bibliography

Benjamin's Writings

Early Writings, 1910–1917. Translated by Howard Eiland. Cambridge, MA: The Belknap Press of Harvard University Press, 2011.
Gesammelte Briefe. 6 vols. Edited by Christoph Gödde and Henri Lonitz. Frankfurt am Main: Suhrkamp, 1995–2000.
Gesammelte Schriften. 7 vols. 3 suppl. Edited by Rolf Tiedemann and Hermann Schweppenhäuser. Frankfurt am Main: Suhrkamp, 1972–89.
Selected Writings. 4 vols. Edited by Howard Eiland and Michael W. Jennings. Cambridge, MA: Belknap Press of Harvard University Press, 1996–2003.
The Complete Correspondence, 1910–1940. Translated by Manfred R. Jacobson and Evelyn M. Jacobson. Chicago: University of Chicago Press, 1994.
Werke und Nachlaß. Kritische Gesamtausgabe. Edited by Christoph Gödde and Henri Lonitz. Frankfurt am Main: Suhrkamp, 2008–.

Education and Pedagogy

Charles, Matthew. "Erziehung: The Critical Theory of Education and Counter-Education." *The Sage Handbook of Frankfurt School Critical Theory*. Edited by Beverly Best, Werner Bonefeld, and Chris O'Kane, 988–1005. London: Sage, 2018.

Charles, Matthew. "Pedagogy as 'Cryptic Politics': Benjamin, Nietzsche, and the End of Education." *boundary 2* 45, no. 2 (2018): 35–62.

Charles, Matthew. "Towards a Critique of Educative Violence: Walter Benjamin and 'Second Education.'" *Pedagogy, Culture & Society* 24, no. 4 (2016): 525–36.

Felman, Shoshana. "Benjamin's Silence." *Critical Inquiry* 25 (1999): 201–34.

Geulen, Eva. "Legislating Education: Kant, Hegel, and Benjamin on 'Pedagogical Violence.'" *Cardozo Law Review* 26, no. 3 (2005): 943–56.

Gladić, Mladen. "Erziehung, zweckfrei: Zur Medialität der Pädagogik bei Walter Benjamin." *Benjamins anthropologisches Denken*. Edited by Carolin Duttlinger, Ben Morgan, and Anthony Phelan, 215–41. Freiburg: Rombach, 2012.

Khatib, Sami R. "Practice Makes Perfect: On Undoing Bourgeois Pedagogy." *boundary 2* 45, no. 2 (2018): 63–86.

Lewis, Tyson E. *Walter Benjamin's Antifascist Education: From Riddles to Radio*. Albany, NY: SUNY Press, 2020.

Lewis, Tyson E. "Walter Benjamin's Radio Pedagogy." *Thesis Eleven* 142, no. 1 (2017): 18–33.

Youth and Youth Movement

Brodersen, Momme. *Spinne im eigenen Netz: Walter Benjamin, Leben und Werk*. Bühl-Moos: Elster, 1990.

Deuber-Mankowsky, Astrid. *Der frühe Walter Benjamin und Hermann Cohen: Jüdische Werte, kritische Philosophie, vergängliche Erfahrung*. Berlin: Vorwerk 8, 2000.

Dudek, Peter. *Liebevolle Züchtigung: Ein Mißbrauch der Autorität im Namen der Reformpädagogik*. Bad Heilbrunn: Klinkhardt, 2012.

Eiland, Howard and Michael W. Jennings. *Walter Benjamin: A Critical Life*. Cambridge, MA: The Belknap Press of Harvard University Press, 2014.

Füller, Christian. "Missbrauch, Gewalt, Ideologie: Wie Ideen sexuelle Gewalt ermöglichen." *Pfadfinderische Beziehungsformen und Interaktionsstile: Vom Scoutismus über die bündische Zeit bis zur Missbrauchsdebatte*. Edited by Wilfried Breyvogel, 237–51. Wiesbaden: Spring, 2017.

Götz von Olenhusen, Albrecht and Irmtraud Götz von Olenhusen. "Walter Benjamin, Gustav Wyneken und die Freistudenten vor dem Ersten Weltkrieg." *Jahrbuch des Archivs der Deutschen Jugendbewegung* 13 (1981): 99–128.

Hillach, Ansgar. "Ein neu entdecktes Lebensgesetz der Jugend: Wynekens Führergeist im Denken des jungen Benjamin." *Global Benjamin. Internationaler Benjamin-Kongress 1992*. Edited by Klaus Garber and Ludger Rehm, vol. 2, 873–90. München: Fink, 1999.

Hotam, Yotam. "Eternal, Transcendent, and Divine: Walter Benjamin's Theory of Youth." *Sophia* 58 (2019): 175–95.

Jay, Martin. "Against Consolation: Walter Benjamin and the Refusal to Mourn." *War and Remembrance in the Twentieth Century*. Edited by Jay Winter and Emmanuel Sivan, 221–39. Cambridge University Press, 1999.

Jay, Martin. "Walter Benjamin, Remembrance, and the First World War." *Review of Japanese Culture and Society* 11/12 (1999): 18–31.

Kupffer, Heinrich. *Gustav Wyneken, 1875–1964*. Stuttgart: Klett, 1970.

McCole, John. *Walter Benjamin and the Antinomies of Tradition*. Ithaca: Cornell University Press, 1993.

McFarland, James. *Constellation: Friedrich Nietzsche and Walter Benjamin in the Now-Time of History*. New York: Fordham University Press, 2013.

Rrenban, Monad. *Wild, Unforgettable Philosophy in Early Works of Walter Benjamin.* Lanham: Lexington, 2005.

Steiner, Uwe. *Die Geburt der Kritik aus dem Geiste der Kunst: Untersuchungen zum Begriff der Kritik in den frühen Schriften Walter Benjamins.* Würzburg: Königshausen & Neumann, 1989.

Steizinger, Johannes. *Revolte, Eros und Sprache: Walter Benjamins "Metaphysik der Jugend."* Berlin: Kadmos, 2013.

Steizinger, Johannes. "Zwischen emanzipatorischem Appell und melancholischem Verstummen: Walter Benjamins Jugendschriften." *Benjamin-Studien 2.* Edited by Daniel Weidner and Sigrid Weigel, 225–38. München: Fink, 2011.

Werner, Nadine. "Zeit und Person." *Benjamin-Handbuch: Leben—Werk—Wirkung.* Edited by Burkhardt Lindner, 3–8. Stuttgart: Metzler, 2011.

Witte, Bernd. *Walter Benjamin.* Reinbek bei Hamburg: Rowohlt, 1985.

Wizisla, Erdmut. "Akademische Freiheit im Kriege? Die Petition Ernst Joël 1916." *Wissenschaftliche Zeitschrift der Humboldt-Universität zu Berlin* 38, no. 6 (1989): 667–73.

Wizisla, Erdmut. "'Die Hochschule ist eben der Ort nicht, zu studieren.' Walter Benjamin in der freistudentischen Bewegung." *Wissenschaftliche Zeitschrift der Humboldt-Universität zu Berlin* 36, no. 7 (1987): 616–23.

Wizisla, Erdmut. "Walter Benjamin—Friedrich Heinle—Ernst Joël: Weltanschauung, Literatur und Politik in der Berliner Freien Studentenschaft 1912–1917." Diplomarbeit, Berlin, Humboldt-Universität, 1987.

Wolin, Richard. *Walter Benjamin: An Aesthetic of Redemption.* New York: Columbia University Press, 1982.

Judaism in the Early Years

Kirchner, Sascha, Vivian Liska, Karl Solibakke et al., eds. *Walter Benjamin und das Wiener Judentum zwischen 1900 und 1938.* Würzburg: Königshausen & Neumann, 2009.

Pignotti, Sandro. *Walter Benjamin—Judentum und Literatur: Tradition, Ursprung, Lehre mit einer kurzen Geschichte des Zionismus.* Freiburg: Rombach, 2009.

Smith, Gary. "Das Jüdische versteht sich immer von selbst. Walter Benjamins frühe Auseinandersetzung mit dem Judentum." *Deutsche Vierteljahrsschrift für Literatur und Geisteswissenschaft* 65, no. 2 (1991): 318–34.

Wohlfarth, Irving. "'Männer aus der Fremde': Walter Benjamin and the 'German-Jewish Parnassus.'" *New German Critique* 70 (1997): 3–85.

C. F. Heinle

Goebel, Rolf J. "Einschreibungen der Trauer: Schrift, Bild und Musik in Walter Benjamins Sonetten auf Christoph Friedrich Heinle." *Weimarer Beiträge: Zeitschrift für Literaturwissenschaft, Ästhetik und Kulturwissenschaften*, 59, no. 1 (2013): 65–78.

Görling, Reinhold. "Die Sonette an Heinle." *Benjamin Handbuch: Leben—Werk—Wirkung.* Edited by Burkhardt Lindner, 585–91. Stuttgart: J.B. Metzler, 2011.

Wizisla, Erdmut. "Fritz Heinle war Dichter. Walter Benjamin und sein Jugendfreund." *Was nie geschrieben wurde, lesen: Frankfurter Benjamin-Vorträge.* Edited by Lorenz Jäger, 115–31. Aisthesis: Bielefeld, 1992.

Part One

Genealogies of Learning

1

Infans

Clemens-Carl Härle

I

The essay "The Life of Students," composed during the summer and fall months of the first year of the war, in several respects marks a turning point in Benjamin's early literary and theoretical production.[1] In the form of self-quotation, he takes up ideas that he had presented in his inaugural address in May 1914 as director of the Berlin Union of Independent Students (*Berliner Freie Studentenschaft*), and also in June of the same year at the assembly of Independent Students in Weimar, but he develops them further with topics that go decidedly beyond those speeches. Compared with his efforts of the preceding year, which were above all dedicated to the aims and vagaries of educational reform, to questions of pedagogy and education, and to more general themes such as the religiosity of the present, Benjamin shifts this text's conceptual point of departure. For him, it is not so much about the idea and the task of, as it were, presenting a politics in the name of the young generation and defending it against an adult world that had outlived its time and was about to plunge itself into war. Rather, the aim of the essay is more matter-of-fact than this, and at the same time more ambitious. The matter to which he specifically turns his attention regards the aporias and shortcomings of a life that is beholden to the dominating authority of a canonical institution, namely the university—a life that at one moment resists this beholdenness, but at another moment succumbs to it. The essay is more ambitious because in it he is grappling with a set of concepts that lends force and emphasis to a critique both of university bureaucracy and of the student life that is determined by it. The essay distinguishes itself from the bulk of Benjamin's writings from his student years in that it regards the university less from the perspective of its imperatives and directives, and more from the perspective of the students he is addressing. To this extent, he remains loyal to the central impetus of the youth movement.

This 1914 text does not merely indicate a caesura, though; more precisely, it enacts one through the way that Benjamin experimentally tries out theoretical—indeed philosophical—positions in the same moment as he tries to distance himself from his earliest journalistic work. The text often only adumbrates, rather than fully fleshing out the positions that he will come back to in later texts and treatises, whether in order to clarify them or further to unfold their unexpected potential. In this striving for conceptual acuity, Benjamin often reaches back to insights and figures of thought from other authors, and imperceptibly reconfigures these in such a way that the force of the borrowings grows through their transplanting and rectification [*Rektifikation*], demonstrating what actually is at stake in student life. In this way, the 1914 essay resembles—perhaps unintentionally—an experimental protocol in which the novelty and scope of what it proclaims becomes recognizable sometimes indirectly, and sometimes only after the fact, in hindsight. It forms a threshold in which distinguishing characteristics of an unforeseeable opening are inscribed. But it must also be acknowledged that concepts that are still decisive for Benjamin in fall 1914, such as "spirit," "necessity," and perhaps also "will," will later be given up, or—as is the case with "life," which is named in the title—will be reconceptualized from the ground up.

Already the opening sentences of "The Life of Students" are noteworthy, for they represent one of Benjamin's first attempts to outline the conception of history that he will soon after explore to its full depth in the so-called "Theological-Political Fragment," and that is geared toward establishing the concept of "a particular condition in which history appears to be concentrated in a single focal point" (37).[2] Benjamin hesitates to give a specific name to this "particular condition"—he will identify it sometimes with "the utopian images of the philosophers," and sometimes with the "messianic domain" or with the "idea of the French Revolution" (37)—but he does explicitly designate it as a "focal point." The use of this expression is not arbitrary. It can be understood as a reference to the *focus imaginarius* that Kant speaks of in the "Appendix to the Transcendental Dialectic" of the *Critique of Pure Reason*, a concept by which he brings attention to the possibility of a "regulative use of the ideas of pure reason."[3] For Kant, this focus indicates a point that "lies entirely outside the bounds of possible experience," but that "nonetheless still serves to obtain for [the concepts of understanding] the greatest unity alongside the greatest extension."[4] It doesn't constitute the origin of the concepts of understanding, but rather makes it possible to lend them maximal extensional and intensional density, which they cannot derive from themselves. Such a focus—which, as an idea in the sense of the critique of reason, does not belong to objective cognition—is "nevertheless indispensably necessary if besides the objects before our eyes we want to see those that lie far in the background, i.e., when, in our case, the understanding wants to go beyond every given experience ... and hence wants to take the measure of its greatest possible and uttermost extension."[5] With this, Kant accounts for a "drive for expansion"[6] and maximization that, above and beyond the laws governing understanding, also prepares the ground for the possibility—indeed the necessity—of a hypothetical use of all ideas of reason that surpass experience, and, to this extent, is inseparable from the main direction of the *Critique*. This does not detract from the drive for expansion, but rather, on the strength of the "ideas as problematic concepts," completes and fulfills it through an only "*projected* unity" that makes it possible to bring "those cases that are not given" into an, as it were, analogical form of cognition.[7] The focal point, or the *focus imaginarius*, specifies the process of this maximization that goes beyond the concepts of experience.[8]

One could say that Benjamin projects the model of the regulative use of reason outlined by Kant in the "Appendix to the Transcendental Dialectic" into the "Transcendental Aesthetic" as a way of expanding the possibilities of cognition—that is to say, the sphere of a priori concepts of time and space—and does so in such a way that the "particular condition in which history appears to be concentrated in a single focal point" corresponds to an expansion of the experience of time that is accounted for in the Aesthetic. Benjamin suggests that "a view of history that puts its faith in the infinite extent of time and thus concerns itself only with the speed, or lack of it, with which people and epochs advance along the path of progress" (75) corresponds to the Transcendental Aesthetic,[9] but he makes unmistakably clear that this notion of the idea of time—and, *mutatis mutandis*, the idea of history—is in no way fully adequate, and therefore requires an elaboration for which no correspondence or basis of any sort can be found in the *Critique*. Moreover, the relation that holds sway between, on the one hand, the conception of time as an infinite motion whose intervals are marked only by differences in epochs and speeds and, on the other hand, the conception of time as the "particular condition" (37) in which all happening is brought to a standstill, can also, in principle, no longer be thought of in terms of the linear, optical model of the focal point. This presumes "lines of direction" that "converge at one point,"[10] notwithstanding the fact that this model, as an idea, belongs to a different sphere than the ensemble of points from which the lines emanate. Of the "elements of the ultimate condition," on the other hand, Benjamin says peremptorily that they "do not manifest themselves as formless progressive tendencies, but are deeply rooted in every present in the form of the most endangered, excoriated, and ridiculed ideas and products of the creative mind" (37). The "elements of the ultimate condition" are thus not *toto caelo* or *per se* distinct from those of the present, but rather are concealed within the latter—or, more precisely, they are contained in a form that is not, or almost not, recognizable, just as if they had disfigured or falsified the "infinite extent of time." Accordingly, the "elements of the ultimate condition" cannot be related to those of the present through lines or rays, nor in the form of a teleology that is enabled by an escalation, completion, or actualization of "tendencies" (37) that are in any way at all primordially or infinitely entangled. Only the conception of a turning that breaks all continuity could do it justice—perhaps a synthesis of non-synthesis, as Benjamin grants in "On the Program of the Coming Philosophy."[11]

With the notion of such a turning, Benjamin distances himself from Kant. He no longer conceives of the focal point merely as the location of the utmost concentration of epistemic intentions; rather, he shifts it into the sphere of the concepts of time. He does this, however, so that it designates an "ultimate condition" in which all happening, all of history, is suspended as a succession of occurrences or epochs, "appears to be concentrated," and breaks off. Benjamin evokes a temporality in which, to be sure, "every present" (37) is correlated to a "future" (38), yet time can no longer be understood as a process of happening and becoming that occurs from within itself as a bringing about of the future in and out of the present in the sense of an ongoing transition. The "ultimate condition" constitutes an "immanent state of perfection," and it "cannot be captured in terms of the pragmatic description of details (the history of institutions, customs, and so on); in fact, it eludes them. Rather, the task is to grasp its metaphysical structure" (37). As such, it functions as a point of reference for the description of the phenomenal world of the present. The "contemporary significance of students and the university, of the form of their present existence" (37) merits contemplation in light of the "end condition," and the cognition and critique of it are only possible insofar as one understands them "as a metaphor, as an image of the highest metaphysical state of history" (37), and insofar as one does not, in so doing, overlook the "most endangered, excoriated, and ridiculed ... creations" that are also embedded in this existence.

The unaccustomed superlatives with which Benjamin stresses the inanity and the aberrancy of the way the present is shaped remind one of formulations from the "Epistemo-Critical Foreword" to the *Trauerspiel* book, namely the point where philological understanding is called upon, "[i]n the most singular and eccentric of phenomena, in the feeblest and clumsiest attempts," to gain certainty regarding events that deserve only for their virtual content[12]—which is separate from the occurrence of discrete content—to be situated within the "preserve of the world of ideas."[13] "[T]he concept of being in philosophical science is satiated not by the phenomenon itself but only by the consumption of its history."[14] The "historical task" (37) evoked in "The Life of Students" is given a different stress. No longer is it only a matter of coming to grips with the world of appearances by means of thought, but rather of "liberat[ing] the future from its deformations in the present by an act of cognition" (38). This liberation of the future from its distortions is not merely an act of thought or of philosophical scholarship. There is a practical aspect mixed into this that cannot be missed, for it takes place in the context of a "crisis that hitherto has lain buried in the nature of things [and that] will lead on to the resolution that will overwhelm the craven-hearted and to which the stout-hearted will submit" (37). Even if it would rather not be understood as a "call to arms or a manifesto" (37), an immanently prescriptive motivation does express itself in the text through these and similar formulations. The list of disfigurations of student life and deformations of the university, which "the stout-hearted" are called upon to rectify and "the craven-hearted" to resist, is long. It addresses the "schoolboyish outlook of the students" (81) as well as the "obscuring of its own ideas" (45) that expresses itself in the "rejection of every form of direct creativity that is unconnected with bureaucratic office" (42) and that reaches its peak by denouncing "the collusion of the university and the state (something that is by no means incompatible with honest barbarity)" (38).

Decisiveness, courage, cowardice, lack of autonomy—the altogether conspicuous accumulation of such expressions points us to a further text by Kant that functions as a second subtext in "The Life of Students," namely "An Answer to the Question: What is Enlightenment?" Kant reminds us of something that is not always noted, namely that, since the "use" of reason that it calls for cannot be expected immediately, but rather must be elicited, there is a prescriptive aspect inscribed into the notion of Enlightenment—not in the form of a command, or even a moral imperative, but rather in the sense of prompting, or of a "motto": "*Sapere aude!* Have courage to make use of your *own* understanding!"[15] The use of reason doesn't begin from within itself, but rather has to reckon with a certain resistance, the overcoming of which the prescriptive aspect calls for. Kant proceeds directly from the appeal "*Sapere aude!*" to the condemnation of "laziness and cowardice" as the reasons why "so great a part of humankind, after nature has long since emancipated them from other people's direction (*naturaliter maiorennes*), nevertheless gladly remains minors for life." He envisions a microphysics of emotions, an invertible relation of forces, so that the use of reason will be set into play in a way that depends on the inversion of affective contrasts. The "everlasting minority" is "self-incurred" not because of a "lack of understanding," but because of a lack of "resolution" and "courage." Benjamin takes up the conceptual framing of the Enlightenment essay, but adjusts its trajectory and the tone of its prescription. In place of the encouragement to use one's own understanding without the guidance of another, there appears a "voice that summons them to build their lives with a unified spirit of creative action, eros, and youth" (46).[16] It is no longer addressed to just anyone, but to an expressly designated recipient, namely, university students— or, more precisely, to "their lives" themselves. And unlike the *sapere aude*, it has the compelling character of "supreme demands" (46) that take precedence over affective resistance. The closing of the essay reads: "At present it is this highly endangered necessity that is still the issue; it requires strict control. Everyone will discover his own imperatives, the commandments that will make the supreme demands on his life" (46).

The way Benjamin dramatizes the modality of prescription is not the only change he makes to Kant's framing of the "Enlightenment" essay. The manner of its justification is no less incisive. Unlike Kant's *sapere aude*, the "supreme demands" are no longer oriented toward one's "own intelligence," toward what incontestably constitutes a "There is thought" as an a priori faculty of understanding that requires no legitimation through experience. Rather, it is oriented toward that "single focal point" or "ultimate condition" that is determined in advance in the opening lines. The "voice that summons" thus retroactively reveals the necessity of its introduction and its function—not only in epistemological, but also in eminently practical terms. The imperative form of the prescription corresponds to the way the "supreme demands" refer back to the "immanent state of perfection"—it not only encourages the use of one's own intelligence, but also commands one "to liberate the future from its deformations in the present by an act of cognition" (38), and "to make it visible and dominant in the present" (37).

II

With this indication of the way Benjamin adopts and transforms philosophemes from the *Critique of Pure Reason*, we have in place the necessary framework to demonstrate what is at stake in student life. One might say, synoptically, that what is at stake is the question of the idea and the possibility of education. Yet Benjamin doesn't use the word "education" (*Bildung*) a single time, and speaks only of the "deformations" (*verbildete Form*) of the future in the present (38). Most likely, he avoids taking up that expression up because, due to the high regard that it had enjoyed within the systems of Idealism and in post-Enlightenment neoclassicism, it seemed to him to be compromised— deformed (*verbildet*). For he doesn't direct the putative question at an indeterminate subject, nor at humanity, nor at a self that he presumes to be as capable of education as it is in need of it, but rather at a single, determinate addressee: the students, the "existence peculiar to [them]" (44), their "life." Benjamin makes clear that it would be fruitless and vain to pose the question of the idea of education without any further qualifications; it can be formulated solely with due attention to the particular conditions of its actualization—i.e., with attention to a particular addressee and to the institutional context, namely the university, to which it owes its existence and to which it is beholden.

This is why the 1914 essay is dedicated to student life, to its manner of existence or being, its chances, its possibilities, its impossibilities.

This life fulfills itself, or at least implies the possibility of such a fulfillment in the "creative life of the mind," in "direct creativity as a form of communal activity" (42). It comprises not only the idea of science, and, beyond that, of knowledge, but also, no less, the incorporation of art. For Benjamin, the inner, "legitimate criticism" of the "modern disciplines" as well as their coopting by the state directly follow from this premise, which is most visibly expressed in the way scholarly research and teaching are subjected to the demands of the profession. Yet the critique is not directed only at the institution of the university and the organization that the state imposes upon it; it is directed no less at all students for whom scholarship is a "vocational training" that "has no bearing on life," and, ultimately, at the sciences themselves. The nature of the profession is grounded so weakly upon scholarly principles that it can in fact afford to ignore these altogether. "For it does not permit you to abandon it; in a way, it places the student under an obligation to become a teacher, but never to embrace the official professions of doctor, lawyer, or university professor" (38). As a result, Max Weber's notion of "Scholarship as a Profession"—expounded in his 1919 text by that name—would surely have garnered Benjamin's utmost distaste, for the kinds of coercion and regimentation that accompany any professional activity, whether public or private, can never be justified by the "idea of knowledge." But lastly—or, rather, primarily—it is the sciences themselves that are to be held accountable for betraying their own idea. Insofar as it develops its very own "professional apparatuses" through the mediation and production of "knowledge and skill," it becomes clear to what extent the modern academic disciplines have "abandon[ed] their original unity in the idea of knowledge, a unity which in their eyes has now become a mystery, if not a fiction." All of those who criticize academia for the betrayal of its idea, but who at the same time demand its "protection and support" by the state, are taking an inconsistent position. Similarly, students' demand for a "tolerance of opinions and teachings, however free" (38) within the space of the university cannot find solid footing "so long as there is no guarantee of a form of life that these ideas—the free ideas no less than the strict ones—imply" (38-9). Such a demand is naive because it refuses to take into account the fact of the "link between the universities and the state." This connection determines "the legal constitution of the university—embodied in the minister of education, who is appointed by the sovereign, not the university," and also sabotages the relationship between students and teachers, since "institutes of higher learning are characterized by a gigantic game of hide-and-seek in which students and teachers, each in his or her own unified identity, constantly push past one another without ever seeing one another" (39).

With this double critique—alleging a "conflict that we have noted in the relationship of the university to the state," and a concomitant "perversion of the creative spirit into the vocational spirit" (41)—Benjamin concurs with the diagnosis Nietzsche gives in his lectures "On the Future of Our Educational Institutions." In May 1914, a few days after his Berlin inaugural address, he tells Herbert Blumenthal of his intention to take up the lectures, which leave traces in the essay both of agreement, and also a very fundamental, if only indirectly articulated critique.[17] Nietzsche, too, assails the contorsion of institutions of higher education into ones teaching "how to win the battle for survival,"[18] and the remorseless subordination of "all educational aspirations to state purposes,"[19] through which the Prussian state presumptuously imposes itself now as an authority governing from a "utilitarian perspective,"[20] now as a "mystagogue of culture."[21] And while Benjamin scathingly criticizes the students for "constantly drift[ing] in the wake of public opinion" (41), he also bemoans the banalization of education through journalism—the "media," as one would say today—that "sticky layer" that is used to "grout the gaps" that have formed between the sciences."[22] Indeed, with his surprising praise of the nobility, which "up to a century ago gave German students a visible profile and enabled them to step forward as the champions of life at its best" (41), he adopts as his own an undertone that Nietzsche all too insistently evokes, namely the "invigorating, uplifting breath of the true German spirit."[23] It is unfortunate that, on the other hand, he ignores one of Nietzsche's insightful observations, namely that the "maximum expansion of education" is "held dear among the present dogmas of political economy," and serves the goal of the "highest possible income."[24]

As the direction he takes in the 1914 essay betrays, Benjamin has not managed to escape those dangers that have not so much to do with the adoption of elements of Nietzsche's diagnosis—for who would question their relevance?—as with the motivation that leads him to it, and even more with the way out of it that he advocates. Although he does place Nietzsche alongside Plato, Spinoza, and the Romantics as a thinker whose metaphysical questions, "through the form of philosophy," elevate university studies "to the universal" (42–3), he at the same time attempts to maintain distance from the vitalism that comes through in Nietzsche's lectures, along with all the fatal implications it carries, and he does so all the more because, for him, what is at stake is nothing less than the "life" of students. The "academic system" and the "educational machinery of the university"[25] are the most visible symptoms of the kind of "degeneration"[26] that leads to a "narrowing" of education[27] and that unrelentingly produces a profusion of people of "degenerate culture,"[28] yet at the same time contains within itself—as does everything living—the power of renewal and rebirth, even if not in each of its exemplars. The students are "miserable innocents who are held to account" (*elend Verschuldet-Unschuldige*)[29] who have been misled by the ideologeme of the autonomy and academic freedom of universities and preparatory schools—"Oh happy age, when the young are wise and educated enough to teach *themselves* how to walk!"[30] He seeks to impress upon them that they must wean themselves from the "un-German barbarism artfully hidden beneath academic erudition of all kinds," and must remember the "old, original *Burschenschaft*," the fraternities that fought during the war for "freedom for the fatherland" and who carried back home with them "the most unexpected, and worthy, trophy of battle"[31] because they didn't try to escape the "hard and rigorous discipline of the great leader."[32] For they had learned there that "we need great leaders, and that all education begins with obedience."[33] This experience, which "the so-called culture now sitting on the throne of the present aims to overturn and destroy," is formalized by Nietzsche: "[J]ust as great leaders need followers, so too must the led have a leader. A certain reciprocal predisposition prevails in the hierarchy of the spirit: yes, a kind of pre-established harmony."[34]

The idea of an "ultimate condition," of an "immanent state of perfection," and the indication of a "historical task"—the latter being "to make it visible and dominant in the present" (37)—would be necessary in order to be able to speak of the existence, indeed of the life of students, and also in order to resist the danger of vitalistically compromising this life. However one may understand this task, it is inseparable from its prescriptive aspect, not in the sense of subjection to an authority figure, a leader (*Führer*)—for every pedagogy entails the threat of making a great leader out of the slave, the *paid-agogos*, who leads the boy to school—but rather to the "countervailing will" (*Gegenwille*), if something else pertains to it, that approaches "the conscious unity of student life." "What distinguishes student life is just the opposite of that: it is the will to submit to a principle, to identify completely with an idea" (38). Only a collectivity of students inspired by such an impetus could open up for itself the chance to

> rally around the university, which itself would be in a position to impart the systematic state of knowledge, together with the cautious and precise but daring applications of new methodologies. Students who conceived their role in this way would greatly resemble the amorphous waves of the populace that surround the prince's palace, which serves as the space for an unceasing spiritual revolution—a point from which new questions would be incubated, in a more ambitious, less clear, less precise way, but perhaps with greater profundity than the traditional scientific questions. (43)

III

This countervailing will demands that "student life" be measured "by the yardstick of this science," or, more exactly, "of knowledge" (38). As a "more exalted" spirit (41), it arises from the possibility that "[s]tudents have not been able to demonstrate its spiritual necessity and for that reason have never been able to establish a truly serious community based on it" (40). Expressions like "spiritual necessity" or "direct creativity as a form of communal activity" (42) are not merely defensive formulas of vitalism, of degeneration, and of regeneration, but rather refer directly to what could be called the virtuality of student existence. It comprises the current forms in which student life appears, its "deformations, whose most appalling effect is that they invariably poison the essence of creative life" (43), and of which the "tyranny of vocational training is not the worst" (43). They misshape life with "various surrogates" that take the place of spirit (43), provoke its "spineless acquiescence" (39), and make the students shrink back from the "hazards of the life of the mind" (43) and from the "radical doubt, fundamental critique, and the most important thing of all—the life that would be willing to dedicate itself to reconstruction" (41). Their "faintheartedness" (46) hinders them from recognizing the virtualities of their existence.

Virtualities are interspersed into life like intervals, achronies, or interludes into that "infinite extent of time" (37) that can be understood as the succession and synthesis of points of actuality, and whose hegemony Benjamin calls into question in the essay's opening. Indeed, being a student is, in principle, itself an indeterminate, perhaps even "illegitimate interlude" (43) in the existence of each individual. These intervals form a multidimensional, mobile openness, yet they are not absolute, but rather are related, at least in the first instance, to that among which they exert their influence. Through attentiveness to these virtualities in life, it is possible to shed light on the way that, through expressions such as "spiritual necessity" (40), "creative spirit" (41), "spiritual strategy" (41), "unceasing spiritual revolution" (43), "creative life of the spirit" (42), and "erotic spirit" (44), which recur throughout the essay,[35] Benjamin makes conspicuous use of the concept of spirit (*Geist*). Although he presents this in a very early text that ascribes the Wickersdorf Free School Community and the program of its founder, Gustav Wyneken, to Hegel,[36] it would be all too simplistic—even irresponsible—to identify the meaning that it acquires in the writings discussed here with the logical-ontological selfhood of spirit, or with the speculative dialectic. The type of intellectuality that Benjamin envisions raises objections against such an identity of the self, and the observations regarding gender and childhood that close the essay—as aphoristic as they are emphatic—only become intelligible once one calls attention to the lack of independence and to the secret heteronomy of spirit that find expression in them.

Benjamin suggests that the "creative spirit" (41) stands in relation to an indelible dependence upon gender. "To transform the necessary independence of the creative spirit and to bring about the necessary inclusion of women, who are not productive in a masculine sense, in a single community of creative persons—through love—this indeed is the goal to which students should aspire, because it is the form of their own lives" (44). Were this not the case, the "torso of the one erotic spirit" would look "lamentable" to us (44). Benjamin does not contest the productivity of women, but believes that this productivity is "of a different kind" (44) than that of men. A little later, in connection with a discussion of the concept of genius, he attempts to determine more clearly the manner in which gender difference plays into the possibility of intellectual productivity. In the short text titled "Socrates," he asserts that intellectual creation as such is genderless, but that even so, it is bound up with the existence of the feminine [*Dasein des Weiblichen*]. "In a society of males, there would be no genius; genius lives through the existence of the feminine. It is true: the existence of the feminine guarantees the asexuality of the spiritual in the world."[37] The 1914 essay stated it only as a double necessity with respect to the *form* of student life: the necessity of the "independence of the creative spirit" and the necessity of the "inclusion of women" (44) are now conceived in such a way that the latter—or, more exactly, the existence of the feminine—functions as a guarantee or facilitation of "asexuality of the spiritual in the world," or of "a life of the mind" that is demanded by the students, and in such a way that it in effect stands in place of it, vouches for it, or stands as its guarantor. Accordingly, the asexuality of the spiritual does not exist as such, but rather only conditionally or virtually. Benjamin acknowledges that the assertion *that* the existence of the feminine sustains creativity is not the same as saying *how* this is so. He simply affirms that "[e]very extremely profound relation between man and woman rests on the ground of this true creativity," and he believes that it follows from this that "it is false to designate the innermost contact between man and woman as covetous love."[38] Precisely because of the ontological split between the *that* (the *quod*) and the *how* (the *quomodo*), he designates as "the greatest secret" the question of "[h]ow the mere existence of the female guarantees the asexuality of the spiritual world" (53). However one may imagine the "inclusion of women" in its particulars, Benjamin makes clear that intellectual productivity cannot be thought of without attention to gender difference. With these considerations, his objection to Nietzsche's vision of the future of our educational institutions comes to its innermost fiber, for his lectures leave no doubt that, following a long tradition, he can only imagine their future—that is, the possibility of a rectification of their present disfiguration—within the context of a "society of males" (53).

In a similar way, Benjamin also conceives of childhood as an alterity to which the "creative life of the mind" (42) stands in innermost connectedness. "Students are not the younger generation; they are the aging generation" (45). A life that is not their own lies in advance of theirs, and another life that will never have been their own lives already and prepares itself to follow it. "[I]t is important to recognize that they have to be creative producers, and therefore lonely, aging people, and that a richer generation of children and youths has already been born, to whom they can only dedicate themselves as teachers" (45). The alterity that Benjamin envisions in childhood is not a distance that could be measured according to chronological time, the same way that the "interlude" (43) does not designate any specific phase of life, any epoch that "advances along" the path of aging (37). Nor is it the object of a recollection that recalls into the present things that have passed. Rather, it names that which withdraws itself from the self-presence of those who remember, in the form of an anteriority that is not given, and that, as a subject, is not capable of giving itself—that does not *exist*, but rather *in*sists. Childhood haunts me insofar as it was there before I, as subjectivity or self-presence, was. The self is initially belated, however young the "aging people" may be who can only renege on their childhood. "Because they do not acknowledge the process of aging, [the students] idle their time away" (46), and conversely, the "regret" regarding this dereliction—Benjamin calls it the "regret for a greatness missed" (46)— is the violation of selfhood, the secret condition of "creativity." He raises the concern that, for this reason, productivity can bear upon another, can bear upon them in the form of "a hazardous self-dedication to learning and youth" (42). But it is dedication only to the extent that it is a giving away of the self, and is not due to the self, but to the way it is acted upon by another. Indeed, Benjamin suggests that the eventuality of such a freedom from the self could become an "expansive friendship between creative minds, with its sense of infinity and its concern for humanity as a whole even when those minds are alone together or when they experience yearning in solitude" (46), and he recognizes, resignedly, that it "has no place in the lives of university students" (46).[39]

Infans is the name of this way of being affected by an alterity that happens inadvertently, as if behind the self's back, and dis-figures (*ent-stellt*) the self and robs it of its standing in "creative life of the mind" (42). It is the name of the deprivation that the "lives of the creative" (46) are subjected to and that obstructs them from being able to organize themselves on the basis of, or in orientation to, a self. It calls attention to the fact that the possibility of creativity, and of speech, lies concealed within an inability to create, or to speak, which compels those who create and who speak—if indeed it compels them—ever again to attempt it anew. To be sure, *infans* designates not that which is to be educated (*das Zu-Bildende*) or the lack of autonomy (*Unmündigkeit*) that aspires seeks to overcome all education (*Bildung*), but rather a state of being beholden to an alterity that disempowers any self-empowerment or affecting of the self.[40]

Unmündigkeit can be regarded as a juridically embellished rendering of "infantia." When Benjamin stresses the dependency of productivity upon remembrance of childhood, he marks his distance to the Enlightenment essay even more clearly than had initially been indicated. For nothing stands more in the way of using one's own understanding and of the imperative to think for oneself than this dependency. This objection maintains its validity as long as one fails to respect the observation that Hölderlin makes in a letter to Böhlendorff, namely that "the most difficult thing is the *free* usage of what is *our own*."[41] Insofar as the expounded formulation, which is directed against the vain attempt "to abstract the rules of art uniquely and solely from the excellence of the Greeks," posits "what is one's own" in opposition to this effort and explicates it expressly with regard to the possibility of its use, it is implicitly alluding to the motto of the Enlightenment essay. But it makes unambiguously clear that that which is one's own—one's own faculty of understanding, in Kant's words—is precisely not in and of itself an accessible, autonomous, transcendental capacity, but rather designates a mere possibility, the scope and purview of which must be explored and experienced from one instance to the next, and through its use—through an experimental use, so to speak, that can be prescribed, justified, or assured by no rule of any type. Precisely because "what is one's own"—or, as the case may be, "the understanding"—is nothing more than, in Freud's phrase, the disquieting scene of a working-through or an anamnesis, its "free use" is the thing that is most difficult. Only then is the activity of creation that Benjamin speaks of truly an activity of creation, and the free surrender of the self that is demanded of it only then attains its capacity, because this process of coming to know what is truly one's own is what is most difficult.

Under the name of *Unmündigkeit*, *infans* is the self-disfiguring that thought always and ever again is talked into, and lets itself be talked into, by those who presume to speak for it. *Infans* is the name of the "admitted … yearning for a beautiful childhood" (46). Of a childhood that disruptively intrudes into the "lives of the creative" (46), and, almost inaudibly, announces something that cannot be thought in advance, and that is always already withdrawn. Of an infinite alterity that strips thought of itself whenever it begins to think and to create. That leads the self to free itself from its "fear of surrendering [itself]" (46), and to surrender itself.

Translated by Michael Saman

Notes

1 "The Life of Students," *SW* 1: 37–47. The essay appeared in 1915 in the *Neuer Merkur* [*New Mercury*], and in its final version in 1916 in the first volume of the annual *Das Ziel: Aufrufe zu tätigem Geist* [*The Goal: Exhortations Toward Active Spirit*], edited by Kurt Hiller. Here, it was supplemented by a dedicatory poem by Stefan George to Hugo von Hofmannsthal, taken from the *Jahr der Seele* [*Year of the Soul*], which Ernst Schoen had brought to Benjamin's attention. Benjamin will distance himself from Kurt Hiller already a year later in a letter to Martin Buber. Page references to "The Life of Students" will be provided in parenthesis after each citation throughout the body of this chapter.

2   On the dating and interpretation of the fragment, see Werner Hamacher, "Das Theologisch-politische Fragment," in *Benjamin-Handbuch*, ed. Burckhard Lindner (Stuttgart/Weimar: Metzler, 2006), 175–92.
3   Immanuel Kant, *Critique of Pure Reason*, trans. and ed. Paul Guyer and Allen W. Wood (New York: Cambridge University Press, 1998), 590.
4   Ibid., 591.
5   Ibid.
6   Ibid., 140.
7   Ibid., 592–3.
8   Already in "School Reform: A Cultural Movement," a commentary that presumably was composed during his first semester at university in Freiburg, Benjamin reached back to the concept of transcendental dialectic in order to explicate the antinomy of nature and culture with which every pedagogy finds itself confronted: "It is a matter of finding a way out of the conflict [*Widerstreit*] between natural, truthful development, on the one hand, and the task of transforming the natural individual into the cultural individual, on the other hand, a task that will never be completed without violence." The text suggests that the resolution of the conflict lies in the idea of youth that Benjamin so emphatically appeals to: "Youth must learn by degrees to work, to take itself seriously, to educate itself: by placing trust in such youth, humanity places trust in its own future, in the irrational which it can only honor, in the youth that is filled not just with the spirit of the future—no!—but with the spirit that feels in itself the joy and the courage of new culture-bearers." "School Reform: A Cultural Movement," *EW* 59–60. Translation slightly modified.
9   In the "Metaphysical Exposition of the Concept of Time," Kant (*Critique of Pure Reason*, 179) adduces the "infinitude of time" as a characteristic of time, and adds that "every determinate magnitude of time is only possible through limitations." In Benjamin's idiom, these qualifications correspond to the "speed" of "people and epochs."
10 Kant, *Critique of Pure Reason*, 591.
11 In his discussion of the Kantian relational categories in "On the Program of the Coming Philosophy," Benjamin expressly indicates that here, "besides the concept of synthesis, another concept, that of a certain nonsynthesis of two concepts in another, will become very important systematically, since another relation between thesis and antithesis is possible besides synthesis" ("On the Program of the Coming Philosophy," *SW* 1: 106).
12 *OT* 25.
13 *OT* 26.
14 *OT* 27.
15 Immanuel Kant, "An Answer to the Question: What is Enlightenment?" in *Practical Philosophy* trans. Mary J. Gregor (New York: Cambridge University Press, 1996), 17.
16 The phrase "voice that summons" (*Ruf der Stimme*) is reminiscent of Heidegger's notion of the call of conscience (*Ruf des Gewissens*), which, as "an *attestation* belonging to the being of Da-sein," opens up the "most primordial potentiality-of-being of Da-sein as being-guilty." See Martin Heidegger, *Being and Time*, trans. Joan Stambaugh (Albany, NY: State University of New York Press 2010), 266. Despite the terminological similarity, it must be recognized that Benjamin's "voice that summons" has the form of an appeal rather than of a demand, and to this extent it is neither directed at a conscience, nor does it carry with it anything that can be interpreted as a obligation. I thank Ilit Ferber for bringing this aspect to my attention.
17 Letter from May 15, 1914, *GB* 1: 226.

18 Friedrich Nietzsche, *Anti-Education: On the Future of Our Educational Institutions*, trans. Damion Searls (New York: New York Review Books, 2016), 55.
19 Ibid., 49.
20 Ibid., 50.
21 Ibid., 49.
22 Ibid., 18–19.
23 Ibid., 82.
24 Ibid., 15–16.
25 Ibid., 75.
26 Ibid., 81.
27 Ibid., 18.
28 Ibid., 81.
29 Ibid.
30 Ibid., 76.
31 Ibid., 82.
32 Ibid., 51.
33 Ibid., 84. The attitude of the young Benjamin with regard to the concept of the leader (*Führer*) is ambiguous. This figure is entrusted with leadership toward a particular goal, but not with determining that goal. With regard to Gustav Wyneken, he writes: "We know him as a leader, but not as a leader toward a goal that he conveys to us, but toward a goal that is immanently given to us" ("Ziele und Wege der studentisch-pädagogischen Gruppen an reichsdeutschen Universitäten [mit besonderer Berücksichtigung der ‚Freiburger Richtung']," *GS* 2: 64). In another passage, he expresses himself more cautiously with regard to the way literary events for student authors are organized: "All leading figures of the student body may, once a year, read a single work of their own production. Then a more strenuous selection of the productions—a selection of the true leaders, I fear—will be possible" ("Studentische Autorenabende," *GS* 1: 71).
34 Nietzsche, 84. In a letter to Ludwig Strauß from November 1912, Benjamin comments on Nietzsche's *Zarathustra*, the significance of which he does not question. This book "is boundlessly dangerous there, where Nietzsche himself is mired in an intellectualized philistinism." Benjamin identifies this "all over" within the terrain of the biological: "Social biologists in Nietzsche's manner fish in murky waters, and transfer into the material realm a heroism that they take from the ideal" (*GB* 1: 78). On the motifs of degeneration, vitalism, and leadership in Nietzsche's lectures from 1872, see Jacques Derrida, *Otobiographies: L'enseignement de Nietzsche et la politique du nom propre* (Paris, 1984), 71–114.
35 Translations of these terms have been partly modified for the sake of lexical consistency.
36 "As is well known, the primary philosophical exponent of this view of things is Hegel," Benjamin remarks with regard to Wyneken's attempt to justify his pedagogical project through references to the dialectical philosophy of spirit. See "The Free School Community," *EW* 39–45. This short text appeared in 1911, in volume 4 of *Der Anfang* (*The Beginning*).
37 "Socrates," *SW* 1: 53. He elaborates on the asexuality of intellectual creativity in a commentary that presumably was composed in June 1916 in connection with a polemic against the figure of Socrates. Benjamin denounces his use of questions as "[a] mere means to compel the conversation," as a dissimulation, and as "an erection of knowledge." "In Socrates the spiritual was sexual through and through" because "[a]ccording to his teaching, the knower is pregnant with knowledge." He constrasts him

against the genius, in which the asexuality of "every truly spiritual creation" (ibid.) comes to expression.

38   Benjamin risks a hierarchy of sorts with regard to gender relations: "of all the stages of such love, including male-female love, the most profound, the most splendid, and the most erotically and mythically perfect, indeed even the most radiate (if it were not so totally of the night), is the love of the female for the female." At the same time, however, he condemns feminine creativity whenever it ventures into intellectual matters, and also whenever it does not present itself as asexual: "Wherever it develops out of this feminine itself, it is flat and weak and does not break through the night" ("Socrates," SW 1: 53). There is an implicit invective against male homosexuality in the observation that the Greeks "resolved the problem by force" and "subordinated procreation to creativity, so that in the long run, by excluding women and children from the life of their state, they brought about its collapse" ("The Life of Students," SW 1: 44).

39   On the motif of devotion, see Jonas Rosenbrück, *Studentenmut und Blödigkeit: Benjamin und die Gefahr der Jugend* (unpublished manuscript).

40   In "Fate and Character," Benjamin points to the muteness and lack of autonomy of the tragic hero and speaks of the "paradox of the birth of genius in moral speechlessness, moral infantility." Taking up considerations on the self of the hero from Rosenzweig and Lukács, this thought is developed further in the *Trauerspiel* book through the observation that "when at the last [the old ordinances] overtake him, [the hero] flings only the mute shadow of his being, of that self, as sacrifice, while his soul is saved and transported into a word of the distant community" (OT 103).

41   Friedrich Hölderlin, letter to Böhlendorff from December 4, 1891, quoted in Friedrich Hölderlin, *Hymns and Fragments*, trans. Richard Sieburth (Princeton: Princeton University Press, 2016), 14.

2

Learning from Experience: Elements of Self-Criticism in Benjamin's Work

Charles Gelman

Introduction

For as long as there has been interest in his work, Walter Benjamin's fitful turn to Marxism beginning in the mid-1920s has been a source of seemingly intractable debate, and with reason.[1] Taken as a case study, Benjamin's relationship to Marxism raises difficult questions, questions that perhaps do not admit of any anodyne response, and that might still give us pause today. These questions are not merely academic or theoretical, nor, I hope it will be acknowledged, are they of only historical interest. Rather, they are eminently practical questions, questions that touch us, as teachers and scholars, that is, as "intellectuals," in our teaching and scholarship, our intellectual work, which is to say, in what we choose to do with our little bit of time on earth, with our energy, and with the resources with which we have been endowed. At bottom, they confront us in a particularly acute way with the eternally nagging question, For what? Of what use is what we do? And to whom? What—or, better, whose—interests (besides our own, inasmuch as it is our livelihood) does our pedagogical and scholarly work serve?

No doubt reflecting on his own trajectory, Benjamin observes in "The Present Social Situation of the French Writer" (1934) that "the intellectual's path to the radical critique of the social order is the longest, just as that of the proletariat is the shortest."[2] The evolution of his thinking, I propose, furnishes us with an example that could not be more instructive of the difficult and not at all predestined path that the intellectual has to follow before arriving at a radical and uncompromising critique of the social order.

"In the mind of an intellectual," the French communist writer Paul Nizan observed in *The Watchdogs: Philosophers and the Established Order* (1932), his devastating critique of the French professoriate, "the future of the intelligentsia itself may lend a singularly powerful interest" to the cause of the working class. For, he continues,

> the situation in which bourgeois thought now finds itself is such that the real fulfillment of the intellectual's special interests is an impossibility. In view of the exhaustion of bourgeois culture, the dead ends into which science has been driven, the degeneration of philosophy, and, finally, the barbarism to which this civilization

has been reduced, a number of intellectuals now feel they have no choice but to dedicate their lives to a future society in which a new leap forward will be possible.[3]

That, it seems to me, well describes Benjamin's case. It is certain at least that he wanted nothing to do with "the complacency of bourgeois scholarship."[4] But a salutary distaste for bourgeois fatuity is still not the same thing as a radical critique of the social order, just as there is a difference between the (politically ambiguous) critique of bourgeois culture and the critique of capitalist exploitation. And Benjamin for his own part was well aware that the "bridge" from his own philosophical standpoint to the method of historical materialism was a "strained and problematical" one.[5] It is precisely in its unevenness and uncertainty that the reorientation of his thinking in the direction of historical materialism is an especially, perhaps uniquely, enlightening example of the difficulties by which intellectuals are beset on the path to the radical critique of the social order. "It is not easy to become a Marxist-Leninist philosopher," Louis Althusser once remarked. "Like every 'intellectual,' a philosophy teacher is a petty bourgeois," meaning:

> When he opens his mouth, it is petty-bourgeois ideology that speaks: its resources and ruses are infinite. You know what Lenin says about "intellectuals." Individually certain of them may (politically) be declared *revolutionaries*, and courageous ones. But as a mass, they remain "incorrigibly" petty-bourgeois in ideology.... To become "ideologists of the working class" (Lenin), "organic intellectuals" of the proletariat (Gramsci), intellectuals have to carry out a radical revolution in their ideas: a long, painful and difficult re-education. An endless external and *internal* struggle.[6]

It is as just such an "*internal* struggle," a "long, painful and difficult" process of self-criticism, that I suggest that we look at the evolution of Benjamin's thinking after 1924, when his attitude to Marxism began to change from antipathy to a sort of probationary acceptance and eventually to commitment.

What is the virtue of posing the question of Benjamin's evolution in this way? As Jürgen Habermas observed half a century ago, the narrowly "academic treatment" of Benjamin's work, although it "furnishes a corrective" to the "factional disputes that have nearly splintered [his] image," nevertheless is "surely not an alternative."[7] With that I fully agree. However, I think that Habermas is following a misguided impulse in attempting to piece back together into a solid whole the "splintered" image of the man to whom Jacques Derrida once gave the apt sobriquet *l'homme-frontière*. I would suggest rather that Benjamin's image best left splintered—that the image is *truer* that way. For what we see in the evolution of his thinking is neither an unbroken continuity nor an absolute rupture, a clean break, but a protracted and uneven process of self-criticism and transformation.

Nevertheless, I do think that it is possible on the basis of textual evidence alone to refute Habermas's view that even Benjamin's late criticism (for example, his work on Baudelaire) is incompatible with the Marxist critique of ideology. That Benjamin himself would have disagreed, he acknowledges, in effect. Benjamin, he says, "deceived himself about the difference between his manner of proceeding and the Marxist critique of ideology."[8] To have thought that he was able to synthesize his "own theory of experience" and the materialist theory of history was "Benjamin's mistake and the wish of his Marxist friends."[9] Habermas here makes common cause with Hannah Arendt, who, as he says, "would protect Benjamin the impressionable, vulnerable aesthete, collector, and private scholar against the ideological claims of his Marxist and Zionist friends."[10] According to Arendt, the Marxist theorem of base and superstructure was for Benjamin merely "the final doctrine of metaphorical thinking."[11] That Benjamin should ever have conceived of history as "a consistent, dialectically sensible, rationally explainable process" seemed to her so self-evidently absurd as not to merit discussion.[12]

On the base-superstructure theorem Benjamin makes only one substantial theoretical statement, the pith of which is that "the material of thought and experience, the superstructure, ... is the expression [*Ausdruck*] of the base. The economic conditions under which society exists are expressed in the superstructure ..."[13] According to Habermas, who is at one with Arendt on this point, expression is a "semantic category" that belongs to "Benjamin's theory of experience" and is "related to those insensible correspondences between animate and inanimate nature on which the gaze of the child and of the artist rests," rather "than to the base-superstructure theorem."[14] It is indeed clear that the concept of expression is closely related to that of experience for Benjamin: "economic conditions," precisely, are *expressed* "in the materials of thought and experience."[15] What neither author can countenance is the possibility of a genuine evolution in Benjamin's thought. To the extent that it is conceded that Benjamin himself thought that his thinking had indeed undergone a real transformation, he is said to have "deceived himself," and that "for political reasons," which is to say, not for good philosophical reasons.[16] For both authors, and the same could be said of others as well, the argument that Benjamin never *really* became a Marxist serves as a screen for the expression of their own philosophical differences with historical materialism—not Benjamin's. For them, if Benjamin was wrong to have "deceived himself" about the nature of his relation to Marxism, in another sense he was "right" *only* to have deceived himself and not actually to have become a Marxist.

In the end, one either affirms the thesis of the determination in the last instance by economic factors—the production and reproduction of species life—or one does not. That is the necessary condition of a Marxist position in philosophy. Benjamin in the end affirmed it. He adopted a Marxist position in philosophy, however tentative, uncertain, and problematic his position may have been in some respects. It is not a coincidence that both authors express their demurrals about Benjamin's Marxism in relation to the base-superstructure theorem. It is the mental resistance to the materialist thesis of the dependence of the ideological superstructure on the economic base that makes the intellectual's path to the radical critique of the social order such a tortuous one. In essence, the work of self-criticism the effects of which can be seen in Benjamin's later writings consists in vigilantly and diligently bringing to light and breaking down this resistance in oneself. Not the least interesting question that Benjamin can help us to answer is why this thesis, on which the possibility of an objective knowledge of ourselves depends, should elicit so much resistance precisely on the part of those who have a special interest in the rigorous and objective pursuit of truth.

I begin by showing in relation to Benjamin's 1915–16 essay "The Life of Students" how the self-consciousness of the intellectual is based on the suppression of the awareness that the intellectual as such occupies a position in a social division of labor. From there I turn to some of Benjamin's criticisms of bourgeois education and to his analysis of the attitude of intellectuals to technology and to the masses—an attitude that makes them susceptible to the appeal of reactionary politics. We will see that questions of education and of the social position of the intelligentsia are at the center of Benjamin's reorientation. Finally, I turn to Benjamin's late essay "On Some Motifs in Baudelaire," in which we see the fruits of his long labor of self-criticism. We will see that, far from having been deluded about the nature of his relationship to Marxism, it was through the discipline of historical materialism that he was able to make sense not only of Baudelaire's experience but of his own, and thus to learn from it. My hope is that we, too, may be able to learn something from his experience.

From "The Life of Students" to "A Communist Pedagogy"

If one were to trace the evolution of Benjamin's thought down to its roots, then one would have to take note of the fact that, not only was he not an "organic intellectual of the working class," but he *knew it and thought about it*. For example, in "The Life of Students" (1916) he writes:

> There is no internal and original connection between the spiritual existence of a student and, say, his concern for the welfare of workers' children of even for other students. No connection, that is, apart from a concept of duty unrelated to his own, most proper labor.... And this duty is carried out not by suffering in the cause of truth, nor by bearing all the scruples of a researcher, or indeed by any intention connected with the person's spiritual life. But by a crude and extremely superficial opposition, comparable to that between the ideal and the material, or the theoretical and the practical.[17]

This passage is among the most noteworthy in Benjamin's early body of work. It is a rare instance in his early writings in which we see him reflect, if only glancingly, not on the metaphysical or religious vocation but on the social position of the student. It testifies at once to his awareness that the student or scholar—in any case, that he himself—occupies a position in a social division of labor and to his suppression of that awareness. For he goes on to distinguish between two types of "labor," precisely. There is the student's "true" (*eigentlich*), his "own, most proper labor [*eigene und eigenste Arbeit*]," and opposite it there is "empty general utility," the production of use-values, labor pure and simple.[18] In the same breath, then, that he rejects as "crude" and "superficial" the "opposition ... between the ideal and the material, or the theoretical and the practical," he avails himself of the "comparable" opposition between *intellectual and manual labor* to assert that the student's intellectual existence has nothing in common with the material/practical existence of workers and their children. The point is that for Benjamin the division between student and worker here is not social—it is as such that it seems to him crude and superficial—but existential and metaphysical. It is a matter of the student's "existence," and the student's existence is "spiritual," made up of other stuff than that of which the existence of workers and their children is compounded. Between them there exists no connection besides "a practice of social welfare," which itself is only "the anxious reaction [*ängstliche Reaktion*] of a spiritual life" and "an evasion of the consequences of the critical, intellectual existence to which the student is duty-bound [*verpflichtet*]."[19]

It is his own "anxious reaction" that Benjamin diagnoses in "The Life of Students," and that he parries away with his sense of "duty." This is neither the first nor the last instance in which it makes its uneasy presence felt in his work. "The consciousness of a proletariat, of progress, all the powers that earlier generations, in order to find peace, were able to appease in orderly fashion through their religious services—these things cause *us* unrest [*beunruhigen uns*]," we read in his remarkable "Dialogue on the Religiosity of the Present" (1912), in which we find already all of the cells out of which his thinking was to develop over the course of the next twelve years, before his fateful encounter with the Latvian Bolshevik dramaturge Asja Lacis on the island of Capri and the beginning of his re-education.[20] He could accept, he goes on to say, an "honest socialism," but not the "conventional one of today ... upheld by everyone who feels something amiss within himself [*der bei sich selbst etwas nicht im Reinen fühlt*]."[21] Evidently, it was he who felt "something amiss within himself," who could feel no solidarity with workers and their children and could see no place for himself in their struggle, and thus could conceive of no reason to join it other than to quiet a gnawing unrest, linked, no doubt, to uncertainty as to the purpose of his "own, most proper labor," that is, as to what purpose it serves other than his own "enjoyment."[22]

A little less than a decade later, as Michael Jennings recalls, Benjamin's position in relation to working class struggle remained essentially unchanged:

> Already in early 1920, he had conceived an essay—which he apparently never completed—with the provisional title "There Are No Intellectual Workers," a pointed reply to the leftist writer Kurt Hiller's brand of activism and, more generally, to the widespread—and wholly ineffectual—attempts on the part of bourgeois writers to identify with and emulate the workers' and soldiers' councils (*Arbeiter- und Soldatenräte*) that had sprung up spontaneously in 1918 and forced the abdication of the Kaiser.[23]

But within only a few more years Benjamin had come to see things very differently. As John McCole puts it, intellectual work became for Benjamin above all a matter of convincing "intellectuals to work toward their own dissolution as a subclass."[24] The role of the intellectual, as he had come to see it, is to affect the "politicization of the intelligentsia," of "the writer's own class."[25] Benjamin never denies the distance separating the intellectual from the proletarian. He is the first to admit that "even the proletarianization of the intellectual hardly ever turns him into a proletarian"; for "from childhood on, the middle class gave him means of production in the form of an education," a "privilege" that binds him to it and it to him by a tie of solidarity that "almost always remains powerful enough to exclude the intellectual from the constant state of alert, the sense of living your life at the front, that is characteristic of the true proletarian."[26] The difference is that he now recognizes this distance, this privilege, which he had earlier, before he knew its real nature, been anxious to preserve, as an indictment of the existing order, and that he is now resolved not to make any excuses for it but, on the contrary, to combat it tooth and nail. In particular, he recognizes in it an indictment of the system of education that—as is every bit still the case—perpetuates "what Lenin called the 'most repulsive feature of the old bourgeois society': its separation of theory and practice," as he says in his 1929 review of Edwin Hoernle's *Grundfragen der proletarischen Erziehung* (*Basic Questions of Proletarian Education*), "A Communist Pedagogy," a minor but inspired text, and one of those in his oeuvre that are unobscured by any of his own old bourgeois habits of thought, on which, on the contrary, it casts a caustic, disillusioning light.[27]

What distinguishes communist pedagogy even from what, as he says, is "best and most honest ... in the bourgeois camp is that it devotes serious attention not just to the child and the child's nature, but also to his social situation, something which the 'educational reformers' can never allow themselves to see as problematic."[28] Benjamin himself, of course, had in his younger days been one of the latter. In one of his earliest articles, for example, we read that "school reform is a struggle of ideas, in which the social moments ... recede."[29] One could adduce any number of citations to the same effect. "A Communist Pedagogy" is significant not least as a document of Benjamin's own re-education. The "two abstract ... data" from which bourgeois education sets out, "the abstract natural disposition" of the child and the "chimerical ideal" of "the complete human being, the citizen," are only the other side of bourgeois education's suppression of the "one concrete reality" on which "the proletarian theory of education is predicated": that "the proletarian child is born into his class."[30] So is the bourgeois child, of course. But, unlike the working-class child, the latter is shielded by the circle of his family "from the harsh lessons of social knowledge" and is able to live in comfortable ignorance of his "social situation"—indeed, of the fact that he has and is the product of a social situation.[31] It is this ignorance that the adult is anxious to preserve—a task for which he is prepared by his education, which consists in "a gradual process of replacing force [*Gewalt*] with cunning."[32] It is cunning that, in bourgeois society, takes the place of the correspondence of theory and practice. The product of bourgeois education becomes an expert in deception and self-deception, particularly when it comes to the consciousness of its own situation.

The same is true of intellectuals, among whom the younger Benjamin was by no means alone in the anxiety evoked in him by the class consciousness of the proletariat. As his contemporary Siegfried Kracauer noted in the early 1930s, "rather than allowing themselves to be forced by the spiritual void (which already reigns in the upper regions) to break out of the corral of bourgeois consciousness, [middle-class intellectuals] instead use all available means to try to preserve this consciousness."[33] They do so, he adds, "less out of faith than out of fear—a fear of being drowned by the proletariat, of becoming spiritually degraded and losing contact with authentic aspects of culture and education."[34] In the interest of "fortifying their position" and continuing "to wield their former intellectual/spiritual power," they lend their energy and intelligence to the preservation of obsolete ideas, which serve only to hold "the threatened superstructure" aloft a little while longer.[35] Thus, they turn not only against the cause of the working class, against social progress, but against science, against intellectual progress, as well, and so betray their own special interest. They become obscurantists, if nothing worse.

What is it at bottom that they fear? Whence their anxiety? And whither does it lead?

Twenty years after "The Life of Students," Benjamin could observe the same anxious concern in the discourse of protofascist intellectuals, whose fear, he observed, was that "culture" should be "betrayed ... and abandoned ... to communism."[36] Perspicaciously, he identifies the source of their unease in their adherence to the "specious," because "lifeless and undialectical," antithesis of "creation and fabrication," the conceptive work of the mind and the exhausting labor of the body.[37] The fact, however, is that the right-wing intellectual for whom "a culture not founded on privileges is unthinkable" has made a sound enough assessment of the facts.[38] Intellectuals' whole way of life is in fact founded on, presupposes privileges, and this effects the way in which they think. A "disdain for manual activities coupled with an overestimation of pure intellectual operations divorced from practical application has remained a hallmark of the theoretical outlook of the upper classes," and for the better part of history there has been no theoretical outlook other than that of the upper classes.[39]

Behind the anxious solicitude for the preservation of culture is an inability or unwillingness to take an interest in "the potential or desirable uses of human industry," in Klaus Theweleit's words—that is, the potential for human emancipation contained in the expansion of human beings' productive forces in modernity.[40] "The social strata ... whose members are denied access to the 'proper' productive use of new materials" are apt to be unable to recognize the productive character of, and the potential for human emancipation contained in, those "new materials."[41] "The proletarian turns against the employer; the petty-bourgeois, against the machine," as Benjamin puts it.[42] But the "productive forces," the development of which "has brought about the crisis that presses toward the socialization of the means of production," include not only "technology" but also "the proletariat" itself.[43] Precisely, what is threatening about the possibility of emancipation thus opened up is not only its materialistic but also, and above all, its *mass* character. What communism threatens to render obsolete is not art or intellectuality but *the individual as separate from and measured against the mass*. It is antithetical to bourgeois society's glorification of independence, of aloofness from the common lot, of distinction. This, it appears, was the source of the young Benjamin's disquiet in the face of "the consciousness of a proletariat": "I have no intention of preaching individualism," he says in the "Dialogue on the Religiosity of the Present."

> I desire only that the man of culture [*der Kulturmensch*] comprehend his relation to society. I think we should break with the unworthy lie according to which the human being is completely fulfilled in the service of society, and according to which the social, in which we undeniably live our lives at present, is also that which in the last analysis determines personality.[44]

Deep down, it is difficult for the bourgeois ego to conceive of—let alone to see as worthy—any sort of striving, any effort that would not have as its outcome the distinction of the individual from the mass of the nameless and unremembered, on whom the light of recognition never falls. It is the longing for success, the desire to stand out from the crowd, instilled by bourgeois childrearing and education that pits the individual against the masses and consequently against progress. For the intellectual in particular, the idea that intellectual labor is not intrinsically worthier, more valuable than manual labor is a bitter pill to have to swallow. That is why "the masses, and, indeed, the reading masses," as Benjamin says, "disquiet [*beunruhigen*] the fascist author like nothing else."[45] He knew something of this disquiet himself, as we saw. But he was eventually able to read the writing on the wall and to see whither it led. Thanks to the roundabout path that his own evolution followed, and above all to his uncompromising honesty with himself, his intellectual integrity, the lucidity that he gained in this particular regard was, and perhaps remains, without parallel. This lucidity is nowhere more fully in effect than in the transformation of his theory of experience in his late work on Baudelaire, to which we now turn.

Learning from Experience

Any judgment of Benjamin's work based on his theory of experience must certainly take account of his late Baudelaire studies. The subject of "On Some Motifs in Baudelaire," the last essay that he completed, is the "transformation of the very structure of human experience."[46] The essay also represents a leap forward in his theory of experience. The unique importance of "On Some Motifs" as a document of the development of his thinking is confirmed by Benjamin himself in a letter to Gretel Adorno, written while he was at work on the essay, in which he tells her: "I have never been certain in any earlier work to this degree of the vanishing point at which (and, as it now seems, from time immemorial) all of my reflections come together from the most divergent points."[47] Among his notes for the essay we also find the following, which is of diagnostic significance for the transformation both of his own experience and of his theory of experience: "In the eye of the philosopher, which understandably closes in the face of this new experience, there appears spontaneously, as it were, as an afterimage [*Nachbild*], a complementary type of experience."[48] It is the "new experience" that the solitary thinker sunk in contemplation cannot make sense of, and to whom it comes, therefore, as a *shock*: "The learning experience is the yield of work. The shock experience is the yield of idleness."[49] The "afterimage" of "a complementary type of experience" arises with the "parrying"—not to be confused with the mastering—of the "shock-experience." Benjamin points to the same defense mechanism in "On Some Motifs in Baudelaire" to explain Bergson's philosophy. Bergson, he writes, "rejects any historical determination of experience [*Erfahrung*]," and thus he avoids above all approaching that experience "from which his own philosophy evolved, or, rather, in reaction to which it arose."[50] It is in the same way that we can and, I think, should understand the development of Benjamin's thinking prior to his turn to Marxism—that is, as a defense against the new experience of industrial modernity, of capitalism, in the face of which he did his best for the better part of a decade to keep his eyes shut (in other words, which he began by rejecting and only later was able to assimilate into his experience and thought, i.e., to make sense of).

Benjamin places at the center of "On Some Motifs" an interpretation of Baudelaire's sonnet "Correspondances." "Correspondances" describes precisely the "derivation of aura"—the forming of a false consciousness—from the "projection of a social experience among human beings [*einer gesellschaftlichen Erfahrung unter Menschen*]"—in the poem, it is the experience of *communication*, the experience of being among human beings itself—"onto nature," by which the human being's "gaze is returned."⁵¹ The "disintegration of aura in immediate shock-experience," which Baudelaire named as "the price for which the sensation of modernity could be had," is inscribed in the poem *en creux*, as it were, in the form of its repression.⁵² The transcendent unity of experience that the verses conjure up is purchased at the price of the possibility of a knowledge of experience—the capacity to learn from what one has lived, and to communicate something of it to one's fellow human beings. It is a unity as obscure as it is profound, in which scents, colors, and sounds respond to one another in the same way that distant echoes blend together and become indistinct; a unity vast like the night and like the light, and in which, to human eyes, everything appears gray.⁵³ What the poem *sings* in its last line—"*qui chantent les transports de l'esprit et des sens*"—is an inability to *speak*, that is, to speak clearly, to communicate, to say something about, to make some sense of the reality of things.

From the breakdown of tradition—the liquefaction of all that was solid and the profanation of all that was sacred—there arises the same "prehistoric dread" that at the beginning of human history gave rise to the belief in magic as a means of controlling the overpowering and mysterious forces of the environment. In its repetitions, ritual reenacts the overcoming of primeval dread in the face of unfathomable nature. "Where there is experience in the strict"—that is, in the "old"—"sense of the word, certain contents of the individual past combine in the memory [*Gedächtnis*] with material from the collective past," writes Benjamin.⁵⁴ "Rituals [*die Kulte*], with their ceremonies and their festivals, ... kept producing the amalgamation of these two elements of memory over and over again."⁵⁵ Through ritual the group is fused together in magical communion. At the far end of the development of the human being's productive forces, the actual conquest of nature, the individual inexorably isolated and cast back on itself by competition is seized by the same fear that gripped its forebears at its beginning. "To his horror, the melancholy man sees the earth revert to a mere state of nature. No breath of prehistory surrounds it—no aura," as Benjamin says.⁵⁶ For the human being who witnesses the disenchantment of nature by technology, large-scale industry, and mass production, and of social relations by class warfare, the "correspondences," the "data of recollection" and of "prehistory," are merely a "consolation," and an "inefficac[ious]" one.⁵⁷ Never again will they seem real. The "experience in which he once shared [having] now collapsed into itself," the individual racked by spleen withdraws further into isolation and takes refuge in "recollection" (*Eingedenken*), above all the kind evoked by scent, the "inaccessible refuge of *mémoire involontaire*," the least communicable and the "most consoling" kind, because more than any other it "deeply anaesthetizes the consciousness of the passage of time [*das Bewußtsein des Zeitverlaufs*]." The time of recollection, "like that of the *mémoire involontaire*," is "historyless."⁵⁸ Recollection—the "experience" of which "forbids us to conceive of history as fundamentally atheological," Benjamin had written a few years earlier—here appears not as an experience of history, but on the contrary as the repression of historical experience.⁵⁹ Perhaps that was the last great lesson that Benjamin was to learn in his life. But, of course, there is no way of knowing that.

What we can say is that the definitive experience of both Baudelaire's life and Benjamin's was that of capitalism's unmerciful, but *disillusioning*, reduction of the human being to its real, disenchanted and prosaic conditions. "No study of Baudelaire can fully explore the vitality of its subject without dealing with the image of his life [*dem Bild seines Lebens*]," says Benjamin.[60] Above all, he stresses time and again the decisive importance for Baudelaire of the fact that the poet was no longer a privileged being, that he would have to compete for patronage on the open market. "In feudal society, the leisure of the poet is a recognized privilege. In contrast, the bourgeoisie once in power, the poet finds himself the out of work person, the 'idler' par excellence," he observes, for example.[61] Unlike those of his contemporaries who tried to escape this fate, Baudelaire "resolved to put his idle existence, deprived of social identity, on display; he made it a sign of his social isolation."[62] Thus alone could he "lay claim to the dignity of the poet"—the dignity that throughout history has gone hand in hand with the exemption from work—"in a society that had no more dignity of any kind to confer."[63] Above all, Baudelaire never came to terms with the shock of finding himself cast out among the nameless masses, whose gaze could not "return . . . except as a competitor."[64] The encounter of the isolated individual with the masses was "the immediate experience to which Baudelaire gave the weight of a learning experience [*das Gewicht einer Erfahrung*]," Benjamin says.[65] But Baudelaire did not learn from his experience. His "portrait" (*Lebensbild*) was fixed once and for all in "petrified unrest [*Unruhe*]"—it "knows no development."[66] He parried the encounter with the masses away from his intellectual faculties by making it into an occasion for his poetry—no doubt some of the most beautiful that has ever been written.

Thanks to the development that did take place in Benjamin's experience, he was able to do for Baudelaire what Baudelaire was never able to do for himself: to communicate the "gist" of his experience "in such a way that its social bearing would become immediately intelligible."[67] He saw what had remained invisible to Baudelaire, and why. "Perhaps [Baudelaire's] clairvoyant condition," he was able to say in the end,

> was no gift of observation at all but the irremediable distress of the solitary in the midst of the crowds. Is it too audacious to claim that these are the same crowds that, in our time, are molded by the hands of dictators? As to the faculty of glimpsing in these subjugated crowds nuclei of resistance—nuclei formed by the revolutionary masses of '48 and the communards—it had not fallen to Baudelaire.[68]

Baudelaire was set on nothing more intently than to prostitute himself in an original way, to make a living, if possible, in a way that would set him apart. It was this intention that fixed him in his place opposite the masses. But his dignity, his sense of his own worth, made him tarry for as long as possible before handing himself over to the market. Whence his resolve to "elevate idleness to the rank of a method of work, his own method," and to put it on display—to transmute, in his own person, use-value into exhibition-value.[69] He made his life into a spectacle of the contradictions of a society that he hated, but which he stopped short of seeking to transform. Because he set himself in opposition to the masses, his lot was instead to share "the fatalism of those who are most remote from the process of production," in relation to which alone the nuclei of any effective resistance to the established order can form.[70]

An attentive reading of Benjamin's late studies, and above all his last study, of Baudelaire, such as I have roughly sketched out here, is sufficient, I think, to refute the claim that his criticism is of a kind that relates "conservatively to its objects," and that it is incompatible with the Marxist critique of ideology.[71] At the core of the question of the nature of Benjamin's criticism is the broader question of the relation between the intellectual and politics, which is to say, as Benjamin himself understood well, between intellectuals and the masses.[72] According to Habermas, Benjamin's criticism has not, like "consciousness-raising critique," an "immanent," but only "a highly mediated relation to political practice. On this, Benjamin did not manage to achieve sufficient clarity," we are told.[73] I have tried to show that, on precisely this point, Benjamin achieved a degree of clarity that is rare. He did not imagine that the social existence of an intellectual is the same as that of a worker (although he himself was often little better off), but he came to see in all that divides them a denunciation of the existing order.

Benjamin knew that the political effect that an intellectual as such has is an "indirect" one, in that its direct effect, if it has any effect at all, is the effect that it has on other intellectuals. He also saw that intellectuals' most urgent task under present conditions, for the sake of their own special interest as well, is to turn their particular "means of production," their education, directly against the system that affords it to them as a privilege. "In Germany," the conclusion of his review of Hoernle's *Basic Questions of Proletarian Education* reads, "there is no orthodox Marxist literature apart from political and economic writings. This is the chief reason for the astonishing ignorance on the part of intellectuals, including left-wing intellectuals, about matters concerning Marxism."[74] The book, Benjamin says, "demonstrates with authoritative acuity, in regard to one of the most fundamental subjects, pedagogy, what orthodox Marxist thinking is and whither it leads. It should be taken to heart."[75] Of the lessons that he learned in his life, that which I have reconstructed in this chapter is the one that it seems to me is most important to take to heart today. Then we may yet learn once more to take up the struggle against a system of production, a social order, in which, among other things, thinkers are not supposed to labor and laborers are not supposed to think—a system that unremittingly divides us from and pits us against one another in the interest of one class, when instead we could be cooperating in the common interest of us all. That will mean taking up in earnest, as Benjamin did, a struggle against the real conditions of our existence, such as they are and such as it is at present.

Conclusion

In his review of Kracauer's ethnography of the Berlin salariat c. 1930, Benjamin remarks that an analogy suggests itself "between the processes in which an unbearably tense economic situation produces a false consciousness and the situations that lead neurotics and the mentally ill along the path from unbearable private conflicts to their false consciousness."[76] It is among those whose way of life large-scale enterprise continually volatilizes, yet who for "cultural" or ideological at least as much as unmediated economic reasons cannot find it within themselves to make common cause with the proletariat, that the contradictions of capitalist development are most apt to be psychically unmetabolizable. For the expansion of human beings' productive forces with the industrialization and socialization of production is experienced by them as a threat to a form of life in denial of its obsolescence and unable or unwilling to be transformed by the new conditions. "A vanished bourgeois way of life haunts them," as Kracauer had said of his white-collar workers. "Perhaps it contains forces with a legitimate demand to endure"—those "authentic aspects of culture and education" with which the intellectual, or simply the cultured person, fears losing touch. "But they survive today only inertly, without getting involved in a dialectic with the prevailing conditions, and so themselves undermine the legitimacy of their continued existence."[77] The resistance to entering into a dialectic with the real conditions of the present, such as might produce a transformation of those conditions and of the experience that they condition, calls into action defense mechanisms. The defense against knowledge of the real conditions of the present does not secure one against those conditions but engenders a counter-dialectic of repression and alienation from reality, which by rendering them unconscious only reinforces the hold of those conditions over the mind.

Benjamin's own thought and experience after 1924, of which his writings are the record, can best be grasped as the stepwise, sometimes halting analysis and unworking of this repression, the waking analysis of the dream-state from which he was step by step emerging. Through the critique of his own earlier ideas, he was able finally to make sense of the experience from which they arose, his own experience: a difficult, and no doubt at times painful, external and *internal* struggle, a struggle with himself that led him to adopt an increasingly definite stance of opposition to the social conditions that made him what he was.

Notes

I am grateful to the editors of this volume for their patient reading of and helpful comments on earlier versions of this chapter.

1. Important contributions on this subject include, for example, Julian Roberts, *Walter Benjamin* (London: Macmillan, 1982); Rolf; Tiedemann, *Dialektik im Stillstand: Versuche zum Spätwerk Walter Benjamins* (Frankfurt am Main: Suhrkamp, 1983); Susan Buck-Morss, *The Dialectics of Seeing: Walter Benjamin and the Arcades Project* (Cambridge: MIT Press, 1989); and, somewhat more recently, T.J. Clark, "Should Benjamin Have Read Marx?" *boundary 2* 30, no. 1 (2003): 31–49. This selection is by no means meant to be exhaustive.
2. *SW* 2: 763; *GS* 2: 804.
3. Paul Nizan, *The Watchdogs: Philosophers and the Established Order*, trans. Paul Fittingoff (New York: Monthly Review Press, 1971), 175; Paul Nizan, *Les Chiens de garde* (Paris: Maspero, 1965), 165. Translation modified.
4. Letter to Max Rychner, March 7, 1931, *C* 372.
5. Ibid.
6. Louis Althusser, "Philosophy as a Revolutionary Weapon," in *Lenin and Philosophy and Other Essays*, trans. Ben Brewster (New York: Monthly Review Press, 2001), 2.

7   Jürgen Habermas, "Walter Benjamin: Consciousness-Raising or Rescuing Critique," in *Philosophical-Political Profiles*, trans. Frederick G. Lawrence (Cambridge: MIT Press, 1983), 130.
8   Habermas, "Walter Benjamin: Consciousness-Raising or Rescuing Critique," 149.
9   Ibid.
10 Ibid., 129–30.
11 Hannah Arendt, "Walter Benjamin: 1892–1940," trans. Harry Zohn, in *Men in Dark Times* (San Diego: Harcourt Brace, 1968), 165–6.
12 Ibid.
13 *AP* 392 (K2,5); *GS* 5: 495.
14 Habermas, "Walter Benjamin: Consciousness-Raising or Rescuing Critique," 152.
15 *AP* 392 (K2,5).
16 Habermas, "Walter Benjamin: Consciousness-Raising or Rescuing Critique," 149.
17 *EW* 200–1.
18 *EW* 201; *GS* 2: 79.
19 *EW* 201; *GS* 2: 78–9. Translation modified.
20 *EW* 64; *GS* 2: 18.
21 *EW* 71; *GS* 2: 26. Translation modified.
22 *EW* 64.
23 Michael Jennings, "Walter Benjamin, Religion, and a Theological Politics, ca. 1922," in *The Weimar Moment: Liberalism, Political Theology, and Law*, eds. Leonard V. Kaplan and Rudy Koshar (Lanham: Lexington, 2012), 115.
24 John McCole, *Walter Benjamin and the Antinomies of Tradition* (Ithaca: Cornell University Press, 1993), 162–3.
25 "An Outsider Makes His Mark," *SW* 2: 309–10.
26 *SW* 2: 309.
27 *SW* 2: 274.
28 Ibid.
29 "Lily Brauns Manifest an die Schuljugend," *GS* 3: 10. My translation.
30 *SW* 2: 273–4.
31 *SW* 2: 274.
32 *SW* 2: 273; *GS* 3: 206.
33 Siegfried Kracauer, "On Bestsellers and Their Audience," in *The Mass Ornament: Weimar Essays*, ed. and trans. Thomas Y. Levin (Cambridge: Harvard University Press, 1995), 94.
34 Ibid.
35 Ibid.
36 Walter Benjamin, "Letter from Paris: André Gide and His New Antagonist," trans. Charles Gelman, *Barricade* 1 (2018): 31.
37 Ibid., 43–4.
38 Ibid., 32.
39 George Novack, *The Origins of Materialism* (New York: Pathfinder Press, 1965), 229.
40 Klaus Theweleit, *Male Fantasies*, vol. 2, *Male Bodies: Psychoanalyzing the White Terror*, trans. Erica Carter and Chris Turner with Stephen Conway (Minneapolis: University of Minnesota Press, 1989), 351.
41 Ibid., 201.
42 Benjamin, "Letter from Paris: André Gide and His New Antagonist," 39.
43 Ibid., 38.
44 *EW* 71; *GS* 2: 25–6.

45 Benjamin, "Letter from Paris: André Gide and His New Antagonist," 42; *GS* 3: 492.
46 "Über einige Motive bei Baudelaire [French Abstract]," *GS* 1: 1187. My translation.
47 Letter to Gretel Adorno, June 26, 1939, *C* 609.
48 "Ms. 1093ᵛ," *GS* 1: 1184. My translation.
49 "Ms. 1093ʳ," *GS* 1: 1183. My translation. On the same page, Benjamin notes the need to distinguish between the "old" and the "new" *Erfahrung*. The old experience is rooted in ritual communion; the new in the experience of work in common.
50 *SW* 4: 314; *GS* 1: 608–9. Translation modified.
51 "Central Park," *SW* 4: 173; *GS* 1: 670. Translation modified.
52 "On Some Motifs in Baudelaire," *SW* 4: 343.
53 "Comme de longues échos qui de loin se confondent / Dans une ténébreuse et profonde unité, / Vaste comme la nuit et comme la clarté, / Les parfums, les couleurs, et les sons se répondent" (Charles Baudelaire, "Correspondances," in *Œuvres complètes*, ed. Claude Pichois, Paris: Gallimard, 1975-6, 1: 11). Cf. "la nature ressemble à un toton qui, mû par une vitesse accélérée, nous apparaît gris, bien qu'il résume en lui toutes les couleurs" (Charles Baudelaire, "Salon de 1846," in *Œuvres complètes*, 2: 423).
54 "On Some Motifs in Baudelaire," *SW* 4: 316; *GS* 1: 611.
55 *SW* 4: 316; *GS* 1: 611.
56 *SW* 4: 336; *GS* 1: 643–4. "Kein Hauch von Vorgeschichte umwittert sie," an allusion to *Faust* I, ln. 7–8: "Mein Busen fühlt sich jugendlich erschüttert / Vom Zauberhauch, der euren Zug umwittert." In Walter Kaufmann's translation (New York: Anchor, 1961): "My breast is stirred and feels with youthful pain / The magic breath that hovers round your train" (65). Cf. "The old prehistoric dread already envelops [*umwittert*] the world of our parents because we ourselves are no longer bound to this world by tradition" (*AP* 462 [N2a,2]; *GS* 5: 576).
57 "On Some Motifs in Baudelaire," *SW* 4: 334–5. Cf. "Mass production is the principal economic cause—and class warfare the principal social cause—of the decline of the aura" (*AP* 343 [J64a,1]).
58 *SW* 4: 335; *GS* 1: 641–2. Translation modified.
59 *AP* 471 (N8,1).
60 "Central Park," *SW* 4: 168; *GS* 1: 665. Benjamin's preoccupation with Baudelaire's *life* goes back a long way. In December 1921, he reports Scholem that his work on Goethe's *Elective Affinities* "is proceeding *very* slowly" and "now ... conflicts with my work on Baudelaire's life, on which I must spend some time" (Letter to Gershom Scholem, December 17, 1921, *C* 198).
61 "Notes sur les Tableaux parisiens de Baudelaire," *GS* 1: 745. My translation.
62 *GS* 1: 746. My translation. See *AP* 802 (m2a,5). See also Baudelaire, "Edgar Allan Poe, sa vie et ses ouvrages," in *Œuvres complètes*, 2: 272.
63 "Central Park," *SW* 4: 168.
64 "Ms. 1090," *GS* 1: 1185. My translation.
65 "On Some Motifs in Baudelaire," *SW* 4: 343; *GS* 1: 652–3. Translation modified. A related formulation appears in his notes for the essay: "The accent that falls on the immediate experience will be the weightier [*gewichtiger*] the further its object is from work. Work is distinguished precisely in that it enables immediate experiences to become learning experiences [*Erfahrungen*]." ("Ms. 1093ʳ," *GS* 1: 1183. My translation.) "Experience [*die Erfahrung*] is the outcome of work; immediate experience [*das Erlebnis*] is the phantasmagoria of the idler" (*AP* 801 [m1a,3]; *GS* 5: 962).
66 "Central Park," *SW* 4: 171; *GS* 1: 668. Translation modified.
67 *AP* 316 (J48,9).

68 "Notes sur les Tableaux parisiens de Baudelaire," *GS* 1: 748. My translation.
69 *GS* 1: 748. My translation.
70 "Left-Wing Melancholy," *SW* 2: 426.
71 Habermas, "Walter Benjamin: Consciousness-Raising or Rescuing Critique," 136.
72 As Benjamin wrote to Scholem, who had been giving him a hard time about his change of attitude in regard to communism, "If it is true, as you claim, that I have actually gotten 'behind some principles' that I knew nothing about in your day, I have gotten 'behind' this one above all: anyone of this generation who feels and understands the historical moment in which he exists in this world, not as mere words, but as a battle, cannot renounce the study and practice of the mechanism through which things (and conditions) and the masses interact" (Letter to Gershom Scholem, May 29, 1926, *C* 300).
73 Habermas, "Walter Benjamin: Consciousness-Raising or Rescuing Critique," 153.
74 "A Communist Pedagogy," *SW* 2: 275; *GS* 3: 209. Translation modified.
75 *SW* 2: 275; *GS* 3: 209. Translation modified.
76 "An Outsider Makes His Mark," *SW* 2: 308.
77 Siegfried Kracauer, *The Salaried Masses: Duty and Distraction in Weimar Germany*, trans. Quintin Hoare (London: Verso, 1998), 82.

3

Leitmotif Siegfried

Laurence A. Rickels

"In the total unconscious fantasy belonging to growth at puberty and in adolescence, there is the death of someone."[1] When in "Contemporary Concepts of Adolescent Development" D. W. Winnicott thus reformulates the murder in adolescence as unidentified dying object, he underscores that the task that comes upon the teen is to take responsibility for the death wish. And so he follows up with emphasis on "personal triumph" as "something inherent in the process of maturation and in the acquisition of adult status," which the teen approaches, however, with "shyness."[2] The combo of murder and triumph that Winnicott sees as basic to adolescence would suggest a psychopathic tendency equally basic were it not for the factor of "immaturity." "Immaturity is an essential element of health at adolescence. There is only one cure for immaturity and that is the *passage of time* and the growth into maturity that time can bring."[3]

In 1964, Winnicott addressed what was in the news: young hooligans acting out in groups:

> There is real danger in the present situation, and the worst result of today's adolescent tendency to group violence would be the beginning of a movement comparable with the beginning phase of the Nazi regime, when Hitler solved the adolescent problem overnight by offering youth the role of superego to the community. This was a false solution, as we can see when we look back, but it did temporarily solve a social problem which in some ways resembled the one in which we are involved now.[4]

The Third Reich jumped the gun and harnessed adolescence to the momentum basic to the new order, power through joy. The short-term solution to teen turbulence was to raise the cursory connections of teen group bonding to the level of society-wide membership. The Teen Age was thus lifted outside its dynamic with midlife criticism. "Lost is all the imaginative activity and striving of immaturity."[5]

According to Winnicott, the teen in the postwar world keeps it real by deferring identification with parental guidance. Only in time can he come around to making a compromise of and for himself. But the holding pattern of deferral must also be contained. Built-in societally controlled release of teen energy ended once the rationale that dedicated youth to preparedness for military conflict was gone with the atom bomb. Add to this effective contraception and adolescence becomes the place in time where sex and violence are contained as its content: "adolescence now has to contain itself."[6] That this suggests a dynamic of inoculation in lieu of treatment or interpretation would be the gist of my work on adolescence and psychopathy.

The circumstances of the early loss of his father in World War I and the father's replacement with a devotee of German culture, who was, moreover, his Oedi-pal, guided Ian Fleming to set the world of James Bond alongside the postwar integration of Germany. When Alexander and Margarete Mitscherlich wonder provocatively in *The Inability to Mourn* where all the energy went that was so generously expended and displayed in Hitler's name I can supply the key: German adolescence was missing in action. The energy or industry associated with adolescence, as I argue in *Germany: A Science Fiction*, was applied by Germans in their majority to the work of reparation that yielded the postwar "economic miracle." That in the world of Bond it is up to the midlifer's libido to occupy the foreground of reality-testing fits a certain brand of athleticism in midlife, which began to be flexed in the 1950s. However, midlife working-out need not cultivate and commemorate the original physicality of one's younger years. The building of the midlife body can also rise up over the incorporation of youth.

Fleming's story "The Living Daylights" is set in postwar Berlin. A Soviet sniper must be stopped from shooting a man who aims to cross over to the west on the evening of one of the next three days. From their room near the border, at once lookout and shooting post, Bond watches the setting through the otherwise closed curtains while the officer in charge, an ambivalently cast father figure named Sender, narrates what to look for, what to recognize, what to remember. "It reminded Bond of a spiritualist séance."[7] While waiting for the evening hour of his assignment, Bond loses himself in the tribulations of the heroine of an S&M porno he picked up just the other day in Berlin:

> James Bond's choice of reading matter, prompted by a spectacular jacket of a half-naked girl strapped to a bed, turned out to have been a happy one for the occasion. It was called *Verderbt, Verdammt, Verraten*. The prefix ver signified that the girl had not only been ruined, damned, and betrayed, but that she had suffered these misfortunes most thoroughly.[8]

Fleming constructs the S&M porno novel out of a hybrid citation and introject. Its recognition value lies in its resemblance to the most famous German-language product in this line, *The Life of Josefine Mutzenbacher: Memoirs of a Viennese Whore*, noteworthy also because the presumed author, Felix Salten, wrote the novel that Disney's *Bambi* adapted. The span of this introjection is historically that of Fleming's generation. However, *Verderbt, Verdammt, Verraten*, the book Bond picks up in Berlin, is the title not of a tribute to Mutzenbacher's Passion but of Georg Reimann's study of the perils of adolescence in postwar Germany, the first volume of which appeared in 1955. Not only is the problem of adolescence thus subsumed by the S&M fantasy projected into it, but the original dominatrix, whose scenarios inverted her male subjects, has been turned into a trainee tied to a fitness regimen.

Another introject or intertext inviting more extensive reflection on the evacuation of German adolescence folds out of a blind spot in the career review of Walter

Benjamin. What also comes out with the spot, the oblivion to which the psychoanalytic setting of Benjamin's thought tends to be consigned, is a case of what I have addressed as the resistance *in* theory.

In 1929, Benjamin published a review of Alexander Mette's psychiatric study from the year before, *On the Relations Between Language Peculiarities in Schizophrenia and Poetic Productions*, and thus entered an exchange that brought his *Origin of the German Mourning-Play* into contact with the clinical literature on psychosis. Two years later, Mette's review of Benjamin's *Origin* book was published in *Imago*.

Benjamin's review opened with a recommendation cited from Rudolf Borchardt: at the onset of the twentieth century, it was high time that a nobler class of readership shake off the fad (even illness) of fascinated identification with Hölderlin. Borchardt makes the comparison with the Ossian craze at the close of the eighteenth century, with which we are still in contact through Goethe's *Werther*, but which was otherwise let go. This not entirely just judgment, says Benjamin, is countered by Mette's study, in particular in the parts endowed, as Benjamin puts it, with winning traits. Benjamin recognizes that Mette's skewering together of schizophrenic and poetic language-invention belongs on the map of German adolescence (and even says it's kind of cute). Mette's "intentions," however, lack the depth and breadth required for "operating" such "dangerous" "linguistic hotchpotch" ("Sprachgemengen").[9] How can one not syndicate in one's own language proximity to the borderline of an untenable comparison if it applies ultimately to every endeavor to give form to thought? That Mette's combination of schizophrenic and lyrical texts amounts to "playing with symptoms" seems to Benjamin "desperate." In Benjamin's more adult view, it is the "primal time" of language in which both schizophrenic and poet submerge themselves, but under very different conditions. The schizophrenic would introduce into a process of collective objectification in language an appointment or appeal ("Berufung") in a matter that was ultimately decided long time ago. The need to grasp essentials, to render immediately what was deeply felt comes to a dead end not because the schizophrenic lacks the spiritual resources of the poet or philosopher, as Mette avers, but, says Benjamin, because the collective trauma of language is predetermined and only a difference in the protective measures taken counts.

The image of the diving bell Benjamin uses to distinguish the lyrical poet's sojourn in prehistory from psychotic abandonment to the same depths fits the image of encapsulation that Benjamin bestows (in his 1928 article, "Books by the Insane: From My Collection") on Daniel Paul Schreber's share in a poet's preparedness.[10] In Benjamin's media theorization, Schreber's diving bell for the wild plummet into prehistory kept him outside the close quarters of poetry and schizophrenia. In his media essays, Benjamin would raise a related question: how does gadget love (and its idiom) allow the adolescent or group member to stagger the psychoticizing impact of technologization and massification? A psychotic like Schreber who succeeds in surviving the end of the world in an escape capsule of his own projection catches up with the industry of adolescence that wasn't originally part of his *Bildung*. Upon his safe landing, with his rights fully restored, Schreber had the score of one of the Siegfried Leitmotivs from Wagner's Ring Cycle etched over the entrance to his home. Adolescence, by daydreaming wish-fulfillment alone, belongs to the future. Wasn't Schreber's transgender experimentation the adolescence-appropriate rehearsal for encapsulation (a far, far better word than adaptation)? Paranomasia, poetry, and schizophrenia tend to break out in adolescence. The teen talent for coining a new idiom is the free gift that comes with in-group membership. While the schizo goes it alone with his over-precision and fabrication, the teen exchanges his neologisms in group. There is a recurring typo in Mette's study that places "wie" (like) where "wir" (we) is required and expected.[11] It would syndicate schizo language if we were not group-bound in language to correct it right away: to let "wie" stand irrevocably in place of "wir" would be schizophrenic. By our initiation via "like" or "as if!" (*als ob*), the quintessential coordinates and particles of teen thought, we apply the group glue and enter the "we."

In his review of the *Origin* book, Mette's one gripe was with Benjamin's dismissal of Nietzsche's view of the Greek chorus.[12] In Mette's theorization of the liminal state of adolescence via the Dionysian in its contrast to Apollonian adulthood, the endurance of the Dionysian chorus on stage is pivotal to the dialectic of developmental stages. Without adolescence: no dialectic, no stage-three accession to tragic heroism.

Following his psychiatric study, Mette published essays and gave lectures in a cosmopolitan-jargonic style within a frame of references to international psychoanalysts. In 1934, Mette published a monograph titled *The Depth-Psychological Foundations of the Tragic, the Apollonian, and the Dionysian* on a topic that was already his standby (the 1928 clinical study was his thesis and station break). The 1934 depth-psychological study, however, was banned in the Third Reich. In the midst of his consideration of the measure in the mix of the divine impulses in exemplary German authors from Classicism and Romanticism Mette directs the reader in note 35 to the cohabitation in the Baroque *Trauerspiel* (in contradistinction to a Classical synthesis) of the psychoanalytically revalorized divine impulses. "I therefore earlier, in a review article on the Benjaminian study, pointed to the connection between two neighboring realms: the melancholic-manic and the schizophrenic."[13]

In the back of the book, among the blurbs endorsing his 1928 monograph, we find an excerpt from Benjamin's review. Although careful reference to the big Jewish names was still possible in 1934, it was already advisable to follow Mette's suit and supplement or subsume Freud, for example, with Nietzsche. However, Mette's references to Benjamin, Siegfried Bernfeld, and Hanns Sachs may well have been judged gratuitous and insupportable. Mette consulted Bernfeld and Sachs because their studies addressed, respectively, the psychology of youth movements and adolescent daydreaming, which Mette was exploring under the aegis of the Dionysian.

In 1936, the psychotherapy institute was founded in Berlin to replace psychoanalysis, which meant however to emplace it, two years later, intact and unnamed as "Working Group A" within an ABC of psychodynamic perspectives that gave form to what was a concession to eclecticism. However, the institute's all-important clinic was the responsibility of "Working Group A," which shows that under different names and neologisms the Nazi government was determined to stick to what worked, which included, in the view from on high, Freudian psychoanalysis.[14] Although Mette did not try for a prominent role within the institute, he was under its protection. Unlike the leading depth psychologists at the institute, Mette didn't enter the Bermuda triangle of reunification of Greater-Psychoanalysis out of a synthesis of Adlerian, Jungian, and Freudian perspectives.

After 1934, Mette developed instead a "literary" style, which paid off. In keeping with tendencies in the discourse of the humanities which were heightened under Nazi censorship, Mette's discourse joined in the gobbledy-spook of Romanticism's unquiet grave. In the back of his 1940 book, his final essay or attempt to illuminate Nietzsche's duo dialectic, select publications by the same press are listed, including Mette's book on dreams from the year before. One blurb endorsing the 1939 study, excerpted from a review in one of the central journals of Nazi German psychiatry, broadcasts words from Mette's sponsor, the head of Berlin's psychotherapy institute, Matthias Göring. In keeping with the institute's reunifying eclecticism, the Adlerian therapist sets aside his reservations: "In the clinical setting elucidation of a dream can proceed only in the context of the whole personality. Just the same, everyone who has depth-psychological understanding will read with pleasure the Mettian book, which is written artistically and graphically."

The adaptation to censorship does not have to equal adaptation to new ideological norms. Censorship can also externalize obstacles faced by anyone apprenticed to the stern mastery of writing. The *Versuchung*, temptation and experiment, of writing can be compelling. Mette's thesis book doubles as manual on the intrapsychic course of obstacles faced in the experiment of being or wanting to be a writer. His first publication, in 1925, was a collection covering his early years as writer-novice, from 1917 through 1922. In addition to his many poems, there is one exposition in which Mette addresses the significance of youth at the same time as he tests his own decision to be an author of critical prose. It's awkward not only in terms of writing development.

Mette opens with a reproach: the young generation swerved from the ideals of the victors in 1870 into the eddy of a concept the future generation never fully owned, with which, however, it came to be associated: the concept of the proletariat.[15] A deeper sense of the impasse is given by the history that came to pass, in which the younger generation faced the fall of the empire with indifference. Well before the unification of Germany, German youth demonstrated a will and path of its own. One need only consider the *Wandervogel* movement. Wasn't it a proletarian trait of the youth movements that in returning to nature they openly turned away from property rights?[16] However, it was an idea that compelled them: the idea of duty-free individuality delivered of all ownership, all material possession, indeed the very thought of it, including economic theory. This new "will to life" that eschews political *organization* may be the highest that a national culture can attain.[17] The younger generation came to a "Hamletian" impasse "not as adversaries of the German spirit, but as representatives of its development, indeed as the only 'historical Germany' that was available in the new century."[18] So ends the first section. Other sections in this pre-psychoanalytic exposition (on extra-moral heroism, on the role of women in the metabolization of youth, on the youth-objective of aesthetic justification of what feels real) are placeholders for what followed in the course of Mette's psychoanalytic revalorization of Nietzsche's Dionysian and Apollonian principles. Between suicidal ideation (Hamlet or Werther) and a hankering for unidentified "heroism" (Siegfried), the German youth movements followed the invention of adolescence into modern group psychology.

Was Mette entering upon so-called inner emigration when, after 1940, he didn't publish again in Nazi Germany? Mette did continue to practice psychotherapy. Right after the war in Weimar, he still trained psychotherapy candidates. In a span between parentheses, Regine Lockot gives the rundown of Mette's GDR career after he gave up his practice: "he pursued an initial interest in health policies, then a university career, and eventually became a member of the chamber of deputies of the German Democratic Republic and a member of the central committee of the Socialist Unity Party."[19] Mette's publications during this period were in a style closer to the cosmopolitan-jargonic style before the Nazi censorship, but adapted to a different superstructure. He adamantly turned his association away from Freud's science and put it there with Pavlov in studies that promoted a politically corrective historiography of the discipline of psychiatry.

Is it possible to discern in Mette's oeuvre and career an afterlife of Benjamin's allegorical affiliations, or at least of their reception, which already took combative form in the couples therapy sessions with Theodor Adorno? Benjamin's investment in Marxist discourse, which he employed not only by Adorno's account metaphorically or perhaps allegorically, was also all about its abandoned status, as seen from the fast lane of the competition on death drive. Benjamin was drawn to lost places deep inside the recent past (the past that always also represents prehistory). He knew about the evil-eye staying powers of condemned discourses.

When the Frankfurt School first put out its shingle, there was really only one main competitor on death drive, the eclectic psychotherapeutic brand and band that had grown up between the wars in the afterglow of Freud's big success story, his science's mythic healing of war neurosis. The military-psychological or psycho-technical competition was way advanced, along the double lines of psychoanalysis and technology that Benjamin explored in the essays on mechanical reproducibility and on Baudelaire. There was no Marxism in the competition's mix, and not because it was the one ism that would have blown it all away. The competition only used what worked toward the accomplishment of a certain set of goals. And that meant Freud and an inside-out understanding of technologization and mass psychology.

The fascist grasp of the intersection between technology and the unconscious was too far along to be outdistanced on its own terms and turf, at least in the shorter run of survival. But the mix Benjamin attempted in the essay on film culture, which culminated in the slogan designed for reproducibility, the one about aestheticization of politics and politicization of art, even won in the longer run. This is how Benjamin sought to intervene in the reversal of psychoanalysis internal to the Nazi techno bond by addressing the same gadget lovers, the distracted teen testers, the teen experts in their own replication or reassembly, who were already plugged into the Nazi takeover of live or life's transmissions on death drive.

Mette's 1939 comeback was a book on dreams; not those of his patients, but the dreams of the authors of non-clinical dream-books published from 1917 to 1935.[20] Like a folklorist, he proceeds by comparing dreams from the various compilations—and between the lines gives a record of unconscious developments, even changes, which were going down in record real time.

In one comparison between dreams, Mette reverses the chronological order, attaching the earlier dream like a gloss or legend to the first dream presentation. Indeed, in the wake and shakeup of the lost war, the 1926 dream is far more demarcated and detailed. In the face of a future that is more fate than fantasy, the 1935 dream is terse, sullen, compacted. In 1935, the dreamer enters the winter forest as hunter (*Jäger*, which she doesn't invest with the female gender). While searching for her missing companions, she finds the severed head of a girl under a thorny bush. She picks up the "tender" head and carries it with her as she continues her search, which is now also the search for the girl's body.[21] She meets up with four of her companions and together they keep looking for those still missing. The dream ends in a walled town, the scene of an absence.

In 1926, we start out with the dreamer and her companion in a place that is "uncanny," mainly "because it is a border area [*Grenzgebiet*]."[22] She looks up at the cliff and recognizes three figures, two hunters and an "unusually beautiful woman," although the dreamer hastens to add that her beauty is alienating.[23] Maybe she's from the South or the East. One of the hunters in the woman's company shoots a deer. The woman radiates a vital joy. Then the dreamer's companion aims his gun. The woman falls from the cliff onto their side of the border. That's why they can secure her remains in a "sanctuary" where she lies piled high with other corpses.[24] The dreamer carries the woman's head in a sack, anxiously taking care of it while conscious of the necessity of ridding herself of it. On a city street she recognizes in the tram the hunters and the woman standing next to them. Upon closer inspection, the dreamer sees that it is a wax mannequin in the dead woman's image. "I stare at the uncanny group anxiously expecting, like a guilty criminal, that at any moment the mask will fall and out of the waxen lifelessness will emerge the old life that binds her to her companions."[25]

Mette reaches back in time for a preliminary interpretation: originally, man struggled as hunter against nature. The conflict with one's foreign neighbor is the continuation in modern times of the prehistorical struggle.[26] Killing our fellow man is horrifying. Only under special conditions, when acting in one's own defense or in war, can the horror be bracketed out. The dreamer evinces a cool attitude that gives way as the dream progresses to a mounting fear of retaliation. The murdered woman is expected to return as a ghost. Her first station stop is the uncanny group with the wax doll.[27] The mannequin's face displays the same expression of triumphant joy as did the woman's visage when she was shot. It crosses the dreamer's mind: that's why she was shot. The dream is set in a border area during the winter, a fitting setting for the theme of annihilation and return.[28]

Mette therefore strikes up the fairy-tale elaboration of separation from childhood, which is abandoned as dead, and of the rebirth that follows into the grown-up world.[29] But what's missing is adolescence, which, Mette says, doesn't heed or need fairy tales.[30] In a fairy-tale episode that comes very close to a dream scene, Mette identifies "a cushioning and mitigating tendency at work," which reserves the fairy tale for the carefree child.[31] The fairy tale doesn't tear apart the setting of childhood, only deepens it.[32] In adolescence, we graduate from fairy tale and approach myth and legend. Beginning in adolescence, processes of maturation and mating stand, "by rule of life" (*lebensgesetzlich*), under the sway of psychic forces.[33] The dream, Mette concludes, is adolescent: it is heir to elemental forces of nature, which are in transition before striking a balance in myth and legend.[34]

By skewering together a dream from the 1917 book and another dream from the 1926 collection, Mette elaborates the prehistory that coincides with the recent past. In 1917, the dreamer travels first by train, then on a boat.[35] Pupils returning from a field trip sing in the background. The ship docks at a public beach where strange images made out of wax depict boys of various ages, each one captioned: portrait of a drowned boy.[36] It crosses his mind that some of them might not have drowned on their own but rather were drowned. In the group of unmoving figures there is one wax figure that seems mechanically wound up to move its torso back and forth.[37] The dreamer recognizes his friend, who shot himself at age eighteen. The suicide tries to drag the dreamer down to the bottom of the sea. They are so closely entwined by the end that the dreamer can feel on his face the suicide's decaying grimace.[38]

In the 1926 dream-comp, the dreamer is on a walking tour out in the country with a large group.[39] Jump cut: she's alone in Berlin. Everything seems alien, and she can hardly recognize a thing. Just the same, she is filled with unbounded joy that she is really in Berlin. She visits relatives who have moved to the city. Together they go for a walk and stop at the fairground, which turns into a cemetery. She goes past a row of unattended graves overgrown with grass, now brown in the winter.[40] "These are children's graves, — graves of teenage ["halberwachsenen," literally: half-grownup] persons, and the thought seizes me with shocking vehemence that these were youths, who lived in Berlin; how did it become so difficult for them that they had to die."[41]

Mette comments: these dead and undead embody the dreamer's past on the cusp of transition.[42] The figures themselves are stuck at the threshold. The horrifying existence of the half-dead, half-living resonates with the atmosphere of initiation rites that submitted teen boys to torture, humiliation, bondage, dismemberment, and haunting.[43]

Touring like the hunting in the other dreams signifies crowd experience. Anxiety inspires one to band together with others.[44] In the 1926 hunting dream, the murdered foreign woman is the feared animal and the masculine principle of gender. In the dream from 1935, the dreamer is a huntress who names herself a male hunter.[45] A woman becomes an Amazon out of fear of the male.[46] The severed heads and the foreign beauty are phallic symbols, I mean "symbols of the masculine gender principle."[47] Depth-psychologically-schooled dream researchers, Mette assures the reader, can readily interpret the application of these symbols as signifying castration.[48] Castration appears in dreams to disavow sexual difference.[49] For all the corpses strewn across these dreams, the main theme, according to Mette, is the removal of the identifying marks of masculinity. Women compiled two of the three dream collections. That different dreams by different dreamers of different genders reveal typical patterns is no more surprising, Mette underscores, than the sameness or androgyny of healthy young bodies in the service of the "law of life" (*Lebensgesetz*).[50]

Mette offers another reversed coupling of dreams from the 1935 and 1926 collections. The 1935 dream opens with a "we" in a mountain village.[51] "Our" boys are away mountain climbing. But when the group of youths returns at noon, the dreamer notices that something is wrong. Her son is no longer with them. All the villagers, thousands of them, join her in searching for him. When she comes upon a slab of stone, it rolls back and her son emerges.[52] She examines him for any injuries, but he pushes her away. It's not me anymore, he tells her. The new one is coming on a raft. The former son offers to save the new one for her. They hurry to the shore. There's the raft on which her son lies sleeping.[53]

The 1926 dream commences in a pleasant landscape that the dreamer, however, finds uncanny, even if it is bright, colorful, and clean.[54] A loud cry announces a boat's arrival. But it's plummeting down a waterfall, and it's not a boat, it's an embracing couple, a couple of youths.[55] The rescued teens, who, it turns out, are *Wandervögel*, are brought inside the hospital while the nurses carry out another dead teen for burial at sea. "We know that they are barely alive and will die in but a few hours."[56]

Mette: "It is once again the destiny of the transitional zone."[57] Dreams of mothers rescuing children in a manner and setting suggestive of birth and rebirth loop the readiness to give birth to new life through the turbulence of adolescence, which consciously is hard to grasp and maintain. It is up to the dreams to represent it. The initiation of girls (also in fairy tales) is more closely aligned with sexual awakening. Threatening masculinity (including that of phallic mothers) must be thwarted so the girl can enter the deep sleep of latency and await Prince Charming. That's why the dreamers seem to dread that renewed contact with heterosexuality would return them to the liminal state of initiation: "The erotic commotion has reawakened inside them in its entirety the crisis zone of transition with all its latent tensions."[58] The dreams also address substitution. The 1926 dream does not succeed fully in bringing back to life the casualties, and in lieu of a substitute there is the dead youth. The psyche, however, remembers that in puberty the old ego dies and a new one rises up anew. The wish to rescue the youth (with whom the dreamer identifies) recalls the earlier process.

Mette is inspired to present another dream from 1935 that also treats the theme of birth and rebirth. The dreamer's five-year-old son has died—vanished from the surface of the earth.[59] She enters the underworld of the dwarves and encounters a woman holding an infant with her lost son standing by. The woman says she must choose between the infant bearing the soul of her son and her bodily son now in possession of a stranger's soul.[60]

Infantile and pre-birth existence are ambivalently processed by the psyche, says Mette, such that, depending on the mood swing of your valuation, birth is death or death birth.[61] The "spiritually established individual, who is fully engaged in the activity of the social processes," however, has an easy choice. "The stronger his consciousness has developed into a dominating agency the more effortlessly he decides for the grownup individual."[62] The choice of the son with the strange soul gives in nuce Klaus Theweleit's genealogy (in *Male Fantasies*) of the heightened state of paramilitary preparation between the world wars that supported the emergence of a Nazi state.[63] The father takes the boy child away from his mother and enrolls him in transit centers of hard-body training. When the youth again stands before his mother, he is a stranger with both feet on the burial ground of young-adult heroism. It is not so much that childhood gets trained out of the young subject once and for all, but rather that childhood is fortified as fairy-tale park and memorial point of departure, the birth of the hero. Adolescence is elided between a riveting childhood and man-of-steel manhood.

The 1940 study that closed the books on Mette's exploration of the Dionysian and Apollonian principles opens upon the uncanny world of the clown.[64] The unending "why?" of the child builds up his conceptual environment in trusting application of the *Satz vom Grund*, the principle of reason.[65] The clown asks why? But he also answers himself with authority, the parental response: Why not! Because! Clown comedy is a hybrid of childlikeness and maturity, incompleteness and accomplishment.

Recent "depth psychological" comparative studies of dream and fairytale motifs—here Mette also refers to his own study from the year before—have found points in common with the initiation rites in puberty that are still performed in primitive societies.[66] The carnival custom of stripping, drowning, destroying a doll or throwing a participant into the water is reminiscent of practices in the initiation ceremonies. The childlike life form must be destroyed in a tortuous staging of sacrifice and then brought back, animated anew as the initiated novice. In comparing the celebration of carnival and the performance of the clown, however, Mette compacts the psychic tension of initiation into the unconscious content of a "transitional phase from childlike being to the stage of maturity."[67] Fairy tales with their dark unconscious images of death and return prepare the child for life's transit zones. But while traits of the prehistorical rites can still be discerned in the customs of carnival, the clown's performance steps back squarely inside early childhood.

Just as Mette could find the Dionysian influence in the carnival festivities of his day, so he discerns contemporary traces of the Apollonian in the overvaluation of sports and, more directly, in the strict hierarchy of our manliest institutions, the authoritarian organization of the state and the military. The psychology behind the discipline is nothing other than the longing for the Apollonian prototype, for emulation of the model without consideration of risk to health or life. Destructiveness is not the prerogative of Dionysus alone. Apollo has cruel traits, too. Consider his uncompromising disdain for what is unformed, flaccid, for whatever is stuck in becoming and mutability.[68] Already in boyhood a dragon slayer, it lies in Apollo's nature to put an end to shapeless becoming and erect in its stead an eternal realm of unchanging beauty and completion. Mette offers a seasonal analogue: the Apollonian preference for the flowing river's transformation into ice.[69] Apollo turns unruly Dionysus into the imperative: die nice as ice.

After he links Apollonian art via and beyond the image to the nobility of the healthy race that represents mankind or which mankind represents, Mette brings up the arrears in this nihilistic optimism: it's a fact of life that the man of culture is more readily able to see the figure of a dead person in light of ideal completion and beauty than the figures or data of those still living.[70] "Only the dead are immune to the decline into raw, unbound, blind instinct-lust."[71] Although the clown's antics might be construed as a tantrum tearing apart the bond between mother and child and therefore as emblematic of transition, Mette stands by his opening interpretation of clown humor in terms of the *Satz vom Grund*, which more aptly registers the clown's distance from the carnival-fool. By breaking and then restoring trust in causality, the clown becomes a well-wrought device for safely experiencing regression to early childhood. In Mette's construction, the clown absorbs adolescence, specifically the creativity in language practiced by teen in-groups. Mette allows that he can say that the clown's performance goes back to and stays with the child's way of finding words and thoughts only if he brackets out another childlike tendency, namely to babble back what was heard and remembered.[72] This babbling brook must freeze over to allow for the two-step march from early childhood to young adulthood.

On the map of the joking that yokes together every variety of mass formation, the humor marking the spot we are in with the clown is the exception. It is not guaranteed the stamp of group approval because not fundamentally group bound. It incorporates an infantile trust in adult superiority, which resonates intrapsychically. You don't take your audience home with you in humor. You are alone with humor, but outsiders can appreciate your situation from a safe distance. In California, the *Heimat* of the Teen Age since the 1930s, likeability betokens a friendliness that never shakes the glue of the "like." The smile for miles or for a laugh lights up the group aspect. Pronounced friendliness, the kind etched into the smiley, ultimately bears up as efficiency in the face of catastrophe. Californian friendliness, which permeates everyday life, is a mode of preparedness, like earthquake preparedness, the mode Freud associated with anxiety, but which Californian group psychology carries forward in the manner of teen likeability.

The German version excavated by Mette is less preparedness and more readiness at the drop(scene) of crisis to join in a humorous camaraderie, which promotes efficiency by acceptance of the fateful setback and the consequent determination to get through it. The bottom line of humor, Freud argued, is gallows humor, in which the superego has the last laugh. Humor redirects unstoppable teen irreverence, like the nickname *Blubo* given the official blood-and-earth, *Blut-und-Boden* discourse of National Socialism. Teens on the psycho path are, Winnicott writes in "The Concept of a Healthy Individual," "candidates for lives of storm and stress or perhaps illness."[73] The possibility of illness registers, on a sliding scale between schizoid and schizophrenic, the other constitutive tendency of adolescence: withdrawal of complicity in order to defend a true self against imposition of a false one (to use a distinction Winnicott fittingly refers to here as "awkward").[74] To follow a final victory against all the evidence in the ego's environment reflects not only psychopathic idealism but also the schizoid variant, which on the laugh track is willing and able to take a joke from the superego. Were the German egos chuckling at the *Blubo*-joke on them as they went along to get through it?

In his 1939 study of dreams, Mette placed the cinematic 1926 dream about the foreign beauty and her wax effigy after the one from 1935 as though it clarified or expanded the more terse presentation allegedly spun around the same complex. Let's heed the 1935 dream narrative as it stands in light of Mette's concluding treatment of the Dionysian and the Apollonian. Looking in the winter woods for her companions, who are missing, the dreamer finds the severed head of a young child. She catches up with four of her fellow hunters, who join her in searching for the others. The dreamer and her lost and found comrades comprise an open crowd. Always falling short of closing a circle, the mass formation denies and subsumes its provenance in adolescence. Propelled by the search for the other adults and for the body of the child, it resolutely enters the city of death.

Notes

1   D. W. Winnicott, "Contemporary Concepts of Adolescent Development and their Implications for Higher Education," *Playing and Reality* (Hove and New York: Brunner – Routledge, 2002), 145.
2   Ibid., 146.
3   Ibid.
4   D. W. Winnicott, "Youth Will Not Sleep," *Deprivation and Delinquency*, ed. Claire Winnicott et al. (London and New York: Routledge, 2000), 156.

5   Winnicott, "Concepts of Adolescent Development," 146.
6   Winnicott, "Struggling through the Doldrums," *Deprivation and Delinquency*, 151.
7   Ian Fleming, "The Living Daylights," *Octopussy: The Last Adventures of James Bond 007* (New York: Signet Books, 1967), 72.
8   Ibid., 79.
9   "Alexander Mette, *Über Beziehungen zwischen Spracheigentümlichkeiten schizophrener und dichterischer Produktion*. Dessau, Dresden: Dion-Verlag, 1928. 99 S.," *GS* 3: 165. Unless otherwise indicated all translations from German into American are my own.
10 "Bücher von Geisteskranken: Aus meiner Sammlung," *GS* 4: 615–19.
11 Alexander Mette, *Über Beziehungen zwischen Spracheigentümlichkeiten Schizophrener und dichterischer Produktion* (Dessau: Dion-Verlag Liebmann & Mette, 1928), 53 (for example).
12 "Walter Benjamin. *Ursprung des deutschen Trauerspiels*." *Imago* 7, no. 4 (1931): 536.
13 Alexander Mette, *Die tiefenpsychologischen Grundlagen des Tragischen, Apollinischen und Dionysischen* (Berlin-Steglitz: Dion-Verlag, 1934), 69.
14 If something works, stick with it. In the idiom of this credo I am referring to the good rap and rep that Freud's science scored with the military authorities of the Central Powers toward the end of the First World War effort. That psychoanalysis was credited with quick-fixing the shell-shocked soldiers and returning them to active duty was the main reason it was not only not banished from the Third Reich but even maintained in a position of privilege. The Jewish practitioners were banished as were their names.
15 Alexander Mette, "Darlegungen," *Gedichte / Darlegungen I* (Dessau: Dion-Verlag Liebmann & Mette, 1925), 57.
16 Ibid., 59.
17 Ibid., 64.
18 Ibid.
19 Regine Lockot, "Germany," *International Dictionary of Psychoanalysis*, 2005.
20 Alexander Mette, *Der Weg zum Traum* (Berlin-Steglitz: Dion-Verlag, 1939).
21 Ibid., 12.
22 Ibid.
23 Ibid., 13.
24 Ibid.
25 Ibid.
26 Ibid., 16.
27 Ibid., 17.
28 Ibid., 14–15.
29 Ibid., 20.
30 Ibid., 21.
31 Ibid., 24, 26.
32 Ibid., 26.
33 Ibid.
34 Ibid.
35 Ibid., 38.
36 Ibid., 39.
37 Ibid.
38 Ibid.
39 Ibid.
40 Ibid.
41 Ibid.

42 Ibid., 40.
43 Ibid., 41.
44 Ibid., 44.
45 Ibid., 47.
46 Ibid., 48.
47 Ibid.
48 Ibid., 49.
49 Ibid., 50.
50 Ibid., 52.
51 Ibid., 10.
52 Ibid.
53 Ibid.
54 Ibid.
55 Ibid.
56 Ibid.
57 Ibid., 41.
58 Ibid., 46.
59 Ibid., 42.
60 Ibid.
61 Ibid.
62 Ibid., 42–3.
63 Klaus Theweleit, *Male Fantasies, Vol. 1: Women, Floods, Bodies, History*, trans. Chris Turner et al. (Minneapolis: University of Minnesota Press, 1987).
64 Alexander Mette, *Die psychologischen Wurzeln des Dionysischen und Apollinischen. Ein neuer Versuch* (Berlin-Steglitz: Dion-Verlag, 1940).
65 Ibid., 6.
66 Ibid., 17.
67 Ibid.
68 Ibid., 43.
69 Ibid., 47.
70 Ibid., 43.
71 Ibid.
72 Ibid., 33.
73 D. W. Winnicott, "The Concept of the Healthy Individual," *Home is Where We Start From. Essays by a Psychoanalyst*, eds. Clare Winnicott, Ray Shepherd, and Madeleine Davis (New York and London: W. W. Norton & Company, 1986), 31.
74 Ibid., 33.

4

The Child in Benjamin: An Enduring Lesson

Henry Sussman

I

Throughout a life that eventually reached every extreme of privilege, luxury, precarity, *déclassement*, misery, and immanent threat, the figure of the child remained an ongoing preoccupation, inspiration, and even obsession to Walter Benjamin. The ultimate child he bore with him on his fitful journey, whose vividness of apprehension he nurtured and whose fresh critical stance he did everything to sustain, was of course himself. Such standout texts as his *Berlin Childhood around 1900*, the first work of exile, as it was preceded by *One-Way Street*, bring home the uncanny affinity that Benjamin, in a summoning forth of early childhood experience at once impressionistic and photographic, shares with Marcel Proust. Childhood is surely as viable an explanation for what drew Benjamin to Proust and initiated the all-encompassing labor of translation as anything else. But it is also fair to say that once Walter Benjamin attains the status of paternity—while still a doctoral student in Berne in April, 1918—the child in whose freshness of vision and language he revels, and over whose readings he frets, is equally his son, Stefan Benjamin (1918-72).

The self-engendering stability of bourgeois marriage may well number among the homelands that Walter Benjamin eventually left behind, whether by coercion or volition. Wherever Walter's wanderings took him, and however attenuated his paternal absences grew, fathering Stefan remained a constant preoccupation, even if its expressions were not exactly conventional. It was as the curator of the exemplary European children's library, as the avant-garde scout for the Humanities of current trends in developmental and cognitive psychologies, and as the historian of childhood (always, in his case, bottom-up, from the perspective of the accrued cultural remains) that Walter Benjamin went about the utterly committed upbringing of his son.

Walter Benjamin's intellectual "children" now span several generations. This is the odd collectivity for whom his writing is seminal to their own inscriptive vocations. This in a multiplicity of its climatic features: whether its unique *scope*, both as modernistic historiography and inter-medial exploration, its dialectically explosive and disorienting *style*; its historical purview *upward* from the sidewalk of cultural remains; the resolute *performativity* that the critical text insists upon from the cultural phenomenon; or its radical recalibration of *translation*—deformation, interruption, defamiliarization as much as rendition. Such factors as the near-loss of Benjamin's cultural production to the historical transcript and the significant time lag his recognition suffered at the expense of World War II has only strengthened these writers' dedication to a crucial intellectual progenitor in multiple senses and to the quality of their own interventions. Yet the loving care lavished by this undeclared Benjaminian collectivity (a Deleuzian "pack" or Borgesian "persecuted brotherhood")[1] from an outrageously diverse range of disciplines and discourses is also protective and, in this sense, parental. Protective of the just acknowledgment and preservation of Benjamin's multifarious cultural contributions, some obvious, some subliminal; of his citizenship both within theory and cultural history, in *their* several scopes and formats. In a gesture redolent of the caring that Walter Benjamin infused into his literary obsessions, his critical *persona*, and his friendships, his broader writerly *children* morph into his *parents*.

This delicate tripwire or toggle by which *recipients* morph into custodians, the impressionable into *authorities*, is also at play when we take up the rather genial occasion of the present collection, "Benjamin's Pedagogy." In an obvious sense, hardly worth even rendering explicit, we who have garnered so much of whatever critical power and relevance we might claim from Walter Benjamin, *learned* most intensively—from his style, his moves, his address, his bearing—by *teaching* his works. No doubt partly in the delusion that we might possess *something*, by way of purview or illumination, worthy of disseminating. In this way, Benjamin's students become his teachers.

In the 1910s, Benjamin launched a critical practice that was already deeply entrenched in educational controversy and in pedagogical theory. Benjamin never outgrew his inaugural public role as *generational avatar*, assumed already in his early ascent to leadership of one of the two main intellectual branches of the German educational *Jugendbewegung* (Youth Movement, 1914), and, in a sense, never relinquished. The figure of the child in Benjamin falls hostage to a series of anomalies— in inspiration, friendship, and intellectual affiliation—that will never leave the critic in peace. The configuration of his composite hypothetical intellectual son created something akin to the one conjured up by the sorcerer in Borges' "The Circular Ruins"—the progeny upon which Benjamin *insists*, that he *commissions*.[2] This is a child encountered, for instance, in "A Child's View of Color" and "Old Forgotten Children's Books." The freshness of apprehension, the ingrained resistance to categorical thinking in multiple guises so deadly to cultural reception, with which they are "uploaded," is a direct derivative of Romantic literature and theory. Yet there can be no doubt of the firm Marxist orientation underlying Benjamin's protectiveness toward the optimal timeframe for the emergence of foundational critical skills in childhood. The major casualties of non-actualization of this developmentally specific "window" will be a palpable disenfranchisement and stunting in cultural citizenship. We will yet be a long time in clearing away the detritus from the conflation of factors conspiring in Donald Trump's 2016 presidential election.

It is a tribute to the complexity and independence of Benjamin's thinking that during his lifetime, he brokered deep and enduring friendships with significant others whose world-views and approaches to intellectual endeavor simply did not match his own. Benjamin's ability to sustain, indeed to exist, as in *Dasein*, *Mitsein*, within intense intellectual friendships fundamentally at odds with one another, at least during his lifetime, has to number among his extraordinary achievements—along with his "mosaic technique" of citation, the dialectic of curatorship (collecting) and allegory that he choreographed, or the synthesis of a cultural historiography grounded in an age or a configuration's *telling* "dialectical images." In the aftermath to World War II, many of the attitudinal differences between the likes of Gershom Scholem, Theodor Adorno, Gretel Karplus Adorno, Bertolt Brecht, and Hannah Arendt softened greatly—in view of the ecstatic miracle of shared survival and in some cases through collaboration in the publication of Benjamin's works.

Not only did Scholem play an instrumental role in Benjamin's attachment to the Judaic, more as a modality of culture-formation and as a repository of images (e.g., stars, constellations) than as a creed; his seminal reclamation of the medieval Jewish mystical literature for modern historiography, scholarship, and criticism resonated exceptionally well with Benjamin's early gravitation to Romanticism as a treasury of literary enchantment, sublimity, expansiveness, and "aura." (The very young Scholem spent an extended stay with the Benjamins, May, 1918 through summer, 1919, precisely as Walter was shaping his doctoral thesis, "The Concept of Criticism in German Romanticism.") Reviewing the various transcripts of these productive if tempestuous times left by both men, it is clear that Benjamin had already discerned a convergence between the mystical vision of the medieval Judaic imaginary excavated by Scholem and the reverence for the image—in its framing, its inexhaustible enigma, and its self-contained ironic knowledge—among the Romantics.[3] This early rapprochement between Benjamin's highly intellectualized take on Judaism and the orientation in his literary readings toward imagery as literary visuality, toward irony, and meta-textual literary performance or allegory goes largely underground in his critical output of the 1920s. But when this Judaic-Romantic affinity resurfaces, as it does with vehemence in Benjamin's 1934 "Franz Kafka: On the Tenth Anniversary of his Death," it does so, as a sustained critical and meta-critical performance, triumphantly.

Scholem was never sympathetic to Benjamin's Marxist streak, especially during the 1930s as the latter engaged with Communism. With Brecht, especially during sojourns to Brecht's residences in Denmark in 1934, 1936, and 1938, Benjamin was free to explore all open possibilities of political engagement, including Communism of Soviet and German stripes. But this alternative was a more fraught issue in Benjamin's correspondence with both Adorno and Felizitas (Karplus). Benjamin and Adorno shared an intense meditation on the translatability of canonical Marxist texts and motifs into state-of-the-art contemporary criticism. As the 1930s wore on, Adorno and Karplus along with Scholem should warn Benjamin away from any irreversible affiliations with the Communists.

Yet Adorno could withhold publication of the 1935 version of Benjamin's introductory "Exposé" to the emergent *Arcades Project* (*Das Passagen-Werk*) on the grounds of its obscuring the operative dialectical-material relationships undergirding modernization in nineteenth-century Paris. Yes, as the correspondence surrounding the "Hornberg letter" of August 2–4, 1935 indicates, Teddie may have outflanked Walter in rendering a philosophically rigorous *transcription* of core Marxian constructs retracing the burgeoning of capital and the accouterments of modernity in nineteenth-century Paris.

But as readers of Walter's *One-Way Street* and "On Some Motifs in Baudelaire" know well, the entire palette of dialectical Marxism was fully "present and accounted for," even in the "Exposé's" 1935 version, under the aesthetic of Baudelairean "poetic prose." These Marxian elocutions played themselves out, first and foremost in the original version, *performatively*. This carefully orchestrated textual *enactment* took such forms as the following: 1) a dialectical counterpoint between the paragraphs composing each section; 2) narrative perspectivism assuring the unfolding of each section from a vitally different historical "camera angle" (from the streets, from the arcades, from the barricades of the Commune, for example); and 3) a montage technique in critical prose pivoting each section around a different "dialectical image" (the photograph in Section II, the world's fairs in Section III, the dialectical image itself in Section VI). Indeed, throughout the long gestation of the 1935 "Exposé" and the entire tractate of which it is an amazingly successful summation, Walter had anticipated Teddie's rather severe critique—*at the level of performativity, not reference* (or as Austin would put it, the constative).[4]

Incompatible, then, as a Romanticism-inspired exaltation in the open-endedness and freshness of childhood thinking with a Marxist commitment to full developmental opportunity for all children may seem, these two architectural foundations of Benjamin's perspective on childhood are a direct consequence of his enduring constellation of seemingly antagonistic but deeply ingrained affiliations.

II

"Walter Benjamin's Pedagogy" names, as fully as possible, the overall "field"—the environment as well as the system—in which Benjamin's experiments and interventions of a lifetime transpired. The entrance to this playing field is, therefore, accessed just as well from a number of directions and parameters. The *sine qua non* that Benjamin would impose on picking up a hand in this particular card-game is, not surprisingly, *discoursing illuminatingly*—for example, on "A Child's View of Color" (1914–15). Benjamin's approach can with little "stretch" be characterized as critico-cognitive. The encounter with color presents young children with a core experience of articulation: the differentiation of signifiers and the modulation of tones also at play in and indispensable to "higher" functions, such as the acquisition and deployment of language. What Benjamin would wish at this inaugural stage of filling in the figure of the child is for an inaugural experience of color "spiritual" in its drift—"soul" here being less an organ of intellect or emotion and far more one of intensity, vividness, and *mood*. Benjamin implicitly militates between these lines for a proto-critical *faculty* of intuition, sensibility, and ecstatic fascination, undergirded by an apprehension of the world's indissoluble interconnection:

> Children's drawings take colorfulness as their point of departure. Their goal is color in its greatest possible transparency, and there is no reference to form, area, or concentration into a single space.... The concern of objects with color is not based on their form: without even touching on them empirically, it goes right to the spiritual heart of the object by isolating the sense of sight. It cancels out the

intellectual cross-references of the soul and creates a pure mood, without thereby sacrificing the world.... But because children see with pure eyes, without allowing themselves to become emotionally disconcerted, it [colorfulness] is something spiritual; the rainbow refers not to a chaste abstraction but to a life in art. The order of art is paradisiacal because there is no thought of the dissolution of boundaries—from excitement—in the object of experience. Instead the world is full of color in a state of identity, innocence, and harmony. Children are not ashamed, since they do not reflect but only see.⁵

In this passage, color is the royal road, the threshold, ushering children into an aesthetic domain so absorptive, captivating, and (we would now say) "virtual" that it defers, if not definitively suspends, intellectual distinctions and emotional judgments. Embedded within the encounter with color is a childhood resistance movement: pushback against predetermined spatial boundaries as against formalism. So vehemently does Benjamin wish to distinguish this experience from conventional pedagogy that he invests it, for all his own skepticism vis-à-vis religious practice, with a "spiritual" elevation. It is in holding out an unadulterated experience of imaginative activity and mood that Benjamin invests color with "purity" and situates it, in cognitive geography, in the "spirit." Children "see with pure eyes." Their imaginative activity is "uncorrupt." This paradisiacal state serves as précis to the less pristine intellectual judgment of developmental maturity, but to ensure optimal critical discernment and full cultural empowerment, Benjamin would wish this state held back, *aufgehoben*.⁶

The "pristine state of color," if one can coin such a construction, is invested with messianic hope—for revelation, correction, and transformation. Ruminating on the child's experience of color affords Benjamin the occasion to cross-reference proto-critical development of a sort elaborated by the Romantics with the vividness of the messianic imagery of divine cyphers, vehicles (Scholem's "*Merkabah*—chariot—*Messianism*"), and constellations.⁷ Benjamin's investigations into color may seem an odd tangential foray, especially in light of the credulity toward theological spiritualism that he is willing to grant at this particular juncture. Yet it turns out that the problematic of color serves as a "roundhouse" encompassing related issues, particularly on a cognitive plane, that Benjamin was broaching as of the same epoch. The way children process color is also, oddly, closely allied to the psychedelic distortion that Benjamin chronicles in his hashish writings and "Crock Notes."

Children like the way colors shimmer in subtle, shifting nuances (as in soap bubbles), or else make definite and explicit changes in intensity, as in oleographs, paintings, the pictures produced by decals and magic lanterns. For them, color is fluid, the medium of all changes, and not a symptom. Their eyes are not concerned with three-dimensionality; this they perceive through their sense of touch.... The child's view of color represents the highest artistic development of the sense of sight; it is sight at its purest, because it is isolated. But children also elevate it to the spiritual level because they perceive objects according to their color content and hence do not isolate them, instead using them as a basis from which to create the interrelated totality of the world of the imagination. The imagination can be developed only by contemplating colors and dealing with them in this fashion; only in this way can it both be satisfied and kept within bounds.[8]

The child's ability simply to "go with the flow" of a shifting color-display, whether through media (in a slide-show) or in a physical phenomenon (soap bubbles), bears a closer resemblance to the reportage of drug experiments in Marseille—whether peering at the pavement or experiencing the "munchies" both physiologically and semiotically, on the menu—than we may be inclined to admit.[9] In the sense elaborated in the extract immediately above, color could at once be exonerated of intellectuality and yet remain aesthetic to the core. The child's experience of the phenomenon as "pure" is not in service to some developmental outcome (touch is more than sufficient to provide for three-dimensional perception, thank you, says Benjamin), just as the encounter is not encoded with pre-packaged signification. "Color content" is sufficient, *an sich*, as it were, to bestow whatever signification the display manages to impart; and so vivid is this content that it affirms and substantiates some corner of experience delegated to spirituality. Yet as tangible and specific as the child's experience of color may be, as a paradigm for the imagination, the experience cannot be bracketed or circumvented. Color is both a base-position without which the imagination cannot function—its "spirituality" is surely a descriptor of its commiseration within the imaginary—and in its specificity, a hold upon the imagination's random free-play. (Color, then, imparts *some* content or specificity to the child's imaginative activity.) In this sense, the encounter with color, in the long-term evolution of critical facility and cultural enfranchisement, is both a necessary and sufficient precondition.

If Benjamin, in spite of his insistence upon a non-formal and non-goal-oriented character to the child's encounter with color, tethers the experience to any broader framework, it is to the realization and the technics of *reproduction* within the codes, art forms, and media of culture (*hervorzubringen*), even as reproducibility is rehearsed in the early psycho-motor activity of perception. In "The World of Children's Books" (1926), a reprise to the earlier passages on childhood sensibility we have been glossing, reproductive activity and sensibility becomes the threshold to an engaged, informed encounter with and participation in culture.

> When you look at colors, the intuitions of fantasy, in contrast to the creative imagination, manifest themselves as a primal phenomenon. All form, every outline that man perceives, corresponds to something in him that enables him to reproduce it. The body imitates itself in the form of dance, the hand imitates and appropriates it through drawing. [*Aller Form nämlich, allem Umriß, den der Mensch wahrnimmt, entspricht er selbst in dem Vermögen, ihn hervorzubringen. Der Körper selbst im Tanz, die hand im Zeichnen bildet ihn nach und eignet ihn sich an*]. But this ability finds its limits in the world of color. The human body cannot produce color. It does relate to it not creatively but receptively: through the shimmering colors of vision. (Anthropologically, too, sight is the watershed of the senses because it perceives color and form simultaneously. And so, on the one hand, the body is the organ of active relations: the perception of form and movement.... Language itself synthesizes this group into a unity in words like "looking," "smelling," tasting,"

which apply intransitively to objects and transitively to human beings.) In short, pure color is the medium of fantasy, a home among clouds for the spoiled child, not the strict canon of the constructive artist.[10]

What Benjamin is seeking most importantly through this elaboration is the removal of the "primal" experience of color from the field of volition: separating it from the psycho-motor *emulations* of music (in dance) and of the visual field (in drawing) by which the subject claims and demonstrates *mastery* over perception. In Bergsonian terms, the encounter with color would be much more allied to *involuntary*, as opposed to "voluntary" memory, the latter being the database of which exam-performance and other exercises of proficiency are made. It is in this sense that the body, endowed with both its own memory and imaginary by Bergson, relates to color "receptively," "passively."[11] It is this "receptive" bearing toward color that hints at a foundational aesthetic experience in the child that eludes Kantian *Zweckmäßigkeit* (purposefulness), circumventing goal-orientation in the widest sense.[12] The motor response to the sensorium, to the visual field and music, can be trained; a training-effect can be extracted, in imitative drawing and dance, from these encounters. In order to allow for an immanent, intuitive, and proto-critical aesthetic substrate in children, Benjamin is willing to couch the encounter with color "passively," to group color along with "lower-level" perceptions such as touch and taste rather than to ally it with sight, "watershed of the senses." His allegiance is to synaesthesia at the baseline.

The child's encounter with color, as Benjamin is setting it out early in his prolegomena to a meta-critically driven pedagogy, is prelapsarian to acculturation, education, moral indoctrination, and vocational training. The unadulterated confrontation of color is a stance from which the encomia to form, manners, discipline, apprenticeship, and conventional morals are arbitrary and even, to a certain degree, violent. Now it may well be that Benjamin's ultimate lifetime vice—even more than his infidelities, his indifference to marriage, his chemical experiments, and his at times abrupt sea-changes in friendship—was his earnestness, an unyieldingness in the high-stakes game of critical interpretation. Yet for all the momentousness that Benjamin may have transferred into the educational reform movement, in which he played a consequential role, the sheer resistance and riot accruing to the Benjaminian child by way of color owes as much to Lewis Carroll, or rather to the Wonderland antics of his Alice, as it does to the more obvious sobriety of purpose. For indeed, even more than her disconcerting size- and location-shifts, it is Alice's incredulity toward everything mannered and predetermined that she leaves with us as her ineradicable imprint. The phantasmatic Queen of Hearts, her absurd games, and her obsequious underlings get their day in court. But the full fury of Carroll's differences with prevalent Victorian mores is reserved for Alice's encounters with anything smacking of school. School is, for Alice as well as the early Benjamin, the disciplinary sinkhole where young minds are dispossessed of their intrinsic critical faculty and sense of the absurd. Carroll works hard, particularly at the outset of *Alice's Adventures in Wonderland*, to contrast the new alogical and fluid relationships into which Alice has been cast with the education into which she has already been inculcated.

"I wish I hadn't cried so much!" said Alice, as she swam about, trying to find her way out. "I shall be punished for it now, I suppose, by being drowned in my own tears! That will be a queer thing, to be sure! However, everything is queer to-day."

Just then she heard something splashing about in the pool a little way off, and she swam nearer to make out what it was: at first she thought it must be a walrus or a hippopotamus, but then she remembered how small she was now, and she soon made out that it was only a mouse that had slipped in like herself.

"Would it be of any use now," thought Alice, "to speak to this mouse? ... "O Mouse, do you know the way out of this pool? I am very tired of swimming about here, O Mouse!" (Alice thought this must be the right way of speaking to a mouse; she had never done such a thing before, but she remembered having seen, in her brother's Latin Grammar, "A mouse—of a mouse—to a mouse—a mouse—O mouse!") The mouse looked at her rather inquisitively, and seemed to her to wink with one of its little eyes, but said nothing.

"Perhaps it doesn't understand English," thought Alice. "I daresay it's a French mouse, come over with William the Conqueror."[13]

III

Yet Benjamin's annotation is no less delegated to issues and media of pedagogy in his vignettes of reminiscence and in some of the fractured folktales that he inserted into watershed critical expositions (the Kafka essay furnishing an exemplary instance). Unlikely as these textual environments may seem, Benjamin also holds out the keys to his pedagogy in such memorable master-texts from *One-Way Street* and *Berlin Childhood around 1900* as "Winter Morning," "The Fever," "The Sock," "The Mummerehlen," "Child Reading," and "Pilfering Child."[14]

The topic also bids us all, in the strongest terms possible, to engage the wider issues of teaching Walter Benjamin under contemporary conditions. The signifier "Benjamin" has become as polymorphous and polyvalent as yet another moniker to which it is often linked, "deconstruction." "Benjamin," like its frequent theoretical partner in crime, has seeped into frameworks and discourses far afield from the Humanities and speculative Social Sciences that were its inaugural catchment areas. In neither of his two preeminent *modi operandi*: the first of these barging forward in journalistic tempo, engaging multiple cultural contributors and artifacts, in no particular sequence, that drove and animated him. As roving critic, he would submerge himself in pertinent subject matter for a certain interstice, then move on. Yet he would subjugate himself for fourteen years, in the other arena of his extended fascination, to the phenomenon of modernization in Paris. From this obsession, he emerged with *The Arcades Project*, an aggressively formless do-it-yourself manual on collision, infatuation, and disruption amid the urban kaleidoscope, rendered from the perspective of history on the ground. In neither of his complementary emanations—the essayist or as the initiator of an *histoire brute*[15] for the modernist era—does Benjamin begin to live up to the scruples of consistency, linear progression in speculation and complexity, and meticulous justification applied to each reference or implication looped in, that, well-ensconced in the twenty-first century, we impose on our own scholarly discourse in the name of "professionalism."

It is not merely an elective affinity in a rogue's gallery based on astonishing erudition, the ability to zero in on the core propositions assuring the durability of intricate epistemological infrastructure, and an astonishing "upper-level" skill at "chunking" systemic blockages recurring in remote epochs and cultural settings that draw Benjamin and Derrida in close vicinity. It is the reading of Marx. Like Benjamin, Derrida experienced Marx first and foremost as a writer—a particularly versatile, fluent, and inventive one. Derrida's explicit referencing of Marx may have transpired relatively later in a career, but it was subtended by extensive experience, both familial and professional, with post-War Eastern European Stalinist regimes: configurations reaching, whether knowingly or not, toward their foregone obsolescence. Given Derrida's tangible experience with the persistent political regimes founded, however tangentially, in Marxist theory, it is all the more astonishing that Karl Marx, in Derrida's 1994 *Specters of Marx*, is invoked as an indispensable sensibility of social justice without which a rapidly evolving European Community cannot fulfill its profoundest aims:[16]

> A deconstructive thinking, the one that matters to me here, has always pointed out the irreducibility of affirmation and therefore the promise, as well as the undeconstructibility of a certain idea of justice (dissociated here from law). Such a thinking cannot operate without justifying the principle of a radical and interminable, infinite (both theoretical and practical, as one used to say) critique. This critique belongs to the movement of an experience open to the absolute future of what is coming, that is to say, a necessarily indeterminate, abstract, desert-like experience that is confided, exposed, given up in its waiting for the other and for the event.[17]

A couple of pages later, Derrida adds:

> Such a deconstruction would have been impossible and unthinkable in a pre-Marxist space. Deconstruction has never had any sense or interest, in my view at least, except as a radicalization, which is to say, also *in the tradition* of a certain Marxism, in a certain *spirit of Marxism*. There has been, then, this attempted radicalization of Marxism called deconstruction (and in which, as some have noted, a certain economic concept of the differantial economy and of expropriation, or even of the gift, plays an organizing role, as does the concept of work tied to differance and to the work in general).[18]

In the first of the above extracts from *Specters of Marx*, Derrida "floats" a certain idea of justice that is the irreducible ("undeconstructible") take-away from the Marxian critique. This Marx-tinged notion of justice, precisely in its endlessness, belongs to the indeterminateness of the *open system*: from the outset, Derrida affiliates justice in its Marxian emanation with futurity, the event, and the gift—all formats for social interaction encompassing unbounded possibility, elaboration, revision, and nuance—in a word, in *ongoing process* (or, possibly, revolution).

And Derrida invokes, in the second citation immediately above, a *spirit of Marxism* to be construed as the *broadest* exigency, well into the twenty-first century, for continuing to read Marx's works and demanding a social justice in large measure driven by the coercions, various assertions of indebtedness, and increasing discrepancies in social and economic power deep-wired both into capitalist process and logic. It is no accident, in this second paragraph, that Derrida's distinctive elocution, *différance*, in various forms, rises in a concatenation of the conditions that Marxian justice *will address*.

Specters of Marx signals two complementary sea changes in Derrida's work that will shift its overall trajectory for the duration: 1) the figure of Karl Marx as an *occasion* for broaching systematic closure on the fronts of imperialist expansionism and globalist economics with a degree of explicitness unprecedented in his work; and 2) an investigation into spectrality, with special attention lavished on Shakespeare, as a breeding ground and generator of widely prevalent *sociological infrastructure*. The deconstructive demonstration, on this tangent, is of the highly spectral, phantasmatic, and speculative underpinnings to such quasi-universal sociological phenomena as hospitality, pardon, promises, and vows. It is even more astonishing, runs the drift of this demonstration, that such tenuous sociological convention could acquire the force of speech acts and performatives—a metamorphosis that had been the subject of intense Derridean study over an even longer duration, since the early 1970s.[19]

Derrida's intense awareness of Benjamin surfaces explicitly elsewhere in his writing.[20] With respect to Marx, what Derrida shares explicitly with Benjamin is both cognizance of a materialism in the constitution and deployment of language without which critique cannot reach its "full service" and pitched attention to messianism as yet another spectral impulse of culture and impulse *behind* cultural critique. It is hardly accidental, then, that Benjamin and Derrida should engage in an intense encounter, whether marked explicitly or not, in the pages of *Specters of Marx*. Let it suffice to zero in on the terms by which Derrida, at the end of a pivotal passage dovetailing the shared interests and bearings of deconstruction and a post-Soviet Marxianism, acknowledges his debt to the writings of Karl Marx. What follows is the final item in a list of crucial current "to dos"—tasks presented and underscored by the persistence of a deconstructive Marxism:

> Lastly and consequentially, a profound and critical reevaluation of the State, of the nation-State, of national sovereignty, and of citizenship must correspond to a phase of decisive mutation. The latter would be impossible without vigilant and systematic reference to a Marxist problematic, if not to the Marxist conclusions regarding the State, the power of the State, and the state apparatus, the illusions of its legal autonomy as concerns socio-economic forces, but also regarding new forms of a withering or rather a reinscription, a re-delimitation of the State in a space that it no longer dominates and moreover that it never dominated by itself.[21]

It is, precisely, "vigilant and systematic reference to a Marxist problematic, if not to the Marxist conclusions regarding the State, the power of the State, and the state apparatus" that furnishes *us*, members of a rhizomatic, interconnected *pack* of deconstructive readers, with our marching orders—particularly amid the transformative conditions of the early 1990s. Marx's writings persist as a program, a "problematic," for engaged cultural critique on the part of theoretically motivated close readers, irrespective of the vicissitudes and conditions of the Marxian State. It is within a Marxian sensibility, a persistent Marxian encomium to a highly rigorous version of social justice, regardless of political happenstance, justice modified, in deconstructive parlance, by such *philosotropes* as *affirmation, promise,* and *the gift,* that Benjamin and Derrida coincide. This interactivity is only catalyzed by their common causes in linguistic materialism and critical messianism (the latter, formulated by Derrida in *Specters of Marx,* as "the messianic without messianism."[22]

In a volume titled *The Task of the Critic,* I distinguished the linear promenade of the critic *proprement dit through* the manifold of auratic cultural artifacts, the *flâneur*'s stroll through art, from the philosopher's attenuated residence, as in Heideggerian *wohnen* (dwelling) in the engine-room of the conceptual operating system, venerable and current.[23] The critic's path, on which Benjamin was definitively set even before the *Habilitationsdebakel* of 1925, perforce has a far greater tolerance for inconclusiveness and being provisional. The question of Benjamin's pedagogy thus necessarily opens up the inquiry into the status and living conditions of the working critic, as I have attempted to characterize them, in the contemporary academy. Specifically with respect to *Das Passagen-Werk,* a volume whose formidable interpretative challenge I accepted at multiple junctures in my own teaching, the unprecedented historical reconstruction customized by this work—casting the reader among the *bribes et morceaux* of epochal materials, with no distinction made for the fragments composed and submitted by the author, or perhaps collator—is itself a powerful strategy of readerly *pedagogy.*

If some of the haunting historical "ifs" could have only been switched in the opposite direction—if, first and foremost, Benjamin could have only taken a more proactive stance to friends' and partners' ongoing admonitions, whether by Scholem or Felizitas, or his wife, Dora, to abandon Europe. Judging by the trajectories of Benjamin's fellow émigré-intellectuals, if only the *deus ex machina* to facilitate a last-minute rescue had worked, he would have eventually landed in the kind of post that had been denied him—at Bard, the New School, perhaps at the nascent Brandeis. But as the academic world has evolved in the seventy-odd years since, what is it of Walter Benjamin that we actually end up teaching? We follow so many of the vertiginous interdisciplinary turns of his discourse proceeding from "high" literature and speculative thought—first into media, perhaps, but then into urban studies, travel, consumption, even fashion. We appropriate and retrofit so many of his formulations, the best endowed with the aporetic impossibility of the "dialectical image"—from "the delight of the urban poet is love—at last sight" to "the highest physiognomic expression." We feel under Benjamin's palpable blessing when we begin to conjure literature and its historical forms as a *medium*—then venturing with awe and sometimes horror into the demilitarized zones of inter-medial transcription. Benjamin remains a powerful force in the roles of master-teacher and inspiration in the quest for the divergent constellations of mediation and nuance crowned in the figure of the dialectical image—itself the horizon and icon of creative impossibility at any given moment.

IV

We continue to learn, on multiple interactive levels, from Benjamin. Projected by his ever self-replenishing interpreters into new media and new predicaments of cultural commentary, Benjamin manages never to relinquish his above-designated role of generational avatar. But what, effectively, are we empowered, under contemporary epistemological, cognitive, and technological conditions, to teach of him? How does the pedagogy we have begun to parse in multiple directions fare amid expectations of comprehensiveness, authority, and coherence—positions all grouped under the aegis of *academic scruple*—we end up perpetuating even while questioning?

To the degree that the student movements of the late 1950s and 1960s, in their demand for reform, their pitched anti-authoritarianism, and their quest for new media of expression and performance, bore striking affinities to Benjamin and early company's *Jugendbewegung*, the results of fervent devotion to the training of a more acutely critical and hence enlightened citizenry have been at best mixed, if not bipolar—contributing to dead-heat political elections in the US, and gridlock in the domains of decision-making and social administration.

Reaching the terminus of a long run in the promotion of precisely those core-values embedded in Benjamin's pedagogy entails for me a number of interrelated afterthoughts:

1. The improvisation of self-enacted discursive criteria for rigorous cultural critique echoing conventions that Benjamin concertedly strove to implement. Above all, his insistence, in keeping with Romantic ideology, on infusing poetic condensation and the byplay of genre into critique; juxtaposing visual, cinematic, and even haptic phenomena with literary images; and subordinating lines of history and argumentation to immersion within cultural materials and materiality.
2. The emergence, whether in the "local climate" of German Studies or under the wider bailiwick of the Humanities, of a significantly updated *map* of cultural dissemination and stewardship. One palpably registering aesthetic improvisations and linguistic practices emerging from zones of former colonial or hegemonic domination, "minor" literatures, and endemically "minority" cultures. This parametric reset within cultural mapping cannot but impinge, in the most salutary way, on the organization of the classroom and upon expectations for teaching and mentoring. Also, upon the broader configuration of the disciplines, their educational *ends*, and the credentialing we perforce engage in.
3. Distortion-effects accruing from the assortment (or "battle") of all generations of students, from freshmen to ABDs, now gathered on campus. We pause, in 2022, at the antiquation that even a current graduate Teaching Assistant may feel in relation to their undergraduate students' cultural libraries and aspirations. Who better to invoke on the occasion of paradigm-shift within the operating systems of mediation than the auratic Benjamin, particularly the composer of "The Work of Art in the Age of its Technological Reproducibility"? But those choosing to tarry, like myself, at the outlying *banlieux* or *barrios* of Benjamin's pedagogy cannot but be struck by the gradations in significance, implication, and grain in his very *figure* between the freshman in Urban Studies or Graphic Design at Pratt or the New School, the *Magister-Student* at Munich, and the doctoral candidate in the Humanities at Berkeley, Brown, or Berlin. If Walter, in his multifarious bearings, qualifies as a *medium* (if not a specter), it is one with varied "outlets" and impacts—within a grid whose irreducible feature is its open-endedness.

The least I owe readers is a map indicating the inroads in and out of this Borgesian archive. A pivotal point of orientation, at least for me, is a passage in which we encounter Marx, toward the end of *Kapital*, Volume I, even more unpredictable than usual. Here he extends his accounting of the multifarious taxes that capitalism exacts from the populations least suited to afford them, namely on the hourly workers who can be hired, fired, reassigned, and relocated at will—and on their children, often forced into child-labor. And in this tangent of his exposé of the factory system, Marx displays surprising acuity with regard to the cognitive development of children, above all to the flashpoints of phase-appropriate skills—lost forever if not acquired in the proper sequence. We can argue all we want about the extent and rigor of Benjamin's readings in Marx, but the passage in question telegraphs ahead apprehensions central to Benjamin's formulations regarding childhood sensibility, aesthetics, and critical predilection.

> At the same time, the capitalist form of large-scale industry reproduces this same division of labor in a still more monstrous shape; in the factory proper, by converting the worker into a living appendage of the machine [*Zubehör einer Teilmaschine*] .... It appears, for example, in the frightful fact that a great part of the children employed in modern factories and manufactures are from their earliest years riveted to the most simple manipulations [*festgeschmiedet an die einfachsten Handgriffe*], and exploited for years, without being taught a single kind of skill that would afterwards make them of use, even in the same factory. In the English letter-press printing trade, there formerly existed a system ... of advancing the apprentices from easy to more and more difficult work. They went through a course of teaching until they were finished printers. To read and write was for every one of them a requirement of their trade. All this was changed by the printing machine. It employs two sorts of worker. On the one hand, there are adults, tenters, and on the other hand there are boys ... whose sole occupation is either to spread the sheets under the machine, or to take from it the printed sheets. They perform this task, especially in London especially, for 14, 15 and 16 hours at a stretch.... A great proportion of them cannot read, and they are, as a rule, utter savages and very extraordinary creatures [*ganz verwilderte, abnorme Geschöpfe*].... As soon as they get too old for such children's work, that is at about 17 years old, at the latest, they are discharged from the printing establishments. They become recruits for crime.[24]

This passage is grounded in Marx's ongoing incredulous rage at the carefully calibrated minimalism—a brutal precarity—at the sustenance that capitalism is willing to mete out to its working affiliates and their dependents. It is crucial and telling that Marx regards the education of the young, by birth drawn into the vertical segmentation of the factory system, as a right rather than a nicety. Cannibalistic child labor violates the basic decency of any imaginable social contract between capital and labor. The "utter savages" and "extraordinary people" resulting from subjugation to menial labor at a shocking age emerge in society because crucial thresholds in learning and cognitive and social development have gone by the board.

The early education that Marx has in mind here is no more sophisticated than the basic sustenance, in terms of calories, environmental safety, and basic concern for rest and recovery from exertion that he would (and does) demand for workers of both genders. Yet the notion engrained in this passage, that childhood attainment and sensibility are the indispensable précis to adult equanimity and productivity, becomes earmarked as a Marxian precept, embedded in everything that Benjamin has to offer regarding childhood itself, regarding, for instance, the early experiences of reading and of color, the *bricolage* by which children enlist material remnants toward their unfolding intellectual agendas.

The primary significance of children, and their sensibility, for Benjamin, is as proto-critics. Critical innovation and intervention as adults is their maximal fulfillment as empowered socio-cultural citizens. As I hope we can acknowledge, this is an irreducibly Marxian idea—also subtending the "awakening" (*das Erwachen*) with which Convolute K of *The Arcades Project* magisterially begins. This latter archive of resources concerning the modernization of Paris during the Second Empire is the second great treasury of Benjamin's formulations and acts of pedagogy:

> Awakening is the graduated process [*Das Erwachen ist ein stufenweiser Prozeβ*] that goes on in the life of the individual as in the life of generations. Sleep its initial stage. A generation's experience of youth has much in common with the experience of dreams. Its historical configuration is a dream configuration.[25]

Very late in the game of Europe's systematic twentieth-century, largely unconscious but for all that, *spirited* "becoming-death," Benjamin still holds out the hope, or at least expresses the wish, that its citizenry will arise from its deep slumber—in *Erwachen* (waking up). This is indeed *very* late in the concatenation of collective illusions, political miscalculations, and mind-boggling cheapening of life that resulted in Europe's near-definitive death-dance.[26] Benjamin's writings on childhood form the backdrop to the inexorable drag on civil society toward barbarism and catastrophe registered in in the speculative Convolutes of his *Arcades Project*. It is already too late to avoid the submerged shoals of annihilation. The scope of destruction is panoramic. Actuality itself (as in *actualités*) is poised for the impending disintegration.

The child's awakening from sleep is an utterly crucial threshold for Benjamin. It affords some of the richest vignettes in the evocation of childhood making up the *Berlin Childhood around 1900*: most notably, "Winter Morning" and "The Fever." In the passage immediately above, still expressing the poignant wish for an awakening from Euro-fascism's long night, the restoration of consciousness takes place *stufenweise*, in steps. We could interpose here "dialectically." Individual and collective awakening are templated upon one another, as in Hegel's *Phenomenology of Spirit*. The child's awakening to a new day of learning is, always already, a Marxian event.

The thrust of Benjamin's pedagogy is irreducibly revolutionary, whether in the writings on childhood, or the quasi-prophetic writings on shock and catastrophe. Benjamin had no qualms about persisting as a devoted Marxian thinker, primarily taking off in this tack from his conversations with Brecht, mostly in the earlier phases of exile. For Benjamin, this was in no way at loggerheads with the positive enchantment with the Judaic imaginary on full display in the 1934 Kafka essay.

> To critique, to call for interminable self-critique, is still to distinguish between everything and almost everything. Now, if there is a spirit of Marxism which I will never be ready to renounce, it is not only the critical idea or the questioning stance (a consistent deconstruction must insist on them even as it also learns that this is not the last or first word.) It is even more a certain emancipatory and *messianic* affirmation, a certain experience of the promise that one can try to liberate from any dogmatics and even from any metaphysico-religious determination, from any *messianism*. And a promise must promise to be kept, that is, not to remain "spiritual" or "abstract," but to produce events, new effective forms of action, practice, organization, and so forth.[27]

The above statement, in the context of the broader drift of deconstructive articulation, of its outset, for instance, in the obscure isomorphism linking philosophemes to poetic deployments of language, comes as close to a credo as we shall find in Derrida. That this credo, this unrestrained affirmation, arises in the camp of Marxian thought is a phenomenon of surprise bordering on astonishment, worthy of consideration in its own right. The only other affirmation, that is to say, all-out *embrace* of a cultural artifact, alongside of, even *in spite of* its intensive hermeneutico-philological parsing, on this order in Derrida's work is the affirmation of Joyce, as much as an institution of letters as a text. And of course, the Joyce of "Penelope" is the "primary source" from which Derrida derives his philosophical trope of affirmation.[28] In keeping with the unrestrained futurity hard-wired into messianic-revolutionary thought, the deconstructive credo in the citation immediately above marshals itself into the speech act of a promise or a vow: "a spirit of Marx which I will never be ready to renounce." The commitment to an inherent "interminable self-critique" transpiring within the Marxian atelier signals an allegorical simultaneity between conceptualization and textual performance. This ongoing process of constructive revision (Thomas Bernhard would call it "correction") is equally part and parcel of how Joyce synthesized text.

What is characteristic of the deconstructive *bearing* here, and in keeping with the *only highly singular and particular* construct of messianism that deconstruction will allow itself, is an explicit firewall by which Derrida insulates this formulation from the foregone strategies of "dogmatics" and "party politics."[29] He thus distinguishes the project of sustained deconstructive "tikkun" or correction, with its embedded messianic drift, from closed-off, self-aggrandizing academic affinity groups, whether espousing deconstruction or excoriating it. There are significant reverberations between a textually gauged messianism, with severe restrictions on its invocation and marshaling, that Derrida allows himself to *affirm* in this passage, and the aspirations that Benjamin continued to nurture, for childhood as well as for critique: the messianism initially dawning upon him through his association with Scholem. Let this nexus remind us that we have already eventuated at a historical juncture at which a certain *spirit of deconstruction* cries out with as much urgency for nurturing, encouragement, and coaxing toward sustainability as the cultural *event* that Derrida *declared*, upon the collapse of Communism in the early 1990s. This was, of course, the *spirit of Marx*, whose arm, in terms of cultural politics, was the *New International*, the latter an indispensable occasion for "processing" the transformations embedded in globalization in its ascendant hegemony.

V

So, oddly, it is an uncharacteristic passage buried within the rambling but never vacant attentiveness of Marx's *Kapital* that becomes the compelling context for the relatively brief, but invariably poignant and compelling sub-literature of childhood pedagogy in Benjamin's writings. It must be, however indirectly, in a Marxian vein that nothing fascinates Benjamin more about his hypothetical children than their *material* culture. Taking a cue from these very same children, he repurposes material from his early writings in his more strikingly "packaged" products. The following extract, from "Old Forgotten Children's Books," will be cited almost verbatim in one of the child vignettes that do so much to imbue a constructive spin on his 1928 *One-Way Street*:

> They are irresistibly drawn by the detritus generated by building, gardening, housework, tailoring, or carpentry. In waste products they recognize the face that the world of things turns directly and solely to them. In using these things, they do not so much imitate the works of adults as bring together, in the artifact produced in play, materials of widely differing kinds in a new, intuitive relationship. Children thus produce their own small world of things within the greater one. The fairy tale is such a waste product—perhaps the most powerful to be found in the spiritual life of humanity; a waste product that emerges from the growth and decay of the saga. Children are able to manipulate fairy tales with the same ease and lack of inhibition that they display in playing with pieces of cloth and building blocks. [*Kinder bilden sich damit ihre Dingwelt, eine kleine in der großen, selbst. Ein solches Abfallprodukt ist das Märchen, das gewaltigste vielleicht, das im geistigen Leben der Menschheit sich findet: Abfall im Entstehungs- und Verfallsprozeß der Sage.*] They build their world out of motifs from the fairy tale, combining its various elements.[30]

This may well be the vignette in which Benjamin most successfully, realistically, and poignantly frames, as in a snapshot, not only how children relate to the environment and function, but also what they *mean*. The passage is an out and out celebration of children's implicit taste for cultural materials and how to marshal them in play, their ability to cordon off the world of "adult" circumspect (utility, rationality, feasibility, etc.) that would stifle this playfulness, the propensity in their experimentation toward a combinatorial playform—one as much at home in the universes of jazz and cubism as of critical apprehension. Children are not only adept in "leveraging" the discrepancy between "material" and "intellectual" relations that would preempt adult thinkers, with their intellectual scruples of categorical rigor and consistency from such open-ended experimentation: any substantial demarcation between physical materials and cultural materials falls simply outside the childhood playbook. It is no accident at the outset of this memorable celebration that the Benjaminian narrator strikes a similar adversarial bearing toward the historians and educators who invoke a "top-down" culture of childhood, one clueless to such a phenomenon as being utterly transported by the experience of color.

On the other side of the historical abyss opened up by World War II, French Structuralism will momentously repurpose the groundwork both toward a working model of intellectual and linguistic *materiality* and toward an understanding of the cultural development that Benjamin sketches out in such a seemingly offhand passage as the above. In his apprehension that children in effect carry over material relations and tactile habits to intellectual (or mythical, or narrative) "property," Benjamin radically preempts Lévi-Strauss's approach to science, experimentation, and classification as conducted by so-called primitive peoples.[31] The Lévi-Straussian *bricoleur*, that jack-of-all-trades who devises complex solutions to the intellectual conundrums facing them within the conceptual and material constraints of the conditions at hand, is an organic development to the Benjaminian child. Lévi-Strauss does not neglect to assign full credit to the indigenous practitioners of "the science of the concrete" for the incredible acumen they have gained in the material sciences. There is a profound *environmental* cast to Benjamin's musings on childhood: it is through the relentless *recycling* of cultural *material*—texts as well as things—that children open new horizons in and for their play. It was already Kafka, in such "fractured folktales" as "Prometheus," "Poseidon," and "The Silence of the Sirens," who demonstrated to Modernism how venerable narrative formulas could literally become the stuff of new constructions and elaborations—even, pace Alice, *contrary* ones. Benjamin was among the first to pick this Kafkan practice up—and Lévi-Strauss would go on to endow the core practice of kaleidoscopic cultural reappropriation with its anthropological sway. Moral fables tease out the permutational play of formulas and fragments of narrative sequences at which children are particularly adept. Children's books, forgotten or not, illustrate—literally—this playful repetition with *différance*.

Reading, and its very possibility, is the zone where children collide into culture, trailing with them everything that they have garnered about the material world. It is the infinite hopefulness regarding children's capabilities for enchantment and eventual critical sensibility and engagement that manages to persist even while Benjamin belatedly sounds the alarm for a general cultural *Awakening*. It is no accident, then, that a very tangible photographic vignette of the "Reading Child" adorns the pre-exilic scrapbook of *One-Way Street*:

> You are given a book from the school library. In the lower classes, books are simply handed out. Often, in envy, you see coveted books pass into other hands.... The child seeks his way along half-hidden paths. Reading, he covers his ears; the book is on a table that is far too high, and one hand is always on the page. To him, the hero's adventures can still be read in the swirling letters like figures and messages in swirling snowflakes. His breath is part of the air of the events narrated, and all of the protagonists breathe it. He mingles with the characters far more closely than the grown-ups do. He is unspeakably touched by the deeds, the words that are exchanged; and, when he gets up, he is covered over and over by the snow of his reading.[32]

More than snow overflows the binding of the book lent out with such deliberation onto the child's outstretched forearms. This passage hails from the very heyday of book culture, evidenced by the care for design, typesetting, illustration, and even paper and cover lavished in the nineteenth and early twentieth centuries on printed volumes. Yet the phrases by which Benjamin's expatiates on what even temporary ownership of an acquired book signifies to a new reader also shimmer in apprehension of the *virtual dimensions* also encompassed by the book. These include the self-contained autonomy of the environment opened up by the book, its tranquility as a protected preserve of the imaginary, its continuity with process (notably narrative improvisation) taking place in the reader's mind, and the interpenetration of surrogates and other constructs generated by fiction into the child's "significant others" of a different order.

The book, as the consummate plaything (*Spielzeug*) of childhood, issues forth in a swirling motion, one reversing and dissolving all kinds of given boundaries: nature/culture, imagination/"reality," property/communal resource, volition/submission. This "swirling" of categories, boundaries, and states of being is for Benjamin the legacy of childhood that is most imperative on an informed citizenry to retain, in the name of its "full" potential politico-cultural franchise, in the name of critical discernment as a public utility. The child's yet-unrealized potential endows its being and its cognitive development with the futurity of the gift, of justice and the vow to pursue it, with which Derrida invested "the spirit of Marx."

VI

Any kind of pedagogy we draw out of a vast battery of Benjamin's signature tactics and moves—from the show-stopping spikes in readerly apprehension concurrent with the intrusion of the dialectical image, to the subjugation of authorial agency to strategic citation, this practice evolving into an art-form in its own right, to the synergy that Benjamin programs between the elucidation at hand and what his text is *performing* in those very passages—is inextricably linked to the highly resonant and complex figure of the child. And over a vast swathe of his writings, Benjamin sustains his devotion to this figure at the limits of his theoretico-literary capability; he persists in his task as a father. The figure of the child in Benjamin underscores the need for some viable construct of literary fathering over and against models—and the metaphysics of—paternity. This is, of course, a fathering in no way gender-specific. Especially at a moment when #MeToo and related interventions have produced sorely needed procedural criteria and traction on the uses and abuses of patriarchal power that were, in the Humanities at least, meaningfully registered over two generations ago. The literary fathering accessible through Benjamin entails a *Sorge* both in the archiving, selection, and display of pertinent cultural materials, and in programming progressive initiation into cultural codes and languages. Such a notion, however arbitrary and vulnerable, is surely not free of its humor and ironies. Benjamin's pervasive intellectual fathering follows, indirectly and at a distance, in the wake of Walter Shandy's aspirations for his Tristrapedia and the "governor's" encomia and ministrations for Rousseau's Emile.[33] Derrida, on the one hand very much a sexual creature of his times, was reaching, in the philosophico-cultural sphere, toward some construct of intellectual fathering when he distilled, in setting out the network of reading and textuality, a rhetoric of *dissemination* and *insemination* (also of *invagination*). This was explicitly at the expense of the metaphysics of paternity, with its embedded claims of authority and legacy.

The dominant feature of Benjamin's trajectory through the world, even while he seeded his insights and illuminations into an almost inconceivable diversity of discourses, formats, and media, is one of progressive *disillusionment*. I introduce this term as D. W. Winnicott, in his writings on mothering, deploys it: as a weaning away, salutary if not always pleasurable, from the delusion of omnipotent control over one's environment.[34] As his academic formation reaches both its apotheosis and stalemate by the mid-1920s, Benjamin loses, in fairly short order, his paternal allowance, his marriage, his parents, his home, his citizenship, and any assurance of economic or political stability. A paradigmatic moment in this persistent life-mantra of progressive debacle is surely the rejection, in 1925, by the Philosophy faculty at the University of Frankfurt, of Benjamin's Habilitation project, *The Origin of German Tragic Drama*.

Give or take a year, from this point on Benjamin writes no longer as a child, from the perspective of they whose needs and interests are a foregone provision. Once his schism from academic Philosophy has been decided, it is the *non-academic nature of Benjamin's social parameters*, his separation from any institution or disciplinary calling, that would afford him stable collegial and/or pedagogical relationships, that would regularly structure his time and activity, and furnish him with logistical support and in the widest sense, an address: it is this being without permanent abode that becomes *the deciding factor* in his rapport to his writing, in his whereabouts, and in relation to significant others. After 1925 or so, the only track on which he is free to pursue his vocation is that of the freelancer, the independent critic, the writerly jack-of-all-trades, the *bricoleur*. It is in significant measure due to the debilitating precarity of this calling that we owe both the incredible diversity of Benjamin's interventions and the poetic virtuosity seizing his formulations the closer he drew to his demise. The great aphoristic works of his later years, from "The Work of Art in the Age of its Technological Reproducibility" to such Convolutes of *The Arcades Project* as K, L, M, and N, were orchestrated as much by the haste in which they were formulated as by anything else.[35] It is abundantly clear that a writerly posture of homelessness leaves nothing more of childlike playfulness to its practitioners. This occupation, with its relentless *preoccupations*—with writerly gigs, vehicles, and audiences, especially as Germany was delivering an unconditional pink slip to unencumbered Humanistic inquiry, left almost nothing *in play*. Benjamin thus continues at the vigil of securing a place for the childhood imaginary in European culture and letters when there is not a trace of the child left in him.

And where does this leave us, whether his students, his intellectual children, or both?

Notes

1   See Gilles Deleuze and Félix Guattari, *A Thousand Plateaus*, trans. Brian Massumi (Minneapolis: University of Minnesota Press, 1987), 28, 33, 243–8; and Jorge Luis Borges, *Ficciones* (New York: Grove Press, 1962), 31.

2. Borges, *Ficciones*, 58–9, 61–2.
3. See Howard Eiland and Michael W. Jennings, *Walter Benjamin: A Critical Life* (Cambridge, MA: Harvard University Press, 2014), 107–8, 136.
4. J. L. Austin, *How to Do Things with Words* (Cambridge, MA: Harvard University Press, 1975), 3–7, 24–7, 94–5, 139.
5. *SW* 1: 51.
6. This German construction is the past participle of the verb at the basis of the Hegelian trope, *Aufhebung*, literally, a "lifting up." Particularly in his foundational *The Phenomenology of Spirit*, Hegel concentrated in this term the temporal complexities embedded in a dialectical model of history.
7. Gershom Scholem, *Major Trends in Jewish Messianism* (New York: Schocken Books, 1974), 40–79. See also Henry Sussman, *Idylls of the Wanderer* (New York: Fordham University Press, 2009), 130–49.
8. *SW* 1: 50. In his "Crock Notes," Benjamin specifically references the assonance between color and the experience of hashish. See Walter Benjamin, *On Hashish* (Cambridge, MA: Harvard University Press, 2006), 83.
9. What particularly comes to mind here is Benjamin's annotations to a hashish experiment he conducted in Marseille on Sunday, September 29, 1928. See Benjamin, *On Hashish*, 50–6.
10. *SW* 1: 442; see *GS* 4: 613.
11. Henri Bergson, *Matter and Memory* (New York: Zone Books, 1991), 77–103, 183–8.
12. Immanuel Kant, *The Critique of Judgment*, trans. J. H. Bernard (New York: Macmillan, 1951) 18, 20, 26–7, 44, 70, 82–3; Henry Sussman, *The Aesthetic Contract: Statutes of Art and Intellectual Work in Modernity* (Stanford, CA: Stanford University Press, 2005), 137–57.
13. Lewis Carroll, *Alice's Adventures in Wonderland & Through the Looking-Glass* (New York: Bantam Classics, 2006), 13–14.
14. "Winter Morning," "The Fever," "The Sock," and "The Mutterehlen" derive from Walter Benjamin, *A Berlin Childhood around 1900* (Cambridge, MA: Harvard University Press, 2006). "Child Reading" and "Pilfering Child" are vignettes spliced into *One-Way Street*, *SW* 1: 463–4.
15. I am playing here on the term *l'art brut*, the term that Jean Dubuffet invented for the artwork—at once naïve, maniacal, and rigidly patterned and repetitive (à la Schreber's thought-processes, in Freud's clinical account) that he and others were discovering among the mentally ill, in and outside of the asylum. I appeal to the category of *l'art brut* to signal the impact of *The Arcades Project*'s fragmentary, non-goal-directed, bottom-up, and impromptu *method* upon "professional" history, in or outside the academy.
16. See, for example, Benôit Peeters, *Derrida: A Biography* (Cambridge: Polity Press, 2013), 332–41.
17. Jacques Derrida, *Specters of Marx: The State of the Debt, the Work of Mourning, and the New International*, trans. Peggy Kamuf (London and New York: Routledge, 2006), 112.
18. Ibid., 115.
19. Particularly crucial in this regard are Derrida's initial assay of the speech act in Austin, and then his rejoinder to John Searle's repudiation of a deconstructive approach. See Jacques Derrida, "Signature Event Context," *Glyph 1* (Baltimore: Johns Hopkins University Press, 1977), 192–208; also, Derrida, "Limited Inc abc . . .," *Glyph 2* (Baltimore: Johns Hopkins University Press, 1977), 162–264.
20. See first and foremost, Jacques Derrida, "Force of Law: The 'Mystical Foundations of Authority,'" in *Acts of Religion*, ed. Gil Anidjar (New York and London: Routledge,

2002), 258–98; also "The Eyes of Language: The Abyss and the Volcano," in *Acts of Religion*, 207–26.
21 Derrida, *Specters of Marx*, 117.
22 Ibid., 92 ("Whether the promise promises this or that, whether it be fulfilled or not, or whether it be unfulfillable, there is necessarily some promise and therefore some historicity as future-to-come. It is what we are nicknaming the messianic without messianism.")
23 Henry Sussman, *The Task of the Critic* (New York: Fordham University Press, 2005), 1–28. See also Martin Heidegger, "Building, Dwelling, Thinking," in *Poetry, Language, Thought*, trans. Albert Hofstadter (New York: Harper and Row, 1971), 145–9, 154–61.
24 Karl Marx, *Capital*, vol. 1, trans. Ben Fowkes (London: Penguin Books, 1990), 615.
25 *AP* 388 (K1,1); *GS* 5: 490.
26 See Deleuze and Guattari, *A Thousand Plateaus*, 180–4, 220, 227–31, 394–403.
27 Derrida, *Specters of Marx*, 111–12.
28 This is the final episode of Joyce's *Ulysses*, ending with Molly Bloom's "and his heart was going like mad and yes I said yes I will Yes."
29 This initiates an all-out parting of the ways with various configurations of community instigating, in its own right, a luminous debate with Jean-Luc Nancy on this very notion. For Derrida's elaborated *skepsis* regarding community, see Jacques Derrida and Maurizio Ferraris, *A Taste for the Secret* (Cambridge: Polity Press, 2001), 24–8, 38–9, 82–6. See also Jean-Luc Nancy, *The Inoperable Community* (Minneapolis: University Minnesota Press, 1991).
30 *SW* 1: 408; *GS* 3: 16–17.
31 With respect to such pivotal structuralist notions as "primitive" classification, *bricolage*, and innovative deployment of the "materials at hand," see Claude Lévi-Strauss, *The Savage Mind* (Chicago: University of Chicago Press, 1962), 16–22, 27–9.
32 *SW* 1: 463.
33 Laurence Sterne, *The Life and Opinions of Tristram Shandy, Gentleman*, ed. and intro. Ian Campbell Ross (Oxford: Oxford University Press, 2009), 298–301.
34 D. W. Winnicott, *Playing and Reality* (London and New York: Tavistock/Routledge, 1971), 10–14, 117–8.
35 Henry Sussman, *Playful Intelligence: Digitizing Tradition* (London and New York: Bloomsbury, 2014), 167–202.

Part Two

Languages of Youth

5

Conversational Pedagogy in Benjamin and Nietzsche

Natasha Hay

Despite the young Walter Benjamin's reputation for austere impracticality as a leading voice of the German student movement, he did help to create an alternative space in which the mission he conceived for student life could have been realized. Benjamin reports with some vexation that the majority of student delegates to the inaugural Free German Youth Day on Mount Meißner in October 1913 were merely advocating for a limited right to self-administration in the manner of student governing councils.[1] In contrast, the *Sprechsaal* or Discussion Hall he organized with fellow students at the University of Berlin sought to create a working model of an independent youth culture for the duration of the academic year 1913–14.[2] During a period in which he distanced himself from the Wynekenians' journal, *Der Anfang*, and became increasingly disillusioned with the prevailing directions of the youth movement, Benjamin continued to participate in the *Sprechsaal* and remained a co-signatory of its Tiergarten lease.[3] For our reconstruction of the political stakes of Benjamin's pedagogy with regard to educational institutions, it is particularly significant that its participants enacted their common sense that "the most urgent requirement for modern pedagogy is to create a space for the emergent culture"[4] by creating a space for intellectual discussions outside the university's infrastructure. They sought to redress the university's self-enclosure from "the non-official, creative life of the mind [*Geistesleben*]"[5] by engaging in readings and discussions that ranged beyond the academic curriculum. Their sessions typically involved oral reading of poetry, essays, and novels followed by informal discussions of themes such as energy and ethics, the modern lyric poem, and the Esperanto movement. Rescuing the potential for "immediate [*unmittelbare*] creativity as a form of community" from "mandarin contempt for the activities of independent artists and scholars who are alienated from and often enemies of the state [*staatsfremden, oft staatsfeindlichen*],"[6] the *Sprechsaal* hoped to foster a free, creative, intellectual community by means of these conversations.

One can easily imagine the frustration of this lofty agenda by the exhausting and tedious forms to which movement talk lamentably tends: charismatic monologues, sectarian feuds, interminable debates. However, these petty conflicts internal to the *Studentenbewegung* were less decisive for Benjamin's ultimate repudiation of the

Sprechsaal than Fritz Heinle's and Rika Seligson's suicide in the very same room that hosted their discussions. In the wake of these lovers' deaths that protested in vain the nation's entry into World War I, the *Sprechsaal* became a tomb in which the retroactively legible failure of "conversational pedagogy" is memorialized. Almost three months into mourning the loss of his dearest interlocutor, Benjamin expresses his grave disenchantment with university studies in a citation from Heinle's diaries that conveys the interdependence of learning and address: "Oh, if only all of them were great men and I could address them familiarly; it is becoming difficult for me to learn from others."[7] By the time that he was writing his *Habilitationsschrift* on the Baroque *Trauerspiel* at the University of Frankfurt, Benjamin confides to a friend that "certain though it is that there does not yet exist outside the university another place where fruitful activity is assured, it seems no less certain that the university itself is today muddying its own wellsprings."[8] Yet having the ability "to step before the young and win them over through living speech"[9] still appeals to him. This persuasive force of the would-be *Privatdozent*'s voice is not a function of the "certificate of public recognition"[10] he might be awarded: it makes a difference "*where* it happens and *whom* it reaches."[11] From these terse observations that bookend Benjamin's post-*Studentenbewegung* time in the university, we learn that the sources, the places, and the addressees for his desire to be a teacher of youth in "living speech" have become corroded and obscure.

The intellectual project of the *Sprechsaal* has a dual purpose meant to intervene in the impoverished modes of freedom of learning (*Lernfreiheit*) and freedom of teaching (*Lehrfreiheit*) in the German university. It is striving to create "a genuinely academic and sophisticated culture of conversation" and to enable its participants to be "teachers and learners at the same time."[12] This guiding sense of an essential connection between the academic culture of conversation and the productive activity of student-teachers resonates with a project for the humanities today proposed by Christopher Fynsk in *The Claim of Language: A Case for the Humanities* (2004). Fynsk recalls his readers to the fact that language is the medium of teaching in the humanities. Acknowledging that "in North America as in Europe, the linguistic turn turned right past the thought of language that made it possible,"[13] he asks that we reflect on the ways that we are working with and against the existing configuration of languages when we respond to the matter of our studies. He contends that we need to invest ourselves in "the material site of the pedagogical relation" and "the local task of teaching" for the sake of the experience with language that becomes possible there.[14] His fundamental claim is that *an experience of language that becomes a question to itself* is the animating heart of the forms of study we call the humanities. In cultivating our receptivity to "the opening of speech" that precedes and exceeds the symbolic order, we encounter the problem of "the communicability of language" whose transmission the governing telos of communicative action in contemporary social theory otherwise tends to obliterate.[15] Among the major voices who "*share a legacy* that derives from a history of speculative thought on language that stretches back well over two centuries,"[16] Fynsk names Benjamin's work on language and translation. Situating Benjamin's philosophical investigations of language vis-à-vis his reflections on university studies demonstrates the salience of Fynsk's claims for this work and intensifies their ethico-political stakes. Drawing out a critical dialogue with Nietzsche's *On the Future of Our Educational*

Institutions (1871) that informs Benjamin's speech on "The Life of Students" (1915),[17] this paper will pursue the speculative line of thought broached in Benjamin's student writings that our relation to language is essential to the pedagogical relation of study, which sustains the ethical and political dimension of academic community in turn.

As Paul Reitter and Chad Wellmon explain in the introduction to their new edition of Nietzsche's lectures, the research seminar was central to the core ideal of intellectual life in Wilhelm von Humboldt's paradigm for university education.[18] Reitter and Wellmon see the perennial defeat of partisans committed to this ideal research seminar, heroically striving to reproduce student cohorts who have learned "a visceral belief in the power of reflective conversation, carried on across space and time, with the record of human experience," as a key element of the permanent crisis confronted by the humanities.[19] In the course of the simultaneous narrowing of research agendas and expansion of undergraduate enrollment in the nineteenth-century German university, "the research seminar began to function as *the* chief site for specialization and professionalization," especially as a proving ground in "training for academia" at the expense of cultivating the holistic art of reflective conversation with texts and ideas.[20] Critics of this repurposing of the research seminar for a "bureaucratic system" were concerned that the inner relationship between scholarship and "a way of life," or, in other words, the reconciling unity of research or *Forschung* and self-cultivation or *Bildung* conceived by Humboldt had been unmade.[21]

At pivotal moments in the staging of the research seminar that resist its formulation as a transhistorical category for theoretical debate, Nietzsche's and Benjamin's reflections on the oral (and aural) dimension of university studies examine how professors' and students' changing relation to language in the humanities classroom crystallizes (de)formations in the receptivity of the human senses. Driven by a similar desire to discover in "the more collaborative oral arts of conversation" a "possible alternative to sophistry, dialogue, and disputation" as the default modes of academic discussion,[22] William Clark's historical survey of the research seminar in *Academic Charisma and the Origins of the Research University* (2006) is discomfited to find that even the seemingly egalitarian gesture in which students have an opportunity to play the role of the teacher involves "leading not a discussion, but rather the lesson."[23] Such a research seminar fashions normalized yet individualized personalities who compete over and are compared with regard to their charismatic originality. Formalistic exchanges of knowledge in a lesson whose power relations remained the same "served well the theatrics of individuation through role-playing and reversals, as each came forward from the chorus to play the lead, while the director remained the director and final critic."[24] As a result of this ever-present framework for instruction that "shapes the student in the director's image," "conversation was not at home, if it ever would be, in the Germanic seminar."[25] Clark's analysis of the remaining documents of the research seminar serves his contrarian view that the self-forming community of pure scholars nostalgically romanticized by the heirs of mandarin critics has never existed.

Drawing out the binding relationship between our use of language and our aesthetic education, Nietzsche's and Benjamin's critical interventions are based on their common intuition that the modes of cultivating speech and listening in the classroom are constitutive for the modes of freedom in teaching and learning that become possible in the university.²⁶ Re-evaluating these meta-educational texts can perhaps disclose future configurations of academic community in the research seminar that go beyond the historical instantiation of the Humboldtian ideal. In the context of the expanding scale of higher education that is converting research seminars into mass lectures, Nietzsche's own public lectures on the future of educational institutions argue that the professorial monologue reduces its student audience to unreflective passivity. For this reason, Nietzsche does not mimic the professorial stance; instead, his lectures make use of a narrative form in which multiple characters give voice to different perspectives on the university. The most vocal of these characters, an emeritus professor who resembles Schopenhauer, is shocked to discover that he has been overheard by students on his walk. He exclaims that he does not want this "chorus of witnesses" who "surely cannot understand us" to trespass on his reunion with a friend.²⁷ Neither the philosophizing students nor the happily retired professor of philosophy whom they encounter have gone to an actual philosophy class lately:

> The old man laughed. "What? You were afraid a philosopher would prevent you from philosophizing? That sort of thing can indeed happen—hasn't it ever happened to you? Not even at your university? You do go to philosophy lectures, don't you?"
> It was an uncomfortable question for us, since we hadn't attended even one. And, like many others, we had the innocent belief that anyone at a university with the office and title of philosopher was in fact a philosopher.²⁸

The students are unsettled by the philosopher's irreverent suggestion that these philosophy lectures would prevent the philosophizing tendencies they are supposed to provoke. The nocturnal collision that Nietzsche stages between the elderly professor, his former protégé, and the young students takes place in the forest and by accident. Had their conversation or indeed Nietzsche's choice of a dialogical form in his lectures followed instead the standard procedures that obtain in the university auditorium, whatever philosophical thrust these exchanges may have for their participants and for Nietzsche's own audience would have been foreclosed.

To denaturalize the educational practices of the German homeland, the professor suggests that the first question a foreigner might ask is "how are the students connected to the university?"²⁹ He asks the eavesdropping students to stay with the amazing strangeness of this underthought connection: "we answer—through the ear. They take part in university life as listeners. The foreigner is amazed and asks: purely by listening? Purely by listening, we repeat. The student attends lectures."³⁰ This is not a frictionless transfer of information between "pure activity" and "pure passivity": the listener's involuntary power of judgment makes itself known in an uncountable number of reactions and decisions that filter and distort the speaker's transmissions. The student "can choose what he wants to hear; he does not necessarily have to believe what he hears; he can shut his ears if he does not want to hear at all."³¹ Control over his ears becomes the measure of his "extraordinary freedom"³² with regard to the expert knowledge dispensed in educational institutions.

The professor emphasizes that this so-called freedom means that university education is completely determined by the student's personal history. The persistence of the recent past at the level of the unconscious tyrannizes over the potentially transformed future that is latent in the present milieu: "the gymnasium education embodied in a young person strides through the university gates as something complete and whole, with its own ambitious claims: *it* makes demands, *it* legislates, *it* passes judgment."³³ Premature autonomy condemns students to perpetual juvenilia. They revert to an infantile state in which they float aimlessly in a uterine lecture chamber and randomly absorb some vital nutrients by means of "a kind of umbilical cord" named "the 'acroamatic' method of instruction."³⁴ The arrested development of this "degenerate culture" marks "our whole educated reading public."³⁵

The student body comes to resemble the "tremendous ear"³⁶ whom Nietzsche's Zarathustra encounters in consternation. A forgetting of acoustic receptivity that swells to monstrous proportions in its hidden dominion over the scene of pedagogy reduces and distorts the spectrum of learning that might be imparted between teacher and student. As a remedy, the professor prescribes "linguistic self-discipline"³⁷ as the only way to recall students to their aesthetic senses. One acquires "a proper linguistic gait"³⁸ by learning "how to listen properly."³⁹ He cautions students against the naïve assumption that mere presence in the lecture halls will impart the disciplined listening needed for a truly aesthetic education:

> Who among you will attain a true feeling for the sacred earnestness of art when you are spoiled with methods that encourage you to stutter on your own when you should be taught to speak, to pursue the beautiful on your own when you should be made to piously worship the artwork, to philosophize on your own when you should be made to *listen* to the great thinkers. The consequence is to keep you forever distant from antiquity, mere slaves to the present.⁴⁰

His argument is that youthful autonomy needs to learn to submit to the authoritative voice of tradition resounding in philosophical and artistic works. The etymological affinity between *hören* ("to hear") and *Gehorsamkeit* ("obedience") is no doubt playfully at work in this precept of proper listening to cultural authority. It is almost an anti-conversational pedagogy: first you must learn to be silent. But it challenges the belief in linguistic autonomy: you learn how to speak by listening.

Rather ironically, the professor's speech in this fifth lecture becomes an extended monologue. Since the sixth lecture was never written or delivered, the problem his monologue investigates is effectively unsolved. Taking up the abortive thread of aural learning in Nietzsche's fifth lecture, an important passage of Benjamin's "The Life of Students" connects the alienated productivity and immature consciousness of his fellow students to the atrophy of their sensorium:

> From the standpoint of aesthetic feeling, the most striking and painful aspect of the university is the mechanical reaction of the students as they listen to a lecture. Only a genuinely academic and sophisticated culture of conversation could compensate for this level of receptivity. And of course the seminars are worlds away from such a thing, since they, too, mainly rely on the lecture format, and it makes little difference whether the speakers are teachers or students.⁴¹

There is a single way of speaking and a single way of listening that are immune from change or differentiation. The "calling to a way of life" for the student that might be imparted in a truly educational conversation remains unspoken and unheard in this scene. Students are "worlds away" from a level of receptivity that could enable a genuine response to alterity in the "mechanical reaction" determined by this format.

Whereas Nietzsche's professor lends no credence to the idea that students might have something to teach lecturers or that they might be capable of research, Benjamin is concerned that the monological form of lectures is symptomatic of the impossibility of a genuine encounter between teacher and student. He observes that "institutes of higher learning are characterized by a gigantic game of hide-and-seek in which students and teachers, each in his or her own unified identity, constantly push past one another without seeing one another."[42] The persistence of "unified identity" or atomized individuality inside and outside the lecture hall suggests that everyone is immersed in their *monologue intérieur*. Because student and teacher pass each other sightlessly and silently, there is no chance for the ecstatic self-loss and unexpected transformation that can occur in pedagogical conversation. In theory, the drama of lecturing means that the student body can alter the academic voice.[43] In practice, the student body becomes an intermediate stage in the invention of the phonograph: it records sounds and can sometimes reproduce them with reasonable fidelity.

Based on the insight that the reduced and distorted *receptivity* of his classmates attests to the university's estrangement from its original ground in the *productivity* of students, Benjamin contends that the university needs to be a place of sanctuary for "the life devoted to total reconstruction" ("dem völligen Neuaufbau sich widmet") awakened in study.[44] The independent productivity of such a form of learning would ultimately be a radical transformation of the institution in which it occurs. He asserts that the original foundation of the university was the creative activity and "complete autonomy" of its students who were "teachers and learners at the same time."[45] This claim that the autonomous productivity of students is the ground of the university is avowedly in contradiction with the *status quo* in which "the students are always inferior to the teachers because they have no official status."[46] An increasingly overt alliance between state power and academic authorities determines an organization of the university in which "the role of learning"[47] that students embody has no official place or voice. Conversely, Benjamin insists on the absolute priority of freedom of learning: every member of the university is a student in potential because there is a moment of learning in all teaching and a moment of teaching in all learning.[48]

Benjamin opines that professional apparatuses meant to produce skilled civil servants have systemically eroded the originary power of ideation evidenced by the conversion of learning into teaching in the course of student life.[49] With the claim that "the vocation of teaching—albeit in forms that are quite different from those that are current today—is an imperative [*geboten*] for any authentic learning,"[50] he reconnects the *calling to study* with its distinctive *way of life*. It is inherent to the very form of philosophy that the student "should be an active producer, philosopher, and teacher all in one."[51] Benjamin expresses the rather paradoxical thought that

[s]cholarship, far from leading inexorably to a profession, may in fact preclude it. For it does not permit you to abandon it; in a way, it places the student under an obligation to become a teacher, but never to embrace the official professions of doctor, lawyer, or university professor.⁵²

Becoming a teacher doesn't mean assuming an academic chair: it means fidelity to the idea in its communication. The student's ability to "take his leave from the community that binds him to other producers,"⁵³ to take his leave from membership in the institution in order to teach in a new way, indexes his role in mediating knowledge by making it communicable. Benjamin thus emphasizes the way in which someone who conceives of their own knowledge as produced by learning can in turn "make [the tradition] communicable by teaching."⁵⁴

Nietzsche not only points out the anatomical monstrosity of a student body that barely supports its tremendous ear, but also sketches the dysfunctional physiology of the academic organism: "One speaking mouth plus many ears and half as many writing hands: that is the academic system as seen from the outside—the educational machinery [*Bildungsmaschine*] of the university in action. And the possessor of this mouth is separated from, and independent of, the possessors of those many ears."⁵⁵ Illustrated by the oxymoronic *Bildungsmaschine* of one mouth separated from many ears, the independence of students and professors from one another dismembers the body politic of the intellectual community to secure the academic freedom of the atomized individual. This semblance of autonomy is a paradigmatic case of the disciplinary power of surveillance:

> the one can say whatever he wants, more or less, and the other can listen to whatever on offer he wants, more or less—except that in the background, a discreet distance away from both parties, the state stands watching with a certain supervisory look on its face, making sure to remind everybody from time to time that *it* is the aim, the purpose, the essence of this whole strange process of speaking and listening.⁵⁶

The concealed presence of the state as the *invisible watcher* over the *free speech* of the faculty and *willful listening* of its students enables a profane annunciation in which the state's discourse pours into their mouth and ears. If the purpose and the aim of the apparent freedom of academic discourse is the tacit governance of the state, then *laissez-faire* exchanges of words in the university inevitably serve the power of a panoptic vision that is secured in its very silence.

Returning to these themes in *Thus Spoke Zarathustra* (1883), Nietzsche spells out the imbrication of this ruse of the state with the babelized tongues of education:

> This sign I give you: every people speaks its tongue of good and evil, which the neighbor does not understand. It has invented its own language of customs and rights. But the state tells lies in all the tongues of good and evil; and whatever it says it lies—and whatever it has it has stolen.... Confusion of tongues of good and evil:

this sign I give you as the sign of the state. Verily, this sign signals the will to death.... "On earth there is nothing greater than I; the ordering finger of God am I"—thus roars the monster.... Behold the superfluous! They steal the works of the inventors and the treasures of the sages for themselves; "education" they call their theft ... Where the state *ends*—look there, my brothers! Do you not see it, the rainbow and the bridges of the overman?[57]

This visual representation of a god in the sign of the state—"The New Idol"—blasphemes against the inspired sources of the sages and the inventors. An all-seeing state is the clandestine infrastructure of a chattering class of journalists and educators. The Ivory Tower becomes a second Tower of Babel—and the divine right of Prussia's constitutional monarchy its *deus absconditus*.[58] As he calls his readers to imagine a cultural education whose lines of inquiry unfold where the state ends, Nietzsche's project is to reclaim the creative power of speaking and listening that has been expropriated by nation-building institutions.

For Benjamin, one major consequence of the official alliance between state and university in the *Kulturstaat* is that the communicability or *Mitteilbarkeit* of pure language in the interdependence of teaching and study is damaged and distorted by the pressure of cognitive judgment regarding the applicability or *Anwendbarkeit* of academic knowledge to the myriad guises of *raison d'état*. The power of these surreptitiously imposed constraints on a seemingly free discourse might be measured when we learn to hear what the members of the university *do not say* and *will not hear*. The study of this tacit dimension of education would be the proper task of a counter-discourse to pedagogies that knowingly or unknowingly sanctify the existing symbolic order. Such a critical study of the use and abuse of language in the university does not have the regulative function of an "ideal speech situation" with regard to our cognitive judgment of everyday communication in the lifeworld. Rather, the peculiarly artificial impediments and strictures on language that we experience in the setting of the classroom can help us to comprehend the otherwise imperceptible norms of ordinary discourse. By attending to the quality and mode of receptivity that is evidenced in the classroom, Benjamin hopes to alter the *way of speaking* and the *way of listening* that have become second nature in university life and in the social world.

Imagining an alternative to these pedagogical scenes, Benjamin does not envision conversation as a reciprocal exchange of reasonable statements between equal subjects about some external object of knowledge. The opening section on conversation in "The Metaphysics of Youth" (1913–14) lays out an asymmetrical relation grounded in and oriented by receptivity, listening, and silence. With the insight that "silence is the internal frontier of conversation" in which liminal exposure between voices can inflect the words used, Benjamin situates the origin of "true language" in a structure of address that goes beyond the speaking "I" and its discursive consciousness.[59] Speaker and listener are essentially related to and in silence: "the listener led the conversation to the edge of language, and the speaker creates the silence of a new language, he, its first auditor."[60] Unpacking the complex relation between past generations and our own time in Benjamin's last manuscript, Michael G. Levine provides the philological note that its convening in the famous "secret assignation" or *geheime Verabredung* stems from the sense of call or address embedded in the root word *Rede*.[61] Though it works with *Schrift* and can work across multiple *Sprachen*, the educative potential of *Rede* is the crux of pedagogy in the research seminar. It is all the more pivotal for Benjamin's account of why the historicity of language is necessary for its power to redeem.

"Every conversation deals with knowledge of the past as that of our youth,"[62] Benjamin writes. We see now what we never saw then: we awaken in horror at "the ruins of our energies" and "the spiritual masses of the rubble fields" remaining from our unconscious struggle with our progenitors.[63] Discovering our unconscious *knowledge of the past* in *the silence of the present* is the promise of conversation. The true language leaves its traces in the historical life of languages as "the nameless in the name"[64] that may become audible each time words fall silent:

> The great motif of integrating many tongues into one true language informs [the translator's] work.... in it the languages themselves, supplemented and reconciled in their way of meaning, draw together. If there is such a thing as a language of truth, a tensionless and even silent depository of all the ultimate secrets for which thought strives, then this language of truth is—the true language.[65]

Reorienting conversation toward the silence in speech not only gives priority to the learner in whom true language has a nascent life, but also attends to the material residue of the creative word that a pedagogical monologue never stops to hear. The generative power of silence is the secret index of an opening to the revealed quality of language that subtends the human exchange of signs: "the speaking spirit is more silent than the listener, just as the praying man is more silent than God."[66] Presence of mind (*Eingedenken*) in conversation might resist the babelized discourse of state power by grasping that even speakers of "the same language" need the work of translation between them.

Importantly, Benjamin's "antinomianism" typically appeals to another order of law: we recall that untranslatability is the law of translation. In order to construct a social ethics whose purpose is other than dutiful service to the Prussian Empire, he turns to the Jewish philosophies of religion developed in Franz Rosenzweig's and Hermann Cohen's work.[67] Cohen and Rosenzweig elucidate a correlation between the human being and God in which the creative reception of divine command (*Gebot*) is not subsumed by and can alter positive law (*Gesetz*).[68] Benjamin borrows from this Jewish tradition of rational messianism to expound the view that "no judgment of the deed can be derived from the commandment"[69] in "Critique of Violence" (1921). So as not to judge the deed on behalf of the actor, the commandment suspends itself: its call to responsibility differs from the punitive function of "the judging word"[70] incurred with the Fall of the spirit of language. The human response to command is bound to the singularity of each case because "ends that in one situation are just, universally acceptable, and valid are so in no other situation."[71] Such a notion of the human interpretation of divine command can serve to elucidate the unique relation of study to the medium of tradition that crystallizes at each moment.

Benjamin's student writings appeal to *Gebot* in order to express a devotion to study that goes beyond professionalization (*Berufsgeist*) and moral duty (*Pflicht*). The commandment to begin to teach corresponds to a love of study that is the origin of intellectual creativity. So, Benjamin's farewell address to the student movement ends:

> Every form of life [*Lebensform*] and its rhythm follows from the commandments [*Geboten*] that determine the lives of the creative ... Everyone will discover his own commandments [*seine eigenen Gebote*] that will make the supreme demand on his life. Through an act of cognition, everyone will succeed in liberating the future from its deformation [*ihre verbildete Form*] in the present.[72]

This messianic temporality in the creative reception of command determines the love of wisdom that drives each student's work. Students learn to hear "the voice that summons them to build their lives with a unified spirit of creativity, eros, and youth."[73] By virtue of their ability to respond to a command borne in the endangered "ideas and products of the creative mind"[74] uniquely addressed to them, their work helps to emancipate the future from its present deformations.

Benjamin portrays the task of students as "a permanent intellectual revolution [*beständige geistige Revolution*]" animating "the university, which itself would be in a position to impart [*mitteilen*] the systematic state of knowledge [at] a point from which new questions would be incubated."[75] He stresses the transformative power of student creativity to "seize upon new ideas, which spring up sooner in art and society than in the university, and mould them into scientific questions [*in wissenschaftlichen Fragen*] under the guidance of their philosophical approach."[76] This practice of study combines creative spontaneity, "to seize upon new ideas," with receptive fertility, "a point from which new questions would be incubated." Study as a form of life exposes a capacity for receptive conception or *Empfängnis* that Benjamin will associate with translation in "On Language as Such and the Language of Man" (1916): "for conception and spontaneity together, which are found in this unique union only in the linguistic realm, language has its own word, and this word applies also to that conception of the nameless in the name. It is the translation of the language of things into that of man."[77] Just as the creative word of God is the guarantee for truth in translation, so is receptive conception in study bindingly related to the commanding word. Its communicability belongs to the spiritual essence of the name for each created being rather than to schematizing cognitive judgments in which the applicability of some theoretical framework is secured. Receptive conception in response to the communicability of the commanding word enables students to become "representatives"[78] of civil society who bear questions, needs, or ideas that have not been granted a hearing by established institutions.

Student life introduces other modes of thinking, creating, and living into a university that would otherwise consolidate the past as the settled possession of the ruling class. Against the university's dissimulation of the true origins of the culture on which it purports to have a monopoly, a responsible student body would form alliances with creative and intellectual labor not yet stamped with institutional legitimacy. The mediating activity of students between civil society and the university experiments with new methodologies so that it can verify the thought it communicates at a unique moment in history. Through its collective labor of transformation, the student body continually alters "the systematic state of knowledge,"[79] ensuring that science will be neither timeless nor closed in itself. In their opening of a communicative medium between the independent arts and the organized sciences, students are not required to generate new solutions or new treatises. The an-archic power of creative study shapes nascent ideas into scientific questions without predetermining their answers. Like the communicability of the spiritual essence of things in the linguistic essence of their names, the fundamental research begun in a studious life imparts itself for the sake of its fulfillment.

Benjamin's speculative philosophy of language entails that there is a language for each expression of human mental life: a language of technology, a language of justice, a language of music.[80] His *Studentenbewegung* corpus attests to a language of teaching in which the intellectual life of study is learning to communicate its spiritual essence. This conversational quality of student life assumes a posture of studious listening to the commanding word whereby "the only nexus of the free union of the old with the new generation"[81] in the communicability of its science becomes possible. A pragmatic stance of receptive conception in the transformative work of student-teachers allows their use of theoretical reason to be an unprecedented judgment bound to the readability of a moment. Bearing in mind that "tradition is the medium in which the person who is learning *continually* transforms himself into the person who is teaching,"[82] and grasping unequivocally that "every age must strive anew to wrest tradition away from the conformism that is working to overpower it,"[83] the unconditional exigency of this paradoxical obligation to become a teacher is to give up the pedagogues' control over the voice of tradition to *all* who may receive it. Complementary to and related in the language of truth, there could then be as many languages of teaching as there are students who wish to learn.

Notes

1 See "Youth Was Silent," *EW* 135–8.
2 On the differing goals of self-governance and independent culture as a catalyst for the schism between the *Freideutsche Jugend*'s reform-oriented and left-wing members, see John McCole, *Walter Benjamin and the Antinomies of Tradition* (Ithaca: Cornell University Press, 1993), 38–40.
3 These details of the *Sprechsaal*'s activities are found in Howard Eiland and Michael Jennings, *Walter Benjamin: A Critical Life* (Cambridge, MA: The Belknap Press, 2014), 61.
4 "School Reform: A Cultural Movement," *EW* 60.
5 "The Life of Students," *SW* 1: 42.
6 Ibid.
7 *C* 75.
8 Cited as an epigraph in Irving Wohlfarth, "Resentment Begins at Home: Nietzsche, Benjamin, and the University," in *On Walter Benjamin*, ed. Gary Smith (Cambridge, MA: MIT Press, 1988), 225.
9 Ibid.
10 *C* 203.
11 Wohlfarth, "Resentment Begins at Home," 225.

12 "The Life of Students," *SW* 1: 42.
13 Christopher Fynsk, *The Claim of Language: A Case for the Humanities* (Minneapolis: University of Minnesota Press, 2004), 57. See also Fynsk, *Language and Relation: . . . that there is language* (Stanford: Stanford University Press, 1996).
14 Ibid., 74–5.
15 Ibid., 65–7. For a highly influential presentation of the "communicability" or *Mitteilbarkeit* of language thematized in Benjamin's work, see Samuel Weber, *Benjamin's -abilities* (Cambridge, MA: Harvard University Press, 2008).
16 Ibid. For an acutely sensitive commentary on the relation of listening and teaching in the work of another thinker who shares this legacy, Emmanuel Levinas, see "Why Listen?" in Robert Gibbs, *Why Ethics? Signs of Responsibilities* (Princeton: Princeton University Press, 2000), 29–46.
17 For biographical justification of this comparison, i.e., that Benjamin read Nietzsche's lectures in preparing his talk, see *A Critical Life*, 65.
18 Paul Reitter and Chad Wellmon, "Introduction," in *Anti-Education: On the Future of our Educational Institutions*, trans. Damion Searls and ed. Reitter and Wellmon (New York: New York Review Books, 2016), xiii. For Reitter and Wellmon's own view of the history and prospects of the humanities, see the recently published *Permanent Crisis: The Humanities in a Disenchanted Age* (Chicago: University of Chicago Press, 2021).
19 Ibid., xxv.
20 Ibid., xiv.
21 Ibid.
22 William Clark, *Academic Charisma and the Origins of the Research University* (Chicago: University of Chicago Press, 2006), 422.
23 Ibid., 175.
24 Ibid.
25 See also Clark's quixotic search for the conversational ethos of Enlightenment salons in the academic context, *Academic Charisma*, 419–22.
26 See Sean Franzel's *Connected by the Ear: The Media, Pedagogy, and Politics of the Romantic Lecture* (Evanston: Northwestern University Press, 2013) for a critical study of the development of the lecture in nineteenth-century Germany.
27 Friedrich Nietzsche, *Anti-Education: On the Future of our Educational Institutions*, trans. Damion Searls and ed. Paul Reitter and Chad Wellmon (New York: New York Review Books, 2016), 74.
28 Ibid., 11. As a first-year university student who was not yet a "card-carrying member of the [philosophers'] union," Benjamin recounts the "grotesque spectacle" of circumspect reasoning and shop talk among "professional philosophers" at a reception in a *Privatdozent*'s home (*C* 29).
29 Ibid., 75.
30 Ibid.
31 Ibid.
32 Ibid., 73.
33 Ibid., 77.
34 Ibid., 75.
35 Ibid., 81.
36 Nietzsche, *Thus Spoke Zarathustra*, trans. Walter Kaufmann (New York: Penguin Books, 1978), 178.
37 *Anti-Education*, 29.
38 Ibid.

39 Ibid., 41.
40 Ibid., 32.
41 "Life of Students," *SW* 1: 42.
42 Ibid., 39.
43 I borrow William Clark's claim. See *Academic Charisma*, 412.
44 "Life of Students," *SW* 1: 41.
45 Ibid.
46 Ibid., 39.
47 Ibid.
48 *C* 94.
49 Wendy Brown's findings on the structural neglect of undergraduate teaching and undergraduate students in the contemporary North American public university are surprisingly resonant with Benjamin's 1915 observations. The final chapter of Brown's *Undoing the Demos* (New York: Zone Books, 2015) recounts that the neoliberal rule of market rationality has "converted higher education from a social and public good into a personal investment in individual futures, futures construed mainly in terms of earning capacity" by students and faculty who are "recognize[d] and interpellate[d] only as human capital" (180–1). Brown finds that undergraduate teaching and academic research are increasingly dissociated under this market imperative. Since advancement in the ranks of the professoriate is tied to publications based on specialized research, the time and care needed for undergraduate teaching is undervalued. Professional success and teaching duties are thus at odds. Outsourcing of the latter to casual labor is the result. She concludes that "neoliberalization has dramatically depressed the status of undergraduate teaching within the academic profession and at public research universities, in particular" (196–7).
50 "Life of Students," *SW* 1: 42.
51 Ibid.
52 Ibid., 38.
53 Ibid., 42.
54 *C* 92.
55 *Anti-Education*, 75.
56 Ibid., 75–6.
57 *Thus Spoke Zarathustra*, 48–51.
58 For a close reading of the conjunction between the "strange process of speaking and listening" in *Anti-Education* and the "confusion of tongues of good and evil" in "The New Idol," see Jacques Derrida, "Otobiographies: The Teaching of Nietzsche and the Politics of the Proper Name," in *The Ear of the Other*, trans. Avital Ronell and ed. Christie McDonald (Lincoln, NE: University of Nebraska Press, 1985), 33–8.
59 "The Metaphysics of Youth," *SW* 1: 7.
60 Ibid.
61 Michael G. Levine, *A Weak Messianic Power: Figures of a Time to Come in Benjamin, Derrida, and Celan* (New York: Fordham University Press, 2014), 8.
62 "Metaphysics of Youth," *SW* 1: 6.
63 Ibid.
64 "On Language as Such and the Language of Man," *SW* 1: 69.
65 "The Task of the Translator," *SW* 1: 259.
66 "Metaphysics of Youth," *SW* 1: 8.
67 For Rosenzweig's reflections on command in epistolary dialogue with Martin Buber, see "The Builders: Concerning the Law," in *On Jewish Learning*, ed. Nahum N. Glatzer

(Madison: University of Wisconsin Press, 2002), 72–92. For the role of prophetic teaching in Cohen's rational messianism, see "Der Stil der Propheten," in *Jüdische Schriften Band 1* (Berlin: C.A. Schwetschke & Sohn, 1924), 262–83. Charmingly, Benjamin's reading of Cohen's *Kant's Theory of Experience* in the company of Gershom Scholem coincides with their fantastical creation of the University of Muri. See *A Critical Life*, 101–2.

68 For a detailed study of correlation, see Robert Gibbs, *Correlations in Rosenzweig and Levinas* (Princeton: Princeton University Press, 1994). Gillian Rose is the first commentator I have found who notices Benjamin's interest in the *educative* potential of a Jewish notion of commandment. She notes that "Benjamin comes near to the idea of Talmud Torah when he contrasts the commandment as a guideline (not a criterion) and its educative potential with the versatility of mythic law-making violence" ("Walter Benjamin—Out of the Sources of Modern Judaism," in *Judaism and Modernity* [London: Blackwell, 1993], 188).
69 "Critique of Violence," *SW* 1: 250.
70 "Language as Such," *SW* 1: 71.
71 "Critique of Violence," *SW* 1: 247.
72 "Life of Students," *SW* 1: 45–6.
73 Ibid., 46.
74 Ibid., 37.
75 Ibid., 43.
76 Ibid.
77 "Language as Such," *SW* 1: 69.
78 "Romanticism: An Undelivered Address to Students," *EW* 101.
79 "Life of Students," *SW* 1: 43.
80 "Language as Such," *SW* 1: 62.
81 *C* 94.
82 Ibid.
83 "On the Concept of History," *SW* 4: 394.

6

Speaking Silence: Historical Subjectivity in Nietzsche and Benjamin

Ian Fleishman

"Our secondary school should refer to Nietzsche and his treatise *On the Advantage and Disadvantage of History*," writes Walter Benjamin, with minimal elaboration, in his own treatise on "Teaching and Value."[1] While passing allusions to Friedrich Nietzsche appear throughout the later philosopher's early work, this is, to my knowledge, the only moment the history essay from 1874 is directly mentioned, its influence summed up in two short sentences encouraging youthful rebelliousness against the purported utility of institutional education: "Defiant, trusting in a youth that follows this philosopher enthusiastically, it [the secondary school] should sweep away the modern pedagogic reforms—instead of becoming modernist itself and trumpeting to all corners a new hidden advantage [*Nützlichkeit*: usefulness] of the institution."[2] Nietzsche thus serves as a model, if somewhat obscurely, for Benjamin's desire to re-form contemporary educational reform. And yet, as I intend to show, what might at first blush seem a rather superficial reception can bring a certain measure of clarity to the murky, even mystical category of *youth* celebrated by both thinkers, ultimately revealing how Benjamin's patient and hopeful attentiveness to silence responds to the crippling effect of hypertrophied historical consciousness bemoaned in Nietzsche's essay.[3]

Here, then, I would like to flesh out the contours of this inheritance, tracing through Benjamin's early reflections on adolescence an unsystematic but nevertheless committed program devoted to the pedagogical project of youthfulness obscurely outlined in the concluding pages of Nietzsche's history essay—in passages that, at times, anticipate Benjamin's nearly verbatim:

> I have faith in *youth*, and I have faith that it has steered me correctly by forcing me into a position of *protest against the historical education of the modern human being in his youth*[.] ... It is necessary to be young in order to understand this protest; indeed, given the premature grayness of our youth today, one can scarcely be young enough and still be able to sense exactly what I am protesting against.[4]

Against the overly historicizing and utilitarian scholarly pedagogical tendencies of his day, Nietzsche, in this early essay, espouses a form of anti-*Bildung* as *resistance*, one that must eschew any definitive form, always remaining (*sich-*)*bildend* ([self-]formative) and never becoming *gebildet* (learned, or, more literally: formed). "That an education with that aim [of formation]," Nietzsche counsels, "is unnatural can only be sensed by those who have not yet been fully shaped by it; only the instincts of youth can sense this, because youth still possesses the instincts of nature."[5] "[A] man is young," agrees Benjamin in one of his own earliest published essays, "so long as he has not yet altogether converted his ideal into reality."[6] What Benjamin borrows from Nietzsche's clarion call for a firstborn generation of dragon slayers is a vague and at times even metaphysical notion of *youth*—or, as he refers to it on one occasion, "superman-youth [Übermenschen-Jugend]"[7]—in radical opposition to the two pillars of moral education identified in the opening sentences "Teaching and Value": history and language, associated by Benjamin, respectively, with ethics and aesthetics. In a sense, the current intervention will trace a movement from the former to the latter, revealing how Benjamin begins to give precarious linguistic form to a productive parabasis at which Nietzsche's essay only hints. Here I will first reveal what Benjamin's hopes for youth owe to Nietzsche's, before examining the pedagogical significance of this legacy and, ultimately, the paradoxical linguistic form—the rhetoric of nonspeaking—Benjamin intends for youth to take.

Youth: Self-Protest

Youth, for both Benjamin and Nietzsche, is less a coherent classification than an unsteady counter-category, ceaselessly suspended in opposition to the fixity associated with adulthood. As Johannes Steizinger, quoting Frank Trommler, notes in his book on Benjamin's "Metaphysics of Youth": "Since Friedrich Nietzsche chose youth as the addressee of his 'antihistorical imperative', it enjoyed a renaissance as a counterforce to power and tradition."[8] Precisely what form this youthful counterforce will take is (always) still to be determined. But if Benjamin's notion of youth, like Nietzsche's, remains vexingly nebulous, this is, I will argue, by design: the anti-utilitarian approach to history advocated by Nietzsche is further radicalized by Benjamin and extended into the linguistic sphere. In the later thinker's "metaphysics" of youth, the inherent defiance of Nietzsche's willful *untimeliness* takes the form of an unspeaking *muteness* (*Schweigen*): a kind of anti-Enlightenment *Unmündigkeit* or immaturity allowing for an ethic of *earnest self-irony*—a paradox I will not attempt to resolve but do hope to elucidate—that Nietzsche's essay was arguably not yet able to achieve persuasively.

Before going any further, it will be important to acknowledge that *youth* appears as kind of *deus ex machina*—and perhaps, as Paul de Man has noted, not an entirely convincing one at that[9]—in the final sections of Nietzsche's history essay. It is first invoked (a few scattered references to youthfulness aside) in its ripening, if not yet fully fledged form at the outset of Nietzsche's penultimate chapter in the context of a dangerous irony verging on an even more perilous sense of cynicism—the flipside of a modern sensibility of prideful historical "cultivation":

> In close proximity to the modern human being's pride stands his *self-irony*, his awareness that he must live in a historicizing and, as it were, twilight atmosphere, his fear that he will not be able to salvage for the future anything whatsoever of his youthful hopes and energies.[10]

The irony Nietzsche outlines here is a kind of stepping out of character and standing beside oneself to regard one's own gloom. Evoking a feeling of futurelessness likely all too familiar to today's youth, Nietzsche's only recourse for remedy is to (re)turn to the perpetual amnesia of the *ahistorical* and the flattening, deflating impact of the *suprahistorical* perspectives outlined earlier in his essay. It is only through this seemingly impossible simultaneity—the admittedly self-contradictory coincidence of cheerful (*heiter* is Nietzsche's preferred word) self-forgetting and earnest (*ernst*) self-knowledge—that youth can take itself seriously and make "use" (a term that will become only more problematic as we continue our investigation) of an awareness of history not only for *life* but for the *future*.

For Nietzsche, before all else, this means a resistance to the purported *utility* of learning from the past: "we want to hold on with our teeth to the rights of our *youth* and will never tire of defending our youth against those iconoclasts who would destroy the images of the future. However, in this struggle we are forced to make an especially painful observation: *that the aberrations of the historical sensibility from which the present suffers are deliberately promoted, encouraged and—utilized.*"[11] Adopting a botanical vocabulary that will appear again in Benjamin, Nietzsche's argument is that such a pragmatic scholarly pedagogical approach stunts the growth of youth by trying to force it to bear fruit too quickly:

> But they [these aberrations of the historical sensibility] are utilized against youth ... to overcome youth's natural aversion.... It is well known—indeed, too well known—what a certain excess of history is capable of: namely *uprooting* the strongest instincts of youth, its fire, defiance, self-oblivion, and love ... of repressing or suppressing its desire to mature slowly by supplanting it with the opposite desire to be quickly finished, quickly *useful*, and quickly productive [*fruchtbar*: literally fruitful] ... it is even capable of cheating youth out of its most beautiful privilege, out of the power to *plant*, overflowing with faith, a great thought within itself and letting it *grow* into an even greater thought.[12]

An excess of history unchecked by youthful defiance, self-forgetting and blind commitment ("Trotz, Selbstvergessen und Liebe") can only lead to cynicism and paralysis—to an inability to action that nips the future in the bud. Youth, in its natural state, is defined as an inherent aversion ("natürliche[r] Widerwillen") without any particular object: to attempt to *form* youth or to make it *useful* would deprive it of its very essence. The lesson Benjamin will learn from this will be to regard *alle Nutzen als Nachteile*, all uses as abuses—"The basic determinant of the moral is renunciation, not motivation through self-interest, nor any utility"[13]—for a youth that has grown into maturity and achieved a stable form would no longer be youth at all.[14] Youthful morality is all about turning away (*Abkehr*); it cannot be codified into a use value but must remain renunciation. In Benjamin's reception of Nietzsche, this insight will entail a pedagogical (non)program of perpetual reform and a peculiar semiotic practice of what Benjamin identifies as nonspeaking (*schweigen*).

Pedagogy: Earnest Irony

It is in his comments on another author entirely—namely, in his "Thoughts on Gerhart Hauptmann's Festival Play"—that Benjamin makes most manifest the direct influence of Nietzsche's history essay:

> So strong is the "historical sense" at the present time, this sense for facts, for restriction and discretion, that our time is perhaps particularly poor in genuine "historical ideas." It calls them for the most part "utopias" and lets them founder on the "eternal laws" of nature. It rejects the task that cannot be comprehended within a reform program and that demands a new movement of *spirits* and a radical new seeing. At such a time, the young cannot but feel alienated and powerless. For they do not yet have a program.[15]

As in Nietzsche, an overdetermined, backward-looking historical sensibility is, in this account, a retardant to the forward flow of history itself, of the history-making potential contained in youth. Not necessarily one to shy away from utopian thinking, Benjamin therefore chooses not to lament the lack of a concrete program of (political) reform but rather to see youth's thoroughly nonprogrammatic nature (perhaps paradoxically) as intrinsic to its teleology.

The young Benjamin echoes Nietzsche's concern regarding the risk of cynicism—and, as we shall see, Nietzsche's precarious solution—less obviously but just as profoundly in his "Dialogue on the Religiosity of the Present," noting that he (or at least the speaker designated as "I [*Ich*]") has lost faith in "the religious sublimity of knowledge[.] ... All the social morality we seek to establish with splendid, youthful zeal is arrested in the skeptical depths of our insights."[16] And thus, as for Nietzsche, the pedagogical goal, for Benjamin, in an essay on school reform as a cultural movement, must be to allow for youth to *live* sincerely, beyond and despite their own historical moment, for and into the future: "propagation of spiritual values [*Fortpflanzung geistiger Werte*] ... It means first of all that we grow beyond our present day. Not only that we think *sub specie aeternitatis* but also that, insofar as we educate ourselves, we live and work *sub specie aeternitatis*."[17] Benjamin adopts the botanical notion of a *Fortpflanzung geistiger Werte* from Rudolf Pannwitz, himself under the influence of Nietzsche and continues to strike a decidedly Nietzschean tone as he calls for a revaluation of values, including, perhaps most importantly, those of the educational institution itself: "But to propagate values means something more.... The question arises as to the values we wish to bequeath to our descendants [*Nachkommen*: offspring] as highest legacy. School reform is not only reform of the propagation of values; it becomes at the same time revision of the values themselves."[18] Reform has become an aim in itself and the ceaseless re-formation of a perpetual revaluation of values has become the ever-shifting ground of the pedagogical project.

Like Nietzsche, Benjamin therefore places his faith in the *autonomy* of youth, arguing that the culture of the future must be allowed to grow wild, organically, with minimal intervention and negligible cultivation:

> After all, the culture of the future is the ultimate goal of the school—and for the reason it must remain silent before the future that comes toward it in the form of youth. It must allow young people to act *on their own* and consequently must rest content with conferring and fostering freedom. And so we see that the most urgent requirement of modern pedagogy is to create space for the emergent youth culture.[19]

The best pedagogical strategy, so Benjamin, is not to educate at all, but rather to get out of the way and to let the younger generation do its thing. This has, if subtly, a *linguistic* structure: the educational apparatus must fall silent, must *not speak* ("so muß sie schweigen") before the promise of the future that *opposes* it ("das in der Jugend ihr entgegentritt"). Only left to its own devices can youth learn—educating itself in a nurturing sense of *Erziehung* rather than the formational sense of *Bildung*—to take itself *seriously*:

> Youth must learn by degrees to work, to take itself seriously, to educate itself: by placing trust in such youth, humanity places trust in its own future, in the irrational which it can only honor, in the youth that is filled not just with the spirit of the future—no!—but with the spirit that feels in itself the joy and the courage of new culture-bearers. Awakening more and more is a consciousness of the unconditional value, the gaiety [*Frohsinn*] and seriousness [*Ernstsinn*] of this new youth.[20]

In its reverent embrace of the irrational, youth embodies not only the spirit of the future but the spirit of historical unfolding itself. And if the cheerfulness (Benjamin's *Frohsinn* recalls a Nietzschean *Heiterkeit*) of this youthful disposition is here unfettered by the skeptical depth of insight that worried Benjamin above, it is not despite this seriousness (*Ernstsinn*) but rather alongside it, as two sides of the same coin.

Benjamin might, then, ultimately offer us some admittedly uncertain way out—the temporary aperture of a perpetually self-closing escape hatch—from what de Man, in his revealing reading of Nietzsche's history essay, has identified as an inescapable "bad faith implied in advocating self-knowledge to a younger generation while demanding from this generation that it act blindly, out of a self-forgetting that one is unwilling or unable to achieve oneself."[21] For Benjamin, the only way out of the despair occasioned by historical awareness is *through* it: "I believe in our own skepticism, our own despair," he contends.[22] A few pages later, cynicism itself is recast as a heroic effort to reassert a sincere subjectivity in and *through* its own undoing[23]—a longing that

> can never have had the last word on anything and hence its terminations are always cheeky. The tragic naïveté of the high-spirited. As I said, it keeps leaping over the chasms it opens up. I love and fear this cynicism—it's so courageous and,

in the end, only a little too vainglorious not to set its own fortuitousness above historical necessity.[24]

Committed to its own contingency over and against historical necessity, this cynicism cannot be taken at its word, can never leave its word alone. Leaping over its own shadow like Nietzsche's *Übermensch*, it always says *more* than it means and sometimes its own opposite.

If history is, for Nietzsche, unintuitively the antidote to the poison of an overly historical self-consciousness, then perhaps, by an analogous gesture, courageous *irony* is itself the cure for the illness of an ironic self-awareness endemic to a generation that has been instructed it is living at the end of history: "*our first generation* must ... educate itself, moreover, against itself."[25] Youthful sincerity is *always* protest and most importantly a protest against itself. Cynicism would not be the inability to take oneself seriously but rather the *necessity* of taking oneself seriously despite oneself, despite one's own inherent cynicism.

Language: A Rhetoric of Nonspeaking

Perhaps this lends some semblance of the tangible (admittedly, a potential act of treason, as this is precisely what has been eschewed all along) to the willfully mysterious metaphysical reflections found in Benjamin's early writings. In what could be described as the most mature work of his juvenilia,[26] his "Metaphysics of Youth," Benjamin outlines—and perhaps performs—the linguistic practice of such self-protest, famously insisting that "the silent one [*der Schweigende*] is the unappropriated source of meaning."[27] I will briefly attempt to explicate and to illustrate this rhetoric of nonspeaking here.

The solution, namely, is not as simple as Nietzsche would appear to imply when he writes that the goal should be "help youth express itself, ... help illuminate, with the lucidity of concepts, the path of their unconscious resistance against this education and transform it into an aware and outspoken consciousness"[28]—even if Benjamin would, momentarily, appear to agree in the concluding words of his critique of the Free German Youth Conference, "Youth Was Silent": "The *fact* of the Youth Congress remains the one thing positive. It is enough to bring us together again better prepared next year—and so for all the years to come, until at some future Free German Youth Congress *youth* speaks."[29] The *fact* alone could never suffice, as it is not just the particular politics of nascent fascism on display at this gathering, as horrific as they are, but *any* political program—any program at all—that runs counter to this Nietzschean "resistance" (*Widerwillen*), to the "will to youth [*Willen zur Jugend*]" that Benjamin celebrates in this same text.[30] Youth, by Benjamin's definition, *must* then, in some sense, stay silent.

In the concluding section to his thoughts on Hauptmann, called "Youth and History," Benjamin hints at the reasons for this necessary reticence:

> School and home dismiss our most earnest ideas as mere cant [*Phrase*].... Now we know that lack of clarity is no reproach, that no one who willed what was serious

[*Ernstes*] had a program ready for the curious and the skeptical. To be sure, we are lacking in "historical sense." But all the same we feel ourselves to be related by blood to history—not to that which is past but to that which is coming. We shall never understand the past without willing the future.[31]

The desire is for an *embodiment* of ideals that, when expressed conventionally, necessarily seems clichéd palaver (what Benjamin repeatedly refers to in German as *Phrase*). Against the accusation of hackneyed principles, tritely expressed, Benjamin suggests a bodily relation to history and a coming of ideals youth feels in its very blood—not so much a liberation of the future from the ballast of the past as an incorporation of the past *into* the future. In the continued spirit of Nietzschean *Sprachkritik* (language skepticism), Benjamin goes on to outline the inevitable erosion and atrophy of established values ("at every present moment the old values grow older; what was momentum becomes inertia, and what was intelligence becomes stupidity"[32]) and the necessity to fight for their renewal ("we struggle for the very possibility of values"[33]) against the indifference to the ostensibly inevitable forward motion of history taught in schools.

Contrary to this dominant view, Benjamin, at the end of his Hauptmann essay, sees history as a battle between a past whose values have already been established and the future whose laws must still be written:

> History is the struggle between the spirited and the inert, between those oriented toward the future and those oriented toward the past, between the free and the unfree. The unfree can always display to us the canon of their laws. But we will not yet be able to give a name to the law under which we stand. That it is a matter of duty is something we feel. In this feeling, youth will have courage for that which the others consider phrasemaking [*Phrase*]. It will take action though others call it confused. Youth is confused like the spirit of history.[34]

Youth, according to this account, is conflictual dialectics itself: the confused progression of history. The established laws alluded to above, which stifle this progression, are, of course, for Nietzsche, worn-out *language*—"such a nonliving and yet incredibly active factory of concepts and words"—and youth is "suffering, furthermore, from the sickness of words and mistrustful of every individual feeling that does not yet bear the stamp of words."[35] Intimating this linguistic element, Benjamin argues that, to act freely, youth must be allowed its coinages, even if these take the appearance of empty currency and hollow phrasemaking ("was die andern Phrase nennen").

Self-serious schooling, Benjamin explains in a short text on the "false romanticism [*falsche Romantik*]" of contemporary education, has left youth feeling everything to be "untrue and unreal [*unwahr und unwirklich*]"[36]—and it is precisely here that Nietzsche makes a quick but significant cameo:

> We therefore, comrades, began impetuously to concern ourselves, with ourselves. We became the much-maligned, individualistic superman-youth. It was really no wonder that we went along jubilantly with the first one who summoned us to

ourselves, to the spirit and to honesty. This was certainly Friedrich Nietzsche's mission among the youth of the schools: to show them something of the tomorrow and yesterday and today of educational tasks. They could not handle it. And they have turned this idea also into a pose, as they have been repeatedly constrained to do.[37]

Even youth's Zarathustran swagger has lost its quality of self-overcoming and instead become stultified into mere affectation. Unable to express itself through the medium of language, youth has *become* a medium for such familiar formulae.

But if Benjamin would appear to be moving past his predecessor here, the solution proposed to this posturing is itself decidedly Nietzschean:

> We need a beautiful and free community, so that the universal can be articulated without becoming commonplace. We do not yet have this possibility; we want to create it for ourselves. We are not ashamed to say that we still have to be trite when we talk about this youth. (Or else, we have to adopt an unworldly academic attitude or an aesthetic posture.) We are still so uncultivated in all that we have in common that honesty and integrity seem banal.[38]

The difficulty alluded to here is to discover a rhetorical form for the *earnest irony* of youth per Nietzsche's definition: a self-articulation that unabashedly adopts the naïve position of the *ahistorical* ("trite [*trivial*]" or "commonplace [*gemein*]"[39] evocations of youth) as a palliative against the ineluctable cynicism of the *suprahistorical* ("an unworldly academic attitude or aesthetic posture [*eine weltfremde akademische oder eine ästhetische Geste*]"). That the posturing or roleplaying—*Geste* is, at base, a dramaturgical term—I am associating here with the suprahistorical sentiment is included parenthetically (and thus under erasure, as it were) gets to the heart of the matter: if the nagging awareness of the suprahistorical perspective cannot be entirely silenced, it must, at the very least, be reduced to a whisper—evoked and then immediately forgotten in the selfsame performative gesture.[40] It is perhaps telling, then, that these last passages are drawn from a short piece with an equally performative, self-cancelling subtitle: "Romanticism: An Undelivered Address to Students."

Conclusion

Elsewhere, Benjamin takes Nietzsche at his (other) word when the earlier thinker counsels that the mission of youth should be to "use no concepts, no party slogans from among the verbal and conceptual coins that are currently in circulation."[41] In fact, Benjamin appears to radicalize this stance as an admonishment even against allowing youth's own coinages to gain currency. Anticipating, at a certain moment, that his audience will ask of him a concrete program and pragmatic praxis, Benjamin contends, with (all too) Nietzschean overtones: "if my words were all too assured, all too exact, they would contradict what I am saying. For youth consciousness is something still becoming in us."[42] Silence, *das Schweigen*, for Benjamin, seems not to be something outside of, but rather contained *in* language: youth, even in its self-expression, must somehow still remain taciturn, unspoken or, at the very most, only provisionally articulated—ultimately communicating only its own provisional nature.

As James McFarland phrases it, for Benjamin, the ideal of youth is "mute ... in principle because the ideal emerges only as the condition and never as the result of communication.... As a condition of expression, youth, whatever it may be, is a possibility within silence. Nietzsche, says Benjamin, is a partner in this silence, a herald of this possibility."[43] The hollow phrasemaking to which youth has been said to have the courage is not empty—at least not exactly—because it lacks content, but rather because its self-contradictions contain what Shoshana Felman has identified in Benjamin's more mature work as "a surcharge of meaning ... quite literally imprisoned in instances of silence."[44] Benjamin's varied, formally diverse early writings on youth similarly work to bring language to its limit, liberating the future from its distortion in the present and lamenting the past to make way for things to come. For, as Benjamin puts it in his "Metaphysics of Youth": "The sole condition for creation is the acknowledged yearning for a beautiful childhood and worthy youth. Without this, no renewal of their lives will be possible: without the lament for a missed opportunity at greatness."[45] It is a strangely hopeful complaint which laments not something lost but rather what has never come to be. An expression of youth, like Benjamin's later descriptions of the critical act, must remain in permanent parabasis, positing and suspending itself by the same gesture, hinting at a future it refuses ever to make fully present.

Notes

1   *EW* 96; *GS* 2: 40 ("Unser Gymnasium sollte sich berufen auf Nietzsche und seinen Traktat 'Vom Nutzen und Nachteil der Historie'").

2   *EW* 96; *GS* 2: 40. ("Trotzig, im Vertrauen auf eine Jugend, die ihm begeistert folgt, sollte es [das Gymnasium; I.F.] die kleinen modernen Reformpädagogen überrennen. Anstatt modernistisch zu werden und aller Ecken eine neue, geheime Nützlichkeit des Betriebs zu rühmen").

3   Howard Eiland and Michael Jennings have noted the influence of this essay on Benjamin's conception of history in "The Life of Students." Howard Eiland and Michael W. Jennings, *Walter Benjamin: A Critical Life* (Cambridge, Massachusetts: Harvard University Press, 2014), 42–3. Generally, however, scholarship has been more attentive to the more evident and more programmatic reception of Nietzsche's lectures "On the Future of Our Educational Institutions" (1872). See, for instance, Eiland and Jennings, *A Critical Life*, 65–6, and James McFarland, *Constellation: Friedrich Nietzsche and Walter Benjamin in the Now-Time of History* (New York: Fordham University Press, 2013), 59–62.

4   Friedrich Nietzsche, *Unfashionable Observations*, trans. Richard Gray (Palo Alto: Stanford University Press, 1995), 158. See Friedrich Nietzsche, *Kritische Studienausgabe* [= *KSA*] (Munich: de Gruyter Deutscher Taschenbuch Verlag, 1999), 1: 324–5 ("[I]ch vertraue der *Jugend*, dass sie mich recht geführt habe, wenn sie mich jetzt zu einem *Proteste gegen die historische Jugenderziehung des modernen Menschen* nöthigt[.] ... Man muss jung sein, um diesen Protest zu verstehen, ja man kann, bei

der zeitigen Grauhaarigkeit unserer jetzigen Jugend, kaum jung genug sein, um noch zu spüren wogegen hier eigentlich protestirt wird").

5   *Unfashionable Observations*, 160; *KSA* 326 ("Das eine Erziehung mit jenem Ziele [der Bildung] ... eine widernatürliche ist, das fühlt nur der in ihr noch nicht fertig gewordene Mensch, das fühlt allein der Instinct der Jugend, weil sie noch den Instinct der Natur hat").

6   *EW* 28; *GS* 2: 11 ("[J]ung ist ein Mensch solange er sein Ideal noch nicht völlig in die Wirklichkeit umgesetzt hat").

7   *EW*, 104; *GS* 2: 45.

8   Johannes Steizinger, *Revolte, Eros und Sprache. Walter Benjamins "Metaphysik der Jugend"* (Berlin: Kulturverlag Kadmos, 2013), 19. My translation ("Seit Friedrich Nietzsche die Jugend zum Adressaten seines 'antihistorischen Imperativ[s]' wählte, feierte sie eine Renaissance als Gegenkraft zu Macht und Tradition").

9   As de Man sees it, Nietzsche "has to delegate the power of renewal and modernity to a mythical entity called 'youth' to which he can only recommend the effort of self-knowledge that has brought him to his own abdication." Paul de Man, "Literary History and Literary Modernity," in *Blindness and Insight: Essays in the Rhetoric of Contemporary Criticism* (based on Oxford University Press edition, 1971), 151. Similarly, while heaping on the praise, de Man ultimately dismisses Benjamin's later reading of (Romantic) irony as too totalizing, insisting that its "radical negation" itself ironically "reveals ... by the undoing of the work, the absolute toward which the work is underway." Paul de Man, "The Concept of Irony," in *Aesthetic Ideology*, ed. Andrzej Warminski (Minneapolis, Minnesota: University of Minnesota Press, 1996), 163–84, 183. Against this charge, Avital Ronell defends Benjamin's "way of recuperating the destructive character of irony" by remaining attentive to "the emergence of a certain irony against which the self is continually tested." Avital Ronell, *Stupidity* (Urbana, Illinois: University of Illinois Press, 2002), 143, 133. Here, I follow the latter view in examining an irony which refuses to disclose itself fully: "Irony suspends the infinite project, its work of appropriating meaning to itself—permanently, which is to say: time and time again." Ronell, *Stupidity*, 144.

10 Nietzsche, *Unfashionable Observations*, 146; *KSA* 312 ("Dicht neben dem Stolze des modernen Menschen steht seine *Ironie* über sich selbst, sein Bewusstsein, dass er in einer historisierenden und gleichsam abendlichen Stimmung leben muss, seine Furcht gar nichts mehr von seinen Jugendhoffnungen und Jugendkräften in die Zukunft retten zu können").

11 *Unfashionable Observations*, 156–7; *KSA* 322–3 ("[W]ir wollen das Recht unserer *Jugend* mit den Zähnen festhalten und nicht müde werden, in unserer Jugend die Zukunft gegen jene Zukunfstbilder-Stürmer zu vertheidigen. Bei diesem Kampfe müssen wir aber auch eine besonders schlimme Wahrnehmung machen: *dass man die Ausschweifungen des historischen Sinnes, an welchen die Gegenwart leidet, absichtlich fördert, ermuthigt und—benutzt*").

12 *Unfashionable Observations*, 157; *KSA* 323 ("Man benutzt sie [die Ausschweifungen des historischen Sinnes] aber gegen die Jugend ... um den natürlichen Widerwillen der Jugend ... zu brechen.... Ja man weiss, was die Historie durch ein gewisses Uebergewicht vermag, man weiss es nur zu genau: die stärksten Instincte der Jugend: Feuer, Trotz, Selbstvergessen und Liebe zu *entwurzeln* ... die Begierde langsam auszureifen durch die Gegenbegierde, schnell fertig, schnell nützlich, schnell *fruchtbar* zu sein, zu unterdrücken oder zurückzudrängen ... ja sie vermag es selbst, die Jugend um ihr schönstes Vorrecht zu betrügen, um ihre Kraft, sich in übervoller Gläubigkeit

einen grossen Gedanken *einzupflanzen* und zu einem noch grösseren aus sich heraus *wachsen* zu lassen"). Emphases added.
13 *EW* 112; *GS* 1: 52–3 ("Die Grundstimmung des Sittlichen ist Abkehr, nicht Motivierung durch den eigenen, noch überhaupt einen Nutzen").
14 McFarland, *Constellation*, 17. McFarland therefore sees Benjamin's juvenilia on the whole as a kind of performative failure in its attempt to define a coherent project despite its programmatic stance against both program and coherence: "In the name of an exemplary youthfulness, these writings would like to promote juvenilia themselves to the status of an autonomous and equally legitimate cultural expression. The desire is self-defeating. If an assertion betrays by its expressive insecurity its immature origin, it forfeits, with all juvenilia, mature authority. But juvenilia disappear in a different way if they achieve a fully adult poise, for they are then no longer juvenilia but simply a precocious adulthood." Ibid., 17.
15 *EW* 120; *GS* 2: 57 ("So stark ist der 'historische Sinn' der Zeit, dieser Sinn für Fakten, Gebundenheit und Vorsicht, daß sie vielleicht ganz besonders arm ist an eigentlich 'historischen Ideen'. Diese nennt sie meist 'Utopien' und läßt sie an den 'ewigen Gesetzen' der Natur scheitern. Sie verwirft eine Aufgabe, die nicht in ein Reformprogramm gefaßt werden kann, die eine neue Bewegung der *Geister* fordert und ein radikales Neu-Sehen. In einer solchen Zeit muß die Jugend sich fremd fühlen und auch machtlos. Denn ein Programm hat sie noch nicht").
16 *EW* 69–70; *GS* 2: 24 ("[D]ie religiöse Erhabenheit des Wissens[.] ... Alle die soziale Sittlichkeit, die wir mit herrlichem, jugendlichem Eifer schaffen wollen, ist gefesselt durch die skeptische Tiefe unserer Einsichten").
17 *EW* 60; *GS* 2: 13 ("Fortpflanzung geistiger Werte ... Das heißt erstens: wir wachsen hinaus über unsere Gegenwart. Nicht nur, daß wir sub specie aeternitatis denken—indem wir erziehen, leben und wirken wir sub specie aeternitatis").
18 *EW* 58; *GS* 2: 14 ("Werte fortpflanzen, das heißt aber noch ein Zweites.... Es erhebt sich die Frage nach den Werten, die wir unsern Nachkommen als höchstes Vermächtnis hinterlassen wollen. Die Schulreform ist nicht nur Reform der Fortpflanzung der Werte, sie wird zugleich Revision der Werte selbst").
19 "School Reform," *EW* 60; *GS* 1: 15 ("Die Kultur der Zukunft ist doch schließlich das Ziel der Schule—und so muß sie schweigen vor dem Zukünftigen, das in der Jugend ihr entgegentritt. *Selbst* wirken lassen muß sie die Jugend, sich begnügen damit, Freiheit zu geben und zu fördern. Und so sehen wir, wie die dringendste Forderung moderner Pädagogik nichts will als Raum für die werdende Kultur schaffen").
20 *EW* 60; *GS* 1: 15 ("In der Jugend, die allmählich lernen soll zu arbeiten, sich selbst ernst zu nehmen, sich selbst zu erziehen, im Vertrauen zu dieser Jugend vertraut die Menschheit ihrer Zukunft, dem Irrationalen, das sie nur verehren kann, die Jugend, die nicht nur soviel mehr erfüllt ist vom Geiste der Zukunft—nein!—die überhaupt soviel mehr erfüllt ist vom Geiste, die die Freude und den Mut neuer Kulturträger in sich fühlt. Es erwacht immer mehr das Bewußtsein vom unbedingten Wert dieser neuen Jugend Froh- und Ernstsinn").
21 Paul de Man, "Literary History," 151.
22 "Dialogue on the Religiosity of the Present," *EW* 69; *GS* 2: 24 ("Ich glaube an unsere eigene Skepsis, unsere eigene Verzweifelung").
23 Benjamin speaks of "witty cynicism [{g}eistreicher Zynismus]" here as "the mighty will to see everything unmoored and not so peacefully and self-evidently anchored in the 'I' as it customarily appears to be [dem gewaltigen Willen, nicht alles so ruhig und

selbstverständlich im Ich verankert zu sehen, wie wir es gewohnt sind]" *EW* 72; *GS* 2: 27. Translation modified.

24 *EW* 72; *GS* 2: 27 ("kann es bei ihrem letzten Wort niemals lassen und setzt den vorlauten Schluß dazu. Die tragische Naivität des Geistreichen. Wie ich schon sagte, es überspringt die Klüfte wieder, die es aufreißt. Ich fürchte und liebe diesen Zynismus, der so mutig ist, und zuletzt nur ein wenig zu eigensüchtig, um nicht die eigene Zufälligkeit über die historische Notwendigkeit zu setzen").

25 Nietzsche, *Unfashionable Observations*, 162; *KSA* 328 ("[U]nsere Generation ... muss ... sich selbst erziehen und zwar sich selbst gegen sich selbst").

26 Both McFarland and Shoshana Felman, in different ways, see this text as an anticipation of "a constant rift in Benjamin's mature thought." McFarland, *Constellation*, 21; Shoshana Felman, "Benjamin's Silence," *Critical Inquiry* 25:2 (Winter, 1999): 201–34.

27 *EW* 145; *GS* 2: 91 ("[D]er Schweigende ist die ungefaßte Quelle des Sinns"). Adi Nester's contribution to this same volume considers Benjamin's early language philosophy as it pertains to his thinking on youth more concretely with reference to this text.

28 Nietzsche, *Unfashionable Observations*, 160; *KSA* 326 ("[D]er Jugend zum Worte [zu] helfen, ... ihrem unbewussten Widerstreben mit der Helligkeit der Begriffe voran[zu]leuchten und es bis zu einem bewussten und laut redenden Bewusstsein [zu] machen").

29 *EW* 136–7; *GS* 2: 67 ("Die Tatsache des Jugendtages bleibt das einzig Positive. Sie genügt, um uns gerüstet das nächste Jahr wieder zusammen zu führen, und so alle Jahre, bis auf einem freideutschen Jugendtage die Jugend spricht").

30 *EW* 135; *GS* 2: 66. John McCole notes that while "Benjamin never invoked the Nietzschean doctrine of the will in so many words ... at times he came very close indeed." John McCole, *Walter Benjamin and the Antinomies of Tradition* (Ithaca, New York: Cornell University Press, 1993), 52.

31 *EW* 123–4; *GS* 2:59 ("Schule und Haus schieben unsere ernstesten Gedanken als Phrase beiseite.... Nun wissen wir, daß Unklarheit kein Vorwurf ist, daß niemand, der Ernstes wollte, ein Programm für die Neugierigen und Skeptiker bereit hatte. Zwar mangelt uns der 'historische Sinn'. Aber doch fühlen wir uns blutsverwandt mit der Geschichte, nicht mit der vergangenen, sondern mit der kommenden. Wir werden nie die Vergangenheit verstehen, ohne die Zukunft zu wollen"). Translation modified.

32 *EW* 123; *GS* 2: 60 ("[D]enn mit jeder Gegenwart werden die alten Werte älter; was Schwungkraft war wird Trägheit, Geist wird Dummheit").

33 *EW* 123; *GS* 2: 60 ("[W]ir kämpfen für die Möglichkeit der Werte überhaupt").

34 *EW* 123; *GS* 2: 60 ("Die Geschichte ist der Kampf zwischen den Begeisterten und den Trägen, den Zukünftigen und den Vergangenen, den Freien und Unfreien. Die Unfreien werden stets den Kanon ihrer Gesetze uns vorweisen können. Wir aber werden das Gesetz, unter dem wir stehen, noch nicht nennen können. Daß es Pflicht ist, fühlen wir. In diesem Gefühl wird die Jugend Mut haben zu dem, was die andern Phrase nennen. Sie wird handeln und mögen andere sie verworren nennen. Sie ist verworren wie der Geist der Geschichte").

35 Nietzsche, *Unfashionable Observations*, 162, 163; *KSA* 329 ("[E]ine solche unlebendige und doch unheimlich regsame Begriffs- und Wort-Fabrik ... [A]n der Krankheit der Worte leidend und ohne Vertrauen zu jeder eignen Empfindung, die noch nicht mit Worten abgestempelt ist").

36 "The Free School Community," *EW* 41; *GS* 2: 44.

37 *EW* 41; *GS* 2: 44–5 ("Also, Kameraden, begannen wir uns stürmisch uns selber zuzuwenden. Wir wurden die viel gelästerte, individualistische und Übermenschen-Jugend. Das war wirklich kein Wunder, daß wir dem Ersten jubelnd zufielen, der uns zu uns selber rief, zum Geist und zur Ehrlichkeit. Das war sicherlich Friedrich Nietzsches Mission unter der Schuljugend, daß er ihr etwas über das Morgen und Gestern und Heute von Schulaufgaben wies. Sie konnte es nicht mehr tragen. Und sie machte auch diese Idee zur Pose, wie man sie stets zu solchem Verfahren gezwungen hatte").

38 *EW* 41; *GS* 2: 45 ("Wir brauchen eine schöne und freie Gemeinschaft, damit das Allgemeine auszusprechen sei, ohne gemein zu werden. Diese Möglichkeit haben wir noch nicht und die wollen wir uns schaffen. Wir scheuen uns nicht, zu sagen, daß wir noch trivial sein müssen, wenn wir von diesem Jugendlichen reden. (Oder wir müssen eine weltfremde akademische oder eine ästhetische Geste annehmen.) Noch sind wir so unkultiviert in unserm Gemeinschaftlichen, daß Ehrlichkeit banal wirkt").

39 Benjamin's punning play on **Gemeinschaft** (community), *das Allgemeine* (the universal) and **gemein** (base or common) is untranslatable but echoes, perhaps, the discussion of the noble and the common (*"Edel und Gemein"*) in §3 of the First Book of *The Gay Science (Die fröhliche Wissenschaft)*.

40 Building on the work of Werner Hamacher, Jan Siebers has identified nonspeaking (*Schweigen*), forgetting and the general strike as analogous forms of productive passivity in Benjamin. Jan Siebers, "Schweigen, Streiken, Vergessen: Zur Aktivierung durch Passivierung bei Walter Benjamin," in *Theorien der Passivität*, ed. Kathrin Busch and Helmut Draxler (Paderborn: Wilhelm Fink, 2013), 216–35. See also Werner Hamacher, "Afformativ, Streik," in *Was heißt "Darstellen"?*, ed. Christiaan L. Hart Nibbrig (Frankfurt am Main: Suhrkamp, 1994), 340–71; "Afformative, Strike: Benjamin's 'Critique of Violence'," trans. Dana Hollander, in *Walter Benjamin's Philosophy: Destruction and Experience*, ed. Andrew Benjamin and Peter Osborne (Manchester: Clinamen Press, 2000), 110–38.

41 Nietzsche, *Unfashionable Observations*, 165; *KSA* 331 ("[S]elbst keinen Begriff, kein Parteiwort aus den umlaufenden Wort- und Begriffsmünzen der Gegenwart zur Bezeichnung ihres Wesens [zu] gebrauchen").

42 *GS* 2: 64. My translation ("wären meine Worte hier allzu sicher, allzu genau, sie würden dem, was ich sagte, widersprechen. Denn das Jugendbewußtsein ist etwas Werdendes in uns").

43 McFarland, *Constellation*, 24.

44 Felman, "Benjamin's Silence," 202.

45 *EW* 208; *GS* 2: 86 ("Ohne dies wird keine Erneuerung [des] Lebens [der Jugend] möglich sein: ohne die Klage um versäumte Größe"). Translation modified. While a necessary investigation of the broader implications for Benjamin's language philosophy unfortunately remains beyond the grasp of the present inquiry, the coincidence of lamentation and silence in Benjamin's "On Language as Such and on the Language of Man" is notable (see *SW* 1: 73; *GS* 2: 155). Felman connects the association between lamentation and silence specifically to Benjamin's traumatic inability to narrate the suicide of his young friend Fritz Heinle, discussed more extensively by Caroline Sautner. See Caroline Sautner, "The Ghost of the Poet: Lament in Walter Benjamin's Early Poetry, Theory and Translation," in Ilit Ferber and Paula Schwebel, ed., *Lament in Jewish Thought: Philosophical, Theological and Literary Perspectives* (Berlin: De Gruyter, 2014), 205–20, especially 219. Eiland and Jennings also draw a parallel between the language essay and Benjamin's "Metaphysics of Youth,"

noting that the later text seems to take up the earlier distinction between "two conceptions of language, one dominated by 'silence,' the other by 'words.'... In his 1916 [language] essay ... Benjamin distinguishes in the same terms between nature and humanity." *A Critical Life*, 5–78. Perhaps, youth, aligned with the natural in both Benjamin and Nietzsche, similarly laments its own fall into language.

7

Silence, Medium, Transmission: Benjamin's Metaphysics of Language and Youth

Adi Nester

Neither youth movements nor communities of learning open Benjamin's 1914 essay "The Metaphysics of Youth," but rather "the conversation." The conversation—namely, the exchange between a speaker, who blasphemes language, and a silent listener, who redemptively holds "true language in readiness"[1]—lays the groundwork for a metaphysical theory of language that Benjamin will present two years later in his language treatise "On Language as Such and on the Language of Man." Yet its significance to Benjamin's thought on youth seems opaque. Why does Benjamin approach the idea of youth via his thinking of language? The underlying claim in the essay "On Language as Such" that all beings partake in language, together with Benjamin's later push towards a concept of knowledge that is derived from the reflection on its linguistic nature in his essay "On the Program of the Coming Philosophy" (1918), indeed suggests that everything can and should be considered through the prism of language. However, the relevance of language to youth here extends beyond these general claims.

Benjamin was, in fact, not the only one to relate youth to language. In 1918, a few years after he had written the bulk of his essays on youth and pedagogy, his then already close friend Gershom Scholem expressed an affinity between youth and language in his "Notes on the Idea of the Youth's Life": "Our youth has no language," Scholem lamented and continued to explain: "It leads an imaginary being, a being in the sphere of semblance and idle chatter ... It is immediately clear that that which we require is a *center* around which the totality of our lives can revolve and from which it can obtain its form."[2] Scholem's search for youth's language—what he later in the essay also designated a *Grundlage*—was a search for a certain form that corresponds with youth. And while his views on youth diverged significantly from those of Benjamin's, the two thinkers shared the same desire to identify the formal principles of this elusive concept. For Benjamin, the kinship between youth and language was mutually beneficial. While the liminal position of youth in the last days of the Wilhelmine era contributed to the articulation of a metaphysical theory of language that exceeds instrumental communication and judgment, an extended view of language in turn allowed Benjamin to think of youth and its education in the context of the conflict between form and freedom, institutional structure and the potentiality of an undefined and formless future.

Situating Benjamin's early writings on youth and pedagogy in relation to his later oeuvre has proven a challenge to Benjamin scholarship. Adorno's condemning evaluation of this corpus as "the psychosocial aberrations of an isolated genius frantically searching for a collective"[3] did not do much to encourage views of continuity between these essays and Benjamin's later work.[4] When such connections were outlined, the early writings were considered undeveloped kernels of later ideas.[5] While the present study does not wish to advance the claim of an overarching unity in Benjamin's work as a whole, it does acknowledge the pertinence of the early essays on youth and pedagogy to his thought on language in a way that exceeds mere inchoate intimations. The following deliberations are in no way exhaustive. Rather, by locating the affinity between Benjamin's reflections on youth and language at the crossroads of three theoretical principles—silence, medium, and transmission—these deliberations mark a preliminary effort to identify an elaborate pedagogical thinking at the foundation of Benjamin's much-discussed theory of language.

Silence

The silence of youth and the absence of a language capable of giving youth an expression were not solely theoretical problems during Benjamin's early years. Around the turn of the century, youth occupied a unique position vis-à-vis bourgeois society. As Johannes Steizinger explains, this position was dictated to a great extent by youth's exclusion from the adult work sphere and thereby from a capitalist reality against whose predetermined material and instrumental values youth was situated.[6] In works like Nietzsche's "On the Uses and Disadvantages of History for Life" (1874) and Frank Wedekind's *Spring Awakening* (1891), youth was regarded as a symbol for an ideal, alternative society to come as well as for a revolt against established institutions—primarily the conservative, patriarchal structures of the Wilhelmine era—precisely due to a certain indeterminacy attributed to youth on account of its liminal position.[7] Yet from both social and legal perspectives, the representation of a potential for renewal did not translate into any special privileges. On the contrary, during Benjamin's school years, youth was considered entirely passive if not oppressed. Being *unmündig* (underage) in the German Empire denoted a very direct correspondence between youth and the absence of language.[8] In addition to being entirely subordinated to their parents in the eyes of the state, students and minors under the age of twenty-one were also deprived of certain fundamental rights including the right to form associations and hold public gatherings independently, as well as the freedom to express opinions publicly.[9]

Youth's silence, its yearning for a language otherwise denied it by society and the state, was therefore first and foremost the product of an immediate predicament. Youth movements were conceived as outlets for a youth that was excluded from the adult linguistic sphere. This was the case, for example, with the "Youth Culture Movement" (*Jugendkulturbewegung*), which Benjamin, inspired by his charismatic teacher at the time, Gustav Wyneken, joined at the age of sixteen. Passionate calls for educational reforms like the ones found in Benjamin's essays "The School Reform: A Cultural Movement" (1912) and "Teaching and Valuation" (1913) were likewise attempts to rethink the educational system in a way that will allow more freedom for youth to find its own expression. In the same vein was the First German Youth Congress (*Erster Freideutscher Jugendtag*), which took place in October 1913 with the aim of promoting self-education for youth in autonomous communities. Benjamin's report from the summit, "Youth was Silent," published the same month under the pseudonym "Ardor" in the radical expressionist journal *Die Aktion*, attests that in his eyes, finding a language for youth was not a task that could be simply carried out in one sitting: "Youth was silent.—It had not yet the intuition before which the great age complex breaks down. That mighty ideology: experience—maturity—reason the good will of adults. It was not perceived at the Youth Congress and was not overthrown."[10]

With the advent of the war, an additional meaning attached itself to youth's silence in Benjamin's writing. Next to the preexisting melancholy of youth's entrapment by the adult ideology of experience and reason, silence was assigned the melancholy of speechlessness in the face of unspeakable terror. Benjamin recalled this years later in his essay "The Storyteller" (1936): "Wasn't it noticeable at the end of the war that men who returned from the battlefield had grown silent—not richer but poorer in communicable experience?"[11] Benjamin encountered melancholic silence both collectively and privately through the double suicide of his close friend Fritz Heinle and Heinle's girlfriend Rika Seligson. The event, which had an immense impact on Benjamin, occurred several days after the outbreak of the war, presumably out of despair in the face of its imminent, devastating outcome. The silence of Heinle's suicide was perceived by Benjamin and his friends as a kind of protest, the only possible response to the horrors of a raging war that exceeded any conventional notion of language.[12] For Benjamin, it also marked the beginning of a prolonged period of silent inactivity which was resolved only in the winter of 1915 with the philosophical-literary essay "Two Poems by Friedrich Hölderlin."[13]

These experiences should not be excluded from a consideration of the connection that Benjamin drew a year later between silence and melancholy in his essay "On Language as Such." The metaphysical theory of language that Benjamin put forth in 1916 no longer considered man as the sole linguistic being. By claiming that everything partakes in language—not just humanity but nature and the inanimate world as well—Benjamin unfettered language from the accepted notion of articulate communications. This reframing of language indicated that silence or muteness as the expression of nature, rather than serving as its opposite or absence, was now a part of language. Benjamin's retelling of the biblical account of creation from the perspective of language attributed melancholy to nature whose silence, denoting an imperfect degree of expression, was consequently dependent on man's naming—a translation from the silent language of nature to that of sound—to become fully known: "Because she is mute, nature mourns ... To be named—even when the namer is godlike and blissful—perhaps always remains an intimation of mourning."[14]

It is no coincidence that the hierarchy between man and nature, born of nature's muteness and man's capacity to name, corresponds with a particular gendered division. Here, the grammatical genus of nature and youth in the German language is significant. *Die Natur* (nature), just like *die Jugend* (youth), are depicted as feminine and silent, dependent on the sounding, masculine expression of man or the adult.[15] This gendered division also plays an important role in the conversation that opens "The Metaphysic of Youth." Yet, as we will see, it is far from denoting a one-sided dependency. This becomes clear when we examine the interaction between nature and man leading to the act of naming in "On Language as Such." On this account, silence is in no way an absorbent passivity. For in order to name nature, that is, in order to allow man to gain true knowledge (*Erkenntnis*) of nature, nature has to communicate itself to man with its silence. "[I]f the lamp and the mountain and the fox did not communicate themselves to man, how should he be able to name them?"[16] If naming is presented here as the attainment of true or absolute knowledge, a knowledge that reaches beyond the superficial capacities of judgment, then Benjamin informs us that its source is not man, the naming being. Rather, knowledge reaches man by way of nature's silent communication. Moreover, nature's communicating silence is not only what fundamentally enables man to fulfill nature's own drive towards expression and in turn grant man access to true knowledge. Man's mental being, man's own essence as name-giver, is fulfilled only when nature assists him in naming her.

We find an earlier version of the exchange between man and nature in the enigmatic opening of Benjamin's "Metaphysics of Youth." The conversation (*Das Gespräch*) there consists of two parties, one who speaks and one who is silent. In this account, the roles of the two are reversed in terms of productivity. The speaker, the one who "sinks the memory of his strength in words,"[17] is described as the unproductive party. Rather than generate meaning through verbalizing, he abuses language and in fact receives true meaning from the silent one, the listener, who is the "unappropriated source of meaning [*die ungefaßte Quelle des Sinns*]."[18] True meaning, and with it an idea of true language (what Benjamin here calls *wahre Sprache*, a precursor to his notion of *reine Sprache*—pure language—that appears in his later essays on language) is beholden to the silence of the listener. The latter leads the conversation "to the edge of language [*zum Rande der Sprache*]"[19] and thereby intimates the existence of an ideal, non-instrumental notion of language.

The conversation requires both parties—speaker and listener.[20] Benjamin indicates that the listener, too, relies on the speaker whose task is to seek forms in which the listener can be revealed. The process that is described is a cyclical one. The speaker blasphemously transmits words to the listener, who in silence produces meaning. The speaker thereafter moves to occupy the position of the receiver by being the first auditor (*Lauscher*) of "the silence of a new language."[21] Yet the conjuring of a new language, a *wahre Sprache*, through the conversation is the result of the listener's refusal to verbalize—that is, the refusal to communicate in the same manner as the speaker. By refraining from articulation, the listener pushes the conversation to confront its own limit, namely, the threshold between the realms of the articulated and the ineffable. The ideal *wahre Sprache*, then, never truly materializes in the conversation; we are made aware of its potential for existence only through non-articulation, since what is articulated—the words of the speaker—is always that which has already been in existence and can never serve as a vessel for a new language that is to come.[22]

While silence had its melancholic aspects—from the insurmountable gap between the adult's language and youth's expressive needs to the collective silence of an entire generation in the face of the war—it nevertheless did not present itself to Benjamin as complete passivity, lack, or absence. The productivity of silence is already fully expressed in "Metaphysics of Youth," which links Benjamin's preoccupation with youth's afflictions to broader metaphysical speculations about a language that is always arriving but never arrives. In assigning silence an active role, as he did in "Metaphysics of Youth" and subsequently in his more elaborate theory of language, Benjamin indicated that youth's productivity lies exactly in its state as potentiality, in silence's ability to indicate the existence of things that are not yet arrived. Ten years later, informed by the writings of Franz Rosenzweig, Benjamin would again insist on the active nature of silence in his book on the German mourning play through his depiction of the tragic hero's silence. In the silence of the tragic hero, his refusal to speak the language of paganism, Benjamin would identify the ushering in of modernity.[23]

Medium

Silence allowed Benjamin to think of both language and youth as openness, a way of liberating the future from a determined past. The language of youth, the "true language" described in "Metaphysics of Youth," could never be fully uttered; its essence was located in the ephemeral intimation rising from the listener's silence as the interval in which what is about to be said has not yet been said. Thus, the conversation in "Metaphysics of Youth" brings together considerations of language and a historical thinking that will continue to guide Benjamin's writing up until the fragments "On the Concept of History" (1940). Elements of Benjamin's non-teleological critique of history as progress, while not yet encompassing the materialist and messianic perspectives of Benjamin's later work, can be traced back to his thoughts on youth and its close relation to his metaphysical linguistic stance. Benjamin's rejection of the already-uttered language of the speaker in the "Metaphysics of Youth," the rejection of the predetermined language and values of the adult, is reiterated in the form of a proto critique of history as progress in essays like "The Life of Students" (1915). Suggesting there to envision "a particular condition in which history rests concentrated, as in a focal point,"[24] Benjamin likens the learning period of university students to that same ephemeral silence that constitutes his metaphysical conversation. Both conceptions critique the idea of youth as a delineated interval externally defined, as well as the complementing conception that the period of youth functions as a means to attaining a fully articulated adulthood. What allows Benjamin to dismiss such conceptions is his new imagining of youth as a unique mode of existence: as potentiality.

A look at Giorgio Agamben's penetrating account in *Potentialities*, itself the product of an ongoing engagement with Benjamin's thought, helps clarify this further. In his own deliberations, Agamben returns to the discussion of potentiality in Aristotle's *Metaphysics*. One of the first distinctions he notes, following Aristotle, is that between the generic potentiality of a child and the existing potentiality of one who already possesses a certain knowledge or faculty within them. "The child, Aristotle says, is potential in the sense that he must suffer an alteration (a becoming other) through learning."[25] The potentiality that interests Aristotle, according to Agamben, is not that of the child, who, by acquiring knowledge, is transformed into something beyond itself.

Aristotle's discussion pertains rather to potentiality insofar as it points to a capacity that is already encompassed within a certain being, a potentiality that, when it is fulfilled as actuality, does not entail that "becoming other": "Whoever already possesses knowledge, by contrast, is not obliged to suffer an alteration; he is instead potential, Aristotle says, thanks to a *hexis*, a 'having,' on the basis of which he can also *not* bring his knowledge into actuality."[26] Contrary as it may sound, Benjamin's notion of youth as potentiality is not that of the child who awaits alteration through knowledge in Aristotle's distinction. Youth for Benjamin is a stable category in the sense that its potentiality relates to something that is immanent to it. For this reason, Benjamin refuses to regard youth in terms of what is to follow, as a gateway or a means to achieving adulthood, that which is outside of or beyond youth.

This is what stood behind Benjamin's wish to identify the inner unity of student life in 1915. Exceeding the bounds of a traditional call for educational reform, "The Life of Students" critiques a prevalent conception of the time students spend at the university as a waiting period on the way to acquiring a vocation and integrating into the bourgeois familial order. The degradation of scholarship (*Wissenschaft*) into vocational training—"The perversion of the creative spirit [*Schöpfergeist*] into the vocational spirit [*Berufsgeist*]"[27]—according to Benjamin, not only meant the rigidification and reduction of autonomous, scholarly life to an institutional prescription of instrumental knowledge resulting in a problematic social reproduction. It also indicated that the temporary period of student existence could be considered only in terms of the awaited societal integration that followed.[28] The close relation that Benjamin found between spiritual and physical creation (*Schöpfung / Zeugung*) as the intertwined roles of Eros and scholarship prompted an equivalent view of the erotic existence of students, which Benjamin's time understood as a temporary period of ostensible freedom before marriage:[29]

> Just as the vocational ideology of the professions fetters the intellectual conscience, as though it were the most natural thing in the world, so the concept of marriage, the idea of the family, weighs upon *eros* with the force of an obscure convention. *Eros* seems to have vanished from an epoch that extends, empty and undefined, between being the son in a family and being the father in a family.[30]

A few sentences later, Benjamin adds:

> German students are ... obsessed with the idea that they should relish their youth. That entirely irrational period of waiting for employment and marriage had to be given some sort of content, and it had to be a playful, pseudo-romantic one that would help pass the time.[31]

In other words, whereas student life was considered a means to a particular end that delineated youth from the outside, be it marriage or vocation, Benjamin was looking to define student life on its own terms. Finding its inner unity meant thinking of this existence as what Benjamin would later, in his 1921 essay "Critique of Violence," call "pure means," independent of an end.[32]

Youth's inner unity in Benjamin's writings is directly related to its form as potentiality. Considering youth without recourse to an eventual alteration, a "turning other," was possible since Benjamin's observations concentrated exactly on what youth had *not* accomplished or experienced: on youth's silent yet decidedly non-passive inactivity. "The adult has always already experienced [*erlebt*] everything: youth, ideals, hopes, woman ... We have not yet experienced [*erfuhren*] anything."[33] To conceive of its inner unity, one cannot consider youth in terms of what it is destined to accomplish as an adult; rather, one has to isolate and examine youth's current inactivity as such. The same tension of non-passive inactivity guides Agamben's reflections on potentiality. Potential, Agamben emphasizes, is not simply the negation of activity. If we follow Aristotle's focus on potentiality as the possession of a faculty, then we are obliged to admit, as Agamben points out, that potential is not a simple privation, simple inactivity, or simple non-Being. It is rather "*the existence of non-Being, the presence of an absence.*"[34] Through Aristotle, Agamben shows that potentiality is always concomitant with—and in fact is—impotentiality:

> To be potential means: to be one's own lack, *to be in relation to one's own incapacity*. Beings that exist in the mode of potentiality *are capable of their own impotentiality*; and only in this way do they become potential.[35]

What we gather from these lines is twofold: potential's inactivity is not passive but active, the active existence of privation; and potential is openness dialectically, that is, insofar as it encompasses both action and non-action, or, more accurately, both capacity and incapacity.

Now we can understand Benjamin's choice to present youth itself as a conversation between the speaker and the silent one. This concurrence of speech and silence, a conversation between action and non-action (a non-passive non-action), gives youth the open form of potentiality by ensuring that it, just like the conversation, will never be fulfilled to its end. Since there is always a part of it that remains unsaid or unaccomplished, youth as potentiality cannot be considered a means leading to an end that marks its completion.[36] Put differently, we could say that youth liberated from adulthood as its end is a form of infinity since its ultimate fulfillment is infinitely postponed.[37] Searching for potentiality and openness in his notion of language just a couple of years later, Benjamin had a similar kind of infinity in mind. What allowed for its conception in language was, again, silence. Identifying silence at the center of youth's potentiality facilitated the future's liberation, by way of an infinite deferral, from a requirement to reproduce the past. In language, silence secured a place for a permanent element of inexpressibility.[38] By extending language's reach to include not only man's utterances but also the muteness of nature and inanimate things, Benjamin was able to present an infinite notion of language encompassing all current utterances as well as all future ones currently non-existent or impossible.

In the 1916 essay "On Language as Such," language's infinity was illustrated by the important and often quoted remark that mental beings communicate themselves *in* rather than *through* language, as well as by the apprehension that language communicates nothing but itself:

[T]he language of a mental entity is directly that which is communicable in it. Whatever is communicable *of* a mental entity, *in* this it communicates itself. Which signifies that all language communicates itself. Or, more precisely, that all language communicates itself *in* itself; it is in the purest sense the "medium" of the communication. Mediation, which is the immediacy [*Unmittel*barkeit] of all mental communication, is the fundamental problem of linguistic theory, and if one chooses to call this immediacy magic, then the primary problem of language is its magic. At the same time, the notion of the magic of language points to something else: its infiniteness. This is conditional on its immediacy. For precisely because nothing is communicated *through* language, what is communicated *in* language cannot be externally limited or measured, and therefore all language contains its own incommensurable, uniquely constituted infinity. Its linguistic being, not its verbal contents, defines its frontier.[39]

Benjamin scholarship has dedicated a great deal of attention to the definition of language as *unmittelbar mitteilbar* (immediately communicable).[40] This immediacy of language's communication (*mitteilen*) dictated language's unique position as *Mittel* (medium) and thereby clarified its infinite nature. What is inferred from this description is that contrary to what Benjamin calls the bourgeois conception of language, language is not a means situated in the middle (*Mitte*) between a certain abstract meaning and an articulated utterance that are both external to language. Benjamin's non-instrumental notion of language dismisses the assumption that language is a means to express an independent content: nothing is expressed *through* language, but all mental being is expressed *in* it. For this reason, language cannot be delineated from the outside; it is rather a kind of infinite medium, and since there is no external content to be communicated, what language expresses is, in fact, itself.

But there is another attribute to this infinity, and this is what unites language's notion as infinite medium with youth. This union emerges with the distinction that the verb *mitteilen* that is assigned to language in Benjamin's essay *imparts* rather than communicates.[41] The divisibility inherent in this verb ensures that im-parting will always be an incomplete action. Whenever language imparts, it simultaneously communicates one thing and conceals another; its imparting maintains its relation to the incommunicable. Like the union of activity and inactivity, utterance and silence in youth, language's imparting is a concurrence of expression and inexpression. Infinity in both conceptions of youth and language is defined as incompletion, in perpetual striving. Thus understood, youth and language are both in a perpetual state of arrival; they are both to come, never to have fully arrived.[42]

Transmission

The perpetual postponement underlying Benjamin's notion of youth as potentiality, that "focal point" suspending the notion of history as linear progress, allowed Benjamin to resist the imposition of the past and the present on the future. Through the category of youth, Benjamin was attempting to secure a future that was truly unfettered and undefined. This attempt had very practical implications since the reflections on youth's potentiality and its relation to an unfettered future ultimately culminated in the pedagogical question concerning a suitable mode of learning that will not stifle the possibility of the new. It is therefore not surprising to see that during the same year in which Benjamin was redefining notions of linguistic communication in his famous essay on language, he had also formulated a short critique on the Socratic method of instruction through dialogue. The 1916 essay "Socrates" discusses the limitation of the transmission of pre-established knowledge to youth.[43] Benjamin's critique of the maieutic method emanates from the same understanding that education of future generations could not take place where the aim of this process of instruction, namely, the aim of the dialogue, is the extraction of knowledge from the "knower" that he is already "pregnant" with, a knowledge that merely awaits its discharge (*Entladung*):

> The Socratic inquiry is not the holy question that awaits an answer and whose echo resounds in the response: it does not, as does the purely erotic or scientific question, intimate the *methodos* of the answer. Rather, a mere means to compel conversation, it forcibly, even impudently dissimulates, ironizes—for it already knows the answer all too precisely. The Socratic question besets the answer from without, it corners it as dogs would a noble stag.[44]

At the center of this critique is again the treatment of both language and eros as means (*Mittel*) to an external end. The Socratic dialogue as a linguistic event renders language an instrument for the extraction of an already-existing answer from Socrates, who, rather than engaging in an authentic exchange with his interlocutor, turns dialogue into a form of monologue. By contrasting the knowledge of the Socratic dialogue to genius, which "lives through the existence of the feminine,"[45] Benjamin alludes to the gendered distinction between articulation and silence made in "Metaphysics of Youth" and "On Language as Such." The active participation of youth's silence, a feminine silence like that of nature, is essential for genius. This is not to be found in the Socratic dialogue, where the feminine and its attributed silence have no role.

The silence of youth was indeed not without perils. For while silence guaranteed openness and potentiality (or in other words, freedom), it was also responsible for a continuous deferral of the new. The rejection of all predetermined values in the name of an undefined future and the unyielding preservation of openness through a perpetual postponement of any fully accomplished reality could promote a notion of the future as a kind of unattainable, absolute ideal. And the tyranny of such an absolute future could be just as burdensome, or even more so, than that of the past, if such a future was guaranteed never to arrive.[46] In Benjamin's early work, these concerns were articulated through the inquiry into the concept of transmission, behind which stood an understanding that a certain kind of knowledge should indeed be transmitted from one generation to another. The question Benjamin was looking to answer, then, involved the nature of such knowledge and the manner of its transmission.

Reflections on the transmission of knowledge guided Benjamin's thought already in one of his earliest essays from 1912, "School Reform: A Cultural Movement." As Benjamin clarified from the outset, the stakes of the essay's advocacy of educational reform exceeded the limited scope of specialized scientific concerns and pertained rather to broader cultural questions or, in fact, to *the* question of culture as that of human cultivation. Situating his call for a school reform at the center of the conflict between nature and culture, Benjamin intensified the problem of the transmission of knowledge and values, which is here depicted as an act of violence and, by implication, as a denial of freedom. In this essay, the school becomes a microcosm for one of the fundamental problems of civilized humanity: the negotiation between form and freedom, and the relation between culture as an expression of freedom (from the dictates of nature) on the one hand, and the danger of restricting freedom through culture on the other. For Benjamin, youth stood at the center of this debate not because it was the passive object of this cultivation process, but exactly since in his view, youth's active potentiality had the capacity to transform these transmitted values:

> [T]he strongest bond between culture and school reform is forged by *youth*. The school is the institution that preserves the accomplishments of humanity while continually presenting them anew. But whatever the school achieves remains merit and achievement of the past. Vis-à-vis the future it can marshal nothing more than strict attention and respect. The young, however, whom the school serves, furnish it with precisely the future … After all, the culture of the future is the ultimate goal of the school—and for this reason it must remain silent before the future that comes toward it in the form of youth.[47]

This stance was voiced again in Benjamin's letter to Scholem from September 1917. The letter dismisses the call to "teach by example" in Scholem's own critique on the work of education conducted by the *Blau-Weiß* youth movement:

> You write: "All work whose goal is not to set an example in nonsense." "If we wish to be serious … then today as, always, the most profound way—as well as the only way—to influence the souls of the future generations is: through example." The concept of example (to say nothing of "influence") should be totally excluded from the theory of education. On the one hand, what inheres in the concept of example is the empirical; on the other hand, the belief in pure power (of suggestion or something similar). Example would mean showing by doing, that something is empirically possible and to spur others to imitation.[48]

Benjamin's rejection of the example as a preferred pedagogical principle bolsters the critical view that underlay his call for a school reform a few years earlier. Teaching by example presupposed imitation as the historical principle that marked the transmission of knowledge through the generations. In Benjamin's communication to Scholem, the critique of this model receives an additional elucidation: education consisting of the transmission of knowledge as the established example is flawed because it assumes that any knowledge that is legitimate (any knowledge that merits transmission) is grounded in the empirical. Seen in this light, we are obliged to understand Benjamin's critique of the Kantian conception of knowledge written around the same time not only in terms of Benjamin's wish to assert the linguistic nature of philosophical inquiries into knowledge, but also in the context of lingering pedagogical concerns.

The aim of the 1918 essay "On the Program of the Coming Philosophy" was to lay out a plan for a future philosophy, which would expand Kant's corresponding concepts of experience and knowledge while still retaining the foundational structure of his system. Elaborating on remarks made the previous year in a fragment on experience and knowledge (*Erfahrung und Erkenntnis*), Benjamin critiqued Kant's exclusion of metaphysics as a form of experience from the definition of knowledge. As Benjamin explains, Kant, in his definition, was interested only in a knowledge whose certainty and integrity were supported by the senses. Such knowledge related only to domains of experience that were perceived empirically and bound to the pure intuitions of space and time. Experiences that were ephemeral and transient were thus excluded from Kant's concept of knowledge, which was, as Benjamin notes, grounded in mathematics.[49] The pedagogical question regarding teaching by empirical example, which Benjamin was evaluating at the time, explains why he saw it necessary to add this correction to what he perceived as Kant's impoverished concept of knowledge. To extend the concept of knowledge beyond the empirical, Benjamin called to abandon a mathematical-mechanical conception, which will in turn also renounce the subject-object division that underlies this concept of knowledge (since space and time as a priori intuitions lie within the subject), and instead relate knowledge to language, something which had been attempted already by Johann Georg Hamann during Kant's lifetime, as Benjamin notes.[50] At the end of the "Program," Benjamin asserts:

> A concept of knowledge gained from reflection on the linguistic nature of knowledge will create a corresponding concept of experience which will also encompass realms that Kant failed to truly systematize. The realm of religion should be mentioned as the foremost of these.[51]

And indeed, with its religious disposition, the 1916 essay on language already evinces an extensive transformation of a linguistically considered concept of knowledge, which turns from judgment to naming. The remainder of Benjamin's conclusion in the "Program," however, points to something that was only hinted at in 1916 but is in fact essential to any consideration of knowledge that also speaks to pedagogical concerns: the question of transmission. The demand upon the coming philosophy, Benjamin concludes, is to "create on the basis of a Kantian system a concept of knowledge to which a concept of experience corresponds, the knowledge of which is teachings [*Lehre*]."[52] Benjamin's choice to designate the new corresponding concepts of knowledge and experience as *Lehre* is significant. As Scholem recalls, *Lehre* featured prominently in Benjamin's thought during those years as a term located somewhere between instruction and doctrine following the Hebrew *Torah*.[53] The relation of knowledge to *Lehre* allowed Benjamin to formulate the need for a new conception not simply of knowledge as such but of knowledge in transmission. For *Lehre* interested Benjamin not as the rigidity of a religious dogma but rather as the question: what can be transmitted as a kind of tradition from one generation to another? *Lehre* thus turned knowledge into a historical problem.

While the question of transmission was already present in Benjamin's reflections on language in 1916, it was not until 1923 with the essay "The Task of the Translator" that a relation between language, knowledge, and transmission was fully articulated. As a kind of transmission, translation revealed itself to Benjamin as a historical phenomenon. For the transmission of a work from one language to another denoted a life and an afterlife of the work:

> Just as the manifestations of life are intimately connected with the phenomenon of life without being of importance to it, a translation issues from the original—not so much from its life as from its afterlife [*Überleben*]. For a translation comes later than the original, and since the important works of world literature never find their chosen translators at the time of their origin, their translation marks their stage of continued life.... The history of the great works of art tells us about their descent from prior models, their realization in the age of the artist, and what in principle should be their eternal afterlife in succeeding generations.[54]

Benjamin's historical understanding of life and afterlife in this context is essential to the understanding of the nature of transmission involved in translation. In his reading of Benjamin, Paul de Man emphasizes that translation is like history "to the extent that history is not to be understood by analogy with any kind of natural process."[55] Translation understood from the perspective of history rather than nature is non-organic and the transmission it involves is non-linear, non-imitative, and non-derivative. This recognition is directly linked to the kind of knowledge that emerges in this process. In translation, as Benjamin shows, there is no transmission of knowledge as a content that gets transferred from one language to the other and from one period to another. What is transmitted, rather, is what Benjamin called *die Art des Meinens*, language's way of meaning. This type of knowledge, however, is not something that occurs in the form of a linear progression. Benjamin demonstrates this through the example of the gap that is opened in the translation of the German word "Brot" into the French "pain":

> In the words *Brot* and *pain*, what is meant is the same, but the way of meaning it is not. This difference in the way of meaning permits the word *Brot* to mean something other to a German than what the word *pain* means to a Frenchman, so that these words are not interchangeable for them; in fact, they strive to exclude each other.[56]

What this type of transmission does is make one aware of the impossibility of translation, of all that is lost from the original sense of the word *Brot* and all that is gained when we find ourselves eventually with the word *pain*. The knowledge that translation makes possible—this knowledge of the *Art des Meinens*—is in fact a knowledge about the original just as much and even more so than it is a knowledge about the translation. As such, it is neither linear nor derivative. Translation makes us aware of the fragmentary nature of the original. It goes back and alters the original. Ultimately, it allows us, as Benjamin says, to come to terms with the foreignness of language, any language, even our own.[57]

Translation allowed Benjamin to articulate a non-linear conception of transmission that corresponded to his pedagogical views. Rather than promoting as knowledge a rigid transference of pre-established content, this transmission instigated a redefinition and alteration of what it was transmitting. Thus, it matched Benjamin's exhortation to Scholem to replace his concept of teaching by example with that of tradition:

> I now hope that you would eliminate the concept of example from the final version of your essay and that indeed, you would want to preserve it in, and elevate it to [*aufheben*], the concept of tradition. I am convinced that tradition is the medium in which the person who is learning *continually* transforms himself into the person who is teaching. In the tradition everyone is an educator and everyone needs to be educated and everything is education [*In der Tradition sind alle Erziehende und zu Erziehende und alles ist Erziehung.*] These relationships are symbolized and synthesized in the development of teachings [*Lehre*].⁵⁸

Tradition could not be separated from Benjamin's idea of *Lehre*, and indeed, a look at the concluding remarks of his translation essay reveals why. The one limitation that Benjamin places on the translation of artworks is that they cannot be further translated. Numerous translations may come out of the original but the translations themselves cannot be translated again due to a certain elusiveness (*Flüchtigkeit*) with which meaning is attached to them. The danger, as Benjamin demonstrates through the translations of Hölderlin, is that the "gates of language" which have been so widely stretched open—indeed, brought to the threshold of overstretching—by the translation may "slam shut and enclose the translator in silence."⁵⁹ This poses a problem from the perspective of transmission, which, insofar as it is considered pedagogically, assumes a certain continuity that is neutralized here. "There is, however, a stop," Benjamin notes: "Where the literal quality of the text takes part directly, without any mediating sense, in true language, in the Truth, or in teaching [*Lehre*], this text is unconditionally translatable [*übersetzbar schlechthin*]."⁶⁰ This is what the concept of *Lehre* facilitated for Benjamin: the continuity of transmission that is necessary for education. Since *Lehre* is unconditionally translatable (and retranslatable), it unites the unique non-linear conception of knowledge in transmission with a continuity that is otherwise absent from the translation of artworks.

The question of transmission united considerations of language and pedagogy that were essential to Benjamin's thinking of youth. Just as language provided Benjamin a form through which to express youth's metaphysical position as potentiality, it allowed him to articulate a concept of transmission and of knowledge in transmission that responded to pedagogical concerns regarding the cultivation of future generations. Thus, rather than succumbing to the risk of an infinite postponement of the future, youth's silence assumed agency in a pedagogical program that allowed it, through its silence, to become an active participant in its own cultivation. Synthesizing learning with teaching in the intertwined concepts of tradition and *Lehre*, Benjamin offers us a pedagogical position in which knowledge is not a pre-established content that is rigidly bequeathed by a teacher to a passive learner. It is rather itself a process of creation and return, alteration and renewal.

Notes

1. *EW* 145.
2. Gershom Scholem, "Notiz über die Idee des jugendlichen Lebens," in *Tagebücher nebst Aufsätzen und Entwürfen bis 1923, vol. 2* (Frankfurt am Main: Jüdischer Verlag im Suhrkamp Verlag, 2000), 186–7. My translation. "Unsere Jugend hat keine Sprache.... [S]ie führt ein imaginäres Dasein, ein Dasein in der Sphäre des Scheins und Geschwätzes ... Es ist unmittelbar klar, daß das, was wir brauchen, ein *Zentrum* ist, auf das sich die Ganzheit unseres Lebens bezieht und von ihm seine Gestalt erhält."
3. Theodor W. Adorno, "Benjamin der Briefschreiber," in *Über Walter Benjamin* (Frankfurt am Main: Suhrkamp, 1970), 85.
4. See Johannes Steizinger, *Revolte, Eros und Sprache. Walter Benjamins "Metaphysik der Jugend"* (Berlin: Kulturverlag Kadmos, 2013), 7.
5. See for example David Ferris, *The Cambridge Introduction to Walter Benjamin* (Cambridge: Cambridge University Press, 2008), 29.
6. For an extensive depiction of the socio-political and cultural circumstances that provided the background for Benjamin's early pedagogical writing see Steizinger, *Revolte, Eros und Sprache*, 15–38.
7. See Steizinger, *Revolte, Eros und Sprache*, 19, as well as Ian Fleishman's essay in this volume. Benjamin refers to Nietzsche's essay on history in his essay "Teaching and Valuation" (1913).
8. The German word "mündig," which denotes political or legal maturity, emphasizes the capacity for speech.
9. Steizinger, *Revolte, Eros und Sprache*, 35.
10. *EW* 136.
11. *SW* 3: 144.
12. The role of silence in Benjamin's work is discussed in Shoshana Felman, "Benjamin's Silence," *Critical Inquiry* 25, no. 2 (1999): 201–34. Felman interprets the silence motive in Benjamin's writing in light of Benjamin's biography. Her discussion of silence and melancholy is accordingly bolstered by a view that links silence to trauma and erasure, and thereby to a decidedly negative interruption or loss of language in the face of events that exceed narration. For Felman, silence is something that seeks a resolution by regaining a voice and returning back to language. However, with this Felman overlooks a positive and performative aspect of silence which takes it out of passivity, as Benjamin had hoped for youth.
13. Years later, Benjamin implied that the Hölderlin essay was dedicated to Heinle. See Howard Eiland and Michael Jennings, *Walter Benjamin: A Critical Life* (Cambridge: Harvard University Press), 71.
14. *SW* 1: 73. Ilit Ferber provides an extensive account of the relation between language and melancholy. Her interpretation of Benjamin's essay emphasizes a hierarchy between man and silent nature that carries with it an ethical commitment of man towards nature through the act of naming. See Ilit Ferber, *Philosophy and Melancholy: Benjamin's Early Reflections on Theater and Language* (Stanford: Stanford University Press, 2013). The relation between nature's silence and mourning appears also in "The Role of Language in *Trauerspiel* and Tragedy," which Benjamin wrote in the same year. This essay presents the early formulations of what was later to become Benjamin's monumental book on the German Mourning Play. It describes nature's lament as a result of being betrayed by allegorical language through which it could no longer be known in its full expression.

15 While Benjamin's ubiquitous remarks on women in early essays like "The Metaphysics of Youth" and "The Life of Students" are far from being unproblematic (one would even call them antifeminist), it should be acknowledged here that his notion of feminine and masculine with regard to speech and silence are conceived symbolically. See Benjamin's often-quoted letter to Herbert Belmore from June 23, 1913, where he distinguishes between man and woman on the one hand and masculine (*Männlich*) and feminine (*Weiblichen*) on the other. The masculine and feminine are elements that can be found in every individual. See *GB* 1: 126-7.
16 *SW* 1: 64.
17 *EW* 145.
18 Ibid.
19 Ibid.
20 See also Sigrid Weigel, *Entstellte Ähnlichkeit. Walter Benjamins theoretische Schreibweise* (Frankfurt am Main: Fischer, 1997), 134. Weigel stresses the dialectical roles of both speaker and listener in the production, *within* the conversation, of "a language beyond the spoken, which tends towards chatter." The speaker blasphemes true language by speaking. Yet, as Weigel observes, true language is dependent on the conversation. It emerges through it rather than existing as its antithesis.
21 *EW* 145.
22 On this "prophetic" attribute of the silence of the listener in the conversation, see Steizinger, *Revolte, Eros und Sprache*, 168.
23 See Samuel Weber's lucid reading of Benjamin's *Trauerspiel* book: "[T]he refusal of the silent hero to speak implicitly announces the coming of a new language and a new community." Samuel Weber, *Theatricality as Medium* (New York: Fordham University Press, 2004), 167. Weber explains Benjamin's remarks on the silence of the tragic hero in relation to the construction of a post-Reformation isolated self, who is no longer guaranteed redemption on the basis of a communal engagement through the good works. See further Samuel Weber, *Benjamin's -abilities* (Cambridge: Harvard University Press, 2008), where Weber notes the performative and defiant aspect of the German verb "schweigen" in contrast to the passive English translation "to fall silent" (145). On the prophetic nature of the silent hero in the *Trauerspiel* book, see also Peter Fenves, *Arresting Language: From Leibniz to Benjamin* (Stanford: Stanford University Press, 2001), 236-9.
24 *EW* 197.
25 Giorgio Agamben, *Potentialities*, trans. Daniel Heller-Roazen (Stanford: Stanford University Press, 1999), 179.
26 Ibid.
27 *EW* 203.
28 See also Antonia Birnbaum, "Beyond Autonomy: Walter Benjamin on the Life of Students," *Boundary 2* 45, no. 2 (May 2018): 157-69. Birnbaum further discusses the critique of student life as a kind of postponement.
29 The relation between creation and the erotic as *Schöpfung* and *Zeugung* is discussed in other essays by Benjamin from this period, including "Socrates" and "The Metaphysics of Youth."
30 *EW* 205.
31 *EW* 207.
32 See also the discussion on pure means in Werner Hamacher, "Afformative, Strike," *Cardozo Law Review* 13, no. 4 (December 1991): 1133-57.
33 "'Experience,'" *SW* 1: 3.
34 Agamben, *Potentialities*, 179.

35 Ibid., 182.
36 Weber complicates the dialectical structure of medium and mediation in Benjamin's work by showing how Benjamin's critique of the medium resists Hegel's notion of mediation (*Vermittlung*), which is the negation that mediates the ultimate identity of every being. In Hegel's dialectic, this mediation of negation has "always already ... taken place." Benjamin's medium, on the other hand, suspends the moment of non-identity. See Weber, *Benjamin's -abilities*, 35–8.
37 See also the extensive discussion of language and infinity in Fenves, *Arresting Language*, 205–15.
38 See Weber, *Benjamin's -abilities*, 14, 43–5, as well as Ferber, *Philosophy and Melancholy*, 123–6 for further discussion of inexpressibility and the potentiality of language.
39 *SW* 1: 64.
40 I am guided here primarily by Samuel Weber and Peter Fenves's writings on Benjamin's language theory.
41 See Weber, *Benjamin's abilities*, 42.
42 In this context, see also the discussion of language as possibility and as realized act in Jacques Derrida, *Limited Inc.* (Evanston: Northwestern University Press, 1988).
43 Socrates will appear again in Benjamin's book on the German mourning play in the context of the end of the mythical era through the figure of the rationalist, ironic pedagogue. See *OT* 113.
44 *EW* 235.
45 *EW* 234.
46 In this context, see also discussion of freedom and the absolute in Howard Caygill, *Walter Benjamin: The Color of Experience* (London: Routledge, 1998), 25.
47 *EW* 59.
48 *C* 93.
49 Experiences manifesting in space and time are mathematizable. See further Eli Friedlander, *Walter Benjamin: A Philosophical Portrait* (Cambridge: Harvard University Press, 2012), 28.
50 Peter Fenves and Howard Caygill both discuss the dismissal of Kant's subject-object division also in relation to Benjamin's philosophy of color, where perception no longer assumes a differentiated subject seeing objects external to her. See Fenves, *Arresting Language*, 174; Caygill, *Walter Benjamin*, 81.
51 *SW* 1: 108.
52 Ibid.
53 "In his early writings he reverted repeatedly to this concept (*Lehre*), which he interpreted in the sense of the original meaning of the Hebrew *Torah* as 'instruction' (*Unterweisung*)." Gershom Scholem, *Walter Benjamin: The Story of a Friendship*, trans. Harry Zohn (Philadelphia: The Jewish Publication Society of America, 1981), 55–6.
54 *SW* 1: 254–5.
55 Paul de Man, "'Conclusions' on Walter Benjamin's 'The Task of the Translator,' Messenger Lecture, Cornell University, March 4 1983," *Yale French Studies*, 97, no. 50 (2000): 10–35, 23.
56 *SW* 1: 257.
57 de Man ("'Conlusions,'" 22) notes the comparison Benjamin makes between translation and the Romantics' notion of criticism as both reveal the fragmentariness of their original object. He further dismisses the suggestion, following the supplementing notion of translation that is often read in Benjamin's "Task of the Translator," that translation does not truly get us closer to the knowledge of "pure

language." What translation does is maintain the fragmentariness of both original and translation. The fragments, even when put together, never constitute a whole. See also Carol Jacobs, "The Monstrosity of Translation," *MLN* 90, no. 6 (December 1975): 755–66, 763, cited by de Man.
58 *C* 94. Translation modified.
59 "The Task of the Translator," *SW* 1: 262.
60 Ibid. Translation modified. In this context, the example provided by Benjamin for such unconditional translatability is the Holy Writ, "in which meaning has ceased to be the watershed for the flow of language and the flow of revelation."

8

"In Voice Land": Benjamin on Air

Ilit Ferber

"Dear radio listeners, welcome once again to the youth hour," says the radio announcer (*Sprecher*) at the beginning of "The Cold Heart," a radio play Walter Benjamin wrote together with Ernst Schoen and was broadcast in 1932 in Frankfurt radio.[1] The announcer skims through the alphabetic list of names of the greatest fairytale writers, he randomly picks the letter H and decides to tell one of Wilhelm Hauff's stories. At this very moment, a loud knock is heard. Reluctantly opening the door, the announcer sees to his surprise all the characters of Hauff's "The Cold Heart" standing there. They introduce themselves, and the announcer asks them why they are disturbing him. Coal Peter (*Kohlenmunk-Peter*) answers: "To tell you the truth, Mr. Announcer, we really wanted to visit Voice Land (*Stimmland*) just once."[2]

What does Coal Peter mean by this "voice land"? What does it mean to visit such a place in which, as he explains to the rest of the characters, "everything that goes on in Voice Land can be *heard* but not seen"?[3] To this strange description the announcer adds a condition: "Whoever enters voice land must be very modest. He must surrender all finery [*Putz*] and relinquish all external beauty, so that nothing is left but voice [*nur die Stimme übrig bleibt*]."[4] If this condition is met, their voices will be heard by "thousands of children simultaneously," which is exactly why the eleven characters jumped out of Hauff's book of fairytales and into the radio.

Two things stand out in this grand opening: first, Benjamin is here thinking about a space in which only sound can be heard, where nothing can be seen, especially not ("relinquish all external beauty") the beauty of the world, the earth where the Black Forest exists together with villages, rivers and clouds.[5] A space that is solely acoustic: "he who strains to listen does not see," as Benjamin writes in a 1938 letter to Scholem about Kafka.[6] Second, this isolation of the voice from everything visual is the condition for children to be able to hear the story: not one child to whom the tale is read at bedtime, but an audience of thousands of listening children, each in his or her own room.[7]

Benjamin is usually considered a thinker of the visual. Taking into account his work on film, photography, and graphics, as well as the array of visual metaphors that govern his work, such as the "optical unconscious" and "dialectical image," this is not surprising. Although the latter do not refer strictly to the visual (Benjamin refers to the dialectical image as taking place in language), in the secondary literature these figures appear, nevertheless, in the context of the discussion of the visual. But Benjamin does not only think in images; he is also attracted to sounds and acoustics, and they accompany his work, though sometimes quietly, from its very beginning. I would like to take this as my starting point and bring the acoustic dimension, or rather, the idea of an acoustic space, together with what I take to be the educational value of radio for Benjamin.

Radio

Between 1927 and 1933, Benjamin wrote various texts which he broadcasted on Berlin and Frankfurt radio stations.[8] They came under several categories: first, there was the "youth hour," fifteen-minute programs in which he told stories about famous artists and writers (Hosemann, Goethe) or fictional figures (Kaspar Hauser, Cagliostro), about special, "secret" places in Berlin (the market and Luna Park), about historical disasters (the Mississippi flood of 1927 and the 1755 Lisbon earthquake, and a debate between the voices of the Enlightenment, Romanticism and the nineteenth century, and finally, radio plays (*Hörspiele*).[9]

Benjamin repeatedly mentions his radio work as a mere means to make a living, writing in a 1930 letter to Scholem that after giving two radio lectures in Frankfurt he is now able to devote himself "to somewhat more useful things."[10] I would nevertheless like to take a look at Benjamin's radio work, not as simply a dispensable side-job, done in order to earn the extra money he needed so badly, but rather, as something worth attention in its own right. I therefore look more closely—or rather, listen carefully—to the sounds of the radio, not only as voiced by Benjamin but also as heard by his young audience.[11] I take the uniqueness of the child's listening abilities to be crucial when we think about Benjamin's radio work. *Berlin Childhood*, Benjamin's central text about childhood, is the best source for his conception of the child's experience of the world: in this case, the city and bourgeois home. It is an extremely sensuous text, referring as it does to all senses: Benjamin the child tastes an apple ("Winter Morning"), smells the lavender in silk sachets in the closet ("A Ghost") and touches the inside of the rolled-up socks ("The Sock"). However, I would like to argue, before anything else, the child is a listener, not a viewer (there are numerous sections in *Berlin Childhood* that are about hearing and sound: "The Telephone," "The Carousel," "The Moon," and others). Benjamin's radio work presents us with a type of learning intended specifically for the child's powerful acoustic (rather than visual) sensibility. The radio is, therefore, not only the acoustic medium par excellence, but manifests itself also as a medium that *suits the child's unique mode of acoustic experience of the world*. For Benjamin, this acoustic predisposition has to do with a *special attentiveness* to sound, an ear for it, which *does not rush to seek its visual referent or corollary*, a sensibility that does not feel that the visual is missing, so to speak.[12]

In his "Two Kinds of Popularity: Fundamental Principles for a Radio Play," Benjamin makes a point about the relationship between the radio and other, more traditional, forms of education, namely schoolbooks or lectures, in terms of their popularity.[13] We tend to think of state-of-the-art, advanced forms of communication as derivative, that is, modifying the content delivered in the preceding medium so that it fits the new medium, in this case, radio.[14] The criterion for a good adaptation would then be to present the materials in a more appealing, popular form by way of omitting the more challenging parts; although the content stays the same, it will always be "second hand."[15] Benjamin therefore thinks of radio as a medium that has failed to realize its potential, which would be to create a wholly new type of listeners, who learn by being engaged and active.[16]

Benjamin then views the radio as a medium that transforms not only the material or subject matter itself (to popularize it), but first and foremost the audience. This is an interesting claim, since, in contrast to theater for example (with which Benjamin was preoccupied at the time especially in relation to Brecht), radio is a medium in which announcer and audience do not share the same physical space, both remaining, most literally invisible ("Dear invisible ones," Benjamin opens his "Children's Literature" broadcast).[17] This configuration is critical for Benjamin's conception of radio as a pedagogical tool: this neutralization of the visual leaves the listener alone with the pauses and silences. In the context of his preoccupation with Brecht's epic theater and its constant interruptions and silences, Benjamin argues that disruptions in continuity create a critical space for the audience to stop and think.[18]

Both the radio plays themselves and his critical texts on radio show an interesting oscillation between voice and hearing. While we might consider the radio plays from the perspective of the announcer's voice (mostly, Benjamin himself), it is worth noting that the German word for radio plays is *Hörspiele* (literally, "hearing-plays").[19] So there is an important reciprocity between mouth and ear, voice and hearing which is also present in Benjamin's critical texts on radio as a medium ("Two Types of Popularity," "Theater and Radio," etc.). In what follows, I concentrate on one radio play in which these two accentuations come together: "Much Ado about Kasper."[20] The intersection between voice and sound, speech and hearing is especially important insofar as the question of education is concerned. It is not only the announcer, the story, and the child listening somewhere to the radio: the plays have a whole array of characters, enacted by different actors who, through speech, dialogue, and noises, create a space. In *Much Ado about Kasper*, this is a space where characters walk in and move about, run from one place to another, enter dangerous zones, hide, etc. This is the space of the story, but it is also an acoustic space that opens up between the storyteller and his audience and which I will discuss below as a "learning environment."

"Much Ado about Kasper"

The story begins with Herr Maulschmidt (whose name is made up of Maul [*snout*] and Schmidt [*Smith*]) trying to convince the main character, Kasper, "the old and famous friend of children," to sit down and speak into the radio microphone.[21] After agreeing at first (Kasper has this wonderful idea that he can talk to his wife Puschi over the radio and tell her he is late), he changes his mind and, making fun of Herr Maulschmidt (Kasper's jokes are all based on word puns and riddles; I will get back to this later), he runs away from him and wanders through the city, making many stops along the way: the railway station, a Chinese food seller in the market, then moving to the carousel, meeting an invisible supernatural spirit, taking aim at human dummies in the "shooting gallery," and finally, in the most amusing scene, he runs into a group of children at the zoo, whom he tricks into believing that he can speak the language of animals.

There is an abundance of sounds in the play: we have, for example, street noises, a telephone ringing, doors slamming, things breaking, whistles of a locomotive, knocking on a door, train station noises, someone being smacked (and not once!), the bells of the carousel, shots, wolves and foxes, children screaming, cries, roars, explosions, the rustling of paper, and, of course, music. But in addition to these noises, the play also includes numerous stage directions relating to the actors' delivery: a joyful cry, soft voice, shouting, pondering tone, wail, rumbling voice, and more. I would like to argue that this profusion of sounds goes together with Benjamin's attempt to constitute an acoustic space for his child-listener. Vision has to be renounced, says the announcer in *The Cold Heart*, but this by no means suggests that the acoustic space cannot be shared by the child; it actually invites the child in.

To understand how Benjamin uses radio as a creative, educational domain, we need to ask first: what type of listening does he want to encourage? In other words, it is one thing to study the content of the broadcasts or plays (which are all wonderful) and another thing altogether to pose the question of listening. The first problem is that radio is a medium that renders its audience passive. This goes along with Marshall McLuhan's famous definition of the radio as a "hot medium," or, in McLuhan's terms, it does "not leave so much to be filled in or completed by the audience," and is "low in participation."[22] Benjamin takes radio elsewhere: for him it is a medium that, rather than anesthetizing the child, fosters his or her creativity and imagination. The fact that there is no actual dialogue is exactly what allows the children to take part, to let the story "in," to make it their own.[23] In a similar context, Benjamin cites Ernst Schoen's slogan (as he calls it): "Give every listener what he wants, and even a bit more (namely, of that which *we* want)."[24]

Let us take a look at some scenes from *Kasper*. Sounds mark each of the stations along the way as Kasper escapes Herr Maulschmidt. When he arrives at the train station, for example, we hear the locomotive's whistle twice and then the sound of the train pulling away; then there is the pitch of the Chinese food seller accompanied by flutes and castanets; again, when Kasper is at the Carousel, we hear it turning around and its bells ringing. Another interesting case is that of the fortune teller who Benjamin addresses with the long title "the supernatural spirit *Lipsuslapsus*, the invisible, all knowing, and great magician."[25] This invisible figure can find your lost objects, teach you a foreign language while you sleep, do your homework for you, and tell the future:

Kasper: If you would be so kind, Lipsuslapsus, I have questions about my future that I would like to ask [*befrage*].

Lipsuslapsus (the echo): Ask! [*Frage!*]

Kasper: What should I do with my life so that later on I will regret nothing? [*mich zu weinen?*]

Lipsuslapsus: Nothing! [*Einen!*]

Kasper: How do I begin to assess my abilities? [*zu prüfen?*]

Lipsuslapsus: Tease! [*prüfen!*]

Kasper: Should I not perhaps study philosophy? For what is a man without wisdom? [*Philosophie?*]

"**Lipsuslapsus:** Dumb! [*Vieh!*]

Kasper: But that's a difficult life. Can you live just from the things you know? [*Genie?*]

Lipsuslapsus: No! [*Nie!*]

Kasper: So I need to find a lucrative line of work? [*Beruf suche?*]

Lipsuslapsus: Work! [*Suche!*]

Kasper: The law is a tough road. I'm not sure I would pass [*wandern lassen*].

Lipsuslapsus: Pass! [*Andern lassen!*]

Kasper: I think becoming a doctor would be fruitful [*Doktor*].

Lipsuslapsus: Fool! [*Tor!*]

Kasper: You don't think medicine would be a decent life course? [*nicht sehr erfreulich?*]

Lipsuslapsus: Of course! [*Freilich!*]

Kasper: With not too much pressure? [*wichtig für das Leben?*]

Lipsuslapsus: Sure! [*Eben!*]

Kasper: Perfect. Is there nothing about life that a doctor doesn't enjoy? [*Arztes Glück?*]

Lipsuslapsus: Joy! [*Glück!*]

Kasper: Then I'll be a statesman. Do you have anything to say against diplomacy? [*Will dir das auch nicht gefallen?*]

Lipsuslapsus: Messy! [*Fallen!*]

Kasper: Right you are, Lipsuslapsus, many more capable men have had little success [*mancher Klügere fiel*].

Lipsuslapsus: Yes! [*Viel!*]

Kasper: So I guess I'll find a rich widow [*Witwe*].

Lipsuslapsus: Uh-oh! [*Weh!*]

Kasper: But then I'd have money. What's stopping me from being fulfilled? [*daß ich mich freue?*]

Lipsuslapsus: Guilt! [*Reue!*]

Kasper: Then what should I do to make money with merit? [*erwerben?*]

Lipsuslapsus: Inherit!" [*Erben!*][26]

Lipsuslapsus, of course, predicts no future. He simply repeats the last syllable of each one of Kasper's questions, turning them into an altogether different word and thereby completely transforming the conversation. When Kasper asks him "What is a man without *philosophie*?" Lipsuslapsus replies "*Vieh!*" (animal or creature); when Kasper tries out another possible future occupation, to be a "ein Doktor," the wizard replies "*Tor!*"; when he says that he has money and asks what stops him from being happy with it (*mich freue*), the wizard answers: "Guilt!" (*Reue!*). Beyond being amusing, this scene is interesting not so much because the booth owner is tricking his audience, but rather, because Benjamin seems to use this scene as a kind of an echo of what will appear a few years later in *Berlin Childhood Around 1900*, namely the child's lapsus linguae or slip of the tongue: when he hears *Mark-Thalle* instead of *Markt-Halle*, and *Blume-zoof* instead of *Blumeshof*, etc.[27] The answers to Kasper's question are not about the future or the possibility of predicting it, they present the way in which language itself replies, in its sounds and tones. But like in *Berlin Childhood*, this is no mere repetition: it opens up whole new possibilities, both about language as well as the world.[28]

Another way to think about this is in terms of riddles. Take for instance Benjamin's following amusing wordplay riddle: "An animal that turns its tail into its head and transforms itself into a heap of angry people. What is it called?" And the answer is: *Otter* and *Rotte*.[29] Another set of riddles appears in the short, outline version of the *Kasper* play recently published in German in the *Rundfunk* critical edition and which has not been translated into English. This version is entitled "Kasper and the Radio" ("Kasperl[l] und der Rundfunk") with the subtitle "A Story with Noise" ("Eine Geschichte mit Lärm").[30] In this text, Benjamin concentrates almost only on the acoustic nature of the play: he moves through the scenes in which Kasper runs from the train station, to the market, carousel, etc. until he reaches the zoo and indicates the sounds that should be heard in each of these scenes. Benjamin describes, for example, the third *Radau* (racket) as follows:

> The clatter of forks and knives, plates clash, glasses clink, fragments of a speech: Long live, hurrah, hurrah, hurrah . . . More clinking of glasses. Fanfare. Sudden big noise of china breaking, cries of anger and dismay: The sauce, my evening dress, you dumb fool. Someone's running—who? Sudden silence. The announcer's voice: . . . I know who it was, it was Kasperl who already made a racket on the radio station earlier today.[31]

The scene is filled with the clatter of cutlery, plates, and glasses knocking against each other (*angestossen*), loud voices ("Schreie der Wut," for instance), breaking China, and moments of silence. Though the scene is described in detail, this version presents only noises, sounds, and silences, not speech; sound here features in its own right. Benjamin begins the text with an introduction in which he describes the main idea of this "noise story": each scene, he explains, should be characterized by way of sound. In other words, each place to which Kasper escapes "appears" on the stage of the radio with particular characteristic sounds. Benjamin continues with an important addition. The *Sprecher* (announcer) gives his *Hörer* (listeners) a task: they are to listen carefully and follow the sounds. By using their imagination and making their wishes, they will be able to identify the sound and picture the scene. Which sound belongs where? Solutions should be sent to the radio station and the winner will receive a prize.[32]

This version of the play is important not only because its center is explicitly acoustic, but also because one may identify a link, crucial to my present argument, between the child's special sensitivity and openness to sound and the reference his or her ability to imagine and wish for something that is not present before them: the sound-riddle and its solution. Radio becomes Benjamin's pedagogical tool, but not in the customary sense. For although he deals with conventional pedagogical topics like historical figures, artists, writers, places—I would like to argue that what is important to him is not this transmitted material but rather lies in retaining the children's unique acoustic entry point into the world as well as cultivating their listening abilities, which will help them to become their own educators.

Storytelling

In his "Two Kinds of Popularity," Benjamin writes that the value of radio is not so much about the "heroes of German intellectual history ... make their appearance," nor is it about mentioning the "greatest possible number of excerpted works." Instead, a depth of learning becomes possible, surprisingly, when "the superficial was taken as a point of departure."[33] This claim is similar to the opening of the "Dr. Faust" broadcast where Benjamin remembers his history textbooks in school: they were divided between sections in large and small print. The children had to study the large print pages describing wars, kings, and dates, whereas he loved the small print—art, culture, architecture—and yearned to learn precisely what was "not required."[34] How are we to understand the relationship between the superficial, the marginal, and perhaps also the rather severe time constraints of the broadcasts, and Benjamin's educational aspirations? We could say that this goes along with Benjamin's more familiar ideas about history and the importance of the marginal in the development of historical consciousness.

Benjamin's love for the "fine print," that is, for what escapes usual descriptions of "grand" historical events, should be considered in light of what he calls "information." Radio as a pedagogical tool should not only be used to impart information or data as educators sometimes do (especially insofar as historical events are concerned). To take one example of Benjamin's unusual way of telling children about historical events, in "The Fall of Herculaneum and Pompeii," Benjamin begins the broadcast with the story of the minotaur's labyrinth and Ariadne's thread, linking it by association to Pompeii's maze of streets in which one can finds one's way only by landmarks (sites, buildings); all of which disappeared with Mount Vesuvius' eruption of 79 AD.[35] Something about the broadcast has to remain open, an openness that is more of an invitation to think and imagine than it is an occasion to memorize or fill one's mind with facts. Radio is not a medium that facilitates dialogue or any other form of direct conversation between the broadcaster and listener. In this sense it does not seem to invite the listeners' active participation. I would nevertheless like to argue that it is precisely the absence of such a possibility of communication that has the potential to instigate the child's imaginative capabilities and provide the finest soil for learning.

This brings to mind a central idea from Benjamin's "The Storyteller."[36] Although this text is not about acoustics or voice (though it refers to "telling," here the story told is not necessarily voiced), it presents a strong claim about the art of storytelling that is pertinent to Benjamin's radio work, and specifically to its pedagogical value. In section VII of the essay, Benjamin follows his claim about radio being an alternative to the more usual transmission of information, arguing that "the value of information does not survive the moment in which it was new. It lives only at the moment."[37] His alternative is the art of storytelling, characterized in this section as what "does not expand itself," and therein lies its strength. Instead of actualizing itself completely at the moment of its transmission (as does information), Benjamin argues that the story "preserves and concentrates its energy and is capable of releasing it even after a long time." For him, "This is what true storytelling is."[38] Put differently and in the context of the stories Benjamin himself broadcasted on the radio: in contrast to a lecture or other forms of instruction, true learning depends on this openness of the story, on its ability to "release" its truth over time.

When a child learns to listen, rather than memorize or simply be taught, he learns to hold the seed of the story within him or her, allowing it to ripen over time, when his or her own *life* requires it. Stated more explicitly and with an emphasis on the listener, Benjamin writes that "The storyteller takes what he tells from experience—his own or that reported by others. And he in turn makes it the experience of those who are listening to his tale."[39] The radio play as well as the other broadcasts operate in a similar way. Here, the child's imagination is given open and ample space to develop, rather than becoming dried out with too much explanation. This comes through in the broadcast "Kaspar Hauser" which Benjamin begins by saying that although the story ostensibly ends with the death of the main protagonist, it "has no real ending, so it has the advantage that it continues on, and that perhaps someday we'll [*alle zusammen*] learn its ending."[40]

In the radio broadcasts, therefore, information is not simply poured into the passive ear, but imagination is stimulated and the ear opens up to admit what is heard into the child's heart and mind. This corresponds to Verma's description of radio as a "theater of the mind."[41] It opens a space in which each listener can constitute his or her own imaginative expanse, "make" something of their own. I take this open-endedness to be a strength rather than a weakness of this medium, a possibility that the visual seems to block. In "Kaspar Hauser," too, Benjamin stages a scene in which vision is blocked in order for learning to be possible: he writes (or rather, says) that while Kaspar was still in the dungeon, a mysterious man entered his cell, stood behind him so that Kaspar could not see him, "took the boy's hand in his [*ihm die Hand geführt*] and taught him to write."[42] This can be understood as an alternative teaching and learning experience, where the educator guides and is present, but remains invisible so that the learning process is no longer about him and his authority. Moreover, what Kaspar Hauser learns in this scene is not information or data of any kind, but the ability to write, a skill that then differently opens him up to the world.

The Possibility of Pedagogy

Radio facilitates new pedagogical possibilities precisely because it constitutes an acoustic space in which the listener becomes the very crux around which learning occurs. Listening is not about the mere facts of a story, but rather, about learning what it means to be in a relationship to a world, to find oneself in it and in its sounds. Learning thus stands revealed as different from instruction and as incompatible with the hierarchical relationship entailed in the teacher-pupil relationship.[43] In this context, Benjamin represents the intriguing figure of the *Sprecher*: he distinctly does not instruct the children, and he also makes a point of unfettering himself from the constraints of the instructor-pupil hierarchy. The implication of this emerges in what I would like to call *the vulnerabilities of the broadcaster*. Evidence of these vulnerabilities is scattered throughout the broadcasts taking different forms.

"The Lisbon Earthquake," to take one example, begins with an interesting allusion to the limited, twenty minutes, length of the broadcast: "Have you ever had to wait at the pharmacy and noticed how the pharmacist fills a prescription? On a scale with very delicate weights, ounce by ounce, dram by dram, he weighs all the substances and specks that make up the final powder. That is how I feel when I tell you something over the radio. My weights are the minutes; very carefully I must weigh how much of this, how much of that, so the mixture is just right. You're probably saying, But why? If you want to tell us about the Lisbon Earthquake, just start at the beginning. Then go ahead and tell us what happened next. But I don't think that would be much fun for you."[44] Benjamin closes the broadcast with the sentence: "my twenty minutes are up; I hope they were not too long for you [*nicht lang geworden*]."[45]

A more theoretical analysis of the vulnerable state of mind of the *Sprecher* (literally, "speaker") appears more explicitly in Benjamin's "Reflections on Radio." Discussing the dramatic change radio has introduced into the relationship between speaker and listener, he writes, discouraged: "the voice is like a guest [*die Stimme gewissermaßen als Gast empfangen*]; upon arrival, it is usually assessed just as quickly and as sharply. And why is it that no one tells the voice what is expected of it, what will be appreciated, what will not be forgiven, etc.?"[46] The speaker has become a "voice," that is, soundwaves without any form of agency. This voice exposes itself in a vulnerable position: what do the listeners want? What do they expect? What should be avoided at any cost? etc. As the speaker or announcer renounces his or her authority over the listeners, the weaknesses of the medium are exposed. But it is exactly these alleged weaknesses that are crucial in transforming radio from an apparatus that imparts information (not to mention propaganda) into what I call here a condition of possibility of education.

The last stop on Kasper's escape route from Herr Maulschmidt is the zoo. On his arrival, Kasper meets a group of children and fools them to believe that he can speak the language of animals. They walk together in the zoo, visiting the wolves, foxes, apes, elephants and lions, while Kasper "translates" what the animals are saying to the excited children. These fake translations are hilarious, however, there is also something dark about them. When the children want to know what the foxes and wolves are howling, Kasper replies that they are talking about what should be done with their furs after they die: a soldier's satchel going to war, a doormat at a hunter's cottage in the middle of the woods and the little fox would like "to become a muff that a little girl sticks her hands in."[47] They continue to the apes. Here the adult ape gives a lecture to the young ones, teaching them how to behave, and in Kasper's "translation": "always act silly when humans are around ... the dumber you seem, the better." To the children's questions, Kasper explains: "If humans don't know how smart we are, and don't notice that we have a language of our own, then they won't force us to work."[48] There is something subversive about this explanation, and one cannot help but think that these are instructions that Kasper, or Benjamin, is giving the children-listeners. It is not that the children have more information or are smarter than their parents. But they have their own language, their own entry point into the world—and it is only theirs to have.

This is similar to Kasper's knowledge of the language of animals, which cannot really serve as a means to translate a howl or roar into an equivalent word. It is a language that reveals nevertheless a whole new world of ideas about parenthood (apes) and moral questions (wolf and fox). This is what the children learn from the radio: not mere information, not data or instructions, but rather a way of seeing a world. It is worthwhile noting here that the zoo scene is extremely critical, at least on the background of the usual absence of social and political critique in Benjamin's writings. To take one example, the apes find a way how not to work, that is, not be a part of the capitalist system, or, keep their own language (or animal culture) and not surrender to human language and values. This criticism comes together with the amusing ending of "Berlin Toy Tour I" where Benjamin tells his listeners to "cover their ears for a moment" and then that he has been receiving angry calls and letters from their parents who are complaining that he is "putting ideas in their [children's] head[s]." Benjamin suggests that the children answer as follows: "The more someone understands something, and the more he knows of a particularly kind of beauty—whether it's flowers, books, clothing or toys—the more he can rejoice in everything that he knows and sees, and the less he's fixated on possessing it, buying it himself, or receiving it as a gift. Those of you who listened to the end, although you shouldn't have, must now explain this to your parents."[49]

This is one of the most important formulations of Benjamin's idea of pedagogy (which he explains to the children rather than to their angry parents): his aim is not to teach them about historical facts or figures or present any other form of "information" and he therefore does not "put ideas in their heads." Instead, Benjamin he teaches the children how to look at the world, to be attentive to it—making it their own. That is, he trains their unique way of experiencing a world reveals that it is not an external space facing them but is rather created by them.

Notes

I would like to thank Dennis Johannßen, Sabine Schiller-Lerg, and Dominik Zechner for their helpful comments. This research was supported by the Israel Science Foundation (grant No. 315/19).

1   Ernst Schoen, who also wrote the music for the play, worked as artistic director for the Frankfurt radio station, and later became its manager, was able to help Benjamin. See also "Conversation with Ernst Schoen," in *The Work of Art in the Age of its Technological*

Reproducibility and Other Writings on Media, ed. M. W. Jennings, B. Doherty, T. Y. Levin (Cambridge: Harvard University Press, 2008), 397–400.

2 Walter Benjamin, *Radio Benjamin*, ed. Lecia Rosenthal, trans. Lisa Harries Schumann and Diana K. Reese (London and New York: Verso, 2014), 223; *GS* 7: 318. A critical edition of Benjamin's radio work was recently published and includes useful material, as well as important comments by the editors: Benjamin, *Werke und Nachlaß. Kritische Gesamtausgabe, Rundfunkarbeiten*, vol. 9, eds. Thomas Küpper and Anja Nowak (Berlin: Suhrkamp, 2017).

3 *Radio Benjamin*, 224. Emphasis added.

4 *Radio Benjamin*, 225; *GS* 7: 320. Translation modified.

5 *Radio Benjamin*, 224; *GS* 7: 319.

6 "Letter to Scholem, June 12, 1938," *SW* 1: 326.

7 See also Benjamin's wonderful "On the Minute," a short text published in the *Frankfurter Zeitung* in 1934 in which he describes the misfortune of an inexperienced radio announcer and his malfunctioning clock. Here, the manager of the radio station gives the young broadcaster some advice, suggesting he imagine he is speaking to thousands of people at once, yet each of them is alone: "One should always act as if one is speaking to a single person," and let me add here, a single, invisible listener (*The Work of Art in the Age of its Technological Reproducibility*, 407). On this text, see also Robert Ryder, "On the Minute, Out of Time," *The Germanic Review* 91, no. 3 (July 2016): 217–35.

8 See Sabine Schiller-Lerg's division of the broadcasts into categories such as Berlin, lectures, stories of catastrophes, *Walter Benjamin und der Rundfunk* (Munich: K. G. Saur, 1984).

9 There is another category to which I am not referring here, namely, broadcasts for adults, or rather, not only for children. Such is, for instance, practical advice on asking for a pay raise ("A Pay raise? Whatever gave you that idea!" *GS* 4: 629–40 [with Wolf Zucker; my translation]; or "Prescriptions for Comedy Writers: A Conversation between Wilhelm Speyer and Walter Benjamin," *Radio Benjamin*, 275–82).

10 "Letter to Scholem, January 25, 1930," *C* 361. Benjamin mentions his radio work in several other letters, see especially: April 22, 1932 (*C* 391) and February 28, 1933 (*C* 403–4).

11 Benjamin's radio work is relatively ignored in the literature, but there are, several very good studies: Sabine Schiller-Lerg's *Walter Benjamin und der Rundfunk* is the most comprehensive monograph on Benjamin's radio work; Wolfgang Hagen provides an informative account of the broadcasts including dates and facts ("'On the Minute': Benjamin's silent work for the German Radio," presentation from *Eye and Ear: Walter Benjamin on Optical and Acoustical Media*, open access; Lecia Rosenthal's introduction to *Radio Benjamin* is a rich and comprehensive account of Benjamin's radio work; as far as I know, Jeffrey Mehlman's *Walter Benjamin for Children: An Essay on his Radio Years* (Chicago: University of Chicago Press, 1993) is the only monograph on Benjamin's radio work in English. It provides an analysis of the broadcasts as well as a discussion of Benjamin's attraction to the medium. Other recent words include Esther Leslie, "Playspaces of Anthropological Materialist Pedagogy: Film, Radio, Toys," *boundary 2* 45, no. 2 (May 2018): 139–56; Tyson E. Lewis, "Walter Benjamin's Radio Pedagogy," *Thesis Eleven* 142, no. 1 (October 2017): 18–33.

12 Lewis argues that Benjamin's radio work poses a challenge to the visual phenomenological orientation of the child, posting the question of what will happen if we shift from the visual to the auditory ("Walter Benjamin's Radio Pedagogy," 20).

13 *Radio Benjamin*, 369–71.

14 The telephone is yet another new sound-related apparatus, with which Benjamin the child is enchanted. See "The Telephone," in "Berlin Childhood Around 1900" (*SW* 3: 349–50).
15 *Radio Benjamin*, 369–70.
16 Ibid., 363.
17 Ibid., 251
18 On Benjamin's interpretation of Brecht's radio plays with an emphasis on sound and interruptions, see also Ilit Ferber, "Interruptions in Brecht and Benjamin: The Case of Brecht's Radio Plays," *Assaph: Studies in Theater*, 19–20 (2005): 35–52.
19 Benjamin also writes about what he called "Listening Models" (*Hörmodelle*); see *Radio Benjamin*, 373–4.
20 The play was first broadcast on March 10, 1932 (Frankfurt radio), and then on September 9, 1932 (Cologne radio); see also *Radio Benjamin*, 219–20. In this essay, I rely on the play's published text but also on the only recording left of it. I thank the DRA: Deutsches Rundfunkarchiv, Stiftung von ARD und Deutschlandradio. The recording contains the part in which Kasper visits the carousel, his encounter with Lipsuslapsus in the "swindlebooth," and his trip to the zoo (unfortunately the recording is not in Benjamin's voice). Benjamin refers to "Much Ado About Kasper" in a letter to Scholem of February 28, 1933, where he describes it as "notable from a technical point of view" (quoted in *Radio Benjamin*, 220). See also Schiller-Lerg, *Walter Benjamin und der Rundfunk*, 252–69. In 2010, Tom Rojo Poller wrote a music piece based on Benjamin's broadcast titled, "Raudau um K. nach einem Hörspiel von Walter Benjamin." See Rojo Poller, "Radau um K." in *Klang und Music bei Walter Benjamin,* eds. Tobias Robert Klein and Asmus Trautsch, (Munich: Wilhelm Fink, 2013).
21 *Radio Benjamin*, 203.
22 Marshall McLuhan, "Media Hot and Cold," in *Understanding Media: The Extensions of Man* (Cambridge, MA: MIT Press, 1994) 22–32.
23 On the role of imagination and fantasy for Benjamin (although not in the context of his radio work), see Eli Friedlander, "Learning from the Colors of Fantasy," *boundary 2* 45, no. 2 (2018): 111–37.
24 "Conversation with Ernst Schoen," *The Work of Art*, 398.
25 Note the magician's name—"lapsus"—which can be related to *lapsus linguae* or slip of the tongue, which is relevant to the scene.
26 *Radio Benjamin* 210–11; *GS* 4: 685–6. Although J. Lutes (together with L. H. Schumann and D. K. Reese) has done a good job in translating this scene, retaining the rhymes, it is nevertheless helpful to see the German as well; I have therefore included the last words of each question and answer in German.
27 *GS* 4: 252, 257.
28 Another important related element is the way in which the wizard's replies constitute the very space of the booth, constituted by the re-sounding echo (an echo being conditioned by an enclosed space). In other words, there is no description of the booth; its inner space is made up by sound. Finally, this scene echoes another of Benjamin's texts, namely the *Trauerspiel* book. There, he quotes a scene from Fritz Homeyer's *Die Glorreiche Marter Joannes von Nepomuck*. In this scene Zytho, one of the conspirators, repeats the speech of his victim, Quido, using the echo ironically, with a somewhat playful cruelty. Zytho repeats only Quido's last syllables, thereby completely changing their meaning. To take just a few examples: *erweisen* (to prove) becomes *Eisen* (iron); *liegt* (lie down) becomes *erliegt* (succumb), etc. After Zytho's repetition, Quido's next sentence begins with a reference to the mistake (here, to

Eisen), which shifts the dialogue into an entirely different direction. I have discussed this scene in *Philosophy and Melancholy: Benjamin's Early Writings on Theater and Language* (Palo Alto: Stanford University Press, 2013), 149–50.
29 "Ein Tier macht seinen Schwanz zum Kopf und verwandelt sich in einen Haufen böser Menschen? Wie heißt es?" *GS* 4: 301–2. My translation.
30 Walter Benjamin, "Kasperl[l] und der Rundfunk: Eine Geschichte mit Lärm," in *Rundfunkarbeiten*, eds. Thomas Kupper, Anja Novak (Berlin: Suhrkamp, 2017), 51–7.
31 Ibid., 53. My translation ("Messer und Gabelklappern, Tellerklirren, Gläser werden angestossen, Brüchstücke einer Festrede: Er lebe hoch, hoch, hoch! Nochmals Glaserklirren, Tusch. Man hört eine Stimme hoch! Nochmals Gläserklirren, Tusch. Plötzlich grosser Lärm von zerbrechenden Porzellan, Schreie der Wut des Entsetzens: die Sauce, mein Abendkleid, Lümmel verdammter. Da rennt er, wer war denn das? Plötzliche Stille. Stimme des Sprechers:... Ich habe ihn erkannt, das war ja der Kasperl, der uns heut auf dem Sender schon Schereeien gemacht hat").
32 Ibid., 51. My translation relies on Rosenthal's version in *Radio Benjamin*, 220.
33 *Radio Benjamin*, 371.
34 Ibid., 119. A similar guiding principle can be found in "Berlin Childhood" with Benjamin's choice to describe the intimate, hidden city spaces rather than its monuments. And even when he does describe the monuments, it is always with a child's eye that notes completely different details. Another example is Benjamin's description of his schoolbooks that "were divided into large and small print. The parts in large print covered princes, wars, peace treaties, alliances, dates, etc., which we had to learn, though I did not enjoy doing so. The parts in small print dealt with so-called cultural history, including the habits and customs of people in earlier times, their convictions, their art, their knowledge, their buildings, and so on. Learning these things wasn't required. We only had to read them over, and this I enjoyed greatly... Our German teacher would say: "We'll hear about that in history class," and our history teacher: "We've already heard about that in German class." In the end, we heard almost nothing about it" (*Radio Benjamin*, 119; *GS* 7: 180–1).
35 *Radio Benjamin*, 152–7.
36 On storytelling in the context of childhood, see also Ilit Ferber, "'Schmerz war ein Staudamm': Benjamin on Pain," *Benjamin-Studien* 3 (2014): 165–77.
37 *SW* 3: 148; *GS* 2: 445.
38 *SW* 3: 148; *GS* 2: 445.
39 *SW* 3: 146.
40 *Radio Benjamin*, 112; *GS* 7: 174.
41 Neil Verma, *Theater of the Mind: Imagination, Aesthetics, and American Radio Drama* (Chicago: University of Chicago Press, 2012), 1. Consider also a nice anecdote Verma mentions in the context of the "golden age" of radio in the United States: he quotes della-Cioppa who refers to a little boy in Tampa who while watching a television story said, "You know mamma, I like stories better on the radio 'cause the pictures up here [pointing to his head] are better" (ibid.).
42 *Radio Benjamin*, 116; *GS* 7: 178.
43 In "Kaspar Hauser" Benjamin describes a scene in which while Kaspar was still in the dungeon, a mysterious man entered his cell, stood behind him so that he could not be seen, "took the boy's hand in his and taught him to write" (*Radio Benjamin*, 116). This can be understood as a kind of an alternative teaching and learning experience, where the educator guides and is present, but remains invisible so that the learning process is no longer about him and does not rely on his authority. Moreover, what Kaspar Hauser

learns in this scene is not information or data of any kind, but the ability to write, a skill that then opens him up to the world differently.
44 *Radio Benjamin*, 158; *GS* 7: 220.
45 *Radio Benjamin*, 163; *GS* 7: 226. In "A Visit to the Brass Works," Benjamin offers another interesting description of the radio broadcast's time constraints and its implications: "And we should think of our few minutes here on the radio as if they were the gondola of a tethered balloon from which we can see into the whole operation down there in the Hirsch-Kupfer Brass Works, and can single out the points that must first be grasped in order to master the whole. Even then it will be difficult enough for us" (*Radio Benjamin*, 70).
46 *Radio Benjamin*, 364; *GS* 2: 1507.
47 *Radio Benjamin*, 214.
48 Ibid.
49 Ibid., 42–3.

Part Three

Envisioning Pedagogical Futures

9

Unfulfilled Historical Time and the Self-Pedagogy of Critique

Gerhard Richter

When we consider Walter Benjamin's earliest period of critical production—the texts he wrote as a young adult between circa 1910 and 1917—we tend to think primarily of their imbrication with his sustained interest in such interrelated topics as the Youth Movement, contemporary institutions of learning, adolescent ways of being in the world, educational reform, moral formation, the erotic dimension of education, or the question of what constitutes a young person's "experience" (*Erfahrung*)—in short, what in the title of a 1913–14 essay he terms a "Metaphysics of Youth." Many of these early preoccupations with childhood, youth, and coming of age through experience and self-formation never leave Benjamin, reappearing in altered form in later works of his mature phase, such as the literary-philosophical thought-images of *Berlin Childhood around 1900*, the revolutionary figure of the child as an embodiment of the radical historical materialist in *One-Way Street*, and his idiosyncratic radio talks for German youth. By the same token, there is no doubt that the traumatizing experience of World War I, which broke out thirteen days after Benjamin turned twenty-two and lasted until he was twenty-six, suffuses—sometimes directly, sometimes indirectly—many of these early texts. After all, this war embodied a watershed moment not only for Benjamin but for the entirety of the contemporary European intelligentsia, who were pushed into profound crisis and who now found themselves living and thinking in the shadow of catastrophe. The most fundamental questions concerning what a human being is demanded to be rethought, along with the Nietzschean question of how one becomes what one is.

To ascertain how one becomes what one is requires, among other things, a sustained inquiry into the methods and assumptions of one's intellectual formation. It is no accident, then, that one of the abiding concerns connecting Benjamin's early writings in particular is the broad question of pedagogy, about which he developed a number of salient ideas, particularly in such essays as his 1915 article for the monthly journal *Der Neue Merkur* (republished in an expanded version in 1916 in Kurt Hiller's journal *Das Ziel*), entitled "The Life of Students." The term "pedagogy" derives from the Ancient Greek *paidagōgia* and *paidagōgos*, leading or directing a child; as such, it describes the methods and strategies by means of which a presumably mature and learned adult leads an immature and uninitiated other on the path of knowledge and insight. Yet there is something in Benjamin's early writings that, for all the attention it bestows on the question of teaching and guiding others, does not quite conform to this classical model of the "other-directedness" of pedagogy. For, even though Benjamin—especially after having been elected by his peers as the president of the *Freistudentschaft*, or Free Student Association—was occupied with proposing pedagogical reforms and progressive models of education for the German educational system as a whole, this formative time also was marked by his ceaseless effort at what I wish to call *self-pedagogy*, that is, by his attempt to articulate for his own sake what it might mean to practice *critique* ("Kritik") as such and to relate to the ever-shifting contours of one's historical time in a reflective and critical manner. Whereas the concept and practice of critique would preoccupy Benjamin through the trajectory of his entire oeuvre in variegated modulations and with changing thematic emphases—from his unfolding of the concept of *Kritik* in German Romanticism as it took shape in his 1919 Bern doctoral dissertation via his essay on Goethe, his reflections in the Baudelaire material and the *Arcades Project*, all the way to the late philosophy of history—his very early engagement with the task of critique can be viewed as a conceptual germ of these subsequent elaborations.[1]

The peculiar logic of a self-pedagogy places the critic in the simultaneous role of student and teacher. More than a mere instance of classical autodidacticism, in which a self teaches itself this or that content or ability, a self-pedagogy is as much concerned with the content of its teachings as it is with the very methods and underlying assumptions of how to impart that content. In other words, the critical self that renders itself both the object and the subject of its own acts of self-pedagogy is engaged in a perpetual double gesture of teaching itself and reflecting on that very teaching both from the perspective of the recipient and from that of the provider. In the practice of self-pedagogy, the self teaches itself *and at the same time* observes itself engaging in the very act of teaching to itself, constantly reflecting—what in a Luhmannian register one might call a second-order observation—on what comes to pass in an originary act of pedagogy. The practice of self-pedagogy is thus always also an act of teaching oneself *how* to teach oneself, in addition to teaching oneself this or that form of knowledge or skill. To engage in self-pedagogy means to fashion oneself simultaneously as a teacher, student, critic, evaluator, creator, and inheritor of a self—the self of a critic who engages, precisely, in acts of critique. Even before Benjamin and his friend Gershom Scholem founded the fictitious University of Muri—a thought-experiment in which they assigned each other all sorts of important posts and functions as a mocking rejection of the traditional university and, by contrast, as something of a haven for the practice of actual thinking and critique—there was, for Benjamin, the self-imposed demand to articulate the principles of any future critique through a relentless pedagogy for, by, and through the self. If the self of this self-pedagogy does not unfold along the lines of a Foucauldian *cura sui*, a care of the self and an attendant aesthetics of life in which the self serves as the creative matter out of which an ethics of existence takes shape like a work of art, this is because Benjamin's radical act of self-pedagogy touches upon a more primordial area of critical experience: a realm in which the very assumptions, premises, and basic features of critique cannot be presupposed as familiar givens but remain perpetually in need of understanding.

It is as though the early Benjamin's latent preoccupation with fashioning a self-pedagogy—even a language and a stance suited to his own emerging critical project—were an implicit response to a sentiment that Nietzsche expressed in his first book, *The Birth of Tragedy*, which, in a certain sense, also marked the birth of Nietzsche. In the "Attempt at Self-Critique" that introduces the book's reissue in 1886, Nietzsche confesses: "I now regret very much that I did not yet have the courage (or immodesty?) at that time to permit myself a *language of my very own* for such personal views and acts of daring, laboring instead to express strange and new evaluations" in terms that were not properly Nietzsche's but someone else's, in this case "Schopenhauerian and Kantian formulations."[2] It is as if Nietzsche's retroactive reflections on his first book, a book that was published in 1872 and composed between 1869 and 1871—that is, between the ages of twenty-five and twenty-seven—served as both a critical guidepost and a warning to Benjamin when he was the same age as the young Nietzsche. Indeed, Benjamin records *The Birth of Tragedy* in his meticulously kept list of books read in their entirety, where it figures as entry 835.[3] More importantly, it is the substantive impact that Nietzsche's reflections had on Benjamin that helps us to frame our considerations here. Like Nietzsche, Benjamin is concerned with developing "a language of my very own" in order to lay the foundation for his trajectory as a mature critic. Not wanting to share Nietzsche's belated regrets over failing to develop his own critical language and sustained self-pedagogy in his first book while remaining confined within the conceptual orbit of other thinkers, Benjamin wishes to devise a self-pedagogy that will allow him to articulate the parameters of what would constitute the true task of a critic. More is at stake here than the general phenomenon that Harold Bloom once memorably termed the "anxiety of influence" with respect to canonical writers and their predecessors. After all, Benjamin, precisely through his gestures of self-pedagogy, also hopes to shape in a decisive manner the contours of an answer to a related and abiding Nietzschean question, one that will never leave either Nietzsche or Benjamin: the genealogically inflected query of "how one becomes what one is," "*wie man wird, was man ist*."

Benjamin's acts of critical self-pedagogy often are carried out as much in his elaborate correspondence as in his formal works. In part, this is so because, as Theodor W. Adorno reminds us in "Benjamin the Letter Writer," Benjamin's "posture as a letter writer inclines to that of the allegorist: letters were for Benjamin natural-history illustrations of what survives the ruin of time."[4] And it is precisely this potential for survival, for an allegorically suffused living-on in a time to come, that propels Benjamin to encode much of his self-pedagogy in the epistolary form. As he consequently emphasizes in a seminal letter to Martin Buber from July 1916, "I am fully aware that the following thoughts are still inchoate and that, where their formulation might sound apodictic, the reason is that what is foremost in my mind is their fundamental relevance to and necessity for my own practical behavior [*ihre prinzipielle Geltung und Notwendigkeit für mein eigenes praktisches Verhalten*]."[5] Benjamin is thus fully awake to the self-pedagogical dimension of his writing at the time, as he attempts to formulate critical guidelines and practical principles with "fundamental relevance and necessity" for fashioning a self that is equal to the challenge of the praxis of critique. What, then, are some of the features that constitute the early Benjamin's self-pedagogy as a critic and as a thinker of historical time?

In a letter that Scholem and Adorno date to late 1916 in their edition of Benjamin's correspondence, Benjamin shares with his friend Herbert Blumenthal some of the thoughts that preoccupy him during this early period of critical self-pedagogy. There— in keeping with the conviction that he articulates in a 1917 letter to another friend, Ernst Schoen, that "[c]orrespondence is the only possible form of expression for many things"[6]—he reflects:

> It is all too great to criticize. It is all the night that bears the light, it is the bleeding body of the spirit. It is also all too small to criticize, not there at all: the dark, total darkness itself—even dignity alone—the gaze of anyone who attempts to contemplate it will grow dim. Inasmuch as the word appears to us on our path, we will prepare the purest and holiest place for it; however, it should dwell among us. We want to preserve it in the final, most precious form we are able to give it; art truth justice: perhaps everything will be taken out of our hands, and it should then at least be form; not criticism. To criticize is the concern of the outermost periphery of the circle of light around the head of every person, not the concern of language. Wherever we encounter it, it means work for us. Language resides only in what is positive, and completely in whatever strives for the most fervent unity with life; which does not maintain the pretense of criticism, of the κρινω of discriminating between good and bad; but transposes everything critical to the inside [*alles Kritische nach innen*], transposes the crisis into the heart of language [*die Krisis in das Herz der Sprache verlegt*].
>
> True criticism does not go against its object [*wahre Kritik geht nicht wider ihren Gegenstand*]: it is like a chemical substance that attacks only in the sense that, decomposing it, it exposes its inner nature, but does not destroy it. The ultrachemical substance that attacks *intellectual* things [*die geistigen Dinge*] in this way (diathetically) is the light. This does not appear in language.[7]

At first glance, it may seem as though the early Benjamin's rather apodictic sentences and elliptic mode of argumentation place his thinking of critique in the realm of the esoteric, even mystical. But when one considers these reflections from the point of view that, through them, he wishes to fashion a preliminary self-pedagogy for critique and for its attendant forms of critical practice, they begin to appear in a more comprehensible light. Critique, as this line of argumentation attempts to think it, cannot take language as its instrument to perform the traditional tasks of critique, which derives from the origins of "critique" in the Greek *krinein*—to separate, to decide, to part. Language, for the early Benjamin, is the realm in which the word does not operate instrumentally, according to a preassigned use-value in the phenomenal world. Language does not affect things in any direct manner, does not separate or decide. Rather, it gathers; it provides the form of phenomena, thoughts, and ideas, even if it is not coextensive with the Platonic Idea. The word, as it dwells in language, affirms by providing form even to what is fleeting, that is, by bestowing formal and, in principle, recognizable contours on that which, like experience itself, appears so elusive as to acquire no form. Within that framework of reflection, language does not "reside in what is positive" because of its failure dialectically to comprehend the simultaneous negativity of a phenomenon, idea, or thought, but rather because it preserves through an affirmation that comes to pass before any act of negation or critique. This "coming before" is not to be understood in the temporal sense according to which there is an affirmation first, and then, in a subsequent step, a negation to follow, as if it were a Hegelian model. Instead, this affirmation, this act of preserving structurally, precedes the very distinction between positivity and negativity. It is in the moral realm, too, that the affirmation structurally precedes the foundational act performed by a separating critique, what Benjamin calls "discriminating between good and bad."

This state of affairs does not mean, however, that language is completely shielded from the entire realm of critique as such. On the contrary, Benjamin argues, it is precisely by not coinciding with critique, by maintaining its relationship of difference with the critical realm, that language also *preserves* critique. Indeed, he avers, it is the very language that maintains its otherness from critique that "transposes everything critical to the inside, transposes the crisis into the heart of language." Crisis, which shares the same etymological and conceptual Greek root as critique, is not preserved by language in the sense of a language that would allow us instrumentally to name critique or to refer to it unequivocally by means of stable signs. Rather, language preserves the crisis that is critique in its very core. The program of the critic's self-pedagogy would thus involve appreciating—and ceaselessly probing—how language affirms critique by separating itself from it as well as how exactly this movement of self-separation is capable of preserving critique at the very core of language. In other words, two interlaced movements of thought are at stake here: the way in which language bears critique in its heart while precisely distinguishing itself from language; and the way in which language names the guarding of the crisis of critique, which is to say, how language itself *is* the mode of crisis.

In order to remain faithful to this critical relationship between language and critique, the critic must learn, in a kind of self-pedagogy of thinking and writing, how critique or criticism (Benjamin's original German word, *die Kritik*, like Kant's, always encompasses both) behave in relation to the object of critique or criticism. If the kind of criticism that this self-pedagogy postulates "does not go against its object," as Benjamin emphasizes, but works to "decompose" it, to "expose its inner nature" without actually "destroying" it, the emerging critic must learn how to proceed in accordance with this thought. Undoing the object from the inside by taking a cue as to how to criticize it from the standpoint of the object itself, the critic does not smash or eradicate what he criticizes. On the contrary, he finds the terms and logic of a certain self-undoing within the object of critique itself, rather than attacking it by means of an external standard or through the use of an instrument that has been brought to the object from the outside and with which it is now confronted on terms that are necessarily alien to it. Here, we might even say that the early Benjamin's image of the critic, along with the act of critique and criticism that comes to pass in his working and thinking, exhibits certain structural similarities with Martin Heidegger's concept of a non-destroying *Destruktion* or *Abbau*, as it would be developed a few years later in *Sein und Zeit*, and, in our own time, with Jacques Derrida's notion of deconstruction as an internal destructuring or laying-bare that was always already silently at work in the text, object, thought, or idea itself. For the early Benjamin, who develops a self-pedagogy that will decisively inform his future work as a practitioner of criticism and critique, the act of laying bare the "inner nature" of the object of critique in the manner that a surgeon attends to the anatomy of a body implies the need to become, as he would later say, a "physiognomist of the object world," in which critique makes visible the hidden tensions and internal contradictions of the objects, thoughts, and ideas that makes one who one is.

In order to grasp more concretely what Benjamin may have in mind with this program of a critical self-pedagogy, it behooves one to look for concrete instances of it in the writing that he carries out at the time and in which the actual act of critique is performed in relation to a particular idea or object. After all, to remain faithful to the ever-shifting requirements of the act of critique, the critic must not view criticism in terms of a pre-established program or ossified method that could simply be applied to any object in the same manner. Rather, the vitality of critique must prove itself with each act and in relation to each object of critique anew, which is to say that it must reinvent the interpretation of its own premises each time in encounters the challenges of a new singular critical object or thought on its own terms. It is thus consequential to recall that at the end of the same 1916 letter to Blumenthal, Benjamin notes that he recently has composed five essays, offering each of them to his friend for possible perusal. This intimate corpus of texts comprises "The Happiness of Ancient Man," "Socrates," "*Trauerspiel* and Tragedy," "The Role of Language in *Trauerspiel* and Tragedy," and "On Language as Such and the Language of Man." Two of these early essays, the ones on the *Trauerspiel*, would serve as initial conceptualizations of some of the ideas that Benjamin later develops in his habilitation thesis, *Origin of the German Mourning Play*.

In the course of the gnomic opening passage of "*Trauerspiel* and Tragedy," Benjamin unfolds a key concern as it pertains to his emerging vocation as a critic: the problem of how to understand, and to relate to, historical time. "Historical time," he avers, "is infinite in every direction and unfulfilled at every moment [*Die Zeit der Geschichte ist unendlich in jeder Richtung und unerfüllt in jedem Augenblick*]. This means we cannot conceive of a particular empirical event that would have a necessary relation to the specific time in which it occurs [*eine notwendige Beziehung zu der bestimmten Zeitlage hätte, in der es vorfällt*]. Time is for the empirical event only a form, but, what is more important, as a form it is unfulfilled." And Benjamin continues by arguing that the "event does not fulfill the formal nature of the time in which it lies. For we should not assume that time is nothing but the measure by which the duration of a mechanical change is reckoned. This sort of time is indeed a relatively empty form, and to think of its being filled makes no sense [*deren Ausfüllung zu denken keinen Sinn bietet*]." To which he adds: "The time of history, however, is something different from that of mechanics. The time of history determines much more than the possibility of spatial changes of a specific magnitude and regularity."[8] The time of history, that which Benjamin calls historical time, cannot be delimited by this or that historico-empirical event or by this or that experience of, or relation to, an historico-empirical occurrence. Instead, historical time becomes readable as a matter of the "infinite," an infinity that extends in every direction. By this formulation, he presumably does not mean that there is no historical time that could ever be experienced or cognized; rather, to open up to historical time is to affirm the ways in which this historical time remains unfilled—and unfilled, precisely, *at every moment*. If Benjamin emphasizes the specification "at every moment," this is because he does not think of historical time in terms of a differential model according to which some empirical events lend themselves to promoting an image of history as finite or fulfilled time, whereas other empirical events—such as, perhaps, what one might traditionally call historic events, including wars, global pandemics, far-reaching disasters, or other transformative ruptures of our ordinary temporalities—escape such delimitation and arrest. The question thus is not one of distinguishing between interpretable historical events and uninterpretable ones, that is, between more common or commensurate ones and others that are deemed, based on certain features they exhibit, to be beyond comprehension. On the contrary, historical time as such is said to be infinite and unfulfilled, which is to say, infinite and unfulfilled in any of its iterations, at any of the historical moments in which we find ourselves.

To learn to understand and to relate to historical time, the critic must first learn to relate to another vexing and shifting relation, the relation between a specific time and the particular event which comes to pass at this specific time. According to Benjamin's model of thought, the problem is not that the event and the specific time in which it occurs are unrelated to each other; rather, the problem is that the relation into which they inevitably do enter can never be a necessary one, which is to say the relation is contingent, optional, even arbitrary. While it is in fact necessary for an empirical event and the time in which it occurs to enter into a relation—otherwise, no consciousness could possibly conceive of, much less witness, an historical event of any kind—the specific nature of that relation is itself exempt from necessity. This relation is not one of necessity, because there is nothing in any particular manifestation of historical time that would cause the coming-to-pass of an event in the world of phenomena at this particular temporal moment rather than at another. The classical historicist way of forging a certain necessity between an empirical event and the time in which it occurred is always a gesture of retroactivity, of delay, of emphasizing a supposed relation that in reality was only invented for the sake of argumentation and exhibition, long after the fact. In Benjamin's model, by contrast, the critic's gaze upon historical time fashions no such putatively necessary relation. Rather, this gaze turns toward the contingency of the relation between *what* comes to pass and the time *in which* it comes to pass in such a way as to remain faithful to the infinity and unfulfilled nature of historical time itself.

When seen from this perspective, Benjamin's understanding of historical time as infinite and unfulfilled also bears upon the question of historical causality. While a traditional historicist account works to construct a model of causality in which historical events are related to one another in a causal manner that is, at least in principle, determinable by historical investigation and through genealogical reconstruction, for Benjamin's critical model no such causality may be assumed, as building one's account on the premise of such causality presumes the non-arbitrary relation between this or that particular empirical event and the time in which it occurs. This is not to say, however, that Benjamin's model works to eschew the historical dimension of critical thought. On the contrary, to remain faithful to the openness of historical time—that is, to think the historical precisely *as* historical—it must not be reduced a priori to a model of thought that rests on the assumption that there is a non-contingent relation between event and occurrence. Only when the non-necessary relation of the two is affirmed—which also always means only when the potentially ghostly and discomforting dimensions of this non-necessity are acknowledged as undergirding the potentiality of historical thought itself—can the non-fixity and non-closure of the historical inform critical thought in the present, that is, in the time and praxis of the critic.

If one were permitted to espy in Benjamin's reflections on the infinite and radically open nature of historical time an indirect engagement with the eleventh of Marx's theses on Feuerbach, one could also say that, for Benjamin, the kind of critical awareness that—beyond merely adding one more layer of interpretation of the world to this very world—is potentially capable of effecting change within that same world possesses this capability precisely to the extent to which the relation between the empirical event and the time of its occurrence is held open. That is to say, interpretation and transformation of the world would no longer be seen by a critical consciousness as binary opposites. In fact, there could be no transformation of the world without a structurally prior—and, in fact, perpetually ongoing—interpretation and reinterpretation of that world. Whatever change within the world comes to be viewed as desirable would be based not on this or that pre-established ideological commitment—nourished, perhaps, by a feeling of wishing to belong, without fail, to an imagined community of the unquestionably good and righteous—but rather by a commitment to keeping the abidingly difficult relation that, from another vantage point, is also a non-relation between an empirical event and its historical point in time as open and as astoundingly aleatory as it in fact is. Effecting a transformation of the world would then, according to this line of thought, proceed not through substitution (say, of change for interpretation) but rather through instigation (interpretation as change).

The thinking of an unfulfilled and open historical time toward which Benjamin here gestures in order to orient the self-pedagogy of the emergent critic could be placed into syntactical relation with later attempts to think the radically open-ended nature of the historical past. For instance, when Emmanuel Levinas engages with the specifically genealogical dimension of his ethical thought, he emphasizes the concept of the absolute past, the *passé absolu*. This absolute past is a form of historical time that was never present to itself and thus cannot be interpreted as if the key to its former intelligibility and hermeneutic fulfillment had been lost but were, at least in principle, recoverable as such. Levinas' idea of an absolute past is also taken up by Derrida, who engages with what he provocatively calls the fiction of anteriority, in other words, the uncritical assumption that the historical past was once transparent and completely present and available to itself. In Derrida's model, there never was an unproblematic immediacy and presence of the historical past to itself; rather, it is we as critics, that is, as historical latecomers, who retroactively construct the phantasm of a historical past that was, during the time that it existed, supposedly legible and understandable by those who happened to live in it.[9] One is reminded in this context of Freud's dictum that the Ancient Egyptians were a mystery even to themselves. What Benjamin's insistence on the unfulfilled and open-ended nature of historical time shares with later critical conceptions such as Levinas' and Derrida's is, for all its simultaneous differences from them, an unyielding concern with respecting the elusive and refractory ways in which the thinking of the past as historical time works to resist the efforts of the critic to endow the time of history with predetermined, stable meanings. While such meanings are said to have been derived in a supposedly causal manner, in truth they were derived from a problematically postulated stable relation between an empirical event and the time in which that event occurred.

One might say that part of what explains the desire for traditional historicism and, indeed, any form of thinking that explicitly insists upon, or tacitly takes for granted, the fulfilled nature of historical time and, by extension, its basic legibility and comprehensibility, can be located in a certain modern desire on the part of the critic to be done with the past as historical time and thus to enthrone the present as the single measuring stick of reflection. In the specific context of literary writing, Paul de Man, in his 1969 lecture "Literary History and Literary Modernity," understands the movement by which this relationship between past and present is established precisely through a gesture of disavowal. "Modernity," he argues there, "exists in the form of a desire to wipe out whatever came earlier, the hope of reaching at last a point that could be called a true present, a point of origin that marks a new departure."[10] De Man, who is here commenting on a passage from Nietzsche's "Vom Nutzen und Nachteil der Historie für das Leben," focuses our attention on the ways in which a self-distancing from a supposedly mastered and understood past is silently instrumentalized as the prerequisite for viewing whatever present the critic happens to find himself in as the true moment of a determinable beginning, what could be described as the "combined interplay of deliberate forgetting with an action that is also a new origin."[11] This new beginning, this transfiguration of the present into a purportedly true origin, requires a deliberate shucking of historical time. To return to the terms that Benjamin employs, we might say that one way of shucking historical time is to be found not in any denial or even destruction of it, but precisely in the claim that historical time has been fulfilled, completed, fully studied and understood, and thus is no longer truly relevant to the critic's own time. To follow Benjamin's self-pedagogy of the critic thus would involve fashioning a perpetually guarded stance vis-à-vis the idea that historical time, as it presents itself in any act of genuine critique, is in any way finite or fulfilled, which is to say, completed and therefore, tacitly, no longer of prime concern.

What the early Benjamin is thinking toward is not to be confused with the models of second-generation Frankfurt School thinkers such as Jürgen Habermas, whose idea of incompletion still implies the principal completability of historical time. That is, when a critic is asked to think of modernity, pace Habermas, in terms of an "unfinished" or "incomplete" project, he also is tacitly called upon to countersign the idea that whatever this historical project may be is fundamentally completable and thus masterable—it will just take a greater philosophical and political effort to do so.[12] For the early Benjamin, however, no such optimism, if that is the right word, is warranted. The idea that historical time is unfulfilled and open is not to be seen as a call for completion, the way perhaps that a magnificent historical building such as the Cologne Cathedral, following some 600 years of intermittent construction, could finally be finished in the nineteenth century. Even if the project in question is something as weighty and needed as the legacy of the Enlightenment itself, no such hope is implied by Benjamin's critical self-pedagogy.

On the contrary, it is precisely *as* something unfinished and unfinishable—that is, as something radically unfulfilled and unfulfillable—that historical time is allowed to remain open and potentially transformative. It is the task of the critic to confront historical time as a past that, on the one hand, remains open and insufficiently understood, and, on the other hand, figures as the time that is always yet to come, that is, a time whose interpretation the critic still awaits and actively works to shape in the very act of criticism.

There is an epigrammatically condensed meditation by the early Benjamin that elaborates on his conceptualization of historical time and its implications for critique. This untitled reflection—an aphoristic observation that Benjamin's German editors, Rolf Tiedemann and Hermann Schweppenhäuser, date to shortly after June 1916— remained unpublished during Benjamin's lifetime. It survives solely in the handwriting of Scholem, to whom Benjamin had entrusted it and who copied by hand a series of ten of his friend's aphorisms for his personal archive. Composed contemporaneously with the five new essays that Benjamin offers in his letter to Blumenthal, including "*Trauerspiel* and Tragedy," the aphoristic observations take up in apodictic form some of the key issues that preoccupy Benjamin's expanding program of critical self-pedagogy as it appears in the more extensive prose texts of the time. In the two lines that comprise the second to last of these ten aphorisms, the one concerning the question of how to relate to the idea of historical time, Benjamin suggests: "The problem of historical time is already given with the peculiar form of historical time. The years can be counted but, in contrast to most things countable, not numbered" ("Das Problem der historischen Zeit ist bereits durch die eigentliche Form der historischen Zeit gegeben. Die Jahre sind zählbar, aber im Unterschied von dem meisten Zählbaren nicht numerierbar").[13] Just what this might mean, and what consequences are to be drawn from it for the task of the critic, Benjamin does not say. Yet one might begin to engage with these lines by commenting upon the idea that the problem of historical time cannot be separated from a thinking of its form. The second line can then be understood as providing neither a continuation of an argument nor an additional positing of a concept, but rather an illustration of what the first line evokes, particularly the *eigentliche Form*, the actual form, in which historical time presents itself. To understand what is essential about the requirements of learning to think historical time, Benjamin seems to be suggesting, one need look no further than to the form of historical time itself. The critic will then find that he does not first need to formulate the problem of historical time but that it is always already given, "*bereits gegeben*." The critical act is merely a retroactive or delayed performance that attempts to catch up with what was already at work, what had already determined—albeit in unarticulated, inchoate, and largely concealed ways—one's relation to historical time.

To confront the problem of historical time thus is to become cognizant, first and foremost, of its previously unacknowledged and unnoticed workings upon critical consciousness. In a second step, the problem of historical time, which emerges as tied to its form, is seen to possess an *eigentliche* form, an actual, authentic, particular, specific form that is germane to it alone. This *Eigentlichkeit* of the form of historical time, the form that it does not share with other phenomena but that is particular only to itself, delimits the framework in which a consideration of historical time is to take place.

What this *eigentliche* form of historical time reveals to a critic, if it reveals anything, is that its units of measurement, its years, are *zählbar*, countable, but not *numerierbar*, numerable, and as such behave differently from other entities that belong to the group or set of countables. To suggest that years, as they give shape to what can be considered the particular form of historical time, are countable but not numerable is to suggest that they can be made the object of an activity that works to indicate units in such a way as to tally the total number of units involved; in this naming of the quantity of units, one arrives at a tallying and reckoning of a total number, which then is said to include all the elements, groups, units, or entities that have been included in the act of counting. Yet if Benjamin's sentences propose that this work of counting should not be confused with a gesture of numbering, it is because the years that give form to historical time cannot be restricted to the implicit hierarchy that makes up any numbering system—that is, to a determined and stable order that assigns years to a specific place according to their relative significance or presumed relevance to the historical consciousness. Such relevance can only be established if one emphasizes the import of one year over another, say, 1914, as the year in which World War I began, over 1913 or 1915. But such a way of relating to historical time presupposes a model in which the empirical event bears a necessary relation to the time in which it occurs; as we have seen, the early Benjamin's thinking, by contrast, emphasizes the idea that no such necessity exists. To follow the path of thinking unfolded here, years, as forms of historical time, can be counted, are *zählbar*, in the sense that their occurrence can be restricted to a definite number but their meaning is not thereby disclosed. Historical time fundamentally remains open and unfulfilled, even if its years are countable, as the question of what these years—along with the form of historical time that they constitute— precisely signify remains very much open.

Another noteworthy element in Benjamin aphoristic observation is the proximity that the root verb of *zählbar*, namely, *zählen*, maintains to the German verb for telling or narrating, *erzählen*. As the later Benjamin will emphasize in his seminal essay "Der Erzähler" ("The Storyteller") from 1936–37—specifically with respect to the historical and personal experience of World War I—the ability to narrate a story, to engage in *das Erzählen* and *die Erzählung*, is a crucial element of any critical consciousness hoping to account for an experience. In the context of Benjamin's aphorism, it is as though historical time could well be narrated or *erzählt* (which, when broken down as *er-zählt*, also means "he counts"), but never given over to a complete, finite understanding, the way that an assigned number might imply. The implicit rhetorical relation that Benjamin's language weaves between the German *zählen* and *erzählen* might be rendered into English in terms of the relation between *counting* and *recounting*, the former being the enumeration of a determinable set of units, the latter being the telling of a story (even though recounting is not limited in its semantic range to story-telling and, unlike the German *erzählen*, also can mean to count again, that is, not to provide an unfolding narrative but rather to start back at the beginning of a completed or interrupted counting activity). *Zählen* and *erzählen*, *counting* and *recounting*, *tallying* and *telling*, are the ceaseless and open-ended ways in which the critic approaches the problem and experience of historical time, keeping watch over fleeting time, keeping watch over the time of history, "keeping watch," as Maurice Blanchot might say, "over absent meaning."[14] It is with a relentless *zählen* and *erzählen* that the act of criticism is forever suffused.

In the July 1916 letter to Buber—designed, as we recall, as a kind of self-pedagogical propaedeutic—Benjamin provides us with a further glimpse of what such an act of criticism would entail for a critic and his understanding of his own relation to the thinking and experience of historical time. Specifically, he returns to the question concerning the role of language and writing in this constellation of critical issues. In order to liberate the thinking of language and the critic's practice of writing from their instrumentalist attachments, the "relationship between language and action" demands to be reconsidered. If acts of critique and criticism are to be capable of engaging the objects of their inquiry—such as the problem of how to understand the conceptual specificity of historical time—in any illuminating way, they must distance themselves from the notion that Benjamin calls "catastrophic," namely that "the entire relationship between word and deed is, to an ever-increasing degree, gaining ground as a mechanism for the realization of the true absolute."[15] As a practical consequence for the critic, language and writing are to be seen in very different terms:

> Every salutary effect, indeed every effect not inherently devastating, that any writing may have resides in its (the word's, language's) mystery. In however many forms language may prove to be effective, it will not be so through the transmission of content [*durch die Vermittelung von Inhalten*], but rather through the purest disclosure of its dignity and its nature. And if I disregard other effective forms here—aside from poetry and prophesy—it repeatedly seems to me that the crystal-pure elimination of the unsayable in language [*des Unsagbaren in der Sprache*] is the most obvious form given to us to be effective within language and, to that extent, through it. This elimination of the unsayable seems to me to coincide precisely with what is actually the objective and dispassionate manner of writing ... My concept of objective and, at the same time, highly political style and writing [*Mein Begriff sachlichen und zugleich hochpolitischen Stils und Schreibens*] is this: to awaken interest in what was denied to the word. Only where this sphere of speechlessness [or: of wordlessness, *des Wortlosen*] reveals itself in unutterably pure power can the magic spark leap between the word and the motivating deed, where the unity between these two equally real entities resides. Only the intensive aiming of words into the core of innermost silence [or: innermost falling-silent, *innersten Verstummen*] is truly effective.[16]

In the early Benjamin's struggle to fashion himself as a critic and to articulate his relationship with language and writing, what is at stake is not the communicative dimension of any act of critique or criticism. Just like in the later preface to his translations of Baudelaire's poems, the 1923 essay on "The Task of the Translator," in which no "poem is intended for the reader, no picture for the beholder, no symphony for the listener," no act of critique—even of such a crucial topic as the critique of historical time—is intended primarily to communicate with a reader who in turn supposedly expects to receive information or stable content.[17] Rather, the critic's self-imposed task is to find a voice for a certain voicelessness, to provide speech to speechlessness, without, however, thereby simply undoing or reversing the effects of speechlessness. The recalcitrant act of critique as Benjamin attempts to teach it to himself involves an affirmation of, and an abiding respect for, the silence into which every word is directed. Yet, by directing the word into the "core of innermost silence" the critic is not to expect to receive an answer from the silent realm of that *Verstummen*— no dialogue, no communication, no symmetrical exchange will sublate the critic's experience of the abyss into a more bearable equilibrium. Whereas other thinkers, such as Benjamin's contemporary Ludwig Wittgenstein, insist on the notion that, as the last line of his *Tractatus* has it, "Whereof one cannot speak, thereof one must remain silent" ("Wovon man nicht sprechen kann, darüber muß man schweigen"), Benjamin's critical propaedeutic seeks out the realm of the unspeakable.[18] It is in a permanent critical engagement with the realm of the unspeakable and the ruins of what has fallen silent that Benjamin's self-pedagogy as a critic unfolds.

The question, however, of whether this realm of the unspeakable represents a powerful potentiality for the critic or rather threatens to become the cause of his disorientation and even demise is difficult to answer. The tension that inhabits this question is to be found in the related question of how to decipher, both figuratively and literally, the words of Benjamin's passage that we just cited. Here, an unexpected philological detail assumes central conceptual significance, and it behooves us to linger with it for a moment. The first publication of Benjamin's letter to Buber occurred in the two-volume selection of Benjamin's letters, edited by Scholem and Adorno in 1966. There, we read the following:

> nur wo diese Sphäre des Wortlosen in unsagbarer reiner Macht sich erschließt, kann der magische Funken zwischen Wort und bewegender Tat überspringen, wo die Einheit dieser beiden gleich wirklichen ist.[19]

Between 1995 and 2000, Christoph Gödde and Henri Lonitz of the Theodor W. Adorno Archive published a newly re-edited and much expanded six-volume edition of Benjamin's correspondence. There, Benjamin's passage from his letter to Buber, included in the first volume of the new edition, which includes the years 1910 through 1918, reads as follows:

> Nur wo diese Sphäre des Wortlosen in unsagbar reiner Nacht sich erschließt kann der magische Funke zwischen Wort und bewegender Tat überspringen, wo die Einheit dieser beiden gleich Wirklichen ist.[20]

Not only does the later edition correct minor deviations by the earlier edition from Benjamin's at times rather idiosyncratic spelling and orthography, it also substitutes a central word: instead of "in unsagbar reiner **Macht**" ("in unutterably pure power") we get "in unsagbar reiner **Nacht**" ("in unutterably pure night"). What has happened? Could it be that one of the editorial pairs misread or misconstrued Benjamin's word— and by extension, his meaning? (A glance at the translations into other languages— such as the standard English translation published by the University of Chicago Press, cited above—that are based on the Scholem and Adorno edition also render the word in question as "power.") A close analysis of Benjamin's actual manuscript reveals that he did indeed write "Nacht" (night).[21] *Macht* vs. *Nacht*, then, might vs. night. According to Scholem's own account, he and Adorno divided up the task of editing and transcribing the letters among themselves, with Scholem being responsible for all letters up to 1921 as well as certain later letters to specific individuals, including Buber. Thus, it is reasonable to conclude that it was Scholem who misrendered *Macht* as *Nacht* in Benjamin's 1916 letter to Buber. Given Benjamin's idiosyncratic modes of argumentation, his often peculiar word choice, his penchant for using existing terms in ways that are often far removed from their commonly accepted meaning, and his famously difficult-to-decipher handwriting, it is certainly understandable how, especially in the context of a massive editorial undertaking, a misunderstanding could occur. And yet, one may still wonder what may have caused a scholar of Scholem's exalted stature and quality, an extraordinarily learned man who was, moreover, exquisitely familiar with his friend's writing and thinking, to misread Benjamin in this way. Was it a mere mistake, that is, only a clerical oversight, or was it an actual error, that is, the tacit expression of a structural (and therefore potentially more interesting) aberration? We will not be able to settle these questions.

Yet whatever else may be said about the elusive movement between *Macht* and *Nacht*, might and night, it appears that it points to rather opposed interpretations of Benjamin's conceptualization of the sphere of speechlessness or wordlessness, *des Wortlosen*. To think of this sphere of speechlessness or wordlessness as possessing *Macht*, an unutterably pure might, is to conceive of this sphere as the powerful, even *purely* (*rein*) powerful agent that is capable, via the magic spark (*der magische Funke*), of causing language to turn into action, rhetoric into praxis. As one of Aristotle's three basic elements of human activity (the other two being *theoria* and *poiesis*), *praxis* (πρᾶξις) is the kind of activity grounded in action, an action that is informed by reflection and that can have transformative effects on the location in which it is performed as well as on the human being who performs it. The Young Hegelians and the Marxian historical materialists would later emphasize this politically transformative dimension of the Ancient Greek πρᾶξις. When seen against this conceptual background, *Macht*, or power, here figures as a self-identical sovereign force that is fully capable of effecting change in the world on its own volition and based on enforceable demands. The hidden premise of this triumphalist understanding of the sphere of the *Wortlosen* is that it can serve to guarantee a transformative link between, on the one hand, what has been conceived exclusively in and as the absence of language, and, on the other hand, the reconstitution of this *Wortlosen* as actually present language capable of effecting this or that empirical change in what we call the world, a world that can in principle be shaped by concrete intervention. But the word that Benjamin actually employs, *Nacht*, calls into presence a decidedly more guarded relation to the supposedly transformative power of the speechless or the wordless. The strange and mystical-sounding phrase "in unsagbar reiner Nacht," "in unutterably pure night," suggests, among many other things, a darkness in which it is not easy to orient oneself, a darkness that is so unutterably pure, a night that is so much night that it also threatens to obscure and to conceal, to hide and to undermine. In this night, one proceeds cautiously, without the benefit of daylight to illuminate one's path ahead; instead of relying on one's sense of vision to move forward decisively, one gradually gropes and cautiously feels one's way around, having to relearn slowly and laboriously how to situate oneself in one's world and how to find one's bearings. It is as if Benjamin's unutterably pure night provided a strategic twist on Kant's reflections on what it might take to orient oneself in thinking ("Was heißt: sich im Denken orientieren?") precisely by emphasizing the impenetrable obscurity that threatens to envelop any act of thinking as it attempts to give rise to critique. By the same token, the critic must also learn anew how to separate and how to decide (the original Greek meaning of critique, *krinein*), lest he fall prey to the misperception of an obscure sameness everywhere, the obscurity and non-differentiation that is brought on by the darkness of night—a night, as Hegel has it in the Preface to his *Phenomenology*, in which all cows are black.

Viewed from this perspective, the struggle between *Macht* and *Nacht* emerges as something significantly more than a mere editorial oversight, more than a momentary lapse of judgment or a corrigible aberration of reading. The tension between the two words and concepts is lodged within the larger movement and logic of the text itself. What is at stake for the early Benjamin's acts of critical self-pedagogy is precisely the question of how to relate, as a critic, to the perpetual struggle between *Macht* and *Nacht*, power and night, disclosure and blindness, potentiality and its withdrawal. Like the one who wishes to understand but first must locate laboriously and cautiously his path in the darkness of night, the critic must first teach himself, arduously and in an irreducibly Sisyphean mode, what it might mean to be a critic, that is, what it might mean to show himself responsible—without ever quite knowing how—to the infinitely demanding and daunting task of critique.

If pedagogy, as *paidagōgia* and *paidagōgos*, figures in our critical consciousness as the realm of methods and assumptions associated with leading or guiding another along the path of learning, what can be said of the act of self-pedagogy? What would it mean to be one's own pedagogue? Would it be akin to figuring as one's own father or mother? Nietzsche, for one, expressed, in *Ecce Homo: How One Becomes What One Is*, the "uniqueness" of his existence "in the form of a riddle [*in Räthselform*]": "As my father I have already died [*bereits gestorben*], as my mother I still live and grow old."[22] In devising a kind of critical self-pedagogy, can the young Benjamin serve as his own father? His own mother? Has he, like Nietzsche, already died as his father yet continues to live on as his mother? Or is it the other way around? Can Benjamin create himself as a critic—that is, can he be not only the "parent" of critique but also his own critical parent? And is this self-fashioning through self-pedagogy not itself an example of the idea of critique and the critical act that were to be the content of the self-pedagogical scene of writing? In the third of the aphoristic observations from the second half of 1916, preserved by Scholem, Benjamin writes a single sentence: "The true aging of the parents is the death of the child" ("Das eigentliche Altern der Eltern ist der Tod des Kindes").[23] In this striking formulation, it is actually the aging of the other, not of the self, that evokes a certain intimation of mortality, even death itself. Here, the aging of the older other—the elder, the *Eltern*—is causally linked to the demise of the younger consciousness. It is as if, under the sign of a critic's aging parents—a group that also includes a critic's intellectual parents, in other words, his theoretical influences and conceptual predecessors—the critic first had to die as a "child" in order to live on, or at least to survive, as a mature, albeit forever orphaned, adult. If the death of the critic as a child names the birth of the critic as an adult, he will face the experience of no longer being able simply to be guided by his elders, that is, of being the recipient of their pedagogy. It is therefore the task of the true critic, as especially the early Benjamin helps us to appreciate, to invent his own self-pedagogy and thus to assume the place of his own parents. In the process, he generates himself, fashioning and even inventing himself out of the very act of critique, even if the result of such critical self-invention can never figure as a stable goal that has been achieved once and for all, a secured and fundamentally complacent form of identity. If Nietzsche forever asks how one becomes what one is, *wie man wird, was man ist*, Benjamin's acts of critical self-pedagogy provide a preliminary, idiosyncratically inflected response, even as they eschew any kind of identity-thinking or precipitous affirmation of a sovereign, (self-)knowing consciousness. This, too, marks the critic's unfulfilled—that is, genuinely historical—time.

Notes

1. For a reconstruction of the function and development of critique throughout the trajectory of Benjamin's work, see Gerhard Richter, "Critique and the Thing: Benjamin and Heidegger," in *Inheriting Walter Benjamin* (London: Bloomsbury, 2016), 59–100.
2. Friedrich Nietzsche, *The Birth of Tragedy and Other Writings*, trans. Ronald Speirs (Cambridge: Cambridge University Press, 1999), 10. On occasion, existing translations have been slightly adjusted to enhance their fidelity to the original.
3. "Verzeichnis der gelesenen Schriften," *GS* 7: 451.
4. Theodor W. Adorno, "Benjamin the Letter Writer," *C* xix.
5. *C* 79; *GB* 1: 325.
6. *C* 85; *GB* 1: 355.
7. *C* 83–4; *GB* 1: 348–9. Translation slightly modified.
8. "*Trauerspiel* and Tragedy," *SW* 1: 55; "Trauerspiel und Tragödie," *GS* 2: 134.
9. For an extended analysis of Derrida's concept, see Gerhard Richter, "Afterness and Experience (III): Mourning, Memory, and the Fictions of Anteriority," in *Afterness: Figures of Following in Modern Thought and Aesthetics* (New York: Columbia University Press, 2011), 186–98.
10. Paul de Man, "Literary History and Literary Modernity," in *Blindness and Insight: Essays in the Rhetoric of Contemporary Criticism* (Minneapolis: University of Minnesota Press, 1983), 148.
11. Ibid.
12. See, for instance, Jürgen Habermas, "Die Moderne—ein unvollendetes Projekt," in *Kleine Politische Schriften (I–IV)*, (Frankfurt am Main: Suhrkamp, 1981), 444–64.
13. "Aphorisms," *EW* 271; "Aphorismen," *GS* 2: 601.
14. Maurice Blanchot, *The Writing of the Disaster*, trans. Ann Smock (Lincoln: University of Nebraska Press, 1995), 42.
15. *C* 80; *GB* 1: 326.
16. *C* 80; *GB* 1: 326–7. Translation modified.
17. "The Task of the Translator," *SW* 1: 253; *GS* 4: 9.
18. Ludwig Wittengenstein, *Tractatus logico-philosophicus*, Werkausgabe, vol. 1 (Frankfurt am Main: Suhrkamp, 1992), 85.

19 Walter Benjamin, *Briefe*, vol. 1, eds. Gershom Scholem and Theodor W. Adorno (Frankfurt am Main: Suhrkamp, 1977), 127.
20 *GB* 1: 326–7.
21 I am grateful to Christoph Gödde of the Theodor W. Adorno Archiv in Frankfurt am Main, and to Ursula Marx of the Walter Benjamin Archiv at the Universität der Künste in Berlin, for kindly granting me access to the manuscript of Benjamin's letter.
22 Friedrich Nietzsche, *Ecce Homo. Wie man wird, was man ist*, *Kritische Studienausgabe*, vol. 6, ed. Giorgio Colli and Mazzino Montinari (Munich: DTV and Berlin: de Gruyter, 1999), 264.
23 "Aphorisms," *EW* 270; "Aphorismen," *GS* 2: 601.

Against the Law: Youth and the Critical Pedagogy of Eternal Rebellion

Michael Powers

In "Sleeping Beauty" (1911), one of his earliest published writings, Walter Benjamin claims that it is a "sure sign of age to see in the existent all there is."[1] To be old means to no longer desire change, to no longer aim beyond what is immediately present, but simply to accept what is as given. In contrast, he defines youthfulness in the following manner: one is "young so long as he has not yet altogether converted his ideal into reality."[2] As the opposite of what already exists, of what has been fully realized and established, youth poses an inherent threat to the status quo. This threat is tied to the promise of a different reality to come that youth discloses in continuously striving toward an unattainable "ideal" (one remains young only "so long as" one's aim remains out of reach). But what specifically does youth strive toward? Or, put differently, what does youth seek to transcend in its unflinching negativity, its unwavering other-directedness? In the same essay—part of a larger complex of texts stemming from the period of Benjamin's involvement with the German Youth Movement (c. 1911–15)—he names three main forces that youth struggles against in its "eternal rebellion": "society, state, [and the] law."[3] Of these three categories, the law may at first sight appear to play only a minor role in Benjamin's writings on youth culture and educational reform. But in many ways, the revolutionary power that Benjamin repeatedly ascribes to youth centers on its ability to unsettle the law in a profound sense.

Built on precedent, on what has already occurred and inscribed itself as rule for future generations to follow, the law marks a historical continuum, a nexus between past, present, and future. Youth, on the other hand, indicates for Benjamin a space that radically precedes the historical force of the law and its abiding unidirectional temporal structure. As yet uninitiated into the rules and conventions that govern the adult world, youth hovers perpetually on the precipice of an undefined future, open in all directions. Benjamin examines this fundamental antagonism between youth and the law at several points in his early writings, although perhaps nowhere as concretely as in his reflections on the school as a privileged site of intergenerational conflict. This essay explores the ways in which Benjamin's early remarks on the constellation of youth, school, and the law set the course for his sustained interest in pedagogy as a historico-political category. While Benjamin engages with the theme of pedagogy in various parts of his oeuvre (for instance his reflections on childhood learning in the aborted project on play, color, and fantasy, or his literary depictions of language acquisition in *Berlin Childhood around 1900*), his early writings on youth and institutionalized learning mark the starting point of a different avenue of focus centered on the youth as an anti-establishment force whose quasi-revolutionary power is waiting to be unleashed. In the following, we trace the development of this trajectory of his thought, from the early writings, through the idea of "educative force" (*erzieherische Gewalt*) that he articulates in "Critique of Violence" (1921), to his attempt to outline a remodeled, proletarian form of childhood learning in "Program for a Proletarian Children's Theater" (1929).

School Reform and Lawless Youth

During his adolescence, Benjamin spent two highly formative years at the boarding school of Haubinda in central Germany. The somewhat unique school was shaped by the pedagogical reforms sweeping Germany at the turn of the century, a phenomenon now broadly known as the German Youth Movement (*Jugendbewegung*). While the *Wandervogel* is the most popular group associated with this movement, it consisted of several heterogeneous participants loosely united through the "notion that youth must lead a general cultural and social regeneration."[4] Among those who shared this view was the educational reformer Gustav Wyneken, one of Benjamin's teachers at Haubinda and a leading figure of a vocal subsection of the *Jugendbewegung*. As has been well attested, Wyneken exerted a strong influence over the young Benjamin and set the tone and subject matter for much of his early work. Immediately upon commencing his university studies, Benjamin became an active member in the Wynekenian faction of the Youth Movement as a member of Freiburg University's School Reform Unit, a new type of student organization established to "supplement official course offerings" and to help advance "liberal educational ideals" within the institution.[5] In connection to his involvement with this group, Benjamin delivered talks and published several texts detailing his views on youth culture and pedagogy.

In one of his most programmatic writings from the period, "School Reform: A Cultural Movement" (1912), an essay included in pamphlets distributed across German universities, Benjamin cites Rudolf Pannwitz's definition of education (*Erziehung*) as the "propagation of spiritual values."[6] In this view, education entails above all the passing down of values and knowledge from one generation to the next, a movement of succession that the young Benjamin examines both in terms of the channels and processes through which such transmission occurs, and the degrees to which the values imparted are imposed upon or freely adopted by pupils. In Benjamin's view, by learning specific, culturally coded values, the student transforms from a "natural individual" into a "cultural individual"—a metamorphosis that, he tells us, can "never be completed without violence (*Gewalt*)."[7] Benjamin says little directly about how we are to understand the precise form of "violence" or "force" (*Gewalt*) at work here. However, he does present us with a vivid image of the existing educational system as a site of combat and adversarial "struggle." Mobilizing war rhetoric, he describes a "savage tumult" taking place on the "battlefield" to decide exactly which values should be imparted to the following generation. Discrete disciplines make up the combating armies in this "grim-visaged war of all against all."[8] Strikingly, Benjamin conjures the Hobbesian formulation "war of all against all," a phrase that Hobbes uses to describe a state of nature prior to civil society, to designate the state of contest taking place in the midst of schools and universities, in other words, in the midst of, not outside of or prior to, the social order. There is a deep irony in Benjamin's applying the phrase to the arbiters of "culture" and "education," namely to those charged with defining the curriculum and thus the course of education for the unformed youth.[9] The strategic redirection of Hobbes's formula calls attention to a certain violence at the root of and embedded in institutionalized learning, a violence that originates from the contested, anarchic (lawless) moment at which the battle was first waged and it was decided to teach *these* things and not others. An underlying question that informs much of Benjamin's critique reveals itself here: by what authority and under whose power does the existing educational system legitimate itself? In variation of one of his well-known phrases, we may ask whether there is any civilized education which is not at the same time a barbaric one—founded on a violence, a force (*Gewalt*) that it continually reasserts.[10]

In contrast to a top-down, hierarchical model of learning (in which the teacher or the chosen values are generally the determinative force), Benjamin promotes an alternative pedagogy based on "fostering freedom" and allowing students the opportunity to "act on their own" in actively forming the course of their education.[11] In this more dynamic, student-oriented model of learning, the youth play the decisive role. This inversion pits the younger generation against the older in a tension that becomes especially salient within the framework of the school:

> The school is the institution that preserves the accomplishments of humanity while continually presenting them anew. But whatever the school achieves remains merit and achievement of the past, even if occasionally of the recent past. Vis-à-vis the future it can marshal nothing more than strict attention and respect. The young, however, whom the school serves, furnish it with precisely the future. The school receives a generation unsure of itself in everything to do with the real and with conscience, self-absorbed perhaps and unknowing, natural and uncultivated (in service to the school, it has to develop [*bilden*] itself), but a generation at the same time full of images [*Bilder*], which it brings with it from the land of the future.[12]

The school is a virtual archive of humanity's accomplishments, a living repository that constantly presents anew what it preserves for each generation, each individual learner. In its archival function, the school remains primarily oriented toward the past, for even where new learning or transmission occurs, it is still the learning of knowledge that has become a fixed part of tradition, ready to be handed down from generation to generation, from teacher to student. The youth, on the other hand, introduce an indefinite, shapeless element into this archive of cultural memory: the future. Benjamin's emphasis on youth's bare, unformed character is telling in this passage: the young are "natural" and "uncultivated." They have no experiential knowledge of the "real" and no "conscience," be it moral, social or otherwise. Indeed, it is possible that such conscience, as the German word *Gewissen* connotes, depends on knowledge (*Wissen*) that can only be learned or acquired over time: *Ge-wissen*. In contrast, youth is "unknowing" (*unwissend*). Youth's naïveté, however, is not portrayed as a flaw, but rather as a promise and a hope for a different future to come.

Immediately following the above passage, Benjamin proceeds to praise youth's rejuvenating effects on the school, and through it on culture as a whole. And yet despite his affirmation of youth's revitalizing potential, he gives no description of the images that young people carry "from the land of the future." This omission not only speaks to the inability to predict or depict the future in advance, but also simultaneously points to the ever-present possibility that the young will interrupt and reorient the school (and culture as a whole) in an absolutely unforeseeable direction. In this sense, we find here an early example of Benjamin's views regarding the unrepresentability of utopia (the *Bildverbot* stance that becomes key in his debates with Adorno).[13] We find another iteration of the same gesture in a related text from the following year ("Thoughts on Gerhart Hauptmann's Festival Play," 1913) in which Benjamin recasts the tension between the young and the old characteristic of the school in terms of youth's relation to both *history* and the *law*:

> History is the struggle between the spirited and the inert, between those oriented toward the future and those oriented toward the past, between the free and the unfree. The unfree can always display to us the canon of their laws. But we will not yet be able to give a name to the law under which we stand.[14]

The intergenerational conflict becomes reformulated as a clash between law and lawlessness, but a lawlessness that is less an infraction of the law than a suspension thereof.[15] The freedom of youth is freedom from the "canon" of law, in other words, historically established law, law that has a past, a shape, a name. But the laws and rules that apply to and govern the past do not yet hold sway over the young. Whereas the "unfree" and "inert" (*Trägen*) are bound by and accept preexisting law *as* law, that is to say, as fixed and immutable, the young know no law, or at the very least none that can be named *as yet* (*noch nicht*). Speaking in the name of the collective youth, Benjamin insists that *we*, in the present, stand under the sign of an essentially different law: an illegible, unwritten, nameless law, a law without history or precedent, and therefore a paradoxically lawless law. For Benjamin, the crux of youth's revolutionary force appears to reside in its connection to and striving toward this radically lawless sphere. In its striving, youth constantly (un-)orients us toward the possibility of an essentially different future—not an alternative future, understood as one of many paths that history already seems to be headed toward, but rather a future that follows no patterns, no laws, including the law of causal, linear time.

Benjamin develops and returns to his understanding of history and exploded time in many of his later writings, most notably in the *Arcades Project* and "On the Concept of History" (1940). But already in his early reflections on youth, we find an embryonic form of the philosophy of history for which he has become known. Indeed, even as Benjamin becomes older, even after he turns away from the Youth Movement and disavows Wyneken (following the latter's euphoric embrace of World War I), Benjamin holds onto his own youthful views regarding the revolutionary potential of the young to interrupt the catastrophic course of culture and history.[16]

Freedom and the Force of Education

In a September 1917 letter to Gershom Scholem, Benjamin reinvokes the idea from his youth writings that education is, at its core, a movement of historical transmission. He is "convinced that tradition is the medium in which the person who is learning *continually* transforms himself into the person who is teaching and that this applies to the entire range of education."[17] Education and the "medium" of tradition are inextricably entwined. This imbrication manifests itself in the transformation of the learner (*Lernende*) into the teacher (*Lehrende*), a process that, he stresses, occurs continually. In other words, there is no *end*, or *Ende*, to education, to the process of transformation that allows the *Lern-ende* to unfold into the *Lehr-ende* over and over again. But to say that there is no end to this medial process of teaching and learning is not the same as to say that there are no breaks, interruptions, or potential moments of deviation within it. Benjamin portrays this process in an extended simile derived from a Talmudic witticism:

> Doctrine [*Lehre*] is like a surging sea, but the only thing that matters to the wave (understood as a metaphor for the person) is to surrender itself to its motion in such a way that it crests [*wächst*] and breaks over [*überstürzt*] with foam. This enormous freedom of the breaking wave [*Übersturzes*] is education in its actual sense: instruction [*Unterricht*], the becoming visible and free of tradition: its breaking like a wave [*Überstürzen*] from living abundance.[18]

Each individual, each learner is little more than a "wave," a ripple in the vast, flowing ocean, the "medium" for the transmission of "doctrine." Education demands giving oneself over to and riding with the flow of knowledge, absorbing and becoming absorbed by it to the point of mastery, when one is capable of taking off and teaching on one's own. For Benjamin, this point of departure marks the crucial moment in the process of education, a moment that occurs immediately upon reaching the peak of a process of development (*wachsen*), a crest that then "topples" or "rushes over" (*überstürzen*) itself. The freefall of *Überstürzen* signals a momentary interruption in the cyclical current of education, a break that unveils "enormous freedom." Benjamin implicitly connects this caesura in the flow of education to his early critique of hierarchic, institutionalized learning through the commonplace German term for "instruction," *Unterricht*, which carries the notions of giving direction (*Richtung*) and imposing law (*Recht*) upon those below (*unter*). In stark juxtaposition, the individual who finds oneself in the midst of *Überstürzen* does not ride beneath or within the wave, but has in a certain sense briefly surpassed it, overstepped it, to the point of coming out of sync with the rhythmic current, the patterns and repetitions that flow from one generation to the next.[19] In precipitously "rushing ahead" or "jumping the gun," another set of meanings contained in *Überstürzen*, the learner-become-teacher momentarily breaks out from under the established, unidirectional continuum of *Unterricht*. Although the motion of "toppling over" implies that such a free individual will inevitably be reabsorbed into tradition, the critical moment of freedom that Benjamin stresses nonetheless opens the possibility of a more profound interruptive, revolutionary rupture—an idea that suggestively resounds with his description, many years later, of the "theory of education as the root of utopia."[20]

Reminiscent of his youth writings, in the wave simile Benjamin hesitates to offer a definitive, static image for the interruptive moment of freedom that the break in the continuous "medium" of tradition reveals. Instead, he describes this pause as a dynamic state of emergence. The "enormous freedom" that characterizes the *Übersturz*, the "break[ing] over with foam," marks the "becoming visible and free of tradition." What the breaking, foaming wave renders visible is not freedom itself, which constitutively escapes confinement (representational or otherwise), but a gesture *toward* freedom from within a system whose progress consists of rhythmically cycling, falling back in upon itself. Benjamin's reluctance to give the pseudo-utopian non-place that he intimates in his writings on pedagogy a positive shape—whether in the form of an image or a name—leads John McCole to note that a certain "ideological ambiguity" accompanies Benjamin's "oracular pathos of 'the coming,'" an ambiguity that places him in close proximity to contemporary "neoconservative ideologists."[21] While McCole's observation is certainly valid, one might add, from a different perspective, that it is precisely Benjamin's refusal to depict the future in advance, to measure or shape it according to current rules or precedents that forms the thrust of his liberal, or rather liberating, stance. Benjamin's motto of acting "always radically, never consistently" ("immer radikal, niemals konsequent") in all important political matters can be said to find expression here in youth's lack of a static, consistent aim for its other-directed negativity.[22] If anything, youth's revolutionary force directs itself adamantly against the category of consistency as such, against what Benjamin in "The Free School Community" (1911) describes as "the uniformity of customs-convention, 'the eternal Yesterday that always was and always returns' and is the worst enemy of everything great."[23] Citing Rousseau's pedagogical treatise *Émile, or On Education* (1762), Benjamin presents youth's unbridled, unfocused energy as its greatest asset: adult concerns and "the day's monotony" have "not yet narrowed the young person's horizon," which affords youth the freedom to pursue grand "ideals."[24] Much like Rousseau, who emphasizes the importance of free, unstructured learning throughout *Émile*, Benjamin demands that the new school must "[confer] and [foster] freedom," for "the most urgent requirement of modern pedagogy is to create space for the emergent culture."[25] Before anything new can be built, the new pedagogy must first clear out the space on which a new culture may arise. "Humanity" must then place its "trust in [the] youth," which means to "trust in its own future, in the irrational," that which makes no sense and follows no logic, i.e., historical precedent.[26]

Benjamin returns to the theme of freedom from the order of historical convention in "Critique of Violence" (1921), a sustained investigation of the interconnected categories of the law (*Recht*) and violence (*Gewalt*)—as we have seen, variations of these two terms appear repeatedly in his reflections on youth pedagogy. In the "Critique of Violence," Benjamin advances what may be described as his idea of a politics of *pure means*, that is to say, a politics stripped of the causal, means to an end logic that structures the profane, historical realm of the law. Much like in his earlier writings, he identifies in the law a cyclical, self-reproducing continuum aligned with tradition. Every infraction or breaking of a law, he argues, ultimately appears to lead to the juridical imposition of a new law, resulting in a seemingly never-ending loop of "law-making" (*rechtsetzend*) and "law-preserving" (*rechtserhaltend*) violence.[27] Instances in which one is compelled to choose between these two forms of violence (*Gewalt*)—for example, in cases of police force, where an officer must often choose between following precedent or adapting their response to the particularities of the situation—illuminate the conflation and complicity of these two forms of legal violence. One either follows the law, or deviates from it, but in the process nonetheless imposes a new law, *ad infinitum*.

Against this continuous cycle of law-preserving and law-creating violence, Benjamin indicates the existence of a fundamentally different form of *Gewalt* (a paradoxically non-violent form of violence) that carries the potential to interrupt the historical continuum of the law: "divine violence."[28] He describes this "pure" form of violence as "law-destroying" (*rechtsvernichtend*)—not in the sense that it offers a different or new law, but insofar as it categorically refuses to manifest itself *as* law. A definitive feature of such pure violence is its "absence of all lawmaking [*Rechtsetzung*]."[29] Divine violence remains pure means, and as such absolutely beyond any means-ends relation, indicating a potential caesura in the unidirectional, historical continuum of the law.

While the proletarian general strike is Benjamin's best-known example of divine violence's ability to interrupt the continuum of the law (in that it marks a total cessation of the preexisting socio-political systems), such revolutionary violence can also exhibit itself in other profane spheres.[30] In a little-remarked passage, he names education as one of the arenas where the pure means of divine violence manifests itself in "present-day life." He writes, "the educative force [*erzieherische Gewalt*], which in its perfected form stands outside the law, is one of [divine violence's] manifestations."[31] Importantly, Benjamin does not state that *all* education is structured by "divine violence," or consists of pure means detached from teleological ends. Rather, we only get a hint of this emphatically medial, non-predetermined mode of learning in the absolutely "perfected form" (*vollendete Form*) of "educative force."[32] Benjamin's view that education, in its highest form, is tied to a notion of nonviolent, revolutionary, "educative force" anticipates his interest in Marxist pedagogy, as well as in improvisation, a state of play-learning whose interruptive, political gesture lies in extemporaneity, in stepping out of time, following no previous law and setting no new law for the future.

Improvisational and Revolutionary Pedagogy

Written more than a decade after the end of his involvement with the German Youth Movement, Benjamin's essay "Program for a Proletarian Children's Theater" (1928) approaches many of the themes outlined above, albeit with a slightly more explicit political bent. This should come as no surprise considering the main source of inspiration for the text: Asja Lacis, the politically engaged Latvian actress and theater director whom Benjamin credits in a 1924 letter to Scholem for his newfound interest in Marxism, as well as his desire no longer to "mask the actual and political elements of my ideas" but rather to "develop them" to "extreme measures."[33] In 1919, Lacis organized a children's theater group in Russia for youth affected by the revolutionary and civil wars.[34] Meant to serve primarily therapeutic purposes, these theater classes focused on restoring to children their lost childhoods and a carefree state of freedom. The theater instruction was grounded on two guiding principles: improvisation (the child's activity) and observation (the instructor's role). In the "Program," Benjamin offers a theoretical articulation of the core ideas that informed Lacis while also adding and further developing his own pedagogical views.

Benjamin begins the piece by recapitulating the intergenerational conflict that he stresses throughout the earlier texts on youth. "Every proletarian movement," he writes, eventually "finds itself confronting many different forces for which it is unprepared. The most powerful of these, as well as the most dangerous, is the younger generation."[35] In order to mobilize the youth toward a revolutionary movement that has a chance at sustainability, however, one must first address the question of how to educate children properly "in a proletarian manner."[36] He explicitly juxtaposes the pedagogy he proceeds to outline from what he terms "bourgeois education": "proletarian education needs first and foremost a framework, an objective space *within* which education can be located. The bourgeoisie, in contrast, requires an idea *toward* which education leads."[37] Whereas proletarian education takes place inside of a free, unstructured space (which we can think of as a medium with depth but no ends, or as the momentary rupture of freedom discussed above), bourgeois education is teleological and purpose-driven—it treats learning as an instrument directed "toward" an external, predetermined goal.[38] Proletarian pedagogy, meanwhile, seeks to make full use of the freedom afforded by the theater framework by stripping it of all external aims. Unlike in the "bourgeois theater," where actors receive a script to follow and are directed on what to do, the proletarian children's theater places an emphasis on extemporaneity, "improvisation reigns [*herrscht*]."[39] Whatever "moral processes" of learning occur, therefore, cannot be attributed to an outside "moral influence," but rather emerge from within, spontaneously through the interactions "undertaken by the children's collective itself."[40] Just as the empty "catchphrases" (*Phrasen*) of the "party program" have no effect upon children, morals and values that are imposed upon them carry little weight, for they do not emerge spontaneously, situationally from the interactions between the children.[41] In the lateral, non-hierarchic form of pedagogy that Benjamin advocates, individuals teach one another, performing the roles of *Lernenende* and *Lehrende* simultaneously.

In addition to providing a loose framework within which children actively, spontaneously learn, the theater plays an important role in awakening the youth's political energies by blurring the distinction between doing and performing, "reality and play."[42] Benjamin interprets the standard bourgeois dismissal of children's theater as an expression of the hidden "fear that the theater will unleash in children the most powerful energies of the future."[43] He goes on to describe these energies that radiate from the collective of children as "not just the most powerful energies [*gewaltigsten Kräfte*], but also the most relevant ones [*die aktuellsten*]."[44] The immediately relevant, forceful (*gewaltig*) powers that emanate from the young materialize in the child's improvisation. Because such extemporized acts follow no law, no conventionalized pattern, they remain fundamentally illegible to those who seek to read through them as self-erasing conveyors of an external meaning. "For the true observer," on the other hand, "every childhood action and gesture becomes a signal" that points to "another world, in which the child lives and commands."[45] Benjamin names Jean Paul as a prototypical example of the sort of "perceptive" teacher-observer best suited to "glimpse" this other world that every "childlike gesture" signals.[46]

Benjamin's invocation of Jean Paul should come as no surprise considering his great admiration of his pedagogical treatise, *Levana, or the Doctrine of Education* (1807), a text he cites often when discussing play, pedagogy, and revolution. Importantly, in *Levana* Jean Paul contemplates a certain notion of play whose qualities parallel Benjamin's conception of non-instrumental, radically undetermined, and thus endlessly disruptive education. In this specific form of play-learning, "the child merely plays the game, does not drive the game nor feel it" ("das Kind das Spiel nur spielt, nicht treibt, noch fühlt").[47] The type of play that Jean Paul describes here is neither active (*treiben*) nor passive (*fühlen*), but rather a mode of play in which the child simultaneously "takes *and* gives," folding reception and creation into one another in a way that privileges neither side of this dichotomy.[48] Unmotivated by external aims or desires, "the child merely plays the game" in a seemingly self-reflexive action that is especially striking in the original German, where the verb *to play* and the noun *game* derive from the same root, rendering the almost tautological phrase, "das Spiel nur spielt."[49]

In the "Program," Benjamin similarly intimates such a self-reflexive, lateral play sphere in his description of improvisation, a state in which the collective of children simultaneously establish (create) the very laws that they follow (receive). "In relation to the process of schooling," writes Benjamin, "the performance is like the radical unleashing of play."[50] Importantly, such play never appears twice in the same way. Each iteration, each performance is different, for "childhood achievement is always aimed not at the 'eternity' of the product but at the 'moment' [*Augenblick*]."[51] This is what renders theater, "the art form of the child," "ephemeral [*vergänglich*]." For a brief moment, the performance introduces a "creative pause in the process of upbringing [*Erziehungswerk*]," a caesura in which the roles are flipped, in which the "children stand on the stage and instruct and teach the attentive educators."[52] This inversion manifests an idea that Marx expresses in his third thesis on Feuerbach. There, he reminds readers that "revolutionary practice" depends not only on raising the consciousness of people by changing their "circumstances and upbringing [*Erziehung*]." In order for revolutionary change to occur, it is also "essential to educate the educator himself."[53] By moving the "educators" into the audience, the model of theater that Benjamin outlines transforms the teachers into students, namely the students of their very own students. This dizzying inversion in which the roles of student and teacher, *Lernende* and *Lehrende*, are unsettled and disrupted, marks yet another one of Benjamin's attempts to theorize an alternate model of pedagogy that could counter the hierarchical, intergenerational structure of "bourgeois education" that centers not only on passing down institutionalized knowledge, but also on immediately fixing, codifying whatever new knowledge is introduced into part of the existing continuum of tradition.

Benjamin's repeated attempts to not only reform but revolutionize pedagogy can be seen to (momentarily) culminate in his reflections on the revolutionary character of ephemeral, improvisational theater. By rethinking education as a lateral, dynamic, unforeseeable exchange between teacher-learners, Benjamin calls on us to reexamine the content, sources, and methods of education, understood as a "propagation of spiritual values," cultural, ethical, and otherwise.[54] The theater, the framework within which the young student-teachers spontaneously perform (or form) their own educations marks an alternative site to the standard institutional learning space. In the children's theater, the youth are allowed an *unprecedented* amount of freedom to shape their own future.

Benjamin's insistence that the improvisational play-acting in the educational theater never outlives the immediate performance, that such improvisation exhausts itself entirely and thus provides no script for future performances, no laws for the future to follow, indicates a schism that underlies his numerous writings on pedagogy. On the one hand, from his early through his late writings Benjamin maintains an emphasis on the present, unformed shape of youth, and thus youth's ability to break with the past and set a new course for the future. On the other hand, such a radical break from what exists and its "force of law"—as Derrida famously names Benjamin's interest in the authority and power of *Gewalt* as historical (juridical) canon[55]—depends, paradoxically in this case, on founding, *instituting* another type of school, namely the theater "framework ... *within* which education can be located."[56] As a counter-institution, the theater space marks an attempt to break out from the hierarchical tradition of education by creating a free space within unfree space, a place where students and teachers may redefine education as well as their roles in the larger cultural-historical process and thus perhaps prepare the way for a different model not only of education, but also of society to come. A further interlinked issue that arises in this context is the problem that any new knowledge or learning that emerges in the ephemeral theater classroom eludes fixation, escapes from becoming a part of a larger ongoing cultural tradition. The extended wave simile discussed above, however, suggests that the transmission of knowledge may itself is not the problem, but rather a homogenous, unidirectional, and thus predetermined movement of progress. The revolutionary character of the young, their "eternal rebellion" against "society, state, [and the] law" disrupts such an idea progress, but it does so in an improvised manner.[57] Ultimately, this means that *rebellious education*—as we may term the sort that occurs without law or precedent in the unstructured children's theater—might appear unable to teach us much, for it does not pass on any formed content or doctrine (*Lehre*). But perhaps this form of pedagogy that Benjamin introduces, and his writings on education more broadly, offer a more profound lesson. Benjamin teaches us how to think from a critical position aligned with the youth in reassessing our pre-existing pedagogical models, methods, and institutions. The youth intimate the possibility of a new future waiting to be unlocked, a future whose contours we do not know, whose name we cannot utter, and whose laws have not yet been written. Benjamin ends the "Program" on precisely such a note of revolution to come, revolution that announces itself in advance by not announcing anything at all, but rather keeps the hopeful image of what is come in reserve: "what is truly revolutionary is the *secret signal* of what is to come that speaks from the gesture of the child."[58]

Notes

1. *EW* 28.
2. Ibid.
3. Ibid., 27.
4. John McCole, "Benjamin and the Idea of Youth," in *Walter Benjamin and the Antinomies of Tradition* (Ithaca: Cornell University Press, 1993), 36.
5. Howard Eiland and Michael W. Jennings, *Walter Benjamin: A Critical Life* (Cambridge, MA: Harvard University Press, 2014), 36-7.
6. *EW* 58. The essay was published in a pamphlet by Freiburg's School Reform Unit "in an edition of 10,000 copies that were distributed free of charge in universities around the country." Eiland and Jennings, *A Critical Life*, 38.
7. "School Reform," *EW* 59; *GS* 2: 14.
8. *EW*, 59.
9. Hobbes uses the phrase "bellum omnium contra omnes" in *On the Citizen* (1642) and *Leviathan* (1651).
10. In "On the Concept of History" (1940), he describes the "lineage" of "horror" that attends cultural "treasures," which "owe their existence not only to the efforts of great geniuses who created them, but also to the anonymous toil of others ... There is no document of culture which is not at the same time a document of barbarism." He concludes the thought by contemplating the question of transmission in a similar manner to his discussion of education, "just as such a document is never free of barbarism, so barbarism taints the manner in which it was transmitted from one hand to another." *SW* 4: 392.
11. *EW* 60.
12. *EW* 59-60; *GS* 2: 15.
13. For an insightful examination of Benjamin's complex views regarding the (im)possibility of representing utopia, see Rebecca Comay, "Materialist Mutations of the *Bildverbot*," in *Sites of Vision: The Discursive Construction of Sight in the History of Philosophy*, ed. David Michael Levin (Cambridge, MA: MIT Press, 1999), 337-78.
14. *EW* 123-4.
15. One might think of this second state as a version of Kant's "lawfulness without a law" (*Gesetzmäßigkeit ohne Gesetz*).
16. In Convolute N of *The Arcades Project*, Benjamin writes, "the concept of progress must be grounded in the idea of catastrophe. That things are 'status quo' *is* the catastrophe." *AP* 473.
17. *C* 94.
18. *C* 94; *GB* 145. Translation modified.
19. Steizinger also comments on the latent futurity suggested by the break of the wave. See Johannes Steizinger, *Revolte, Eros und Sprache: Walter Benjamins "Metaphysik der Jugend"* (Berlin: Kulturverlag Kadmos, 2013), 141-2.
20. *AP* 915.
21. McCole, "Idea of Youth," 53-4.
22. *C* 300; *GB* 425. Translation modified. Benjamin states this in a May 1926 letter to Scholem in which he explains his reluctance to join the Communist Party of Germany (KPD).
23. *EW* 41. Convention recurs as a motif throughout these early texts, often in opposition to youth and its accompanying spirit of the new. For instance, in "Dialogue on the Religiosity of the Present" (1912), he suggests that religion today has been degraded to

little more than empty ritual. Only "when we again have the strength to shape convention, to give it serious and worthy form in place of our social sham world, *then* we shall have the symptom of the new religion" (*EW* 74–5). In "Experience" (1913), he similarly criticizes the philistine (which he associates with an adult mode of relating to the world) for their lack of a "relationship to anything other than the commonplace, the established routine" (*EW* 117).

24. "Free School Community," *EW* 41.
25. "School Reform," *EW* 60. A tension persists throughout Rousseau's text between giving the child the space to develop on his own, and closely supervising or even controlling the child's development. This tension is captured in Rousseau's concept of "well-regulated freedom." Rousseau, *Émile*, 92. For an overview of Rousseau's views on this topic, and an attempt to correct the prevailing account of his pedagogy as "romantic noninterventionist" in the image of Fröbel or Pestalozzi, see Iheoma, "Rousseau's Views," 69–81.
26. "School Reform," *EW* 60.
27. *GS* 2: 197–8.
28. Ibid., 200.
29. Ibid. For more on this absence and the "deposing" (*Entsetzung*), law-annihilating character of pure violence, see Werner Hamacher, "Afformative, Strike: Benjamin's 'Critique of Violence,'" in *Walter Benjamin's Philosophy: Destruction and Experience*, ed. Andrew E. Benjamin and Peter Osborne (Manchester: Clinamen Press, 2000), 108–36.
30. *GS* 2: 194–5.
31. Ibid., 200.
32. Hamacher indicates the sort of pure mediality that is at stake here: "Thus, it is only in annihilation—not, certainly, the annihilation of mediacy, but the annihilation of the sphere of positing and its institutions by means of its reduction to mediacy that the proletarian strike is 'the highest manifestation of pure violence by humanity.'" Hamacher, "Afformative, Strike," 119.
33. *C* 257.
34. For Lacis's account of this theater group, see *GS* 2: 1491–5.
35. *SW* 2: 201.
36. Ibid.
37. Ibid., 202.
38. This structural distinction parallels one we see Benjamin make in several other contexts, including not only education and the law, but also in his philosophy of language and in his color studies. In both of the latter cases, he develops an understanding of the medium as a sphere of transmission *in* which communication and perception occur.
39. *SW* 2: 204; *GS* 2: 767.
40. *SW* 2: 203.
41. *SW* 2: 201; *GS* 2: 763.
42. *SW* 2: 202. Benjamin develops this idea further in "Spielzeug und Spielen" (1928). For more on Benjamin's concept of play, see my article, "The Smallest Remainder: Benjamin and Freud on Play," *MLN* 133, no. 3 (April 2018): 720–42.
43. *SW* 2: 202.
44. *SW* 2: 203; *GS* 2: 766.
45. *SW* 2: 203–4.
46. The term and concept of the *gesture* or *Geste* becomes central for Benjamin in his engagement with Brecht's epic theater. Benjamin's use of this term in the "Program,"

however, predates his friendship with Brecht (their first meeting was facilitated by Lacis). Nonetheless, the affinities between the notion of revolutionary theater developed here suggest a link to Brecht's thought. For more on this connection, and the other potential theatrical influences on Benjamin in composing this text, see Karin Burk, *Kindertheater als Möglichkeitsraum* (Bielefeld: transcript, 2015), especially 276–95.

47 Jean Paul, *Levana; or, the Doctrine of Education* (London: George Bell & Sons, 1897), 152. Translation modified. For the German, see Jean Paul, *Werke*, ed. Norbert Müller, 6 vols. (München; Carl Hanser, 1959–63), 5: 602–3.
48 Ibid. Emphasis added.
49 For a reading of the role of this non-instrumental form of play in Jean Paul's pedagogical and aesthetic writings, see my chapter, "Between Speaking and Listening: Jean Paul's Wordplay," in *Play in the Age of Goethe: Theories, Narratives, and Practices of Play around 1800*, eds. Edgar Landgraf and Elliott Schreiber (Lewisburg: Bucknell UP, 2020), 213–35.
50 *SW* 2: 205.
51 *SW* 2: 204; *GS* 2: 767.
52 *SW* 2: 205; *GS* 2: 768.
53 Karl Marx, *The Marx-Engels Reader*, ed. Robert C. Tucker (New York: W.W. Norton & Co., 1978), 144.
54 *EW* 58.
55 See Jacques Derrida, "Force of Law: The Mystical Foundation of Authority," in *Deconstruction and the Possibility of Justice,* eds. Drucilla Cornell, Michel Rosenfeld, and David Gray Carlson (New York: Routledge, 1992), 3–67.
56 *SW* 2: 202.
57 *EW* 10.
58 *SW* 2: 206.

11

Improvision

Thomas Schestag

Probably in late 1928, but most certainly, at the latest, in early 1929 in Berlin, Walter Benjamin improvised a program. A program at the core of which improvisation reigns: "Die Improvisation herrscht." Its title (half improvised, half programmatic): *Programm eines proletarischen Kindertheaters* ("Program of a Proletarian Children's Theater").[1] It is a small text, as if to be folded and put into a child's hand, feeling the paper, its folds, inside its fist holding on to it, like a secret message to be opened, fold for fold, and looked at, letter for letter, later. The program, though, is not so much written *for* a (future) children's theater, and not so much for children as either spectators or actors. It rather approaches the participants in such a theater (to improvise a word) as *spectactors*. The program, although (according to the letter of its prefix *pro-*) *pro*spective at first glance, is in fact no less *retro*spective. Its every letter—*grámma*—split between past and future: Janus-faced. Not just *for* nor simply *in view of* a proletarian children's theater (yet to come), neither simply *pre*scriptive nor *pro*spective, but rather distilled from and condensing past—yet incomplete—experiences (as will be seen), Benjamin's *Programm* is nonetheless a program written (almost clandestinely) *for* or on behalf of … Benjamin wrote the *program* for Asja Lacis who, in late 1928, just arrived from Russia to Berlin, where she was to direct the section on *Film* in the Department of Commerce at the Russian Embassy (until 1930), talks about her former experiments with a children's theater in Russia to Johannes R. Becher and Gerhart Eisler, who both come up with the proposal for the foundation of such a children's theater at the Liebknechthaus in Berlin. In a memo or memoir, written in German, years later (in 1968), for the journal *Alternative*, Asja Lacis remembers how Benjamin came to offer to write (and was forced to rewrite) the program:

> I was asked to work out the program. Already in Capri (1924) Walter Benjamin had heard about my children's theater and shown an extraordinary interest in it. 'I will write the program', he said, 'to explain and support your practical work theoretically.' And indeed, he wrote it. But this first version presented my theses in a most complicated (almost monstrous) way. When they read in the *Liebknechthaus*, they laughed: But Benjamin has written this for you! I gave the program back to Walter Benjamin, asking for a more comprehensive text. This is how the '*Program of a Proletarian Children's Theater*' in a second version (the first has not yet been rediscovered) was accomplished.[2]

The *program* (in its second, more comprehensive or *improved* version) springs from a (monstrously) complicated back and forth ... Its *pro-* no less than each letter of its text (who is *re*ferring here to or *pro*viding, and *pro*grammatically so, whose theses?) being fissured in ways almost impossible to reconstruct. It is as if at the core of the accomplished second version of this program improvisation reigned.

Years earlier, in late 1918, Asja Lacis had arrived in Orel to start working at the city's theater as a stage-director. She was on her way in the direction of directing. "A beaten path" (*ein gebahnter Weg*), she later writes (in the same memo or memoir from 1968). But something unforeseen and unexpected happens, leading her astray. It is her encounter with abandoned, ragged, and wayward children, living in loose bands not only *on the streets* of Orel but on market places, in cemeteries, basements, ruined houses. In the language of those not living on the street they have a name: *besprizorniki*.[3] Asja Lacis describes them in these words:

> Among them were lads with blackish faces, unwashed for months, in ragged jackets with leaking strings of cotton, broad and long cotton pants, held together with a cord, armed with sticks and crowbars. They always went in groups, each one led by a chief, they stole, they robbed, and they knocked down. In short, they were bands of robbers—victims of the world war and of civil war. The Sovjet government tried to settle these vagrant children in community homes and workshops. But they escaped time and again.[4]

The other group of children Asja Lacis will encounter in Orel are orphans who lost their parents during the war (*Kriegswaisen*), and who now live in protectories provided by the city. Looking at these children without childhood, looking at how they were looking, seeing their open eyes without opening their eyes—"they looked like old people: sad and tired eyes, no interest in anything" ("sie blickten drein wie Greise: müde, traurige Augen, nichts interessierte sie")—Asja Lacis decides to draw them out of their lethargy. A task was needed seizing their *entire* life, to set free their traumatized abilities:

> I knew about the monstrous force inherent in playing theater.... I was convinced that the play was a possibility to wake up and evolve [develop] these children.... I wanted to induce the children to better use their eyes, to tune their ears, to help their hands give shape to useful things from formless material. Therefore I divided the work up into sections. To develop their eyes, and sense of seeing, the children were painting and drawing. This section was led by Viktor Schestakow ... Other sections of my experimental school model in Orel included rhythmics and gymnastics, speech training and improvisation. Hidden forces which were set free during the working process, and developing skills went into *improvisation*. This is where and how the play originated. Children were playing for children.[5]

In her memo from 1968, Asja Lacis calls this educational model, as if alluding to Friedrich Schiller's programmatic series of letters entitled *Über die ästhetische Erziehung des Menschen*, a model of aesthetic education, to help develop these children's—orphans and *besprizorniki*: vagrants, robbers, thieves—aesthetic and moral skills. But what happens—unforeseen—in Orel around 1918 is that Asja Lacis, drawn away from the beaten track toward stage-directing by (looking at) bands of vagrant children, deviates from Schiller's project in that this experiment does not focus on the aesthetic education of *man*, but on the aesthetic education of *children*. The Orel experiment centers around a training period, split into different specific sections. The word *section* here alludes (whether deliberately—and programmatically—or unconsciously) to the forty-eight *sections* of the Parisian Commune during the French Revolution, in 1790, echoing similar notions in other languages, such as *Räte* in German, *Sovjet* in Russian, *tanács* in Hungarian, or *ward divisions* in American English.[6] In such sections the children *work* (under the guidance less of a teacher than a *counselor*) on different skills and senses, less in view of a more nuanced perception and control of their skills and senses (fit for application), but in view of *improvisation*. This particular experimental school's *program* does not aim to grow children into grown-ups, adult and useful members of a work force in a party or production line, but towards *improvisation*. In other words (and to give more relief to its paradoxical shape): this school's program, its prescriptive and prospective trajectory, the one-way (street) it indicates, in short, its ***pro***-, is to experience the unforeseeable and unforeseen: ***impro***-; the improvised undoing of its programmatic outline.[7] Condensed by Asja Lacis into a most ambiguous yet seemingly familiar (composite) word: *Theaterspielen* (playing theater). This one word, in its two parts or sections, at first glance simply indicates, true to its familiar *mimetic* scheme, that the quintessence of *theater* is to *play*: a play performed on stage by imitating actors, acting *as if* acting, and acting *out*, a plot unfolding between a finite number of *personae* in real time. But *Theaterspielen* may also indicate, less visibly and less foreseeably, thus opening cracks (as if into walls) towards improvised readings of this very word, that the quintessence of the *play* is *theater*. In other words: this particular play's objective is to *play* theater: to play *as if* playing theater, to imitate (or mimic) imitation as it happens on and off stage: in short, to imitate an imitating actor. Or still otherwise: to *play*—to play. The difference in diction (or accentuation) (between both readings) is minimal, but decisive: to play *theater* is not to *play* theater. The eruptive, explosive *force* encapsulated in the composite *Theaterspielen* is only freed when *working* towards *playing* theater: "Ich wußte, welche ungeheure Kraft im Theaterspielen steckt."

Again: Benjamin's *Programm*, improvised at the latest in early 1929 in Berlin, is not only written *for* Asja Lacis, but also in reminiscence *of* what she had told him earlier, when they first met, in the summer of 1924 in Capri, where Benjamin wrote sections of (and for) his book *Ursprung des deutschen Trauerspiels*, about her Orel experiment and experiences in *Theaterspielen* with orphaned and abandoned children, *besprizorniki*, back in 1918. The *program* is neither prospective, nor simply in view of a proletarian children's theater (to come), nor simply written in retrospect, in remembrance of discussions with Asja Lacis, but it is written *for* the *unfor-*: for improvisation (in view of what blocks or cracks the view) at the core of *a* proletarian children's theater, which may have become—transitorily—manifest once in Orel, but which also may have happened earlier, at random times and places, in forgotten languages, and which may happen later, in some unforeseen and unexpected time—out of time—and place—out of place. But how precisely to prepare—and programmatically, that is, prescriptively so—for the unforeseeable, for some enormous, monstrous hidden force, encapsulated in (children) *playing theater*?

Pro-. The *program* written by Walter Benjamin for Asja Lacis in early 1929, stems from experiences with, and is improvised in view of, another *pro-*: a *pro*letarian children's theater. It addresses children as *proles* and as *proletarian* children. But what is a *proles*, who are *proletarians*, what (kind of) *for* is at play in the word *proletarian*, and where does the word come from? This question already reappears from within book XVI of Aulus Gellius' *Attican Nights* (first published around 177): "Then the question was raised there, what *proletarius* meant" ("tum ibi quari coeptum est, quid esset 'proletarius'"). The answer is provided further down by a famous Roman lawyer, Julius Paulus, just passing by. He explains the notion *proletarii civis* (proletarian citizen), inscribed in the *Twelve Tables*, as follows:

> Those of the Roman commons who were humblest and of smallest means ... were called *proletarii*, but those who were rated as having no property at all, or next to none, were termed *capite censi*, or 'counted by head.' ... However, the class of *proletarii* [*proletariorum ordo*] was somewhat more honourable in fact and in name [*et re et nomine*] than that of the *capite censi* ... And they were called, not *capite censi*, but by a more auspicious name [*prosperiore vocabulo*] derived from their duty and function of producing offspring [*prolis edendae*], for although they could not greatly aid the State [*rempublicam*] with what small property they had, yet they added to the population of their country by their power [*copia*] of begetting children [*subolis gignendae*].[8]

Proletarians, thus, are those bearing a more auspicious or *prosperous* word designating their (political) task (as members of a class). A more promising name, full of expectation, for *prosperus* literally means in view of, tending towards, tempted by hope: *pro *spēre*. The members, men and women, of this class are called *proletarii* because of their power (*copia*) to beget children (*suboles*). The passage explaining the word *proletarii* oscillates between children, the very aim of hope or expectation, as either *proles* or *suboles*, hesitating between wherefrom—from underneath: *sub*—and whereto—forth or forward: *pro*—the offspring—*oles*—springs. *Proletarii* designates members of a political class defined by nothing but the (sexual) power of begetting children: because of having sex *in view* of women's pregnancy and children to be born (and raised) for the state. They are called proletarians *because* of the children they produce. The passage in *Attican Nights*, explaining the origin of the word *proletarii* (answering the—children's— question: *where does it come from?*) sketches (almost inconspicuously) the rhetorical figure of *hysteron proteron*. Children—neither *sub-* nor *pro-*, just *-oles*—are the condition of possibility for those bearing the name *proletarii*. Without children—no proletarians. Children—*-oles*—are neither *proletarians* nor *suboletarians*. Their coming (to the world) provides those who *have* them, retrospectively, with the name *proletarii*. There are proletarians only because of the children they *have*, but the children— *-oles*—are not *proletarians'* children. No child—*-oles*—is a proletarian's child. The political designation (nothing more than an ideological slogan or catchword: as if called up to catch the child and turning it into a member of a proletarian class or movement) of *proletarius* is ruined by the child for it only retrospectively (in other words: *too late*) provides the *-oletarians* with their (more improvised than programmatic) *pro-*. What a scene! What a theater! What a (proletarian) children's theater! The children Asja Lacis was working and playing with back in 1918 in Orel were neither *suboletarian* nor *proletarian* children, barely *-oles*; they escape both designations: *proles* and *suboles*. They may remain indifferent to, not care about, the (children's) question, where they are coming from and going to. Straying bands of urchins, improvising life in the street—*Straßenkinder*—in the margins of public markets, in ruined basements, cemeteries, on the one hand, and on the other hand abandoned orphaned children (provisionally) gathered in shelters provided by the city. Those children don't belong to any *class*. Their (*para*political) state (of being) is classlessness. They live in (loose) groups of (free) association. *Associety*.

But Benjamin's improvised program seems to hold on, at first glance at least, to the programmatic notion, if not slogan, of a *proletarian* children's theater. The little text, for the sake of clarity (and most probably to prevent more laughter from the political leaders at the *Liebknechthaus*) is divided into three sections: a third *pro-*—*Vorbemerkung* or Prefatory Remark—preceding two schemes: *Schema der Spannung* (scheme of tension), and *Schema der Lösung* (scheme of solution). The prefatory remark, though, in its first sentence, introduces a third scheme: the scheme of parliamentary discussion (*Schema der parlamentarischen Diskussion*). The *Vor-*—or *Pre-*—of Benjamin's *Vorbemerkung*, although coming after the two (programmatically if not ideologically charged) *pro-*words of this text's title—*Program* and *Proletarian*—reaches back before what the title promises, provides or prepares for: back before this text's programmatic and proletarian outline. The prefatory remark in its first sentence is about the unpreparedness—*unvorbereitet*—of any proletarian movement, for children: nothing but *-oles*, cut off from any guiding principle or prefix, be that *pro-* or *sub-* or *ad-*, *-oles* (cent). It leaves the readers with a most powerful and most dangerous force alone: in front of, face to face with, – *children*. Alone with children. With children alone. Almost abandoned: "Every proletarian movement, whenever it has for once [rather: as if once and for all] escaped the scheme of parliamentary discussion, finds itself confronted with many different forces for which it is unprepared. The most powerful of these, as well as the most dangerous, is the new generation" ("Jede proletarische Bewegung, die einmal dem Schema der parlamentarischen Diskussion entronnen ist, sieht unter den vielen Kräften, denen sie plötzlich unvorbereitet gegenübersteht, als die allerstärkste aber auch allergefährlichste vor sich die neue Generation"). The first scheme, back before the (programmatic) schemes of tension and solution, is *linguistic* through and through: it is the scheme of political speech in the realm of *parliament*. A space reserved for *adult* speakers in their function as party members and professional politicians, protecting the prevalence of a certain use of language against the intrusion of *children*. The self-certainty and stupidity of political speech stems from the fact that in parliament, or more generally speaking according to a certain parliamentary scheme or speech pattern dominating the (political) sphere of human beings as speaking animals living in society, adults remain among themselves: "daß die Erwachsenen unter sich bleiben." The fact that children are prevented not only from participating in political debates but from publicly raising their voices (and being listened to), alludes to another Latin word, besides *proles*, no less ubiquitous, even more famous and widespread, that has traveled languages and continents and centuries, detecting speechlessness as all children's main characteristics: child, according to this word and its explanation, is the one, that does not (yet) speak (like adults speak): *infans*. The child, between *proles* and *infans*, embodies in both words both a promise and a threat. In *proles*: the promise to grow into the political class of *proletarians* as a future adult member; and the threat to undo the *proletarian* character of this very class, for children—*-oles*—do not embody the *progenitive* faculty of human beings; they interrupt it. In *infans*: the promise to grow into a *speaker*, joining the *parliament* of human society; and the threat not to canalize and silence the *idiotic*, idiosyncratic use of words (and syllables and sounds, and letters: almost like poets do), challenging existing parliamentary schemes or speech patterns, in other words: the validity of language in its *grammatical* and *programmatical* shape. Children *threaten*—this is (almost) the quintessence of their *theater*—the unquestionable recognition of both *pro*-words which the title of Benjamin's little text brings to the fore: the political authority of *Proletarian*, and the linguistic authority of *Programm*.

Every proletarian movement that successfully escapes the scheme of parliamentary discussion enters the (extraordinary, if not enormous, monstrous) sphere not only of extraparliamentary, but extragrammatical, extra*programmatical*—not only the sphere of extra*pro*letarian, but extrapolitical—life. (Where the wild things are.) *Mere* life (without *proles*, without *Polis*, without grammar and program). Mere *life*: the sphere (or atmosphere) of sheer improvisation. Bereft of its identity as one political class among others (up to fight for the destruction of all other classes, including its own, and to prepare for the establishment of a classless society); bereft of its language—*logos* turned into *ideology*—every proletarian movement, once it has escaped the patterns of (political) speech, seizes and sees—*sieht* ... *vor sich*—in front of it, out of a sudden, like an obstacle—a barrier or barricade—unforeseen and unprepared for—*unvorbereitet*—among many other forces, as the most powerful, but also most dangerous force the new generation: *-oles* (without *pro*-): children (including their own; if not, also, and more explosively so, them*selves—as* children). The movement described by this first prefatory (provisional, almost improvised) sentence corresponds in strange ways to Asja Lacis' description of her arrival in Orel in 1918, on her way to the (house of) *Theater*, determined to become its stage-director, but suddenly distracted and turned away from the direction she took by (loose) bands of children crossing her path. In Benjamin's first sentence, written in Berlin, in either late 1928 or early 1929, a proletarian movement escapes the (house of) *Parliament*, seeing itself out there, and out of a sudden, confronted with children, embodying a most powerful, dangerous force. Proletarians escaping the house of Parliament; Asja Lacis heading towards the city theater of Orel as its future (stage) director: both movements are—unexpectedly, abruptly—forced to stop: confronted by (passing) children. They embody the unforeseen. They escape (and block) the (political-teleological) calculus of *providence*. No catchword or catchphrase—*Phrase*—is able, is powerful enough to catch these children's, *all* children's attention. Children remain *immune* to language considered and used as a tool of *communication*, built of a (variable) set of grammatical, *programmatical* slogans, in view of building (political) *communities* of listeners and speakers: "Mere catchphrases have no power over children" ("Über Kinder ... haben Phrasen gar keine Gewalt"). Language, in its *pro-*, *-grammatical*, and *ideo-*, *-logical* outline, condensed here into the (catch)word *Phrase*, is useless, no tool—*Instrument*—to approach and reach, and *instruct*—a child's ear. This declared uselessness of language in its programmatical and ideological, that is in its *educational* tendency, as a main if not the only tool in—proletarian—children's education, raises a question: which instruments are there to help raising—proletarian—children? A perpetual questioning, rather than a question (waiting for an answer): "We are simply asking, but will not cease to ask, for instruments serving the class-conscious education of proletarian children" ("Wir fragen ganz einfach, aber wir werden auch nicht aufhören zu fragen, nach den Instrumenten der klassenbewußten Erziehung proletarischer Kinder"). The task, thus, sketched out in the *Vorbemerkung*, is not only the search for extra-linguistic instruments providing and supporting the *proletarian* education of children: "For ... children ... must be brought up in a proletarian manner" ("weil ... Kinder ... proletarisch erzogen werden müssen"). The task is less to find an instrument or instruments orchestrating (or improvising) proletarian *education*, but to ask for a *proletarian* education that has escaped the ideology of (proletarian) party programs and parliamentary patterns of speech. The task is to read, and reread the word *proletarian* differently, to undo its political and programmatic character. To shake (or shock) its usefulness for ideological ends. Taking a closer look at this word's letters helps: *proletarian* education is not the education *of* proletarian children into class-consciousness, preparing them for the future inclusion into the political class of *proletarians*. Proletarian education, as sketched out in the *Vorbemerkung*, is *pro-oletarian*, that is, stammering the word apart: education *for* children. To break the programmatic character of the word *proletarian*, its ideological use as a slogan, it has to be taken literally (and its literality apart): *pro-ole-tarian*: in view of the unforeseen: in view of children. Only *pro-oletarian* education will help to ignite another, slightly different class consciousness: the class of children is the class (or school) of those who don't belong to any class (or school): the (extracurricular) class of classlessness.

No less than the catchword *proletarian*, also the word *program* has to suffer (as if touched by a child's hands) a slight (almost invisible) deformation (of its literal body). *Pro-oletarian* education has to have a *system*. But the word *system*, another slogan, has to be taken differently here: "System aber heißt hier Rahmen" ("system" here means "framework"). And: "Proletarian education needs first and foremost a framework, an objective area *within* which education can take place" ("Die proletarische Erziehung braucht also unter allen Umständen zuerst einmal einen Rahmen, ein sachliches Gebiet, in dem erzogen wird"). The frame—*Rahmen*—of proletarian education is the proletarian children's *theater*:

> The education of a child requires *that its entire life be engaged.* / Proletarian education requires *that the child be educated within a limited area....* It is only in the theater that the entire life, framed in all its unforeseeable plenitude—*in seiner unabsehbaren Fülle*— can appear as a limited area; and this is why the proletarian children's theater is the dialectically determined—or *voiced*—site of education.[9]

This is not (despite its appearance) a *program*. The program here is taken out of its grammatical frame and deviates, slightly disfigured, into a certain *Rahmen*, or, in a more improvised (and precise, almost childlike) manner: *Programm* here (disfiguring its every letter—*grámma*—) means *Prográhmen*.

Life in its entirety is unforeseeable—*unabsehbar*—without beginning and end. Children embody the unforeseeability of (their entire) life. Its improvised character. Life being (without *being*) the unlimited, illiterate area of improvisation. A proletarian children's theater is the limited area or territory to feel and to unfold (though not programmatically) this unforeseeability.

At the end of its prefatory remark—*Vorbemerkung*—the title of this little text—*Programm eines proletarischen Kindertheaters*—appears in a different light, rather unforeseen. It allows, if not necessitates, to be read otherwise. *Programm*, another word for *Rahmen*, but a *pre-* or *para*grammatical, *Prográhmen*, has to be taken here as a synonym (as if relating to a children's dictionary) of *Theater*; both words framing the title's core section: *eines proletarischen Kinder-*; in other words, a children's ... for children: *pro-oles*. What happens at the core of this *Rahmen* or *Theater* relates to a lapidary note in the memo written years later, in 1968, by Asja Lacis: "children were playing for children" ("Kinder spielten für Kinder"). At the core of this core, improvisation reigns: "Die Improvisation herrscht." But how to (*pre-* if not *para*grammatically) prepare for the entire life in its unforeseeability? How to prepare for—improvisation?

Impro-. For the proletarian child, the proletarian children's theater—children playing for children—is the dialectically determined site of education—*Erziehung*. But this site being split into two sides, relating to one another as the scheme of tension—*Schema der Spannung*—and the scheme of solution—*Schema der Lösung*—the very word *Erziehung*—to literally draw somebody upwards, thus creating a certain tension between the one who draws and the one being drawn—is itself related, almost dialectically, to *Erlösung*. The aim of a proletarian child's education—*Erziehung*—is the -solution, rather *dis*solution than *re*solution, alluding to redemption and relief, of tensions having been built in view of a performance—*Aufführung*— taking place exclusively inside the frame of a proletarian children's theater, where children play for children (*spectactors* on both sides): the (provisional) dissolution of (the scheme of) tension. Children playing for children: the (improvised) redemption from education. They play the building and undoing of both schemes: of tension and -solution: *Erziehung* and *Erlösung*. Their performances—*Aufführungen*—do not per*form*, they per*forate* both schemes, leaving each *Aufführung* bereft of leadership: *Auf-* without *-führung*. These stage events are Aufführungen, not performances, for they do not deliver and represent an elaborated theatrical production. *Aufführungen* are visualized (but improvised) *Auflösungen*—dissolutions—or Auflösungs*erscheinungen*—dis*appearances*—of tensions embodied in the figure of the educator—*Erzieher*—or leader—*Leiter*:

> One might say that here [in a proletarian children's theater] *Aufführungen* come about incidentally, one could say as an oversight [*aus Versehen*], almost as a children's prank, and in this way the children interrupt the course of study that

remains incomplete forever. The leader doesn't really care about completion. He is more interested in the tensions that are dissolved in such *Aufführungen*. The tensions of collective labor are the educators.[10]

Aufführungen are not the result of collectively elaborated stage-productions, they interrupt—*unterbrechen*—the children's study, their only object of study being the abundant unforeseeability of (their entire) life, remaining incomplete forever. These interruptions happen almost accidentally: *aus Versehen*. Not out of providence, but unexpected: unforeseen. Instead of the *study* of life (the sphere or atmosphere of improvisation) improvisation (embodied in children playing for children) takes place.

Children, playing for children, embodying the unforeseen, do not per*form*, they per*for*-. But this *disposition* is not the privilege of a *proletarian* children's theater. It *strikes* at the core of every child's relation to itself, that is to (its entire) life in its unforeseeability. Every child is a proletarian child (no matter into which class it has been born) in that its birth is *pro-*: not back into a family, a clan, or even class, be it the class of workers or proletarians (as a newborn member: *one* among others). Each child's birth, instead, takes place *pro-oles*: for (other) children *playing*, that is improvising (their entire) life, with and for other children. Each child born *pro-oles* is—as if—(for) another child. Each child's birth takes place *pro-*, but the quintessence of this *pro-* remains *impro-*. The release (in a proletarian children's theater) of unforeseeability at the core of each child's relation to itself (that is—as if—to *other* children) prevents each single child from being (perceived as) *one* (and the same). It immunizes (up to a certain point) each child, *pro-oles*, against the political-teleological aim of education: the formation of a *moral* personality (as member of a social order, class, or corporation). Children are *im*moral, that is *in*nocent, in other words *shameless*. They do not form a class of their own. Not even the one class of those who don't belong to any class. Instead, each child – a *collective*: "But the child, too, is such a collective" ("Solch ein Kollektivum ist aber auch das Kind"). But no child *forms* nor *performs* a collective entity. What then does the child as *such* a collective provide? It *provides* indeed—if only on the brink of (in)visibility—something, at first glance at least, for the *eye*. But back before this evidence the word *collective* here, no less than *proletarian* and *program*, is not *one*. Its programmatic reading suggests its substitution by one (other) word: the class (*die Klasse*). A public as collective, the collective as class (in a strictly ideological understanding) is *conditio sine qua non*, categorically indispensable for all proletarian children's theaters fruitful outcome. This is the passage, in Benjamin's little text, from one (reading of the word) *collective* to another:

> To have a fruitful outcome, proletarian children's theaters make a collective public categorically indispensable. In one word: the class. Just as only the working class has an infallible sense for the existence of collectives. Such collectives may be the public meeting, the army, the factory. But the child, too, is such a collective. And it is the prerogative of the working class to have a most open eye—*das offenste Auge*—for the childlike collective—*das kindliche Kollektivum*—whereas the bourgeoisie is unable to catch its sight. This collective radiates not just the most powerful energies, but also the most acute [burning] ones. In fact, the actuality of childlike modeling and gesturing—*kindlichen Formens und Gebarens*—is unsurpassable.[11]

Among all (political) classes only the working class (the one class working towards the overcoming of all classes, towards *classless* society; the one class, up to end all classes) disposes of an infallible *organ*, an extreme sense for the existence of collectives. An (open) eye for the many, bordering on countlessness. The list enumerating (accumulating) such collectives—public gatherings of the people; the army, the factory—also counts the child among its (growing) number. But the child not only continues, it interrupts and incompletes the list it adds up to (for every single member of any other class mentioned, also remains—if only by remembrance—child). For the child, according to Benjamin's ambiguous formulation—*Solch ein Kollektivum ist aber auch das Kind*—exploiting a *grammatical* no less than *programmatical* linguistic ambiguity, perceived as an all-embracing general notion, allows to imagine a class of all children; but the child, each single child, allows to be perceived as a—rather loosely connected, almost disintegrating—multitude. Only the class of *proletarians* has—but only when reading the name of this one class apart and discovering amidst its name or (programmatic) designation a crowd of children—a particular sense for the child—*pro oles*: each child a class-like collective (bordering the unforeseeable: classlessness). This exquisite sense is called by Benjamin *das offenste Auge*. It is not simply the eye as the organ of sight—and as such the *theoretical*, namely *theatrical* sense par excellence—and not only the eye wide open, but an eye *widest* open; no longer just the sense of vision and provision, bound by respective and prospective obligations, and blinded by the desire to see what it expects; but open for the unforeseen—*improvisions*—when looking at children playing for children. This collective, not only (most evidently) children playing for children, but (less visible): each single child playing *for* and *with* another—unforeseen—child at the place of this one child, playing *as* more than one and playing *for* more than one *other* child, in other words, each child a multitude of children playing *for* (and *with*, and *as*) children; this collective not only emanates the most powerful force, but the most acute and *momentary* energy. This radiating energy, embodied in each child—an erupting multitude (countless, unaccountable for), is not *directed* (towards the future of a classless society); it consumes and consummates the moment (of its emanation); in German: den *Augenblick*. The *most* open eye of the (proletarian) observer is an eye (open) for such moments: less Augen*blick* than Augen*blitz* (an eye's lightning). The most extreme manifestation of such a moment in the playing child is the child's gesture—*Geste*—or gesturing—*Gebaren*. Benjamin calls it *unerreicht*: unequaled, unattained, un-reached. The educators' task, as leaders—*Leiter*—of the various *sections* in which the children experience and experiment with different forms of expression, "the making of stage props, painting, recitation, music, dance," is a task of *(Augen)Blitzableitung*. Each *Leiter*: *Blitzableiter* (lightning conductor). For these educators' solely task is to reach (out) for each child's un-reached—*unerreicht*—acuteness and actuality of its gesturing; to free—*erlösen* is Benjamin's word—each child's gestures "from the hazardous magical world of sheer phantasy" ("aus dem gefährlichen Zauberreich der bloßen Phantasie zu erlösen"), and to bring the children's un-reached gesturing *in touch* with a variety of materials (provoking *im*provised, unforeseeable results). These leaders—*observing* the children's gestures, in each section differently—are readers: they learn to translate the children's gestures—*kindliche Gesten*—into children's signals—*kindliche Signale*. But these *un-reached* signals are not reaching for help or attention from outside. They are signals from a world no less than into and throughout a world in which the child lives and commands (*in welcher das Kind lebt und befiehlt*). Benjamin condenses the quintessence of these observations (developed in the Russian children's clubs) into a sentence (to be taught, and studied): "The child inhabits its world as a dictator" ("das Kind lebt in seiner Welt als Diktator"). And: "Almost every gesture of the child is command and signal in a surrounding world, or environment, for which only rarely men of genius were able to open the eye, to catch a glance" ("Fast jede kindliche Geste ist Befehl und Signal in einer Umwelt, in welche nur selten geniale Menschen einen Blick eröffnet haben"). This world, in which the child lives (and commands as a dictator) is the world of its entire life. What the child dictates, and what its every gesture signals, is this: improvisation. *Die Improvisation herrscht* (improvisation reigns). The world in which the child does live (its entire life), and which it overlooks, is *unforeseen*. This is the reason for Benjamin's insistence on the *most* open eye—*das offenste Auge*—to catch a first, provisional glance—einen Blick eröffnet haben. The child as dictator does not embody the programmatic ideological slogan of the dictatorship of the proletariat—*die Diktatur des Proletariats*. It embodies some unforeseen aspect (as if hidden) at the verso of this programmatic slogan's every word, but only if read apart, letter for letter, to catch a first glimpse of ... *for children*, at the core of the word *proletariat*: *pro oles*. The child embodies the dictatorship of what in a child's world—children playing for children—reigns: *die Diktatur der Improvisation*.

Pro-: Impro-. The sole aim of the educating leaders, leading the various (extracurricular) sections in which the gesturing children—un-reached in their gestures' acuteness and incisive force: cutting into the most open eye—get in touch with different materials in order to execute (or manifest) their gestures' *improvisional* (exploratory, if not explosive) force, is *centered* on one section only which, for that very reason, is not just one section among others but the one and only section cutting into all other sections and cutting each single section's sectarian character apart. Improvisation—improvising nothing but -*cisions* into what matters (in education): unforeseen cuts into all other sections—assures the improvisional character of each section's programmatic outline. (Proletarian) education tends to have the dictatorial *legislative* order in every child's world—*Improvise!*—get in touch with the *executive* experience of its categorical (categorically improvised) imperative's application to matter. Each child's dictatorship consists (inconsistently) in this: the improvisation of *decision*-making. But *improvised* decisions (almost) categorically long for (improvised) cuts into the (texture of) decision or device: to dispose each *dictum* (taking the shape of *datum* and *factum*), resulting from improvised decision-making, for *discussion* (in its *pre*- or *para*parliamentary, that is childlike, pregnancy). This is the decisive section (on improvisation) in Benjamin's *Schema der Spannung* (scheme of tension):

> The development of children's gestures in the different forms of expression—the making of stage props, painting, recitation, music, dance, improvisation—is the task of the different sections. / In all of them improvisation remains central; for, at last, the *Aufführung* is nothing but an improvised synthesis of all of them. Improvisation reigns; it is the disposition (or constitution) from which the signals, signifying gestures, emerge. And the synthesis of these gestures must be *Aufführung*

or theater, because this synthesis alone has the unexpected (sudden and unmistakable)—*unversehentliche*—uniqueness in which the child's gesture stands as in its own real space.¹²

In a child's dictatorial world, improvisation is the *Verfassung*: disposition no less than constitution (consisting in one single *para*linguistic gesture: *Improvise!*). The only paragraph of this constitution—*Improvise!*—is not a *given*, no *pre*scription. Its gesture is *pre-*, *para*grammatical: the unconditionally improvised interruption of *writing* as programmatic prescription, and *speaking* as dictatorship. To *dictate* improvisation is to *improvise*—in other words *to play*—not only *juris*diction but any kind of *diction*. Every gesture emanating from improvisation also emanates improvisation: exposing itself as improvised: without beginning nor end, not *one* nor *self* (never one and the *same*), inconsistent, incomplete(able), unforeseen and without expectations: interrupted by, no less than interrupting, another (improvised) gesture. *Theater* is the *improvised synthesis* of all these gestures (taught to get in touch with a variety of materials in different sections, each section intersected with each other through improvisation). This *synthesis* has to be called *improvised* or provisional for what takes place at its core is (ana)*lysis*: the (improvised) (dis)*solution* of its (improvised) gathering. A proletarian children's theater is the improvised *analysis* of an improvised *synthesis*: the dissolution of the scheme of tension, in other words of education (*die Aufführung führt nichts als die Auflösung einer improvisierten Synthese auf: (vorübergehende) Erlösung von (vorübergehender) Erziehung*). Benjamin calls the uniqueness of this *theatrical* event *unversehentlich*: an unexpected, improvised word, not to be found in any German dictionary: the crossing of two common [familiar] words (interrupting each other): *unversehens* (out of a sudden, unforeseen), and *versehentlich* (through oversight). At play in both words—as can be seen—is the German verb *sehen* ("to see"; a possible translation of the Ancient Greek verb *théorein*). But also at play (not *at work*) in both words is the verb *versehen*: to provide (someone with something); echoing the noun *Versehen* (error). The gesture supporting the emanation of this *hapax*, the word *unversehentlich*, oscillates between *unmistakably unoverseen* and *unexpected*; between *expected* and *unexpected*; between *unforeseen* (*unversehens*) and **ununforeseen** (**un**versehentlich); indicating that even the expectation of the unexpected remains unprotected from unexpected interventions into the very (familiar) notion of *the unexpected* and *the improvised*. Such an intervention takes place at the precise place of the prefix *un-* (as in **un**versehentlich and its most accurate English translation *ununforeseen*), at the core of which a gesticulating crowd of prefixes, interrupting each other, intervenes: . . . **unununun** . . . As much as this *hapax* oscillates between *un*foreseen and *unun*foreseen: it oscillates no less (even more) between *unun*foreseen and *ununun*foreseen. And so (unforeseeably) forth. This is the (*para*grammatical) *force* at the core (in every gesture) of a proletarian children's theater. The proliferation of these gathering gesticulating *un-* at the unique, *ununforeseeably* unique moment of *Aufführung* as the theatrical appearance of education's dissolution: *Auflösungs*erscheinung, hits the spectator's eye and transperforates a proletarian children's theater into what Benjamin calls "*Augenblick*": an event that is no longer *spectacle*: no longer exclusively bound to the *eye* as the theoretico-theatrical organ and sense of sight. Each eye, including the *most* open eye (inconspicuously) opens around the ... unforeseen: "Children's achievement is always aimed not at the 'eternity' of the products but at the 'moment' of the gesture. Theater as the ephemeral art is the children's art" ("Nicht auf die 'Ewigkeit' der Produkte', sondern auf den 'Augenblick' der Geste stellt alle kindliche Leistung es ab. Das Theater als die vergängliche Kunst ist die kindliche"). The *Augenblick*, put into quotation marks—"..."—the *so-called* Augenblick of unleashing the improvising gesture cuts into the impression of self-sufficiency and domination of the sense of sight. This "*Augenblick*" opens the eye for the hand: the sense of sight *in touch* with the sense of feeling. Children get in touch with this perforation of the border between the sense of seeing (condensed in the *eye*) with the sense of feeling (condensed in the *hand*) in the section on painting: "[The painter] is, rather, a man who sees more accurately with his hand when his eye fails him, who is able to transfer the receptive innervation of the eye muscles into the creative innervation of the hand. What characterizes every child's gesture is that creative innervation is exactly proportioned to receptive innervation" ("[Der Maler ist] ein Mann, der mit der Hand da näher zusieht, wo das Auge erlahmt, der die aufnehmende Innervation der Sehmuskeln in die schöpferische Innervation der Hand überführt. Schöpferische Innervation in exaktem Zusammenhang mit der rezeptiven ist jede kindliche Geste"). The emblematic proof of where this transfer occurs, not in the painter but in the *writer*, in Benjamin's little text, as if a child's hand were taking over the (adult) writer's eye at this particular "*Augenblick*," is the writing of the word *unversehentlich*.

Education—the scheme of (building) tensions—takes place between two *solutions*: first, in the sections it frees—*erlöst*—the children's improvising gestures from their im- or amaterial touch: they get in touch with manifold textures (*Stoffen*) to execute and bring the incisive unforeseeability of their gestures, bound to specific matters, to the fore; second, in theater, at the moment—"*Augenblick*"—of *Aufführung*, the child's gesturing breaks free from the scheme of (building) tension, as well as from the *theater* in its *spectacular* aspect as a *Schau*platz for the happening of *Schau*spiel. The moment— "*Augenblick*"—of *Aufführung* opens a gap or *pause* between *Schau*- and -*platz*, between *Schau*- and -*spiel*, emancipating both, -*platz* and -*spiel* from the observing, watching, over- and foreseeing eye of the (adult) spectator as *theorós*. Only the eye *widest* open, only the opening (cutting apart) of the open eye, is able to experience this *pause*. Benjamin calls this moment, as if alluding to (the moment) of *birth*, "radikale Entbindung" (the radical unleashing or, more literally: *accouchement*), and "wilde Entbindung" (wild delivery): "Opposite to the educational process of schooling, the *Aufführung* is the radical delivery—one may call it *ammaterialisation*—of sheer play, something which the adult can only look at" ("Die Aufführung steht der erzieherischen Schulung gegenüber als die radikale Entbindung des Spiels dem der Erwachsene einzig und allein zusehen kann").

Earlier, at one point in the section "scheme of tension," Benjamin prepares for the unforeseen and surprising use of the word *unversehentlich*, when explaining that a proletarian children's theater doesn't emanate from the collective work in the children's clubs. It rather *interrupts* the study in the sections: "Here, *Aufführungen* come about, one might say: incidentally, as an oversight, almost as a children's prank, and in this way the children interrupt the course of study, which remains incomplete forever" ("Hier kommen Aufführungen nebenbei, man könnte sagen: aus Versehen, zustande, beinahe als ein Schabernack der Kinder, die auf diese Weise einmal das grundsätzlich niemals abgeschlossene Studium unterbrechen"). *Aus Versehen*: incidentally, as an oversight, *unforeseen*. But what precedes is no less important: *man könnte sagen* (one might say). The notion *aus Versehen* challenges the desire to understand: *zu verstehen*. It is not clear whether *to say* "man könnte sagen" actually says what at first glance only *could* be said (but isn't), and therefore energizing the dynamics of the notion *aus Versehen*, or whether *man könnte sagen* helds back the actual saying of what it says nevertheless, *as if* it said: *aus Versehen*. [It is never clear whether what *is* said *is* said or *as if* it were said whether the *saying* (for instance of the turn of phrase *man könnte sagen*) takes place on or off stage.]

The irritating notion *man könnte sagen: aus Versehen* indicates that the unexpected happening of a proletarian children's theater can't be put into words for its unforeseeability includes its unforesayability: literally the *in*fantility of what might happen to language, words, and syllables and letters when the (proletarian children's) genius of improvisation gets in touch with them. The notion *man könnte sagen: aus Versehen* seems to speak without saying something (understandable): almost a *Schabernack* (prank) as if inserted by a child's hand into the *Programm* ..., thus interrupting its *grammatical* coherence. This is part of the *program* of a proletarian children's theater: to *interrupt* the (pro)grammatical coherence of the (ideological) language of adults, and thus of the *Programm* ..., as if written by an adult, itself. A proletarian children's theater has no *intermissions*. It is itself nothing but intermission, -ruption, cut. Near the end of the section "scheme of (dis)solution," Benjamin refers back to a proletarian children's theater as caesura, by calling it a *pause*:

> The *Aufführung* is the great creative pause in the work of education. It is in the realm of children what the carnival has been in the old cults. Everything is turned upside down, and just as in Rome the master served the slaves during the Saturnalia, in the same way in their *Aufführungen* children stand on the stage and instruct and educate the attentive educators. New forces, new innervations appear, ones the leader had no inkling of while working [in the sections]. He learns about them only in the course of this wild delivery of the child's imagination. Children that have played theater in this way, have been set free in such *Aufführungen*. Through playing, their childhood has been fulfilled.[13]

By referring to similarities between a proletarian children's theater as a "creative pause" (*schöpferische Pause*)—whether such a pause interrupts creativity or is itself creative remains (as if) unsaid—and carnival, Benjamin introduces (without doing so explicitly) a passage from Florens Christian Rang's essay *Historische Psychologie des Karnevals* ("Historical Psychology of Carnival"; written in 1909, but published only in 1928, a text with which Benjamin was familiar at least since 1921):

> Carnival is a *pause*, the interregnum between abdication of and accession to the throne (the formula known to us from constitutional law: le roi est mort, vive le roi! has no validity in Oriental sultanates; therefore it is a procession, a pageant: the image of a celestial procedure: the procession of stars, until the ruling star of the old year has completely vanished, and the ruling star of the new year has climbed to take the throne.[14]

And in a preceding passage, Rang emphasizes the astrological logic of *carnival* as *interval*: "Astrology yields carnival a place in the calendar, the breaking of the law has to cover a miscalculation; this is astrology's logic: carnival covers the leap-time. Which originally was situated *between* the two calendar years" ("Die Astrologie gibt dem Karneval einen Platz im Kalender, der Gesetzesbruch muß ihr einen Rechenbruch decken; das ist die Logik der Astrologik: Karneval deckt die Schaltzeit. Die ursprünglich *zwischen* den beiden Kalender-Jahren lag"). According to this astrological logic, carnival covers—overacts, or *überspielt*—a break between the course of the years following the *revolution* of the stars; a break or intervention, opening an interstice in the *revolutionary* cycle of the calendar, that *carnival*—at the same time, so to say— exposes. Therefore (as if out of embarrassment) Rang calls the interim time (meantime) or time-out of the carnival, oximoronically, "gesetzliche Gesetz*los*igkeit" (lawful law*less*ness).[15] Carnival, according to this reading, oscillates between a *proviso clause* and *improvision*. This *critical* pause, once applied to Benjamin's *Programm*, may allow to say this: A proletarian children's theater is not a *revolutionary* theater, it is not part of a (proletarian) revolution, but *revolts* against (the mechanics of) revolution in its *astro-*, *des*astro*-political* sense. A (proletarian) children's theater, considered a *pause* (and compared to *carnival*), is neither (des)astrologically nor politically oriented. Its inclination differs from both. Rang alludes (though involuntarily) to this other inclination by quoting the juridical formula in use throughout the reign of French Absolutism: *le roi est mort, vive le roi!* This formulaic sentence (or *dictum*), though almost invisibly, as if incidentally—*aus Versehen*—is syncopated by another pause. This pause is not astrological, it is *diacritical*: a *comma*, indicating *silence* (though not semantically saturated)—another moment of *infan*tility—between *le roi est mort* and *vive le roi!* The comma indicates a pause, but remains without any suggestion about the time or duration of this pause. This pause cannot be filled, nor fulfilled. It doesn't bridge the gap between the living and the dead; between living and dead kings or children. It is not revolutionary. Rather *truly* revolutionary (*wahrhaft revolutionär*) according to the last sentence in Benjamin's program: "What is truly revolutionary is the *secret signal* of what is to come that speaks from the gesture of the child" ("Wahrhaft revolutionär wirkt das *geheime Signal* des Kommenden, das aus der kindlichen Geste spricht"). The *secret signal* of what comes—*des Kommenden*—is condensed into the comma— *Komma*—(thus echoing *das Kommende*), between the two sentences, *le roi est mort* and *vive le roi!* This coming—always to come without preparing for the coming to an *end* of what comes: Komm*ende*—the actuality of which is marked by the comma, speaks— without speaking: *improvising* speech—from inside the child's gesture, out: into the open. This pause marks a (fissured) *fermata*. In other words, an opening: *Ouverture*.

-vision. A proletarian children's theater is not, as the word *theater* suggests, dominated by the sense of sight, nor by any other sense. It is less *Schau-* (*spect-*), and more *-spiel* (*-acle*). What reigns—relating all five senses to one another in *unforeseen* ways, by having them get in touch with *matter*—is *improvisation*. Improvisation is the (forceful, *most pregnant*) quintessence of children's *play*: not only children playing with and for children, but children playing—*playing children*. This irritating split (or doubling) of play—*play* not simply contrasting *work*, but exposed to a play called "playing"—is the (explosive) "moment"—"Augenblick"—of the radical or wild delivery (unleashing or acouchement: *Entbindung*) of *play* at the core of a proletarian children's theater, "which the adult," as Benjamin writes, "can only look at" (*dem der Erwachsene einzig und allein zusehen kann*): under the spell of the sense of sight, as if chained to the rear wall of his eye socket, an orbit cavity. Children's *theater*, a play—-*spiel*—detached from the domination of *théorein—Schau-*—is not simply contrasting the sense of sight, but entertains a certain relation to the eye as well as to all other senses. Which relation? In the second passage of his *program*, "scheme of tension," Benjamin mentions, almost in passing, Jean Paul as the first among very few men of genius who were able to open the eye for the world (or environment: *Umwelt*) of children's play where improvisation, the improvised gesture, reigns: "Almost every gesture of the child is command and signal in a surrounding world, or environment, for which only rarely men of genius were able to open the eye, to catch a glance. Above all, Jean Paul did this" ("Fast jede kindliche Geste ist Befehl und Signal in einer Umwelt, in welche nur selten geniale Menschen einen Blick eröffnet haben. Allen voran tat es Jean Paul"). This opening happens at one point in Jean Paul's *Levana oder Erziehlehre* (*Levana, or, The Doctrine of Education*), in a section or paragraph on children's plays (*Spiele der Kinder*). This paragraph is not an analysis of children's plays. It *improvises* (mimics or mocks) such an analysis. The paragraph is written *as if* it were written (by a German who is up to write an opusculum on children's plays): "If now a German were to write an opusculum on children's plays . . ., he would divide them up . . . only in two classes" ("Schriebe nun ein Deutscher ein Werkchen über die Kinderspiele . . ., so würde er sie . . . nur in zwei Klassen teilen"). But such a scientific man, Jean Paul continues, thus undermining the binary pattern dividing all children's plays along the line of investing *active* or *passive* force, impression or expression, the force to activate (force), and the force to retain (force)—such a man would have to, as if forced to, establish a third class of plays: "Namely that class where the child neither performs nor feels the play, but plays as if it were playing, that class namely, where the child is comfortably taking and giving form and sound—for example looking out a window, lying on the grass, overhearing the nurse and other children" ("die nämlich, worin das Kind das Spiel nur spielt, nicht treibt noch fühlt, nämlich die, wo es behaglich Gestalt und Ton nimmt und gibt—z.B. aus dem Fenster schauet, auf dem Grase liegt, die Amme und andere Kinder hört"). This class to which Jean Paul alludes already further up in the same paragraph—"though children also have a play they consider mere play, for instance joking, meaningless speech, in order to pronounce (or dictate) something to themselves etc." ("wiewohl auch die Kinder ein Spiel haben, das ihnen eines ist, z.B. das Scherzen, sinnloses Sprechen, um sich selber etwas vorzusprechen etc.")[16]—does not simply cover a third variety of children's plays. It annihilates the validity of the first two classes in that every play covered by both classes can be played *as if* it were (seriously) played. Children play *to act* (*treiben*), and children play *to feel* (*fühlen*). This third class is not a class among others, it undoes the scientific approach (which is just another—children's—play) to observe and classify all children's plays. Among the examples provided by Jean Paul to characterize children playing—*playing children* is also this: to look out a window (*aus dem Fenster schaun*). This is Jean Paul's *Programhmen*. To play looking out a window (secretly) signals an improvised gesture at play in what is called *seeing*: to play to see does not add a sixth or seventh sense. It provides a presentiment of the senselessness of counting senses. Children playing ... don't count (on) five senses, for to (play to) count is just another play among (countless) others. *To-play-to-see* opens behind (if not amidst) your eyes a world(lessness) unembraced by sockets containing (and counting) their globes. A (proletarian) children's theater is not *Globe Theater*. It opens (secretly) around a comma , or colon :

Notes

1   "Programm eines proletarischen Kindertheaters," *GS* 2: 763–9. An English translation, "Program for a Proletarian Children's Theater," by Rodney Livingstone, has been published in *SW* 2: 201–6. Quotations from this translation are altered and discussed throughout this text.
2   "Ich sollte das Programm ausarbeiten. Walter Benjamin hatte schon in Capri (1924) von meinem Kindertheater erfahren und ein außerordentliches Interesse daran gezeigt. 'Ich werde das Programm schreiben', sagte er, 'und deine praktische Arbeit theoretisch darlegen und begründen.' Er schrieb es wirklich. Aber in der ersten Fassung wurden meine Thesen ungeheuer kompliziert dargestellt. Im Liebknechthaus las man und lachte: Das hat dir ja Benjamin geschrieben! Ich gab Walter Benjamin das Programm zurück, er solle verständlicher schreiben. So entstand das *'Programm eines proletarischen Kindertheaters'* in einer zweiten Fassung (die erste ist noch nicht wieder aufgefunden)" Asja Lacis, *Revolutionär im Beruf. Berichte über proletarisches Theater, über Meyerhold, Brecht, Benjamin und Piscator* (München, Rogner & Bernhard, 1976 [1971]), 24–30. My translation. An earlier version of this memoir's section on Benjamin in *Alternative* 59/60 [April/June 1968]: 64–7 [Asja Lazis, *Das "Programm eines proletarischen Kindertheaters." Erinnerungen beim Wiederlesen*]. Benjamin's "Programm" was published for the first time in Walter Benjamin, *Über Kinder, Jugend und Erziehung* (Frankfurt am Main: Suhrkamp Verlag, 1969), 79–86.
3   The Russian noun *besprizornik* meaning, most literally, *the-one-who-is-not-looked-after*. The *pro*gram will have been written for those, in a way, who are not looked after, and who are not after a *pro*gram explaining to themselves and others what they are after (or not) ...—For a detailed historical account of *besprizornik* in Soviet Russia, see Alan M. Ball, *And Now My Soul Is Hardened. Abandoned Children in Soviet Russia, 1918-1930* (Berkeley/Los Angeles/London: University of California Press, 1994).
4   "Darunter waren Burschen mit schwarzen, monatelang nicht gewaschenen Gesichtern, zerlumpten Jacken, aus denen die Watte in Strähnen hing, breiten langen Wattehosen, die mit einem Strick festgebunden waren, bewaffnet mit Stöcken und Eisenstangen. Sie gingen immer in Gruppen, hatten einen Häuptling, stahlen, raubten, schlugen nieder. Kurz gesagt, es waren Räuberbanden—Opfer des Weltkriegs und Bürgerkriegs. Die sowjetische Regierung bemühte sich, die streunenden Kinder in Erziehungshäusern und Werkstätten seßhaft zu machen. Aber sie brachen immer wieder aus." My translation.
5   "Ich wußte, welche ungeheure Kraft im Theaterspielen steckt.... Ich war überzeugt, daß man die Kinder durch das Spiel wecken und entwickeln könne.... Ich wollte die Kinder dazu bringen, daß ihr Auge besser sieht, ihr Ohr feiner hört, ihre Hände aus dem ungeformten Material nützliche Sachen gestalten. Dazu teilte ich die Arbeit in Sektionen ein. Um das Auge, das Sehen zu entwickeln, malten und zeichneten die Kinder. Diese Sektion leitete Viktor Schestakow ... Weitere Sektionen meines

Schulmodells in Orel waren Rhythmus und Gymnastik, Diktion und Improvisation. Verborgene Kräfte, die durch den Arbeitsprozeß freigesetzt, die Fähigkeiten, die ausgebildet wurden, vereinigten wir durch die *Improvisation*. So entstand das Spiel. Kinder spielten für Kinder." My translation.

6 On the spontaneous—improvised—origin and character of the various and variable, incoherent and heterogeneous *council systems* during the early stages of all European revolutions since 1790, always in open or veiled conflict with the *party system*, see Hannah Arendt, *On Revolution* [1963] (London: Penguin, 2006), 247–67; and in particular Oskar Anweiler, *Die Rätebewegung in Russland 1905–1921* (Leiden: E.J. Brill, 1958).

7 In early 1928, Walter Benjamin had published *Einbahnstraße*. This book—or street—opens with a printed dedication: "DIESE STRASSE HEISST / ASJA-LACIS-STRASSE / NACH DER DIE SIE / ALS INGENIEUR / IM AUTOR DURCHGEBROCHEN HAT" ("This street is called / Asja-Lacis-Street / according to her who / as an engineer / has forced its way through inside the author"). The dedication improvises, almost providentially, the subtle extension of *Programm* into Pro*grahmen*, by breaking a certain *Bann*—proscription, ban—inside the author and opening a way—Ein*bahn*-—where writing had seemed to remain confined to aporetic waylessness.

8 *The Attic Nights of Aulus Gellius*, Books XIV–XX, with an English translation by John C. Rolfe (Cambridge, MA/London, England: Harvard University Press, 1993), 166–71 (16.10.1–14).

9 "Die Erziehung des Kindes erfordert: *es muß sein ganzes Leben ergriffen werden.* / Die proletarische Erziehung erfordert: *es muß in einem begrenzten Gebiet erzogen werden.* ... Weil nun das ganze Leben in seiner unabsehbaren Fülle gerahmt und als Gebiet einzig und allein auf dem Theater erscheint, darum ist das proletarische Kindertheater für das proletarische Kind der dialektisch bestimmte Ort der Erziehung."

10 "Hier kommen Aufführungen nebenbei, man könnte sagen: aus Versehen, zustande, beinahe als ein Schabernack der Kinder, die auf diese Weise einmal das grundsätzlich niemals abgeschlossene Studium unterbrechen. Der Leiter legt auf diesen Abschluß weniger Wert. Ihm kommt es auf die Spannungen an, welche in solchen Aufführungen sich lösen. Die Spannungen der kollektiven Arbeit sind die Erzieher."

11 "Proletarische Kindertheater erfordern, um fruchtbar zu wirken, ein Kollektiv als Publikum ganz unerbittlich. Mit einem Worte: die Klasse. Wie denn andererseits nur die Arbeiterklasse ein unfehlbares Organ für das Dasein der Kollektiva besitzt. Solche Kollektiva sind die Volksversammlung, das Heer, die Fabrik. Solch ein Kollektivum ist aber auch das Kind. Und es ist ein Vorrecht der Arbeiterklasse, für das kindliche Kollektivum, welches der Bourgeoisie nie zu Gesicht kommen kann, das offenste Auge zu haben. Dieses Kollektivum strahlt nicht nur die gewaltigsten Kräfte aus, sondern die aktuellsten. Unerreicht ist in der Tat die Aktualität kindlichen Formens und Gebarens."

12 "Die Entwicklung dieser kindlichen Geste zu den verschiedenen Formen des Ausdrucks, als Anfertigung von Requisiten, Malerei, Rezitation, Musik, Tanz, Improvisation, fällt den verschiedenen Sektionen zu. / In ihnen allen bleibt die Improvisation zentral; denn schließlich ist die Aufführung nur die improvisierte Synthese aus ihnen. Die Improvisation herrscht; sie ist die Verfassung, aus der die Signale, die signalisierenden Gesten auftauchen. Und Aufführung oder Theater muß eben darum die Synthese dieser Gesten sein, weil nur sie die unversehentliche Einmaligkeit hat, in welcher die kindliche Geste als in ihrem echten Raume steht."

13 "Die Aufführung ist die große schöpferische Pause im Erziehungswerk. Sie ist im Reiche der Kinder, was der Karneval in alten Kulten gewesen ist. Das Oberste wird zuunterst gekehrt und wie in Rom an den Saturnalien der Herr den Sklaven bediente, so stehen während der Aufführung Kinder auf der Bühne und belehren und erziehen die aufmerksamen Erzieher. Neue Kräfte, neue Innervationen treten auf, von denen oft dem Leiter unter der Arbeit nichts ahnte. Erst in dieser wilden Entbindung der kindlichen Phantasie lernt er sie kennen. Kinder, die so Theater gespielt haben, sind in dergleichen Aufführungen frei geworden. Im Spielen hat sich ihre Kindheit erfüllt."

14 "Karneval ist eine *Pause*, das Interregnum zwischen einer Thron-Entsagung und Thron-Besteigung (unser Staatsrecht-Satz: le roi est mort, vive le roi! gilt ja für Sultanate des Orients nicht; ist darum eine Prozession, ein Umzug: das Abbild eines himmlischen Prozesses: der Prozession der Sterne, bis das Herrscher-Gestirn des Altjahrs völlig untergegangen ist und das Herrscher-Gestirn des neuen Jahrs auf die Thron-Höhe geklommen." My translation.

15 Florens Christian Rang, *Historische Psychologie des Karnevals* [1909], ed. Lorenz Jäger (Berlin: Brinkmann & Bose, 1983), 13–14. See also Lorenz Jäger, *Messianische Kritik. Studien zu Leben und Werk von Florens Christian Rang* (Köln/Weimar/Wien: Böhlau, 1998), 79–93.

16 Jean Paul, *Levana oder Erziehlehre* [1806], in Jean Paul, *Sämtliche Werke*, ed. Norbert Miller (Munich: Hanser Verlag, 1987), I/5: 602–3.

12

Walter Benjamin and the Anthropocene

Nitzan Lebovic

Less than a century after the invention of the industrialized total war, a host of environmental catastrophes offered a fertile ground for postapocalyptic imagination; one theoretician has commented, "Everything is now in play. Every cubic meter of air and water, and every hectare of land."[1] Human life and nature converge, once again, in man's made catastrophe and a renewed sense of finality as a part of "deep time" or "geological time." As the temporality of the twentieth century assumed a form quite different from previous centuries, "our usual historical practices for visualizing time, past and future, times inaccessible to us personally ... are thrown into a deep contradiction and confusion."[2] The Anthropocene, the era in which human actions have profoundly changed the Earth's geology, water, and atmosphere, has been marked by a disarray in both space and time. In the present, the disarray extends back into human lives. Scholars such as Anne Fremaux and John Barry show that "Humanity is leaving the 'safe operating space' of the stable, accommodating environment offered by the Holocene, [moving toward] a radical break, a point of no return, a dangerous upheaval that calls for the rethinking of our paradigms of thought and action."[3] Those who believe that human beings, thanks to their rationality, can cope with any problem are, as Clive Hamilton declared in a lecture entitled "Human Destiny in the Anthropocene" (2013), "like Walter Benjamin's Angel of History, flying into the future but facing backwards, fleeing from a horrible past of suffering and oppression but unable to see the destruction that lies ahead."[4]

1. Benjamin, Aura, and Anthropocene

Elizabeth DeLoughrey, Thomas Ford, and Tobias Menely have recently discussed the Anthropocene in direct connection with Benjamin's theory of history. DeLoughrey argues that "Benjamin has laid the groundwork for theorizing Anthropocene discourse in that the latter also remarks on a disjuncture between humans (history) and the planet (nature)." For her, Benjamin's understanding of history and nature is always framed in relation to decline and ruins: "Decline is represented in Benjaminian allegory and Anthropocene scholarship as ruins."[5] Ford and Menely discuss the importance of decline for Benjamin as well, but they avoid a direct link between forms of representation, decline, and the Anthropocene. Instead, they focus on Benjamin's understanding of the aura, a "strange weave of space and time," exposed during times of industrial reproduction and cultural decline.[6] Ford thinks that the dialectical concept of the Anthropocene originated at the time of industrial reproduction, i.e., when the aura was in decline. The fundamental element of both is the convergence and collapse of time-frames "at the same moment when discrepant temporal scales suddenly intersect, and distinct ways of telling time are folded, concretely, into each other."[7] By that he means not only the breaking and folding of traditional divisions between time-scales (geological and existential), of temporal frames (the deep past and the living present), or objects of knowledge (natural and cultural), force, cause, and agency (geophysical and political), but also the collapse of time-scales in the Anthropocene. Ford identifies Benjamin's temporal convergence in the auratic time—the fusion of distance and nearness, self and other—with the origins of the Anthropocene. Benjamin's critique follows a post-Nietzschean critique of progress, historicism, metaphysics, and "unhistorical atmosphere" and predicts the fundamental engagement with the time of the Anthropocene. The era of decline keeps building on "action from distance" and is doomed to end, according to both Nietzsche and Benjamin, with "a star without atmosphere," i.e., without aura, breath, or a proper understanding of a planetary time-scale.[8] Menely reads the aura as an expression of "the phenomenology of air," a "breath of lost time," and its decline and commodification as a warning sign regarding the accumulative nature of catastrophe, or simply "the accumulative principle."[9] In contrast to most crises, which suddenly diverge from the past, he explains, the decline of the aura shows "the accretion of the past, a thickening of the air"; blending time and physical properties, Menely declares that "the temporality of the Anthropocene [is] the delayed and disaggregated effect of fossil capitalism, the accumulation of greenhouse gases, the acidification and heating of the oceans."[10] All three researchers see Benjamin's history of the aura as a cautionary tale, and in spite of their different emphases, all identify decline—a Roman concept revived in the nineteenth century—with the catastrophe of the Anthropocene, a twenty-first-century concept.[11]

Reading Benjamin in the context of the Anthropocene requires, as the commentators I mention above do, a daring hermeneutic move. However, the question of context matters here, too. After all, as Ian Balfour demonstrated, "the moment of decline or transition is, paradoxically, the moment when totality presents itself."[12] For Romantic poetry, such as Hölderlin—an important poet for the young Benjamin—it signified a linguistic totality.[13]

Benjamin's catastrophic reading of history, his aesthetics of ruins, his view of the angel of history, and his analysis of decline were inspired by nineteenth-century pessimism on the one hand and its sense of language on the other hand. It is impossible to understand his catastrophic interpretation of progress without the heavy input of Romanticism and Nietzscheanism. But does Benjamin's understanding of history and nature, his investment in Romantic and Nietzschean terminology, help us in the time of the Anthropocene? Are we still trapped between decline and linguistic totality? Building on the recent theoretical works mentioned previously, the four principal arguments of this chapter are both historical and analytical. First, in line with the three texts mentioned above, I claim that a key component of the twenty-first-century rhetoric of catastrophe, the Anthropocene included, follows a Romantic, post-Nietzschean, Benjaminian, critique of progress. Yet, beyond the scope of previous research, an understanding of decline and of the catastrophe of the Anthropocene rely on a similar critique but not on the same means of correction. Put simply, Benjamin could not have foreseen the repercussions of post-1950s industrialization and neoliberal economics. Second, and within the scope of Benjamin studies, I argue that already in his early pedagogical essays Benjamin explained the fundamental basis of his critique of progress. Even if unfamiliar with the conditions of globalized economy, he wanted to alert his readers to the mistake of falling prey to linear, anthropocentric, positivistic time-frames that separated science and mankind from nature. Here I demonstrate that Benjamin's early, post-Romantic and post-Nietzschean emphasis on a planetary temporality was meant to resist the Anthropogenic order and an anthropocentric analysis of both history and nature. Third, I develop an analytical argument to unite my two historical claims above, relying on Benjamin's interest in temporal categories—for example, *Rhythmus* (rhythm) and *Aufblitzen* (flash)—as a further development of the nineteenth century's interest in the dialectic of man-nature relations, i.e., progress and decline. This interest is an uncommonly coherent thread that runs through Benjamin's oeuvre; a careful review shows that the theme developed gradually, in response to politics, social changes, economic movements, and aesthetic pressures. Finally, the use of temporality—rather than concepts connected to ideology, materialism, or dialectics (think of the famous "dialectics in standstill")—allowed Benjamin to consider the limitations of his own critique. A set of temporal terms function, in his writing, as a counterbalance to the critically charged Nietzschean Last Man and the "destructive character." Benjamin's focus on temporality as a principle of critical reflection is responsible for his main contribution to the idea of an Anthropocene.

2. Pedagogy and Time

2.a. "The Metaphysics of Youth"

A coherent argument that runs through Benjamin's whole oeuvre, from early to late, holds that progress—and indeed all linear time—entails a catastrophe, or "an interval" in the flow of time. In a passage from "The Metaphysics of Youth" (1913–14), written more than twenty-five years before "Theses on the Philosophy of History," Benjamin wrote that "the new storm rages in the agitated self."[14] The storm, a Romantic image, introduces a permanent threat arising from within the landscape of the self, and leads one to reconsider the relation of past and future.

> If the "I" is sent out as time, within it things storm on, countering it in their distancing, humble bearing, on course toward the center of the interval, toward the womb of time, whence the self radiates outward ... To it all future is past. The past of things is the future of "I"-time. But past things become futural. They send forth the time of the self anew when they have entered into the distance, into the interval.[15]

Benjamin's cryptic discourse on the time of the self assumes that at the heart or "womb of time" lies an outside force, be it a storm or an interval. The interval contrasts with the usual, linear understanding of progress and Enlightened self. In other words, a natural force resists, actively, any reasonable attempt to domesticate the self. Its preferred weapon of resistance is the anarchic distribution of intervals.

2.b. Neo-Kantianism and Post-Nietzscheanism

Benjamin's biographers tell us that the origins of the temporal concepts developed in his youth came from neo-Kantian and post-Nietzschean circles. The first he studied in order to oppose. The latter he studied in order to adapt and change. At Freiburg University, Benjamin took courses in religion, literature, history, and philosophy. He was smitten by Kantian and anti-Kantian philosophy, and, in a course taught by the neo-Kantian Heinrich Rickert, he met Martin Heidegger, his senior by three years. The two young thinkers took a few classes with Rickert, among them a seminar on Henri Bergson.[16] It is during that period that Benjamin was drawn to the pedagogical reforms of Gustav Wyneken and the thought of Friedrich Nietzsche, which he used to counter Wyneken's support of World War I. The paradoxical nature of Nietzsche's philosophy and its subversive interest in identity—"Our own 'I' (is uncertain)"—would have a deep influence on Benjamin.[17]

The change in Benjamin's rhetoric during this period becomes quite clearly articulated when one notes his use of temporal concepts to question both Kantian progressivism and Nietzschean cultural pessimism. Interestingly, for Benjamin this double critique functioned as a pedagogical lesson. A year after "Metaphysics of Youth," he discussed education as "liv[ing] and work[ing] *sub specie aeternitatis*."[18] What seems to be an advocacy of an a-timely idea carries in fact the opposite temporal order: what Benjamin meant by eternity stood in direct contrast to the Kantian understanding of self-cultivation and language of self-realization. The very opening of "Metaphysics of Youth" is a rebellious cry against the inheritance of the Idealist legacy: "What we do and think is filled with the being of our fathers and ancestors. An uncomprehended symbolism enslaves us without ceremony."[19] Against this "enslavement," Benjamin's prescription was to awaken to the power of time; a biographer concluded, "Benjamin's youthful writings constitute the workshop of his later philosophy ... At stake in [his] historical dialectic is 'the art of experiencing the present as waking world,' what he will come to call 'now time.'"[20] It is a time made of catastrophes and storms, intervals and the sign of eternity, i.e., the cancellation of traditional temporality as a whole.

2.c. Permanent Catastrophe

If in early observations the self is still the organizing framework for all "intervals," later texts, especially those composed after 1918, talk about the interval as an existing condition, no longer dependent on the self. In a letter written in 1913, Benjamin reported that during a period when he had read *The Critique of Pure Reason* and Rickert's "Logic of Numbers," he had found in himself all absence of "any kind of pleasure in nature."[21] He turned to consider temporal breaks as an alternative route to that pleasurable, or any, experience of nature. Later, his analyses would extend "the interval" into the catastrophe and the Kantian pleasureless into disaster that "is given" (*das Gegebene*). "Critique of Violence" (1921) may list divergent types of murderous states, but one never loses sight for a single minute of the violence at the core of every state. Violence, whether human or divine, judicial or executive, presents the structure of governance with the idea of a recurrent break in the order of things. An absence of pleasure has been systematized and organized as an institutional form.

For Benjamin, it was impossible to understand politics after World War I without understanding the relation between progress, the status quo, and catastrophe: "The concept of progress must be grounded in the idea of catastrophe. That things are 'status quo' *is* the catastrophe."[22] This rendered self and world, past and future, history and nature all one single catastrophe.[23] The catastrophe, or the broken temporality, enabled Benjamin to point at the artificiality of reproduction, the "strange weaving of space and time," mentioned above, but now extending beyond the early stages of Capitalism into an all-encompassing totality. Michael Jennings explains: "The development of a new mode of production under capitalism, much like the overt state of conflict that dominated the seventeenth century, produces only a 'vast rubble heap' that spirals downward into new losses and degradation."[24] It was there, when state violence met the rise of mechanical reproduction, that Benjamin brought Nietzsche's posthumanist catastrophism ("I am no man; I am dynamite") to confront the present moment. As Deborah Cohen explains, "It is only in 'the moment of danger' that this catastrophic 'memory' comes into focus, as history suddenly becomes apparent as something other than the triumphant story told by its victors."[25] Benjamin used temporal principles such as rhythm and "the flash" in order to overcome the constraints that humanist progressive thought adopted willingly.

3. *Rhythmus*

3.a. Anti-Idealism/Existentialism

Benjamin's concept of catastrophic time is grounded in the rejection of progress, linearity, idealism, and ideology.[26] From his early rebellion against the Kantian-Fichtean obsession with the self—"The new storm rages in the agitated self"—to the extension of "the interval" to "the last day of humankind" ("Karl Kraus," 1931), or "the Last Man" (*Arcades*), who's also "the good European," Benjamin conceived of a truly revolutionary temporality.[27] The Nietzschean critique of idealism in the early texts, the eschatology of the Karl Kraus essay, and the metahistorical, almost mythic, perspective of the unfinished Arcades project appear to have little in common, but weaving all of those together is a coherent, long-term, politically motivated rejection of norms, including Enlightenment conventions and counter-Enlightenment reactionary myth-making—all undergirded by an appreciation of broken and repetitive time. As Beatrice Hanssen put it, Benjamin's view of nature and history rebelled against both the neo-Kantian understanding of temporality and the existential one. By connecting, much like Nietzsche, the concepts of life and afterlife (*Überleben, Fortleben*), or creation and origin (*Ursprung*), Benjamin traced "that which emerges from the process of becoming and disappearance."[28]

Viewing human history as a permanent storm, a permanent catastrophe, breaks with any utilitarian argument, shifting that history from an anthropocentric to an environmental notion of time. In that respect, Benjamin's basic assumption, dating back to the early 1900s, was remarkably close to what one reads nowadays in relation to the Anthropocene.

Anticipating the break of man-history-nature relations, Benjamin proposed over a century ago an antiprogressive, posthumanist political theory that could confront the double danger of either the progressive, capitalistic, blind trust in growth, or its counter, the conservative yearning for a non-existing past. As a guiding pedagogical principle, Benjamin reiterated: "A Brechtian maxim: to not build on the good old days, but on the bad new ones."[29] The task of the student—the good European who turns into the Last Man—is to see reality for what it is and propose change, rather than deny it or take refuge in past myths. In order to do that, Benjamin argued, one had to consider the wrong rhythms of past experience and the proper rhythm of change.

3.b. Studying Rhythm

Benjamin understood modernity first and foremost as an issue of time. Instead of the repetitiousness of the past, which made predictions easy, the modern man found himself dancing to unstable rhythms. The concept of rhythm shows how the "eternal recurrence" of the body's beating heart, and the cycle of natural seasons, contrasts and completes the Nietzschean will to power. As Nietzsche put it, "the world ... lives on itself: its excrements are its nourishment," on the insight that nature, unlike mankind, is "without goal ... without will," and that eternal recurrence may be defined as that moment when "all features of the world become motionless, a frozen death throe."[30] The cycle of life and death, excrement and nourishment, stands against the human will and its wish the break away from that cycle.

Benjamin's understanding of the inherent interval in "the womb of time" takes us one step further: the interval exposes the promise and rhythm of the flow, or its absence.[31] This is the reason Benjamin turned rhythm into a hermeneutic principle: in such early works as "The Metaphysics of Youth," "'Experience'" (1913), "Two Poems by Friedrich Hölderlin" (1914), and "The Life of Students" (1915), rhythm was the mark of time, or as Benjamin put it in "Metaphysics of Youth": "When our time expelled us from our isolation into the landscape and our beloved strode toward us ... we could feel how time, which sent us forth, flooded back toward us. This rhythm of time, which returns home to us from all corners of the earth, lulls us to sleep."[32] As Johannes Steizinger wrote in *Revolte, Eros und Sprache* (2013), "The young Benjamin found himself [committed to] the critique of progress and its historical model ... Grounding history in a disruptive rhythm meant this model was predicated on a creative break [*schöpferischen Bruch*] instead of a linear, continuous, and causal process."[33]

Benjamin continued to develop the hermeneutics of rhythm and time in his next works. In "On Language as Such and on the Language of Man" (1916), the concept of rhythm is central to his ontology of language, next to its power of naming as creation.

Adding to his comment on "the curious revolution in the act of creation, where it concerns man," he wrote of "the manifold rhythm of the act of creation" and "the rhythm by which the creation of nature (in Genesis 1) is accomplished."[34] Here, the word "rhythm" indicated the integral pluralism of creation, and in "Goethe's *Elective Affinities*" (1919–22) Benjamin mentioned the "rhythmic sequence of representations" and the "communal rhythms" of architecture.[35] In "The Right to Use Force" (1920) he explained that "what is at issue is the violent rhythm of impatience in which the law exists and has its temporal order, as opposed to the good rhythm of expectation in which messianic events unfold."[36] Rhythm, we recall, is an operative principle that stands beyond good and evil. But it also stands beyond mankind. Its pluralism does not need to follow our imagined shapes and our needs.

Benjamin learned how to use *Rhythmus* as an antihistoricist term from the circle around the poet Stefan George, and specifically from his disciple, the post-Nietzschean thinker Ludwig Klages (1872–1956). In 1912, he traveled to Heidelberg, where, from a distance, he watched George walking with his group of disciples around him. He tried to meet Klages a few times, until the latter agreed, finally, in 1914. Benjamin's biographers identified this interest with "the cultic view of the poet ... reaching from Nietzsche's Zarathustra through the knightly figures of *Jugendstil* to Stefan George."[37] As I have discussed elsewhere, for Klages rhythm was an ecstatic outlet essential to life. He hoped that this life rhythm would enable men to live life to its fullest, confronting death in a direct and unflinching way.[38] Benjamin continued to exchange ideas with Klages, in spite of his explicit anti-Semitism, and in 1930 he recommended him to Gershom Scholem as a great thinker.[39] *Rhythmus* was, for George and Klages, a Nietzschean principle of non-linear movement that defied progressive, enlightened, rational norms, following instead aesthetic, irrational impulses, and it implied an essential point where man and nature overlapped. Politically, the idea of rhythm was embraced by radicals from different social sectors, political ideologies, and ethno-religious identities. It is not by coincidence that the circle around George and Klages included key thinkers and artists from both the radical left and the radical right, conservationists and youth movement activists, bohemians and militants. What all those different people shared was a belief that industrialized progress and the bourgeois state spelled doom for both humanity and nature. Benjamin used rhythm to mark both the beat of creation, and the ecstatic dance of the Last Man. Looking at language itself from the perspective of beginning and end allowed him to avoid any teleology or triumphalism.

3.c. The Last Man/The Good European

In *The Arcades Project*, Benjamin connected three separate ideas: Baudelaire's conviction that the world would imminently end, Nietzsche's notion of "the Last Man," from the prologue to *Thus Spoke Zarathustra*, and Nietzsche's "the good European" from *Human, All Too Human* and *Beyond Good and Evil*.[40] In these fragments, Benjamin rejected the temptation to move to dialectics by freezing it.[41] Instead, he turned to the notion of rhythm, a critical tool that allowed him to avoid an idealist teleology; connecting Baudelaire's "La Fin du monde" and Nietzsche's "the last man" allowed Benjamin to discuss "the coming society," which for him signaled the worst of all possible societies: "this critique displays, in part, prophetic features ... [when] any justice will forbid the existence of citizens who are unable to make a fortune."[42] In this society, "Rulers will be compelled, in order to maintain their position and create a semblance of order, to resort to methods that would appall present-day mankind."[43] Against the idealist emphasis on realization through self-cultivation (*Bildung*) or the capitalist sanctification of growth and wealth he proposed the cyclical rhythm of nature or theological fatalism. The last man, like the angel of history, is the one who's being thrown into the future with his back to it, committed to his last breath to the commemoration of a falling, declining world he leaves behind—but cannot completely let go. Similar to the aura, the image of a declining world is the last remnant of past hope and (failed) promise.

3.d. The Destructive Character

Benjamin's critique of idealism should be read as an attempt to liberate the self from the boundaries imposed on it by humanist anthropomorphism. As his earliest texts prove, he was dedicated to pedagogy and solidarity before any last thoughts about the Last Man and his destruction. From "The Life of the Students" (1916) to "The Destructive Character" (1931) Benjamin advocated for the liberation of the future "from its deformation in the present," urging instead what he called "destructive dwelling—a mode of dwelling that undoubtedly prevents the development of any habits."[44] First among those habits is our assumption that language carries a telos, a message. The analysis of language, his biographers write, is "inseparable from the problematic of time," for the wrong temporal rhythm (habit) will not lead one to the right "mode of dwelling."[45]

4. *Aufblitzen* (Flashing Up)

4.a. Dialectic in Standstill

As mentioned above, the Anthropocene is marked by the collapse of traditional divisions, first and foremost that which separates man from nature. As leading historians and critics have indicated, the Anthropocene forces us to reconsider the divisions between and limits of human, technological, and geological time.[46] Benjamin's attempt to educate his fellow students about the hermeneutics of time was in line with what one would identify nowadays as deconstruction, but his effort proceeded along more basic, ontological lines. Benjamin's plea to leave behind old anthropogenic notions, and his deep suspicion of all institutions, opened the path to a different form of hermeneutics, one based on temporal categories. His investigation relied on nonteleological concepts.[47] As a supplement to his antiteleological sense of rhythm, he proposed *Aufblitzen*, borrowed from Wyneken. "Like Nietzsche," wrote Benjamin's biographers, "Wyneken criticizes 'the old humanistic order,' [preferring] *Aufblitzen*, a sudden flashing up of ideas"; such intuitions arose from "the dark stream of life."[48] The flash is a concept that predates Benjamin's later analysis of shock, his reflections on fascism, or his critique of Martin Heidegger and Ernst Jünger; this tells us something about his earlier motivation.⁴⁹ As he put it in a plan for educational reform: "It is a matter of finding a way out of the opposition between natural, truthful development, on the one hand, and the task of transforming the natural individual into the cultural individual ... [This] will never be completed without violence."⁵⁰ What sort of violence? Overcoming the opposition between biological/natural time and the order of enlightened *Bildung* could only be achieved by creating a new system of education and reflection grounded on broken rhythm and the power of immediacy. Sounding the Nietzschean bells, Benjamin rejected the violence of the state in favor of a revolution in values: "School reform ... becomes the revision of the values themselves," which means, first and foremost, "travelling in all directions."⁵¹ The change of values implied, principally, a reconsideration of human temporality.

Once again, the question of context matters here: the flash became one of Benjamin's central ideas after World War I. It united his work on aesthetics in general (and photography, or montage, in particular), his understanding of the war, politics, the epistemology of recognition, and most importantly the *Jetztzeit*, his ontology of "now-time." Considering the "flashing up" in conjunction with the historical shock of mass violence, and the philosophical understanding of modern self and world, connects his early and late work. As he explained in Convolute N of *The Arcades*, in part a reaction to his own early 1910s interest in Klages's concept of *Traumbewusstsein* (dream consciousness): "The moment of awakening would be identical with 'the now of recognizability,' in which things put on their true—surrealist—face."⁵² Benjamin continued by attacking the principle of dialectics and the dialectics of history itself: "The Hegelian dialectic knows time solely as the properly historical, if not psychological, time of thinking.... All in all, the temporal moment (*Zeitmoment*) in the dialectical image can be determined only through confrontation with another concept. This concept is the 'now of recognizability' (*Jetzt der Erkennbarkeit*)."⁵³ According to the translators and editors of *The Arcades Project*, "The famous 'now of recognizability' ... has the character of a lightning flash [where] historical time is broken up into kaleidoscopic distractions and momentary come-ons."⁵⁴ If this is the case, then Benjamin was trying, since his earliest writings about pedagogy, and as late as his analysis of dialectics in the later writing, to break our understanding of time as a vehicle connecting self and world, individual and collective, nature and history. Like Nietzsche and Baudelaire, he was trying to move beyond dialectics, by exposing it as the function of an anthropocentric worldview. If dialectics is in "standstill," then its very oppositional relation answers the temporal condition of its existence. The flash throws a sudden, bright light that exposes the limitations of its apparent movement.

5. A Qualitative Leap into the Twenty-First Century

In order to understand what limits Benjamin set on his work and what those limitations mean, we need to understand not only how he conceived of progress and linearity, history and nature, but also where his analysis halted. Understanding those limitations is a necessary task for the generation of the Anthropocene. As Nietzsche, and Benjamin after him, called for the end of metaphysics and the rise of the Last Man—"the one who prefers a nothingness of will, who prefers to fade away passively"—they seem to have gotten their own with the advent of the Anthropocene.[55] Anything coming after Nietzsche and Benjamin's call belongs to a different logic altogether, a logic without metaphysics, but also without or beyond Benjamin.

The first step in overcoming the boundaries of nineteenth-century progressivism was the realization that the Romantic understanding of nature was tightly bound to its own understanding of history, nationalism, and individualism, in toto: "Place and local, let alone nation, entail subject positions—places from which Romantic ideas of place make sense. For this reason," Timothy Morton explained in his acclaimed *Ecology without Nature*, "it is all the more important to consider deeply the idea of place, and in general the Romantic attitude to nature prevalent today."[56] "What better time," Morton observed halfway through the book, "to focus upon Benjamin, who has been claimed variously by deconstruction and Marxism, as a theorist with whom ecocritique could engage productively."[57] Morton did not elaborate much—Benjamin was not the center of his analysis, after all—but even in his brief discussion he mentioned aura and the concept of distraction (*Zerstreuung*). He discussed the former in relation to industrialization, reproduction, and decline, the latter in relation to "the dissolving subject-object dualism upon which depend both aestheticization and the domination of nature."[58] In other words, while Benjamin's analysis relied on Romantic terms, he still contributed to the rise of ecocritique by emphasizing a temporality that offered an alternative to the Romantic opposition of man to nature, subject to object. This alternative was based on Benjamin's ability to turn his critical eye toward both progress and Romantic quasi-mystical holism: "Instead of confirming a holistic world in which object and subject fit each other like a hand in glove, the reduction of perception to a sequence of dots enables us to demystify it."[59]

Morton tackled the shift from the terminology of the early 1900s to the present, which has witnessed a collapse of categories. *The Encyclopedia of the Anthropocene* agrees with a plea to "move towards a new humanism in the age of climate change."[60] Benjamin's notions of rhythm, flash, and shock predated World War I, anticipating the events that turned many away from empiricism; he recognized that humanity had by 1914 already reinvented itself as a different life-form. Historians of modernity have pointed to the impact on transportation and communication of steam power and electricity, the telegraph and the cinema, and new weapons, but they rarely notice the temporal concepts that presuppose the material realization. The problem recently became acute. "The escalation since 1945," wrote J. R. McNeill and Peter Engelke, "has been so fast that it sometimes goes by the name the Great Acceleration. Within the last three human generations, three-quarters of the human-caused loading of the atmosphere with carbon dioxide took place.... This period since 1945 corresponds roughly to the average life expectancy of a human being."[61] While it is clear that the conditions created during the nineteenth century shaped the "qualitative leap" into industrialized killing and, later, the destruction of the environment as a whole, a twenty-first-century analysis must address a different context than Benjamin's.[62] In order to understand the difference, it is important to note how Benjamin divided history from nature and how the nineteenth century's view of continuity differed from our own.

To conclude, considering the political implications of our new conditions, the authors of *Climate Leviathan*, Geoff Mann and Joel Wainwright, cited Benjamin's critique of idealism for helping shape a "politically resolute witness to crisis, a stance that finds affirmation in contemporary appeals to a 'coming community' and destituent power."[63] While the relevance of new political, temporal, aesthetic, and ecological categories is becoming clearer and clearer, we manage to take pleasure in the celebration of a man-nature bond, or the conclusion that human life (materially considered) has improved over time. In the Anthropocene, mankind may be forced to consider again how to engage with that bond, and with it the pleasure of heeding the critics of nineteenth-century idealism. Listening to Benjamin's exceptional understanding of his day means also listening carefully to where he sets the boundaries of his own analysis. If his was a time to plumb the nineteenth century, ours must address the humanist tradition and its critics. That might very well be the most important pedagogical lesson Benjamin left behind, an emblem of the Last Man who is also the good European.

Notes

1. Clive Hamilton, "Human Destiny in the Anthropocene," in *The Anthropocene and the Global Environmental Crisis: Rethinking Modernity in a New Epoch*, ed. Clive Hamilton, Christophe Bonneuil, and François Gemenne (New York: Routledge, 2015), 36.
2. Dipesh Chakrabarty, "The Climate of History: Four Theses," *Critical Inquiry* 35, no. 2 (2009), 198.
3. The state and social institutions, charged with educating the people, have been accused by recent scholars of fostering an "accommodating environment" and an "eco-managerial governance." Anne Fremaux and John Barry, "The 'Good Anthropocene' and Green Political Theory: Rethinking Environmentalism, Resisting Eco-modernism," in *Anthropocene Encounters: New Directions in Green Political Thinking*, ed. Frank Biermann and Eva Lövbrand (Cambridge: Cambridge University Press, 2019), 172.
4. Hamilton, "Human Destiny in the Anthropocene," 43.
5. DeLoughrey is more interested in allegories than she is in Benjamin, but the latter had a crucial role in the realization that "modern allegory triggered a new relationship with nonhuman nature that recognized it as a historical rather than an abstract ideal. When modern allegory engages nature as history (what Benjamin termed 'nature-history'), then history becomes subject to nature and therefore to decline." Elizabeth M. DeLoughrey, *Allegories of the Anthropocene* (Durham, NC: Duke University Press, 2019), 6.
6. "Little History of Photography," *SW* 2: 518, quoted in Thomas H. Ford, "Aura in the Anthropocene," *Symploke* 21, no. 1 (2013), 71.
7. Ford, "Aura in the Anthropocene," 66.
8. Ford showed that Nietzsche mentioned "the star without atmosphere" twice, and that Benjamin read both of the texts in which the phrase occurred. Benjamin recycled this metaphor. See "On Some Motifs in Baudelaire," *SW* 4: 343. See also Ford, "Aura in the Anthropocene," 77.
9. Tobias Menely, "Anthropocene Air," *Minnesota Review* 83 (2014), 93.

10 Ibid., 100.
11 For the concept of decline in Cicero's political rhetoric, see Maridien Schneider, *Cicero: 'Haruspex' vicissitudinum mutationisque rei publicae: A Study of Cicero's Merit as Political Analyst*, a Dissertation submitted to the University of Stellenbosch (2000): https://core.ac.uk/download/pdf/37373232.pdf. Last accessed July 10, 2019. For the use of decline in Romantic poetry, see for example the recent Jonathan Sachs, *The Poetics of Decline in British Romanticism* (Cambridge: Cambridge University Press, 2018).
12 Ian Balfour, *The Rhetoric of Romantic Prophecy* (Stanford: Stanford University Press, 2002), 242.
13 Ibid.
14 *SW* 1: 15.
15 Ibid.
16 Howard Eiland and Michael W. Jennings, *Walter Benjamin: A Critical Life* (Cambridge, MA: Belknap Press of Harvard University Press, 2014), 33.
17 Ibid., 48.
18 "School Reform: A Cultural Movement," *EW* 58.
19 "Metaphysics of Youth," *SW* 1: 6.
20 Eiland and Jennings, *A Critical Life*, 42.
21 For the early testimony, see Walter Benjamin to Herbert Belmore, July 30, 1913, *C* 48. For the later discussion of catastrophe, see "Central Park," *SW* 4: 185.
22 "Central Park," *SW* 4: 184.
23 "On the Concept of History," *SW* 4: 392.
24 Michael W. Jennings, *Dialectical Images: Walter Benjamin's Theory of Literary Criticism* (Ithaca, NY: Cornell University Press, 1987), 56.
25 Deborah R. Coen, "The Storyteller and the Seismograph," in *Catastrophes: A History and Theory of an Operative Concept*, ed. Andreas Killen and Nitzan Lebovic (Berlin: DeGruyter, 2014), 15.
26 On Benjamin as a critic of ideology, see Sigrid Weigel, *Body- and Image-Space: Re-Reading Walter Benjamin*, trans. Georgina Paul (London: Routledge, 1996).
27 "Karl Kraus," *SW* 2: 444; *AP* 315 (J47a,3). Benjamin presents Kraus's position as one of "the last judgment" but a secular one at that, for "this is the last official act of this zealot: to place the legal system itself under accusation." In the passage from *The Arcades Project*, Benjamin connected Baudelaire—"This world is coming to an end"—and Nietzsche—"the Last Man" (ibid.).
28 Hanssen, like Eiland and Jennings, contrasts this understanding of time with Heidegger's "process by which the existent came into being." Beatrice Hanssen, *Walter Benjamin's Other History: Of Stones, Animals, Human Beings, and Angels* (Berkeley: University of California Press, 1998), 41.
29 Walter Benjamin, "Conversations with Brecht," in *Reflections: Essays, Aphorisms, Autobiographical Writings*, trans. Edmund Jephcott (New York: Harcourt Brace Jovanovich, 1978), 219.
30 Friedrich Nietzsche, *The Will to Power*, in *Gesammelte Werke* (München, 1925), vol. 14 (Unpublished Papers, 1882–8, 188. I rely here on the translation supplied in *AP* 115 (D2,4–6).
31 This is what Rancière came to identify as *On the Shores of Politics*: "time then, is a headlong flight, becomes the substance of the last utopia. All we need is to have no lack of it ... We would have it that the age of promises and progress is over ... But what has expired is not so much a progressivist faith in the powers of time as the link

which that faith once maintained with the idea of a yardstick, a telos." Jacques Rancière, *On the Shores of Politics*, trans. Liz Heron (London: Verso, 1995), 25.
32 "Metaphysics of Youth," *SW* 1: 13.
33 Johannes Steizinger, *Revolte, Eros und Sprache: Walter Benjamins 'Metaphysik der Jugend'* (Berlin: Kadmos, 2013), 56. Samuel Weber explained that the student helps to disrupt the convergence of law and life, or the one of charismatic Führer and his biopolitical order. The student's gesture "leads to nothing separable from its own repetitive and spectral reenactment ... which subverts the very notion of 'act' as 'actualization.'" Samuel Weber, *Benjamin's -abilities* (Cambridge, MA: Harvard University Press, 2008), 206.
34 "On Language as Such and on the Language of Man," *SW* 1: 68.
35 "The manifold rhythm of the act of creation ... establishes a kind of basic form, from which the act that creates man diverges significantly" ("On Language as Such," *SW* 1: 68). For "communal rhythm," see "Naples," *SW* 1: 416.
36 "The Right to Use Force," in *SW* 1: 231.
37 Eiland and Jennings, *A Critical Life*, 73.
38 Nitzan Lebovic, *The Philosophy of Life and Death: Ludwig Klages and the Rise of a Nazi Biopolitics* (New York: Palgrave Macmillan, 2013), 191–5, 260–70.
39 Ibid., 8.
40 "To be a good European means, for Nietzsche, to be someone who is part of this self-overcoming of Christianity. One thereby embraces the notion of the free spirit." See "Good Europeanism" in Peter R. Sedgwick, *Nietzsche: The Key Concepts* (London: Routledge, 2009), 56.
41 "We must take seriously the anti-dialectical character of Nietzsche's philosophy." Gilles Deleuze, *Nietzsche and Philosophy*, trans. Hugh Tomlinson (New York: Columbia University Press, 2006), 8.
42 *AP* 315 (J47a,3).
43 Ibid.
44 "The Life of Students," *EW* 198; "May–June 1931," *SW* 2: 480. A common mistake made by Benjamin interpreters is to view his reflective reading of the destructive character as affirmative. While Benjamin undoubtedly approved of defamiliarizing social norms, the characterization of the destructive character is more nihilistic than his own. For why Benjamin's temporality differs from the temporality of destruction, see Nitzan Lebovic, "Benjamin's Nihilism. Rhythm and Political Stasis," in *Benjamin-Studien 2*, ed. Daniel Weidner and Sigrid Weigel (Munich: Fink, 2011), 145–58.
45 Eiland and Jennings, *A Critical Life*, 91.
46 See for example the plea for interdisciplinary research found on the website maintained by The Anthropocene Curriculum: https://www.anthropocene-curriculum.org. Last accessed July 8, 2019.
47 John McCole identifies many of those concepts with an antinomian, rather than a dialectic, system. See John McCole, *Walter Benjamin and the Antinomies of Tradition* (Ithaca, NY: Cornell University Press, 1993).
48 Eiland and Jennings, *A Critical Life*, 26. Jennings and Eiland show that Wyneken's attraction to *Aufblitzen* was linked to his own mystical inclinations, especially "a new critical-historical religiosity beyond the invidious dogmas of the churches." We know that Benjamin's critique of Martin Buber rejected any form of religiosity as *Unsinn*. See "Welt und Zeit," *SW* 1: 226–7.
49 For David Ferris, "Benjamin already defines his relation to Heidegger according to his own frequent use of the verb denoting a flash of light (*aufblitzen*) whenever he speaks

of history. It is this repeated image that situates Heidegger within Benjamin's theory of knowledge of history." David S. Ferris, "Introduction: Aura, Resistance, and the Event of History," in *Walter Benjamin: Theoretical Questions*, ed. David S. Ferris (Stanford, CA: Stanford University Press, 1996), 6.

50 "School Reform," *EW* 59. Benjamin returned to the concept of *Aufblitzen* in his 1931 essay "On the Mimetic Faculty," which emphasized the flash of self-recognizability.
51 Ibid., 58, 60.
52 *AP* 464 (N3,a3).
53 *AP* 867 (Q,21).
54 *AP* xii.
55 Deleuze goes a step beyond Benjamin's identification of the last man and the destructive character. In his close reading of Nietzsche he separates "the last man" from "self destruction, active destruction ... [by] the man who wants to parish." While the last man "the final product of becoming. Reactive," the active will of annihilation of the man who wants to parish is "the product of a selection which undoubtedly passes through the last men but does not stop there. Zarathustra praises the man of active destruction." Deleuze, *Nietzsche and Philosophy*, 174.
56 Timothy Morton, *Ecology without Nature: Rethinking Environmental Aesthetics* (Cambridge, MA: Harvard University Press, 2007), 84.
57 Ibid., 161.
58 Ibid., 164.
59 Ibid., 166.
60 Dominick A. DellaSala and Michael I. Goldstein, eds., *The Encyclopedia of the Anthropocene* (Oxford: Elsevier, 2017), 158.
61 J. R. McNeill and Peter Engelke, *The Great Acceleration: An Environmental History of the Anthropocene since 1945* (Cambridge, MA: Belknap Press of Harvard University Press, 2016), 4.
62 "The qualitative leap" is a concept used by historians of the Holocaust and genocide to explain the leap between sporadic and systematic killing during the summer and fall of 1941. See the way Göetz Aly discussed this "leap" in his *Final Solution: Nazi Population Policy and the Murder of European Jews*, trans. Belinda Cooper and Allison Brown (New York: Arnold, 1999), 232; or Anton Weiss-Wendt's discussion of the Armenian genocide in *Historiography of Genocide* ed. Dan Stone (New York: Palgrave Macmillan, 2008), 55.
63 Joel Wainwright and Geoff Mann, *Climate Leviathan: A Political Theory of Our Planetary Future* (London: Verso, 2018), 183.

Contributors

Ilit Ferber is Professor of Philosophy at Tel-Aviv University. She is the author of *Philosophy and Melancholy: Benjamin's Early Reflections on Theater and Language* (Stanford University Press, 2013) and *Language Pangs: On Pain and the Origin of Language* (Oxford University Press, 2019), which is now being translated into German. She has published articles on Benjamin, Heidegger, Leibniz, Scholem, Herder, Freud, Améry, and others, and co-edited four books in English, Hebrew, and Spanish on moods in philosophy, lament in Jewish thought, and the relation between language and violence.

Ian Fleishman is Associate Professor of German and Cinema & Media Studies at the University of Pennsylvania, where he is also affiliated with the Programs in Gender, Sexuality & Women's Studies, Comparative Literature & Theory, and the Penn Program in the Environmental Humanities. He has published widely on topics ranging from the Baroque to contemporary moving-image pornography. His first monograph, *An Aesthetics of Injury: The Narrative Wound from Baudelaire to Tarantino* (Northwestern, 2018), was the winner of the Northeast Modern Language Association Best Book Award.

Charles Gelman teaches at the Gallatin School of Individualized Study, New York University. He received his PhD in Comparative Literature from New York University in 2019. His work has previously appeared in the journals *Barricade*, *Décalages*, and *Law and Literature*.

Clemens-Carl Härle is Professor Emeritus of German Literature and Aesthetics at the University of Siena, Italy. He is editor of *Ai limiti dell'immagine* (Quodlibet, 2005), *Shoah. Percorsi della memoria* (Cronopio, 2006), and *Confini del racconto* (Quodlibet, 2010; French translation: *Aux confins du récit*, Puv, 2014). With Giorgio Agamben and Barbara Chitussi, he curated the edition of the collected fragments of Benjamin's unfinished book on Baudelaire: *Walter Benjamin. Charles Baudelaire. Un poeta lirico nell'età del capitalismo avanzato* (Neri Pozza, 2012; French edition: *Baudelaire*, La Fabrique, 2013).

Natasha Hay holds a PhD in Comparative Literature from the University of Toronto. At present, she is teaching sessionally in the University of Toronto's Department of Philosophy. Her work has been published in *Trans-: Revue de littérature générale et comparée* and is forthcoming with *New German Critique*.

Michael W. Jennings is Class of 1900 Professor of Modern Languages Emeritus at Princeton University. He is the author of two books on Walter Benjamin (*Dialectical

Images: Walter Benjamin's Theory of Literary Criticism and, with Howard Eiland, *Walter Benjamin: A Critical Life*). He served as the General Editor of the standard English-language edition of Benjamin's work, *Selected Writings* (four volumes, 1996–2003).

Dennis Johannßen is Assistant Professor of German in the Department of Languages and Literary Studies at Lafayette College, where he is also affiliated with the Program in Film and Media Studies. His essays on Walter Benjamin, the Frankfurt School, media theory, and Weimar and postwar thought have appeared in *Anthropology & Materialism*, *The German Quarterly*, *MLN*, *Perspectiva*, and *Zeitschrift für kritische Theorie*.

Nitzan Lebovic is Professor of History and the Apter Chair of Holocaust Studies and Ethical Values at Lehigh University. He is the author of *The Philosophy of Life and Death: Ludwig Klages and the Rise of a Nazi Biopolitics* (Palgrave Macmillan, 2013) and *Zionism and Melancholy: The Short Life of Israel Zarchi* (Indiana University Press, 2019). He is also the co-editor of *The Politics of Nihilism* (Bloomsbury, 2014), and *Catastrophes: A History and Theory of an Operative Concept* (DeGruyter, 2014), and the editor of special issues of *Rethinking History* (Nihilism), *Zmanim* (Religion and Power), *The New German Critique* (Political Theology), *Comparative Literature and Culture* (Complicity and Dissent), and *Political Theology* (Prophetic Politics).

Adi Nester is an Assistant Professor of German and the Levine-Sklut Fellow in Jewish Studies in the Department of Germanic and Slavic Languages and Literatures at the University of North Carolina, Chapel Hill.

Michael Powers is Visiting Assistant Professor of German Studies at Macalester College, where he also teaches in the Program in Critical Theory. He has published essays on Benjamin, Jean Paul, Goethe, Bloch, Kracauer, Freud, and Merleau-Ponty.

Gerhard Richter is the L. Herbert Ballou University Professor of German Studies and Comparative Literature at Brown University. He is the author or editor of seventeen books in European critical thought and aesthetics, several of them on Walter Benjamin. Richter was elected to the Board of the International Walter Benjamin Association at its inaugural conference in Amsterdam in 1997 and served on it for a decade. He co-organized and hosted, in California, the 2008 World Congress of the International Walter Benjamin Society. He serves on the editorial boards of a number of journals and book series, including *Walter Benjamin Studies*. His most recent book is *This Great Allegory: On Word-Decay and World-Opening in the Work of Art* (MIT Press, 2022).

Laurence A. Rickels divides his time between the two coasts he postulated in *The Case of California* (1991), residing in Berlin and Palm Springs. The cultural anthropology of what he coined—in earshot of Freud's the uncanny—"unmourning," can be followed out in *Aberrations of Mourning* (1988), *Nazi Psychoanalysis* (2001), *Ulrike Ottinger. The Autobiography of Art Cinema* (2008), *I Think I Am. Philip K. Dick* (2010), *SPECTRE* (2013), *Germany. A Science Fiction* (2015), and *Critique of Fantasy* (2020–21). Before a decade of teaching in Germany, Rickels was Professor of German and Comparative

Literature at the University of California, Santa Barbara for thirty years. *The Vampire Lectures* (1999), *The Devil Notebooks* (2008), and *The Psycho Records* (2016) document his legendary course of instruction.

Thomas Schestag is Professor of German at Brown University. His most recent publications include *Namenlose* (Matthes & Seitz, 2020), *erlaubt, entlaubt* (Engeler Verlag, 2021), and as an editor and translator: Francis Ponge, *Le Soleil / Die Sonne* (Matthes & Seitz, 2020).

Henry Sussman is Professor Emeritus of Comparative Literature at the University of Buffalo, Retired Visiting Professor of Germanic Languages & Literatures at Yale University, and a Visiting Scholar in the Department of Germanic, Russian, and East European Languages and Literatures at Rutgers, The State University of New Jersey. His books include *Playful Intelligence: Digitizing Tradition* (Bloomsbury, 2014), *Idylls of the Wanderer* (Fordham University Press, 2011), *The Task of The Critic* (Fordham University Press, 2005), *Kafka's Unholy Trinity: The Trial* (Twaynes Publishers, 1993), *The Aesthetic Contract* (Stanford University Press, 1997), *Afterimages of Modernity* (Johns Hopkins University Press, 1990), *High Resolution: Critical Theory and the Problem of Literacy* (Oxford University Press, 1989), and *The Hegelian Aftermath* (Johns Hopkins University Press, 1981).

Dominik Zechner is Assistant Professor in the Department of German, Russian, and East European Languages and Literatures at Rutgers, The State University of New Jersey. He received his PhD in Germanic Languages and Literatures from New York University in 2019. Before joining Rutgers, he was the Artemis A.W. and Martha Joukowsky Postdoctoral Research Fellow at Brown University's Pembroke Center. He is the editor of a special issue of *MLN* and his work has appeared in *differences*, *Oxford Literary Review*, *Philosophy Today*, *The German Quarterly*, *The Yearbook of Comparative Literature*, *Translation & Literature*, *Triëdere*, and *Zeitschrift für Literaturwissenschaft und Linguistik*, among other venues.

Index

Academic Charisma and the Origins of the Research University (Clark) 99, 108n.22
Academic Committee for School Reform (ACS) 19, 20, 23n.14
"A Child's View of Color" (Benjamin) 74, 76–77
"A Communist Pedagogy" (Benjamin) 10, 46–50, 57n.74
adolescence 59, 62
Adorno, Gretel, *née* Karplus 50, 75
Adorno, Theodor W. 16, 64, 75, 126, 161–62, 171–72, 180
Agamben, Giorgio 129, 131, 139nn.25, 34
Alice's Adventures in Wonderland (Carroll) 79–80, 92n.13
Althusser, Louis 44, 54n.6
Anthropocene, the 211–13, 218–20, 221n.3
anti-idealism 215–16
"antinomianism" 105
anti-Semitism 18, 20, 217
  see also Judaism
Anwendbarkeit 104
"anxiety of influence" (Bloom) 161
Apollo 62–63, 67–69
"Appendix to the Transcendental Dialectic" (Kant) 30–31
The Arcades Project (Benjamin) 54n.1, 80, 86, 91, 92n.15, 160, 180, 187n.16, 217, 219, 222n.27
Arendt, Hannah 45, 55n.11, 75, 208n.6
Aristotle 129–31, 172
Art des Meinens (Benjamin) 136
astrology 205
"At Night" (Benjamin) 18
atom bomb 59–60
Attican Nights (Aulus Gellius) 194
Aufführung 198–99, 201–4, 208nn.12, 13
aufgehoben 77, 92n.6
Augenblick 166, 185, 200, 202–3, 206

Aulus Gellius 194
aura 10–11, 15, 50–51, 75, 101, 211–12, 218, 220

Bambi (Disney) 60
Barbizon, George 21
Barry, John 211
base-superstructure theorem 45
Basic Questions of Proletarian Education (Hoernle) 48, 53, 184, 197
Baudelaire, Charles 5, 22, 44, 46, 50–53, 56nn.53, 65, 64, 76, 160, 170, 217–19
Becher, Johannes R. 191
Belmore, Herbert 18, 139n.15
Benjamin, Dora 16, 22, 83
Benjamin, Emil 16
Benjamin, Georg 16
"Benjamin the Letter Writer" (Adorno) 161, 174n.4
Benjamin's -abilities (Weber) 108, n.15, 131, 139n.23, 140nn.36, 38, 223n.33
Benjamin, Stefan Raphael 21, 73
Benjamin, Walter,
  and the Anthropocene 211–13, 218–20, 221n.3
  Aufblitzen 213, 218–19, 223–24nn.48, 49
  broadcasting 143–49, 153nn.7, 9, 12
  the child in 73–91, 92n.15
  conversational pedagogy 97–107, 108nn.16, 28, 109n.49, 110n.68
  early life of 15–22, 22n.2
  freedom 181–83, 188–89n.23
  historical subjectivity 111–12
  improvisational/revolutionary pedagogy 183–86, 188–89nn.38, 46
  improvision 191–207, 208n.7
  language 116–19, 123–24n.45
  learning from experience 50–54, 56nn.49, 53, 56, 60, 57n.72

and Marxism 64
pedagogy 114–16, 121–22n.23, 177–78, 187n.10
pedagogy and time 213–15
psychoanalytic setting of 61–62
school reform/lawless youth 178–81
self-criticism 43–46
self-pedagogy 159–74
silence 125–32, 138–39nn.12–15, 20
storytelling 149–50, 155n.34
transmission 132–38, 141n.60
turning point 29–39, 39n.1, 40nn.8, 11, 16, 41–42nn.33–4, 36–8, 40
the Twenty-First Century 219–21
on youth 177–78
youth: self-protest 112–14
Bergson, Henri 19, 50, 79, 214
Berlin Childhood around 1900 (Benjamin) 16, 73, 80, 86, 92n.14, 148, 154n.14, 159, 178
"Berlin Toy Tour I" broadcast (Benjamin) 152
Berlin Union of Independent Students 29
Bernfeld, Siegfried 19–21, 62
Bernhard, Thomas 87
besprizornik 192–93, 207n.3
Bildung 33, 38, 61, 99, 111, 115, 218–19
Bildungsmaschine 103
The Birth of Tragedy (Nietzsche) 161, 174n.1
Blanchot, Maurice 169–70, 174n.14
Blau-Weiß youth movement 134
Bloom, Harold 161
Blumenthal, Herbert 34, 162, 164, 168
Blut-und-Boden 69
Böhlendorf, Casimir 39, 42n.41
"Bologna Process" (EU) 1–2
"Books by the Insane: From My Collection" (Benjamin) 61
Borchardt, Rudolf 61
boundary 2 (Eiland/Charles) 9, 14nn.21, 23, 54n.1
bourgeoisie 43–44, 46, 48–49, 52
Brecht, Bertolt 75, 86, 145
bricoleur (Lévi-Strauss) 89, 91
broadcasting 11, 63, 143–46, 149–51
Brown, Wendy 13n.5, 102, 109n.49
Buber, Martin 21, 161, 170–72
Burschenschaft (fraternity) 35

capitalism 50, 52–54, 85, 215, 218
carnival 68, 204–5
Carroll, Lewis 79, 92n.13
castration 66
censorship 63
Charles, Matthew 9, 14nn.22, 23
childhood/children,
    and Benjamin 73–91
    Benjamin haunted by 38–39
    Benjamin's radio audience 144, 159
    the child in Benjamin 73–91, 92n.15
    energies that radiate from 184–86
    learning to listen 150–52
    and Mette 68
    Schiller's project 192–93
    theater as their art 203–6
"Children's Literature" broadcast (Benjamin) 145
"The Circular Ruins" (Borges) 74
The Claim of Language: A Case for the Humanities (Fynsk) 98, 108n.13
Clark, William 99, 108nn.22, 25
climate change 220–21
Climate Leviathan (Mann/Wainwright) 221, 224n.63
clowns 67–68
Cohen, Hermann 105, 110n.67
"The Cold Heart" (Benjamin/Schoen) 143, 146
color 74, 76–79, 89
Communism 48–49, 75, 87
    see also Marxism
"The Concept of Criticism in German Romanticism" (Benjamin) 75
"The Concept of a Healthy Individual" (Winnicott) 69
"Contemporary Concepts of Adolescent Development" (Winnicott) 59, 69n.1
"Correspondances" (Baudelaire) 50–51, 56n.53
counter-Enlightenment 215
COVID-19 pandemic 1–2
Critique of Pure Reason (Kant) 30, 33, 40nn.3, 9, 19, 214
"Critique of Violence" (Benjamin) 5–6, 13n.14, 14n.21, 105, 110nn.69, 71, 130, 178, 182–83, 215
"Crock Notes" (Benjamin) 77–78, 92n.8

Das Kapital (Marx) 85, 88
Das Passagen-Werk (Benjamin) 75, 83
deconstruction 80–82, 87, 163, 220
Deleuze, Gilles 220, 223n.41, 224n.55
DeLoughrey, Elizabeth 211, 221n.5
de Man, Paul 112, 115, 120n.9, 136, 140–41nn.55, 57, 167
The Depth-Psychological Foundations of the Tragic, the Apollonian, and the Dionysian (Mette) 62
Der Anfang (journal) 18–21, 41n.36, 97
Der Neue Merkur (journal) 159
Derrida, Jacques 1, 44, 81–83, 87, 90–91, 93n.29, 163, 166–67
"The Destructive Character" (Benjamin) 218
dialectics 37, 45, 54, 63, 75–76, 83, 90, 117, 131, 219
"Dialogue on the Religiosity of the Present" (Benjamin) 47, 49, 1114, 121n.22
Die Aktion (journal) 127
Die Angestellten (Kracauer) 53
différance 81–82, 89
dreams 63–69
"Dr. Faust" broadcast (Benjamin) 149
dualism 8, 220
Dürer, Albrecht 19

Ecce Homo: How One Becomes What One Is (Nietzsche) 173, 175n.22
Ecology Without Nature (Morton) 220, 224n.56
eigentliche Form 168–69
Eisler, Gerhart 191
Elective Affinities (Goethe) 56n.60, 217
Émile, or On Education (Rousseau) 90, 182, 188n.25
Empfängnis 106
The Encyclopedia of the Anthropocene (DellaSala/Goldstein *Emile*) 220, 224n.60
Engelke, Peter 220, 224n.61
Enlightenment 32–33, 39, 167, 215
"Epilogue" (Benjamin) 18
Eros 30
erzieherische Gewalt (educative power/violence) 6–8, 14n.20–21, 178, 183
Esperanto movement 97
European children's library 73

existentialism 215–16
""Experience"" (Benjamin) 13n.12, 19, 56n.65, 216

fairy tales 65, 68
"The Fall of Herculaneum and Pompeii" broadcast (Benjamin) 149
fascism 86, 116, 219
Felman, Shoshana 119, 128, 138n.12
Feuerbach, Ludwig 166, 185
Fichte, Johann Gottlieb 215
First German Youth Congress (1913) 127
Fleming, Ian 60
Ford, Thomas 211–12, 221n.8
Foucault, Michel 160
Frankfurt School 64, 167
"Franz Kafka: On the Tenth Anniversary of his Death" (Benjamin) 75
Free German Youth Day (October 1913) 97, 116
Free German Youth Movement 17, 20, 22
"Free School Community" (Benjamin) 16–18, 122n.36, 182
Free Student Association (*Freistudentschaft*) 21, 160
"Freiburg Orientation" (lecture) 20
Freiburg School Reform branch 19
Freiburg University 18, 214
Freie Schulgemeinde Wickersdorf (group) 20
Freire, Paulo 3
Freistätten (universities) 1
Fremaux, Anne 211
French Revolution 193, 208n.6
Freud, Sigmund 39, 62, 64, 69, 166
Fynsk, Christopher 98

Gehorsamkeit (obedience) 101
Geiger, Moritz 22
George, Stefan 217
Germany 63–64, 91, 126, 130, 160
German Youth Movement 4–5, 8–9, 15, 17, 21, 177–81, 183
Geste 118, 123n.38, 188n.46, 200–6, 208n.12
Gewissen 40n.16, 180
globalization 88
Gödde, Christoph 171
Goethe, Johann Wolfgang von 160, 217

Göring, Mathias 63
Great Acceleration 220
Great Recession 2
Greek chorus 62
Gretor, Georg 21
Grundfragen der proletarischen Erziehung (Hoernle) 48
Gumpert, Martin 22
Guttmann, Simon 21

Habermas, Jürgen 44–45, 53, 167
Habilitationsschrift 98
Hamacher, Werner 1, 13n.3, 14n.19, 40n.2, 123n.40, 139n.32, 188nn.29, 32
Hamann, Johann Georg 135
Hamilton, Clive 211
Hanssen, Beatrice 215
Haubinda boarding school 15–18, 178
Hauff, Wilhelm 143
Hauptmann, Gerhart 116–17, 180
Hegel, Georg Wilhelm 17, 20, 86, 163, 173
Heidegger, Martin 19, 33, 40n.16, 163, 214, 219
Heimat 69
Heinle, Christoph Friedrich 18–22, 98, 127
Hiller, Kurt 21, 47, 159
Historische Psychologie des Karnevals (Rang) 204, 209n.15
Hitler, Adolf 60
Hobbes, Thomas 179
Hoernle, Edwin 48, 53
Hölderlin, Friedrich 39, 61, 137, 212
holism 220
hören (to hear) 101
"Hornberg letter" 75
Hörspiele (radio plays) 144–45
"Human Destiny in the Anthropocene" (Hamilton) 211, 221n.4
humanism 220
Humboldt, Wilhelm von 1, 99–100

"The Idea of the Free School Community"(Wyneken) 17
idealism 15, 33, 69, 215, 218, 221
improvisation 11, 84, 90, 183–86, 191–93, 196–99, 201–2, 204–6
The Inability to Mourn (Mitscherlich/Mitscherlich) 60
individualism 49, 220

Jennings, Michael 9, 47, 215
Jephcott, Edmund 5
Jetztzeit 219
Joël, Ernst 19, 21
Johnson, Barbara 3
Joyce, James 87
Judaism 15, 18, 45, 75
  see also anti-Semitism
Jugendbewegung (Youth Movement) 17, 74, 84, 178
Julius Paulus 194
Jünger, Ernst 219

K-12 education 4
Kafka, Franz 86, 89
Kaiser-Friedrich-Schule 16–17
Kant, Immanuel 30–33, 39, 40n.9, 134–35, 161, 173, 214–15
"Kaspar Hauser" broadcast (Benjamin) 146–52, 155–56n.43
Kellner, Philipp 19
kindliche Signale 200–201
Klages, Ludwig 21, 217, 219
Kracauer, Siegfried 48, 53–54
Kraft (weak messianic power) 5, 13nn.13, 15
Kraft, Werner 22
Kraus, Karl 22n.27, 215
Kulturstaat 104

labor 46–47, 49–50, 53, 73, 85, 106
Lacis, Asja 47, 183–84, 191–96
"La Fin du monde" (Baudelaire) 217–18
Landerziehungsheime 17
Landerziehungsheim Haubinda boarding school *see* Haubinda boarding school
Language Peculiarities in Schizophrenia and Poetic Productions (Mette) 10
the Last Man 213, 215–16, 218, 220, 220–21
Lehre 135, 137, 140n.53, 181, 186
Lenin, Vladimir 44, 48
Levana, or the Doctrine of Education (Paul) 185, 189n.47, 206, 209n.16
Levinas, Emmanuel 166–67
Levine, Michael G. 104
Lévi-Strauss, Claude 89
Lewis, Tyson E. 9, 92n.13, 153n.11

l'homme-frontière (Derrida) 44
Liebknechthaus, Berlin 191
Lietz, Hermann 16
The Life of Josefine Mutzenbacher: Memoirs of a Viennese Whore (Salten) 60
"The Life of Students" (Benjamin) 21, 30, 32, 39n.1, 45–49, 99, 101, 129–30, 159, 216–18, 223n.44
"The Lisbon Earthquake" broadcast (Benjamin) 151
"The Living Daylights'(Fleming) 60, 70n.7
Lockot, Regine 64
"Logic of Numbers" (Rickert) 214
Lonitz, Henri 171
Luhmann, Niklas 160

McCole, John 47, 182
McFarland, James 21n.14, 113, 119
Macht/Nacht 171–73
McLuhan, Marshall 146
McNeill, J. R. 220
Mann, Geoff 221
Marxism,
  and Benjamin 64, 220
  Benjamin's attachment to 74–76
  Benjamin's engagement with 15, 43–45, 50
  and children 85–88
  and Derrida 81–82, 90
  and Feuerbach 166, 185
  incompatible with critique of ideology 53
  influence of Asja Lacis 183–84
  introduction 2
  and pedagogy 183
Marxist-Leninism 44
Mauthausen Concentration Camp 16
mediation 132
Meinecke, Friedrich 18
Melancholia I (Dürer) 19
Menely, Tobias 211–12
messianism 83, 93n.22
Metaphysics (Aristotle) 129
"The Metaphysics of Youth" (Benjamin) 5, 104, 112, 116, 119, 125, 128–29, 133, 159, 213–14, 216
#MeToo movement 2, 90
Mette, Alexander 10, 61–66, 68–69
Mitteilbarkeit 104, 108n.15

Modernism 89
modernity 167
Morton, Timothy 220
"Much Ado about Kasper'(Benjamin) 145–49, 154–55nn.20, 28

National Socialism 22, 69
Nazis 15, 62–64, 67
  see also Third Reich
neoclassicism 33
New International 87–88, 92n.17
Nietzsche, Friedrich 10, 34–35, 38, 62–63, 98–104, 111–19, 119nn.3–4, 126, 159
  end of metaphysics 219–20
  moving beyond dialectics 219
  post-Nietzscheanism 212–18, 223n.40
  and self-pedagogy 161, 167, 173
  will to power 216
  and Wyneken 218
Nizan, Paul 43–44
Noeggerath, Felix 22
non-Being 131
"Notes on the Idea of the Youth's Life" (Scholem) 125

"Old Forgotten Children's books" (Benjamin) 74, 88
On the Advantage and Disadvantage of History for Life (Nietzsche) 10, 111, 126, 167
"On the Concept of History" (Benjamin) 1, 11, 129, 180, 187n.10
One-Way Street (Benjamin) 73, 76, 80, 88–89, 92n.14, 159
On the Future of Our Educational Institutions (Nietzsche) 10, 34, 41n.18, 98–99, 108nn.18, 27
"On Language as Such and the Language of Man" (Benjamin) 106, 125, 127–28, 131, 133, 135–36, 164, 216
"On the Minute" (Benjamin) 143, 153nn.7, 11
"On the Program of the Coming Philosophy" (Benjamin) 31, 40n.11, 125, 135
On the Relations Between Language Peculiarities in Schizophrenia . . . (Mette) 61

On the Shores of Politics (Rancière) 216, 222–23n.31
"On Some Motifs in Baudelaire" (Benjamin) 46, 50, 56nn.52, 54, 57, 76
Origin of the German Trauerspiel (Benjamin) 32, 62, 70n.12, 91, 98, 139n.23, 164, 168, 193
Ossian craze 61

Pannwitz, Rudolf 114, 178
paranomasia 62
"Passagenwerk" or "Arcades Project" (Benjamin) 75, 80, 86, 91, 160
Paul, Jean 185, 206
"pedagogical imperative" (Johnson) 3, 6
Pedagogical Student Conference, Breslau 20
pedagogy,
    and Benjamin 114–16, 121–22n.23, 177–78, 187n.10
    conversational 97–107, 108nn.16, 28, 109n.49, 110n.68
    engaging with the theme of 177–78
    improvisational/revolutionary 183–86, 188–89nn.38, 46
    meaning 159–60
    self 159–74
    and time 213–15
Phenomenology of Spirit (Hegel) 86, 92n.6, 173
Plato 35, 162
"The Poet" (Benjamin) 18
poetry 52, 61–62, 93, 170, 212
Pollak, Dora Sophie, née Kellner 21
post-Enlightenment neoclassicism 33
Potentialities (Agamben) 129, 139n.25
"The Present Social Situation of the French Writer" (Benjamin) 43
Privatdozent 98, 108n.28
productivity 37–39, 86, 101–2, 128–29
"Program for a Proletarian Children's Theater" (Benjamin) 178, 183, 185–86, 191–96, 205, 207n.1
proletariat *see* working class
Proust, Marcel 73
Prussian Empire 105

The qualitative leap 220, 224n.62

radio *see* broadcasting
"The Rainbow" (Benjamin) 22
Rang, Florens Christian 204
rechtsvernichtend 7, 183
"Rechtszweck" 7
Rede 105
Reimann, Georg 60
Reitter, Paul 99
Revolte, Eros und Sprache (Steizinger) 9, 120n.8, 216, 223n.33
rhythm (*Rhythmus*) 208, 213, 215–18
rhythmus 215–18, 223n.35
Rickert, Heinrich 18–19, 214
"The Right to Use Force" (Benjamin) 217, 223n.36
Rilke, Rainer Maria 22
"Ring Cycle" (Wagner) 61
"The Role of Language in *Trauerspiel* and Tragedy" (Benjamin) 138n.14, 164
Romanticism 35, 75–77, 84, 160, 212–13, 220
"Romanticism: An Undelivered Address to Students" (Benjamin) 110n.78, 118
Rosenzweig, Franz 105, 129
Rousseau, Jean-Jacques 90, 182, 188n.25

Sachs, Hanns 62
Salten, Felix 60
Sapere aude! 32–33
Satz vom Grund 67–68
Schema der Spannung (scheme of tension) (Benjamin) 195, 198, 201–2
Schiller, Friedrich 192–93
schizophrenia 61–62
Schoen, Ernst 143, 146, 162
Schoenflies, Pauline 16
"Scholarship as a Profession" (Weber) 34
Scholem, Gershom,
    and Asja Lacis 183–84
    and Benjamin 22, 83, 87, 134, 137, 181
    and Benjamin on air 143–44
    and Klages 217
    and "Notes on the Idea of the Youth's Life" 125
    and "University of Muri" 160
    unpublished works of Benjamin 168, 171–73
    and World War II 75

"The School Reform: A Cultural Movement" (Benjamin) 6–7, 18, 126, 133, 178
School Reform Unit, Freiburg University 178
Schopenhauer, Arthur 100, 161
Schreber, Daniel Paul 61–62
"the science of the concrete" 89
secret assignation (*geheime Verabredung*) 104–5
Self-Criticism 43
Seligson, Carla 20–21
Seligson, Rika (Frederika) 20–21, 98, 127
Shandy, Walter 90
"Sleeping Beauty" (Benjamin) 18, 177
Socialist Unity Party 64
social media 4
sociological infrastructure 82
Socrates 37, 41n.37, 133, 139n.29, 140n.43, 164
Socrates (Benjamin) 133
Specters of Marx (Derrida) 81–83, 88, 92n.17, 93nn.21, 27
Spinoza, Baruch 35
Spitteler, Carl 19
Sprachkritik (language skepticism) 117
Sprechsaal Berliner Schüler 19
Sprechsaal (discussion group) 10, 19–22, 97–98, 108n.3
"Spring Awakening" (Wedekind) 126
Steizinger, Johannes 9, 112, 126, 216
"The Storyteller'(Benjamin) 127, 150, 169
storytelling 149–50, 155n.34
Strauß, Ludwig 18
structuralism 89
Studentenbewegung 97–98, 107

Tableaux Parisiens (Baudelaire) 22, 56n.61
The Task of the Critic (Eagleton) 83, 93n.23
"The Task of the Translator" (Benjamin) 136, 170, 174n.17
"Teaching and Valuation'(Benjamin) 111–12, 126–27, 138n.7
theater 9, 11, 15–16, 145, 150, 183–86, 191–99, 202–6
Theaterspielen 193
Theodor W. Adorno Archive 171
"Theological-Political Fragment" (Benjamin) 30

"Theses on the Philosophy of History" (Benjamin) 213
"The Storyteller" (Benjamin) 127, 150, 169
"The Task of the Translator" (Benjamin) 136, 170, 174n.17
Theweleit, Klaus 49, 67
Third Reich 59, 62
see also Nazis
"Thoughts on Gerhart Hauptmann's Festival Play" (Benjamin) 114, 180
Thus Spoke Zarathustra (Nietzsche) 41n.34, 103, 217
time 31, 164–65, 215–16
Torah 135, 140n.53
Tractatus (Wittgenstein) 171, 174n.18
"Transcendental Aesthetic" 30–31
transgender experimentation 61–62
"*Trauerspiel* and Tragedy" (Benjamin) 138n.14, 164, 168, 174n.8
Traumbewusstsein (dream consciousness) (Klages) 219
Trommler, Frank 112
"Two Kinds of Popularity: Fundamental Principles for a Radio Play" (Benjamin) 144, 149
"Two Poems by Friedrich Hölderlin" (Benjamin) 22, 127, 216

Über die ästhetische Erziehung des Menschen (Schiller) 192–93
University of Muri (thought-experiment) 160
Unterricht (instruction) 181–82
utopia 180

Verderbt, Verdammt, Verraten (Reimann) 60
Verma, Neil 150, 155n.41
virtuality 36

wahre Sprache 128
Wainwright, Joel 221
Walter Benjamin, Briefe vol. 1 (Scholem/Adorno) 171, 175n.19
"Walter Benjamin and the Possibility of a Global Pedagogy" (conference) 9
Wandervogel group 17, 63, 67, 178
"War and Youth" (Wyneken) 22

The Watchdogs: Philosophers and the Established Order (Nizan) 43–44, 54n.3
Weber, Max 34
Weber, Samuel 129, 139n.23
Wedekind, Frank 126
Weigel, Sigrid 128, 139n.20
Wellmon, Chad 99
Werther (Goethe) 61
Wilhelmine Empire 3, 17
Winnicott, D. W. 59, 69, 91
Wittgenstein, Ludwig 171
Wölfflin, Heinrich 22
The Work of Art in the Age of its Technological Reproducibility (Benjamin) 84, 91, 152n.1, 153n.7
working class 43–48, 53, 63, 194–96, 200
"The World of Children's Books'(Benjamin) 78–79
World War I 159, 169, 180–81, 214–15, 219–20
Wyneken, Gustav 6, 15–22, 126, 178, 180–81, 214, 218, 223n.48

youth,
    an inherent threat to the status quo 177
    and Benjamin 112, 137, 177–78, 180, 182
    confused nature of 117–19
    metaphysics of 125–34, 159, 213–14
    self-protest 112–14
Youth Culture Movement 126, 180–81
"Youth and History" (Benjamin) 116–17
"Youth Was Silent" (Benjamin) 20, 107n.1, 116, 127

zählbar 168–69
Zarathustra (Nietzsche) 41n.34, 103, 108n.36, 217
Zionism *see* Judaism

www.ingramcontent.com/pod-product-compliance
Lightning Source LLC
Chambersburg PA
CBHW062142300426
44115CB00012BA/2007